Charles I. Jones

Macroeconomics

SECOND EDITION

Charles I. Jones

Macroeconomics

SECOND EDITION

David Gillette

TRUMAN STATE UNIVERSITY

W • W • NORTON & COMPANY • NEW YORK • LONDON

W. W. Norton & Company has been independent since its founding in 1923, when William Warder Norton and Mary D. Herter Norton first published lectures delivered at the People's Institute, the adult education division of New York City's Cooper Union. The Nortons soon expanded their program beyond the Institute, publishing books by celebrated academics from America and abroad. By mid-century, the two major pillars of Norton's publishing program—trade books and college texts—were firmly established. In the 1950s, the Norton family transferred control of the company to its employees, and today—with a staff of four hundred and a comparable number of trade, college, and professional titles published each year—W. W. Norton & Company stands as the largest and oldest publishing house owned wholly by its employees.

Printed in the United States of America

Manufacturing by Sterling Pierce

Composition and layout: R. Flechner Graphics

Editor: Lorraine Klimowich

Production Manager: Christopher Granville

Second Edition

ISBN 978-0-393-91178-7 (pbk.)

W. W. Norton & Company, Inc., 500 Fifth Avenue, New York, NY 10110
www.wwnorton.com

W. W. Norton & Company Ltd., Castle House, 75/76 Wells Street, London W1T 3QT

1 2 3 4 5 6 7 8 9 0

CONTENTS

Preface

The purpose of this study guide is to enhance your learning experience as you work through Charles Jones's *Macro - economics*. Each section of each chapter has been carefully developed and reviewed by several students to best accomplish this goal. My assumptions in writing each chapter are that you will have already read the text material before turning to the study guide, that you are now ready to learn how much you know, and that you want to find out where you still need to know more.

Each chapter of the study guide starts with a statement responding to the learning objectives presented at the beginning of each chapter in the textbook. This statement provides a succinct chapter summary in which you should recognize all the major topics. I suggest you test yourself by thinking about how much more detail concerning each topic you could fill in with no further prompting.

The second part of each chapter in the study guide contains a more in-depth explanation for each of the chapter's key concepts. These explanations are meant to ensure that no major concepts are missed as you read the chapter and, in some cases, provide quick examples or further explanation to supplement the material in the text. This information on its own is not a substitute for actually reading the chapter.

The third and fourth sections provide an opportunity to test your understanding of chapter material by answering some true/false and multiple-choice questions before moving on to the exercises and problems. To make studying as efficient as possible, most concepts receive only a one-question allotment, so challenge yourself. Treat these questions as a self-test and try answering each of them without referring back to the chapter or to the answers at the end of the study guide. All the answers for each true/false and multiple-choice question at the end of the study guide include a section reference back to the text, in case you need to do some follow-up studying, and most of them also have an explanation about why an answer is correct. Some even explain why a few very tempting answers are incorrect.

The next two sections of each chapter present exercises and problems intended to help prepare you for the end-of-the-chapter exercises in the textbook. Try to work through them on your own at first but do not get discouraged if you get stuck. Early experiences with the modeling aspects of economics can sometimes be quite difficult. Therefore, each exercise and problem also has a solution provided at the end of each chapter, unless it is one of the worked problems, whose solution follows immediately and serves as a guide for the material that follows.

Best wishes as you pursue your study of macroeconomics.

Acknowledgments

I wish to express my appreciation to all those who have helped make this study guide become a reality. My thanks go first to my best friend Gabriele for her continued friendship and support over many years and specifically during this project, and then to Jack Repcheck and Lorraine Klimowich of Norton for their encouragement and confidence throughout this process.

I would especially like to thank Daniel Campbell, Justin Jenkel, Samantha Sanchez, Kathleen Schulte, and Elise Dye of Truman State University, who in addition to their other coursework faithfully read and critiqued each element of this study guide. It benefited immensely from their efforts. Any surviving errors, of course, remain my responsibility.

CHAPTER 1 | Introduction to Macroeconomics

OVERVIEW

The objectives for Chapter 1 are to learn what macroeconomics is, what kinds of questions the text will teach you to address, the nature of an economic model, and how economists use it to answer important questions. Macroeconomists study issues regarding the economy as a whole: economic growth, inflation, unemployment, interest rates, expansions, contractions, fiscal and monetary policies, budget and trade deficits, exchange rates, and the like. This chapter introduces the questions surrounding these issues such as the growth of inflation during the 1970s and the corresponding roles of both monetary and fiscal policy. Other questions concern the behavior and sustainability of our current trade and budget deficits. This chapter also reviews the basics of model building.

KEY CONCEPTS

Macroeconomics is the study of collections of people and firms and how their interactions through markets determine the overall performance of the economy.

Microeconomics is the study of individual people, firms, or markets and how they interact to determine the allocation of particular economic goods.

Economic models allow economists to abstract from an innumerable set of forces at play in the real world in order to narrow the focus to a smaller set of forces thought to be most relevant to the issue at hand. For example, an entire market might be represented by two simple equations, one for demand, $Q_d = a - bP + cY$, and one for supply, $Q_s = e - fP$, and represented on a demand and supply diagram with price, P, on the vertical axis and quantity, Q, on the horizontal axis.

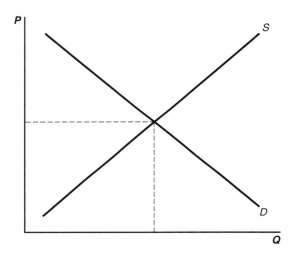

Parameters are components of the model, sometimes called *behavioral* or *sensitivity parameters*, that generally remain fixed or constant over time unless explicitly changed by the model builder. For example, if we consider the demand equation $Q_d = a - bP + cY$, the letters a, b, and c are parameters that define the behavior of demand, either independent of P and Y, as in the case of a, or in response to changes in P and Y, as in the cases of b and c, respectively.

Exogenous variables are components of the model that are allowed to change over time but only in specific ways, as determined in advance by the model builder. For example, in the preceding demand equation, Y might be income that changes by 100, or by 10 percent, and causes the demand curve to shift by an amount determined in part by the parameter c.

Endogenous variables are the outcomes generated by the model. For example, a competitive market model

1

combining the demand equation $Q_d = a - bP + cY$ with the supply equation $Q_s = e - fP$ would yield a solution for price, P, and quantity, Q, in terms of the model parameters and exogenous variables for that particular market.

Long-run economic analysis occurs when there has been sufficient time for all factors of production to adjust to changes and disturbances in the economy. For example, in the long run, the size of a factory can be expanded to meet an increase in demand due to an increase in population.

Short-run economic analysis occurs when one or more of the factors of production in the economic process cannot be changed in response to changes and disturbances in the economy. For example, in the short run, workers in a factory might have to work overtime to meet an increase in demand until the factory can be expanded.

Potential output (GDP) describes the maximum amount that an economy could produce if all of its factors of production were fully and efficiently employed. It generally is thought of as growing at a steady rate over time and associated with the long-run behavior of an economy.

Economic fluctuations occur in the short run and describe the behavior of actual output relative to potential output. Sometimes, a fluctuation will generate a positive output gap, where actual GDP exceeds potential GDP for a short period of time; at other times, an output fluctuation will leave actual GDP below potential GDP, generating a negative GDP gap.

Inflation measures the growth (in percentage terms) of the price level (an index number) over time and can derive from either demand or supply side changes.

TRUE/FALSE QUESTIONS

1. Macroeconomics is to microeconomics as a building is to construction materials.

2. Microeconomics concerns issues of the consumer, firm, and industry, while macroeconomics concerns issues of the economy as a whole.

3. For 150 years, the U.S. GDP per capita exceeded that of most industrialized countries, including the United Kingdom, Germany, and Japan.

4. Unemployment generally increased during the last half of the twentieth century for Europe, Japan, and the United States.

5. Budget deficits have been a constantly growing problem ever since the early 1970s.

6. The solutions of an economic model are specific values of the endogenous variables.

7. Per capita GDP growth in the United States has averaged close to 3 percent for the past 140 years.

8. News announcements about quarterly GDP growth shed light on long-run economic trends.

MULTIPLE-CHOICE QUESTIONS

1. The study of modern macroeconomic theory requires the use of techniques from
   a. game theory.
   b. all of the social sciences.
   c. only macroeconomic principles.
   d. only microeconomic principles.
   e. both macroeconomic principles and the study of individual behavior.

2. Which of the following issues is not addressed by the study of macroeconomics?
   a. inflation
   b. firm behavior
   c. budget deficits
   d. per capita wealth
   e. economic growth

3. Which of the following issues is not addressed by the study of microeconomics?
   a. government intervention
   b. exchange rates
   c. opportunity cost
   d. unemployment
   e. labor markets

4. The study of macroeconomics addresses each of the following issues except
   a. recessions.
   b. unemployment.
   c. personal income.
   d. the national debt.
   e. economic growth.

5. Which of the following issues is not addressed by the study of macroeconomics?
   a. government intervention
   b. trade barriers
   c. exchange rates
   d. stock prices
   e. stock market bubbles

6. Macroeconomists generally follow a four-step process when performing their analysis. Which of the following is not one of those steps?
   a. Develop a survey.
   b. Document the facts.
   c. Develop a model.
   d. Compare the predictions of the model to the original facts.
   e. Use the model to make other predictions that may eventually be tested.

7. To be considered successful, a model must
   a. provide solutions for the endogenous economic variables in question.
   b. provide correct qualitative descriptions of changes in the endogenous variables in response to the model's behavioral parameters.
   c. generate correct quantitative predictions for the endogenous variables in response to changes in the exogenous variables.
   d. do all of the above.
   e. do only a and c.

EXERCISES

This first problem is intended to help familiarize you with the Snapshots resource.

1. Go to http://elsa.berkeley.edu/~chad/snapshots.html; download the Country Snapshots file by clicking on the snapshots.pdf link and open it. (Some browsers will allow you to work with the file without downloading it.) Note that pages 3–4 in this file contain detailed instructions on its use and sources. After opening Country Snapshots, locate the country "Hungary" in the list of countries on page 1 and click on it.
   a. How many years of GDP data are provided?
   b. What is GDP per capita in the year 2000?
   c. What does the number you obtain for your answer on part b mean? (Hint: Click on the link "Click here for notes" on page 1, then go to the third bullet.)
   d. How much does it differ from GDP per worker in the year 2000?
   e. How do GDP per capita and GDP per worker differ in principle?
   f. What is the GDP growth rate for the year 2000?

Worked Exercise

The following exercise will lead you step by step through the process of using a spreadsheet to create a graph. It assumes very little spreadsheet experience but does require basic computer application familiarity, such as selecting content, copying, and pasting. The instructions assume the use of Microsoft Excel on either a PC or a Mac, but the procedures are similar to other spreadsheet packages as well.

2. Continuing with the country of Hungary, once you have found the Snapshots page for Hungary you should see "Hungary(Population=10.0m)(data)" printed at the top of it. Click on the word "data" to download the Excel file for Hungary. (Depending on your computer configuration you may need to right-click and select the appropriate option. Otherwise, the URL is http://elsa.berkeley.edu/~chad/snapshots/HUN.xls) Open it. The file should look as follows (on page 4):

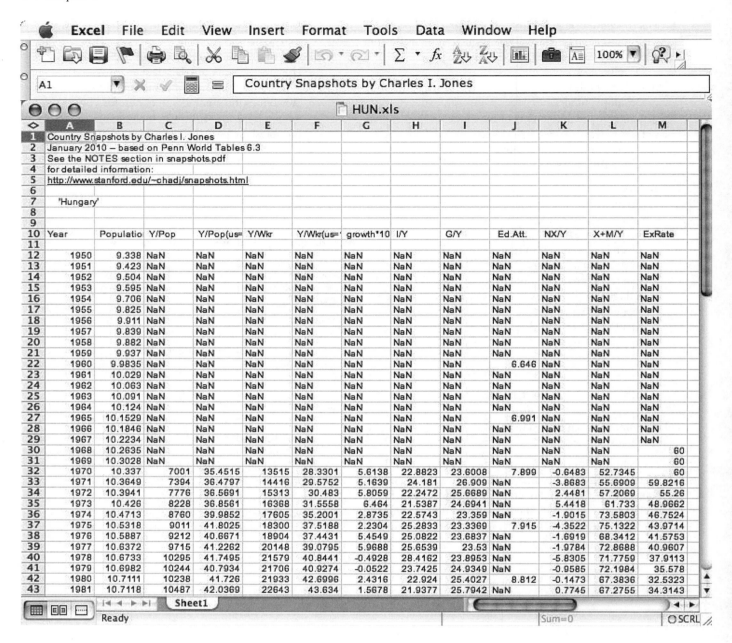

First, organize the data in a more graphing-friendly format for Excel. There are several ways to accomplish this, so if you know another one that works well for you, please feel free to use it, but for the novice spreadsheet user, this one should provide a good place to start. Notice when you first open the original file that there is only one tab, titled "Sheet1," at the bottom of the file. Go to the application menu bar and click on the "Insert" pull-down menu and select "Worksheet."

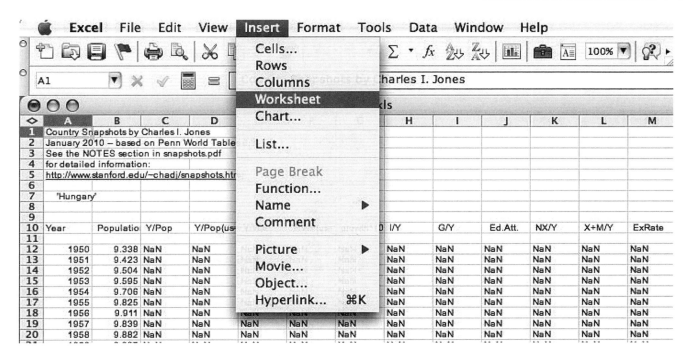

A second tab will appear titled "Sheet2."

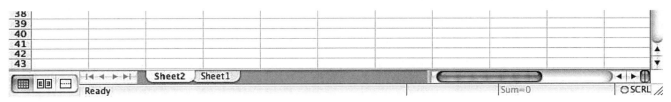

Choose "Sheet1" and, beginning with row 6, column A, select rows 7 through 69 and columns A through M inclusive. Using the "Edit" pull-down menu, copy these cells.

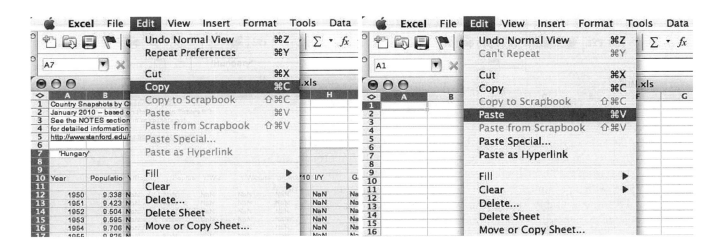

Select the "Sheet2" tab you just created, put the cursor in cell A1, and select "Paste." Your spreadsheet should now look like this:

	A	B	C	D	E	F	G	H	I	J	K	L	M
1	'Hungary'												
2													
3													
4	Year	Population	Y/Pop	Y/Pop(us=10	Y/Wkr	Y/Wkr(us=10(	growth*100	I/Y	G/Y	Ed.Att.	NX/Y	X+M/Y	ExRate
5													
6	1950	9.338	NaN	NaN	NaN	NaN	NaN	NaN	NaN	NaN	NaN	NaN	NaN
7	1951	9.423	NaN	NaN	NaN	NaN	NaN	NaN	NaN	NaN	NaN	NaN	NaN
8	1952	9.504	NaN	NaN	NaN	NaN	NaN	NaN	NaN	NaN	NaN	NaN	NaN
9	1953	9.595	NaN	NaN	NaN	NaN	NaN	NaN	NaN	NaN	NaN	NaN	NaN
10	1954	9.706	NaN	NaN	NaN	NaN	NaN	NaN	NaN	NaN	NaN	NaN	NaN
11	1955	9.825	NaN	NaN	NaN	NaN	NaN	NaN	NaN	NaN	NaN	NaN	NaN
12	1956	9.911	NaN	NaN	NaN	NaN	NaN	NaN	NaN	NaN	NaN	NaN	NaN
13	1957	9.839	NaN	NaN	NaN	NaN	NaN	NaN	NaN	NaN	NaN	NaN	NaN
14	1958	9.882	NaN	NaN	NaN	NaN	NaN	NaN	NaN	NaN	NaN	NaN	NaN
15	1959	9.937	NaN	NaN	NaN	NaN	NaN	NaN	NaN	NaN	NaN	NaN	NaN
16	1960	9.9835	NaN	NaN	NaN	NaN	NaN	NaN	NaN	6.646	NaN	NaN	NaN
17	1961	10.029	NaN	NaN	NaN	NaN	NaN	NaN	NaN	NaN	NaN	NaN	NaN
18	1962	10.063	NaN	NaN	NaN	NaN	NaN	NaN	NaN	NaN	NaN	NaN	NaN
19	1963	10.091	NaN	NaN	NaN	NaN	NaN	NaN	NaN	NaN	NaN	NaN	NaN
20	1964	10.124	NaN	NaN	NaN	NaN	NaN	NaN	NaN	NaN	NaN	NaN	NaN
21	1965	10.1529	NaN	NaN	NaN	NaN	NaN	NaN	NaN	6.991	NaN	NaN	NaN
22	1966	10.1846	NaN	NaN	NaN	NaN	NaN	NaN	NaN	NaN	NaN	NaN	NaN
23	1967	10.2234	NaN	NaN	NaN	NaN	NaN	NaN	NaN	NaN	NaN	NaN	NaN
24	1968	10.2635	NaN	NaN	NaN	NaN	NaN	NaN	NaN	NaN	NaN	NaN	60
25	1969	10.3028	NaN	NaN	NaN	NaN	NaN	NaN	NaN	NaN	NaN	NaN	60
26	1970	10.337	7001	35.4515	13515	28.3301	5.6138	22.8823	23.6008	7.899	-0.6483	52.7345	60
27	1971	10.3649	7394	36.4797	14416	29.5752	5.1639	24.181	26.909	NaN	-3.8683	55.6909	59.8216
28	1972	10.3941	7776	36.5691	15313	30.483	5.8059	22.2472	25.6689	NaN	2.4481	57.2069	55.26
29	1973	10.426	8228	36.8561	16368	31.5558	6.464	21.5387	24.6941	NaN	5.4418	61.733	48.9662
30	1974	10.4713	8760	39.9852	17605	35.2001	2.8735	22.5743	23.359	NaN	-1.9015	73.5803	46.7524
31	1975	10.5318	9011	41.8025	18300	37.5188	2.2304	25.2833	23.3369	7.915	-4.3522	75.1322	43.9714
32	1976	10.5887	9212	40.6671	18904	37.4431	5.4549	25.0822	23.6837	NaN	-1.6919	68.3412	41.5753
33	1977	10.6372	9715	41.2262	20148	39.0795	5.9688	25.6539	23.53	NaN	-1.9784	72.8688	40.9607
34	1978	10.6733	10295	41.7495	21579	40.8441	-0.4928	28.4162	23.8953	NaN	-5.8305	71.7759	37.9113
35	1979	10.6982	10244	40.7934	21706	40.9274	-0.0522	23.7425	24.9349	NaN	-0.9585	72.1984	35.578
36	1980	10.7111	10238	41.726	21933	42.6996	2.4316	22.924	25.4027	8.812	-0.1473	67.3836	32.5323
37	1981	10.7118	10487	42.0369	22643	43.634	1.5678	21.9377	25.7942	NaN	0.7745	67.2755	34.3143
38	1982	10.7055	10652	44.0514	23142	46.2177	-0.0353	20.8528	26.0875	NaN	2.2366	63.3323	36.6305
39	1983	10.6895	10648	42.2694	23291	44.7847	1.6709	19.355	26.3381	NaN	3.2489	66.3018	42.6711
40	1984	10.6681	10826	40.0198	23827	43.0495	0.759	18.6172	26.3162	NaN	4.3152	66.8298	48.0422
41	1985	10.6487	10908	39.124	24156	42.6651	2.8342	17.8696	27.0647	8.197	3.4568	69.4099	50.1194
42	1986	10.6306	11217	39.3269	24994	43.6269	3.5877	18.907	27.2756	NaN	0.4828	67.6402	45.8321
43	1987	10.6127	11620	39.7961	26048	44.7752	0.2403	18.8602	26.7239	NaN	1.1767	64.0946	46.9705
44	1988	10.4425	11648	38.7219	26263	44.0476	1.1225	18.5059	27.5956	NaN	3.8231	61.223	50.4132
45	1989	10.398	11778	38.167	26699	44.0102	-2.8602	18.6036	26.9879	NaN	4.3422	59.4275	59.0663
46	1990	10.3719	11442	36.9156	26010	42.8574	-9.1591	18.3906	27.6486	8.708	3.5296	51.6201	63.2059
47	1991	10.3647	10394	34.1765	23809	39.5976	-2.066	16.0393	29.7107	NaN	-0.8953	64.2098	74.7354
48	1992	10.3487	10179	32.7198	23315	37.8906	2.8709	13.0931	30.1525	NaN	-0.2211	60.9656	78.9884
49	1993	10.329	10471	33.035	24956	39.5829	1.6744	16.8674	32.1708	NaN	-7.8636	58.7655	91.9332
50	1994	10.3127	10646	32.4605	26199	40.2153	-1.4554	19.8935	29.4031	NaN	-6.2029	62.0107	105.1605
51	1995	10.2959	10492	31.5119	26463	39.8959	1.2995	20.4631	26.8573	8.518	0.0085	86.2915	125.6814
52	1996	10.2736	10628	30.9969	27071	39.6332	4.9753	23.1902	25.9013	NaN	0.5066	93.3047	152.6467
53	1997	10.2447	11157	31.3251	28736	40.7051	6.0062	25.2406	25.4919	NaN	1.0569	105.684	186.7892
54	1998	10.2111	11827	32.094	30273	41.3638	4.7066	28.9768	24.4875	NaN	-1.3123	121.1275	214.4017
55	1999	10.1727	12383	32.4492	30952	40.8579	5.1844	29.7326	23.8088	NaN	-2.5474	126.9341	237.1458
56	2000	10.1374	13025	33.1932	32282	41.9229	3.8322	31.5639	22.2273	8.811	-3.624	147.763	282.1792
57	2001	10.1095	13525	34.7359	33590	43.8603	4.935	29.1501	21.9736	NaN	-1.2319	143.4189	286.49
58	2002	10.0833	14192	36.3372	35079	45.5842	4.5734	27.5503	22.2482	NaN	-1.9588	127.9201	257.8867

Assume for the sake of this exercise that the two observations for educational attainment in cells J16 and J21 will not be needed. Select cells A5 through M25 inclusive. Then, from the "Edit" pull-down menu, select "Delete" and the "Shift cells up" option when prompted, so that your sheet now looks as above. Notice, too, that cell A4 now is empty. (Be sure to remove the word "Year" from cell A4 using the delete key rather than using the space bar to make it go away; a cell with a "space" in it is not empty, and Excel knows this.) The point here is that an empty cell at the top of the leftmost column tells Excel that the values in this column are horizontal axis labels rather than the first series that you wish to graph. Your spreadsheet should now look like this:

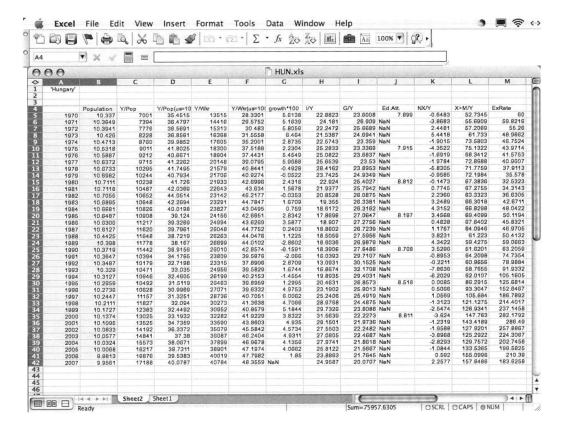

'Hungary'

	Population	Y/Pop	Y/Pop(us=10	Y/Wkr	Y/Wkr(us=10	growth*100	I/Y	G/Y	Ed.Att.	NX/Y	X+M/Y	ExRate
1970	10.337	7001	35.4515	13515	28.3301	5.6138	22.8823	23.6008	7.899	-0.6483	52.7345	60
1971	10.3649	7394	36.4797	14416	29.5752	5.1639	24.181	26.909	NaN	-3.8683	55.6909	59.8216
1972	10.3941	7776	36.5691	15313	30.483	5.8059	22.2472	25.6689	NaN	2.4481	57.2069	55.26
1973	10.426	8228	36.8561	16368	31.5558	6.464	21.5387	24.6941	NaN	5.4418	61.733	48.9662
1974	10.4713	8760	39.9852	17605	35.2001	2.8735	22.5743	23.359	NaN	-1.9015	73.5803	46.7524
1975	10.5318	9011	41.8025	18300	37.5188	2.2304	25.2833	23.3369	7.915	-4.3522	75.1322	43.9714
1976	10.5887	9212	40.6671	18904	37.4431	5.4549	25.0822	23.6837	NaN	-1.6919	68.3412	41.5753
1977	10.6372	9715	41.2262	20148	39.0795	5.9688	25.6539	23.53	NaN	-1.9784	72.8688	40.9607
1978	10.6733	10295	41.7495	21579	40.8441	-0.4928	28.4162	23.8953	NaN	-5.8305	71.7759	37.9113
1979	10.6982	10244	40.7934	21706	40.9274	-0.0522	23.7425	24.9349	NaN	-0.9585	72.1984	35.578
1980	10.7111	10238	41.726	21933	42.6996	2.4316	22.924	25.4027	8.812	-0.1473	67.3836	32.5323
1981	10.7118	10487	42.0369	22643	43.634	1.5678	21.9377	25.7942	NaN	0.7745	67.2755	34.3143
1982	10.7055	10652	44.0514	23142	46.2177	-0.0353	20.8528	26.0875	NaN	2.2366	63.3323	36.6305
1983	10.6895	10648	42.2694	23291	44.7847	1.6709	19.355	26.3381	NaN	3.2489	66.3018	42.6711
1984	10.6681	10826	40.0198	23827	43.0495	0.759	18.6172	26.3162	NaN	4.3152	66.8298	48.0422
1985	10.6487	10908	39.124	24156	42.6651	2.8342	17.8696	27.0647	8.197	3.4568	69.4099	50.1194
1986	10.6306	11217	39.3269	24994	43.6269	3.5877	18.907	27.2756	NaN	0.4828	67.6402	45.8321
1987	10.6127	11620	39.7961	26048	44.7752	0.2403	18.8602	26.7239	NaN	1.1767	64.0946	46.9705
1988	10.4425	11648	38.7219	26263	44.0476	1.1225	18.5059	27.5956	NaN	3.8231	61.223	50.4132
1989	10.398	11778	38.167	26699	44.0102	-2.8602	18.6036	26.9879	NaN	4.3422	59.4275	59.0663
1990	10.3719	11442	36.9156	26010	42.8574	-9.1591	18.3906	27.6486	8.708	3.5296	51.6201	63.2059
1991	10.3647	10394	34.1765	23809	39.5976	-2.066	16.0393	29.7107	NaN	-0.8953	64.2098	74.7354
1992	10.3487	10179	32.7198	23315	37.8906	2.8709	13.0931	30.1525	NaN	-0.2211	60.9656	78.9884
1993	10.329	10471	33.035	24956	39.5829	1.6744	16.8674	32.1708	NaN	-7.8636	58.7655	91.9332
1994	10.3127	10646	32.4605	26199	40.2153	-1.4554	19.8935	29.4031	NaN	-6.2029	62.0107	105.1605
1995	10.2959	10492	31.5119	26463	39.8959	1.2995	20.4631	26.8573	8.518	0.0085	86.2915	125.6814
1996	10.2736	10628	30.9969	27071	39.6332	4.9753	23.1902	25.9013	NaN	0.5066	93.3047	152.6467
1997	10.2447	11157	31.3251	28736	40.7051	6.0062	25.2406	25.4919	NaN	1.0569	105.684	186.7892
1998	10.2111	11827	32.094	30273	41.3638	4.7066	28.9768	24.4875	NaN	-1.3123	121.1275	214.4017
1999	10.1727	12383	32.4492	30952	40.8579	5.1844	29.7326	23.8088	NaN	-2.5474	126.9341	237.1458
2000	10.1374	13025	33.1932	32282	41.9229	3.8322	31.5639	22.2273	8.811	-3.624	147.763	282.1792
2001	10.1095	13525	34.7359	33590	43.8603	4.935	29.1501	21.9736	NaN	-1.2319	143.4189	286.49
2002	10.0833	14192	36.3372	35079	45.5842	4.5734	27.5503	22.2482	NaN	-1.9588	127.9201	257.8867
2003	10.0577	14841	37.38	36087	46.2404	4.9311	27.0805	22.4687	NaN	-3.8968	125.2922	224.3067
2004	10.0324	15573	38.0671	37899	46.9678	4.1356	27.9741	21.8618	NaN	-2.8293	129.7572	202.7458
2005	10.0068	16217	38.7311	38901	47.1974	4.0662	25.8122	21.5667	NaN	-1.0844	133.5365	199.5825
2006	9.9813	16876	39.5383	40019	47.7982	1.85	23.8863	21.7645	NaN	0.592	155.0996	210.39
2007	9.9561	17188	40.0787	40784	48.3559	NaN	24.9587	20.0707	NaN	2.2577	157.6486	183.6258

Your spreadsheet now is ready to easily generate a graph. (Have you saved yet?) Excel's Chart Wizard has four steps. To begin using it, we create a graph of Hungary's population from 1970 to 2007. Use your cursor to select cells A4:B42, as shown next.

Now click on the "Chart Wizard" icon. It is the little bar chart icon below the letter "H" in "Help" in the following diagram, or you can find it in the "Insert" pull-down menu, which also follows, if the icon is not showing on your application.

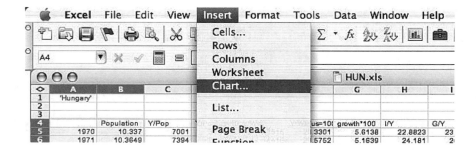

Step 1 will ask you to choose a chart type. For this exercise, select "Line" and the first chart sub-type. Step 2 lets you verify the data range and alter it if you wish, or tell Excel that the data are in columns if it has guessed wrong based on the cells you highlighted. Normally, you will not need to do anything in Step 2.

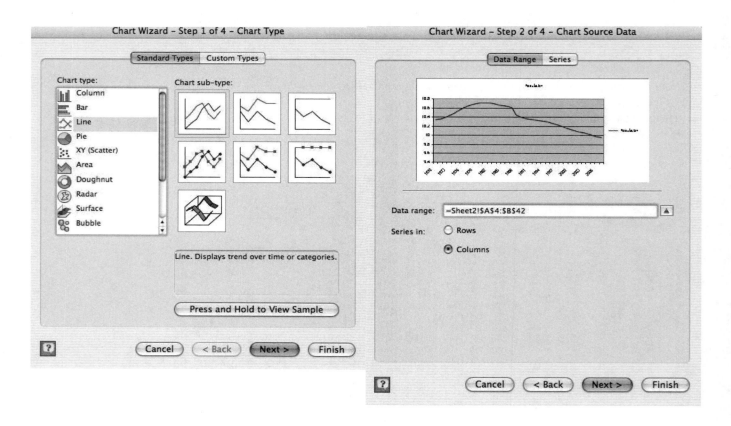

Step 3 lets you choose various options regarding the graph's appearance. The best way to learn about this option is to simply click on all the tabs and see what they allow you to do. For now, since there is only one series and its title is at the top of the graph, there is no need for a legend; so click on the "Legend" tab and uncheck the "Legend" box. By clicking on the "Titles" tab, you can add axis labels such as "Year" and "Millions of People" to the graph so that its reader understands what the graph represents.

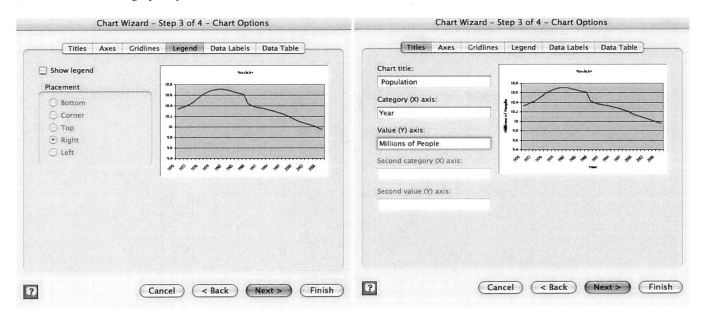

Step 4 asks you to make an important decision regarding where you want the graph placed. The choice depends on what you want to do with it. If you just want to work with the graph by itself and print it out or copy and paste it to another application, placing it as a new sheet makes it easier to work with. After clicking on "Finish," the graph will be complete.

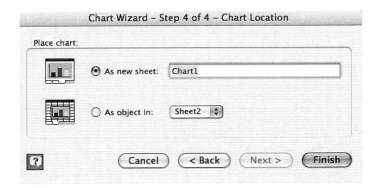

A couple of tips for working with graphs and making them as readable as possible include going to the "View" menu and clicking on "Sized with Window," so that the graph expands to fill the entire space available, as shown in the next two diagrams.

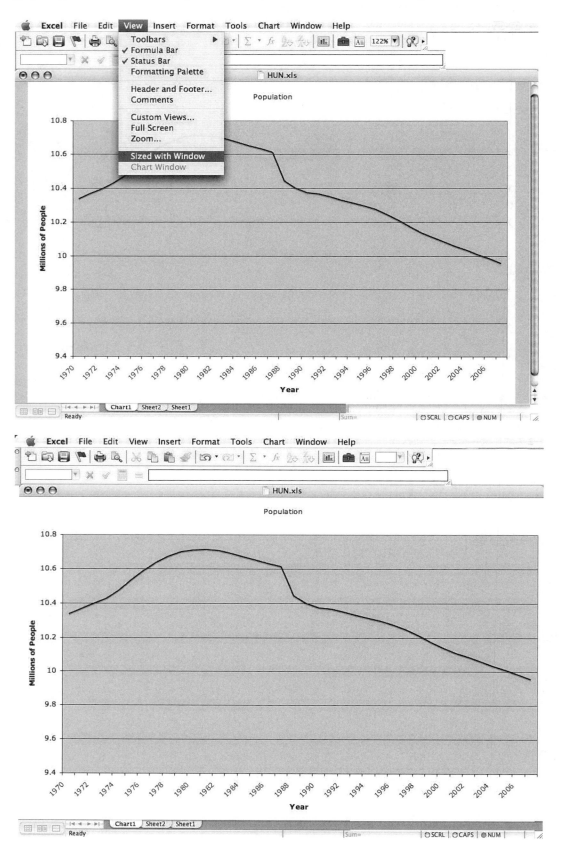

At this point, the graph technically is finished, but you can still experiment with the various presentation options by clicking on the different elements of the graph and determining the available options. For example, by double-clicking, or right-clicking on the gray area, it can be changed to white (saving a lot of ink when printing). Clicking on the axes and other labels can enhance their appearance by making them bold or increasing their size. Any number of the graph's attributes can be changed; the best way to learn, short of reading an instruction manual, is just to click and explore. The important part about this process is to produce an easily read and interpreted graph. For example, from the graph that follows, we easily can see that the Hungarian population grew during the 1970s and steadily decreased during the 1980s and 1990s.

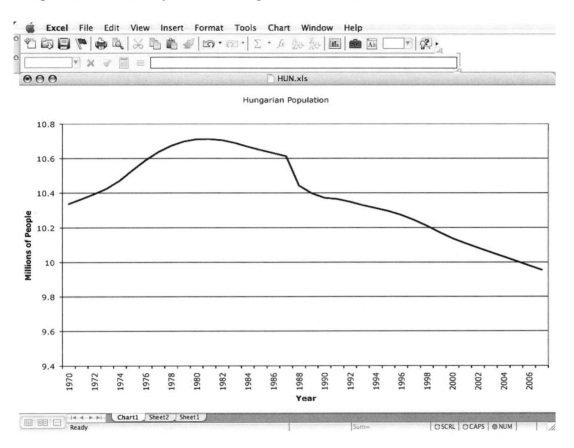

As a concluding exercise to the production of this first graph, look back at the last three graphs and decide for yourself which one is the most appealing to study and learn from.

Finally, suppose you need to graph more than one data series and those data series do not lie in adjacent columns. Copying and pasting them so that they do is one approach to making such a graph. Another, more efficient method, is exactly the same except for the initial step of data selection for the graph. First, select the data in cells A4:A42 on Sheet2, then hold down the control key on a PC or the command key on a Mac (the one with the apple on it) and, while holding it down, select the data in cells D4:D42 and then repeat the process to select the data in cells F4:F42 so that your spreadsheet appears as follows. You can repeat this process to include as many data series as desired.

	Population	Y/Pop	Y/Pop(us=10	Y/Wkr	Y/Wkr(us=10(	growth*100	I/Y	G/Y	Ed.Att.	NX/Y	X+M/Y	ExRate
1970	10.337	7001	35.4515	13515	28.3301	5.6138	22.8823	23.6008	7.899	-0.6483	52.7345	60
1971	10.3649	7394	36.4797	14416	29.5752	5.1639	24.181	26.909 NaN		-3.8883	55.6909	59.8216
1972	10.3941	7776	36.5691	15313	30.483	5.8059	22.2472	25.6689 NaN		2.4481	57.2069	55.26
1973	10.426	8228	36.8561	16368	31.5558	6.464	21.5387	24.6941 NaN		5.4418	61.733	48.9662
1974	10.4713	8760	39.9852	17605	35.2001	2.8735	22.5743	23.359 NaN		-1.9015	73.5803	46.7524
1975	10.5318	9011	41.8025	18300	37.5188	2.2304	25.2833	23.3369	7.915	-4.3522	75.1322	43.9714
1976	10.5887	9212	40.6671	18904	37.4431	5.4549	25.0822	23.6837 NaN		-1.6919	68.3412	41.5753
1977	10.6372	9715	41.2262	20148	39.0795	5.9688	25.6539	23.53 NaN		-1.9784	72.8688	40.9607
1978	10.6733	10295	41.7495	21579	40.8441	-0.4928	28.4162	23.8953 NaN		-5.8305	71.7759	37.9113
1979	10.6982	10244	40.7934	21706	40.9274	-0.0522	23.7425	24.9349 NaN		-0.9585	72.1984	35.578
1980	10.7111	10238	41.726	21933	42.6996	2.4316	22.924	25.4027	8.812	-0.1473	67.3836	32.5323
1981	10.7118	10487	42.0369	22643	43.634	1.5678	21.9377	25.7942 NaN		0.7745	67.2755	34.3143
1982	10.7055	10652	44.0514	23142	46.2177	-0.0353	20.8528	26.0875 NaN		2.2366	63.3323	36.6305
1983	10.6895	10848	42.2694	23291	44.7847	1.6709	19.355	26.3381 NaN		3.2489	66.3018	42.6711
1984	10.6681	10826	40.0198	23827	43.0495	0.759	18.6172	26.3162 NaN		4.3152	66.8298	48.0422
1985	10.6487	10908	39.124	24156	42.6651	2.8342	17.8696	27.0647	8.197	3.4568	69.4099	50.1194
1986	10.6306	11217	39.3269	24994	43.6269	3.5877	18.907	27.2756 NaN		0.4828	67.6402	45.8321
1987	10.6127	11620	39.7961	26048	44.7752	0.2403	18.8602	26.7239 NaN		1.1767	64.0946	46.9705
1988	10.4425	11648	38.7219	26263	44.0476	1.1225	18.5059	27.5956 NaN		3.8231	61.223	50.4132
1989	10.398	11778	38.167	26699	44.0102	-2.8602	18.6036	26.9879 NaN		4.3422	59.4275	59.0663
1990	10.3719	11442	36.9156	26010	42.8574	-9.1591	18.3906	27.6486	8.708	3.5296	51.6201	63.2059
1991	10.3647	10394	34.1765	23809	39.5976	-2.066	16.0393	29.7107 NaN		-0.8953	64.2098	74.7354
1992	10.3487	10179	32.7198	23315	37.8906	2.8709	13.0931	30.1525 NaN		-0.2211	60.9656	78.9884
1993	10.329	10471	33.035	24956	39.5829	1.6744	16.8674	32.1708 NaN		-7.8636	58.7655	91.9332
1994	10.3127	10646	32.4605	26199	40.2153	-1.4554	19.8935	29.4031 NaN		-6.2029	62.0107	105.1605
1995	10.2959	10492	31.5119	26463	39.8959	1.2995	20.4631	26.8573	8.518	0.0085	86.2915	125.6814
1996	10.2736	10628	30.9969	27071	39.6332	4.9753	23.1902	25.9013 NaN		0.5066	93.3047	152.6467
1997	10.2447	11157	31.3251	28736	40.7051	6.0062	25.2406	25.4919 NaN		1.0569	105.684	186.7892
1998	10.2111	11827	32.094	30273	41.3638	4.7066	28.9768	24.4875 NaN		-1.3123	121.1275	214.4017
1999	10.1727	12383	32.4492	30952	40.8579	5.1844	29.7326	23.8088 NaN		-2.5474	126.9341	237.1458
2000	10.1374	13025	33.1932	32282	41.9229	3.8322	31.5639	22.2273	8.811	-3.624	147.763	282.1792
2001	10.1095	13525	34.7359	33590	43.8603	4.935	29.1501	21.9736 NaN		-1.2319	143.4189	286.49
2002	10.0833	14192	36.3372	35079	45.5842	4.5734	27.5503	22.2482 NaN		-1.9588	127.9201	257.8867
2003	10.0577	14841	37.38	36087	46.2404	4.9311	27.0805	22.4687 NaN		-3.8968	125.2922	224.3067
2004	10.0324	15573	38.0671	37899	46.9678	4.1356	27.9741	21.8618 NaN		-2.8293	129.7572	202.7458
2005	10.0068	16217	38.7311	38901	47.1974	4.0662	25.8122	21.5667 NaN		-1.0844	133.5365	199.5825
2006	9.9813	16876	39.5383	40019	47.7982	1.85	23.8863	21.7645 NaN		0.592	155.0996	210.39
2007	9.9561	17188	40.0787	40784	48.3559 NaN		24.9587	20.0707 NaN		2.2577	157.6486	183.6258

Now click on the Chart Wizard and repeat the process used to produce your first graph. Experiment by clicking on the various components of the graph (center gray area, axes, legend, titles, series, etc.), changing them until you have matched the graph that follows next. Note that, if you just click on the legend once, you can drag it around and place it wherever you want it.

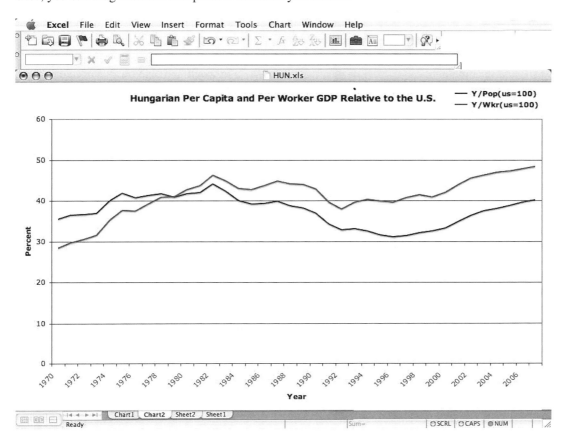

PROBLEMS

Worked Problem

This problem addresses the issue of modeling that Chapter 1 asks you to review from your previous economics coursework. Economists build models using mathematics—particularly algebra, its corresponding graphs, and calculus—to help understand the economy. Consider for example, a model of the market for laptop computers. We are fairly certain that the supply of laptop computers depends on the price for which they sell and the price of the materials required for their production. We also are fairly certain the demand for laptop computers depends on the price of laptop computers, the price of desktop computers, and consumers' income. We use symbols and notation to express concepts such as these more compactly. Recall from your math classes that $Y = F(W, X, Z)$ represents a multivariate function where Y is affected by the three variables W, X, and Z. In economics, we adopt this format and express demand and supply functions as $Q_d = D(P, P_{DT}, Y, \ldots)$;

$Q_s = S(P, P_M, \ldots)$. These demand and supply functions indicate that several variables have an impact on quantities both demanded and supplied. Q_s, Q_d, P, P_{DT}, P_M, and Y are all *variables*, denoting, respectively, the quantity of laptops supplied and demanded, the price of laptops, the price of desktop computers, the price of materials, and aggregate consumer income. In a specific product market like this one, P and Q (both Q_d and Q_s) are the endogenous variables because the model determines their outcomes. We use other letters, generally lowercase or Greek, to denote constants, exogenous variables (determined outside the model), and behavioral, or sensitivity, parameters that describe one variable's response to another. Very often in economics, we do not know the exact nature of the relationships among variables so we prefer this type of general functional notation. We also illustrate these relationships on a diagram, where an upward sloping supply curve shows that the quantity of laptops supplied increases and a downward sloping demand curve shows that the quantity of laptops demanded decreases as the price of laptops rises. P_{DT}, P_M, and Y are placed inside the parentheses to show that Q_d and Q_s also depend on other variables as well as the price of laptops. When working with graphs, like demand and supply diagrams, the number of endogenous variables is limited to two: price and quantity (P and Q), and they are always found on the graph's axes. Any exogenous variables shift either the demand or the supply curve, and behavioral parameters affect the slopes.

1. Suppose the following model represents supply and demand in the market for laptop computers:

$$Q_d = a - bP + cY \ ? \ dP_{DT} \qquad Q_s = eP + fP_M$$

In the problem and calculations that follow, do not let the question mark distract you; we will get to it later. For now, just let $a = 300$, $b = 10$, $c = 40$, $d = 30$, $e = 300$, and $f = 100$.

a. Which variables are exogenous and which are endogenous? How can you tell?

The variables P, Q_s, and Q_d are the endogenous variables in this model because they are the outputs determined by the model through the solution process. The variables P_M, P_{DT}, and Y are the exogenous variables in this model and must be known in advance (given) in order to find a solution. It also helps to note that we find the endogenous variables on the axes (price and quantity) in our demand and supply diagram.

b. What do the parameters a–f represent, and what is their function in the model?

The lowercase letters, a–f, are behavioral, or sensitivity, parameters. They indicate how an endogenous variable responds to changes of either exogenous or endogenous variables found in the model. For example, the parameter c in the demand equation determines how much quantity demanded changes in response to an increase in consumer income.

c. Which sign (+ or –) should replace the question mark in the demand equation? Why? What would a plus or minus sign signify in the laptop computer market?

The question mark should be replaced with a + sign because laptops and desktops are substitute products for performing computing operations. When the price of desktops goes up, so does the quantity of laptops demanded, because they become relatively less expensive to purchase. Similarly, the use of a – sign would indicate the presence of a complementary product, such as a piece of computer software. When the price of complementary products such as software and other peripherals rises, the quantity of laptops demanded decreases.

d. What are the equilibrium price and quantity in a market-clearing model for computers given the assumption of flexible prices?

Let income (Y) equal 10,000, the price of materials (P_M) equal 1,000, and the price of desktops (P_{DT}) equal 1,200.

First, to generate a solution to this demand and supply model, it is necessary to impose the equilibrium condition of demand equals supply. Begin, therefore, by setting demand equal to supply, that is, set Q_d equal to Q_s, then solve first for P then for Q as follows:

$$300 - 10P + 40Y + 30P_{DT} = 300P + 100P_M$$
$$300 - 10P + 400,000 + 36,000 = 300P + 100,000$$
$$310P = 336,300$$
$$P = 1,084.84$$
$$Q = 425,452 = 300(1,084.84)$$
$$+ 100,000$$

e. Graph the markets for laptops and desktops labeling each diagram as completely as possible given the available information.

With flexible prices your diagram should look like this:

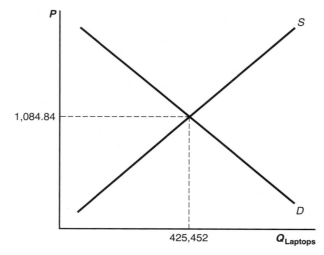

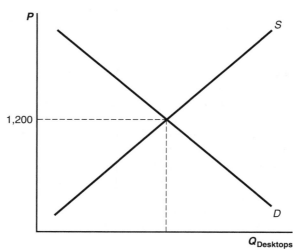

Note that you do not have enough information to complete the diagram for the market for desktop computers.

f. Suppose income increases to 11,000 and prices in the laptop market are sticky in the short run. What will be the price and quantity outcomes in the laptop market under these conditions? Show them on the laptop diagram from part e.

With sticky prices your diagram should look like this:

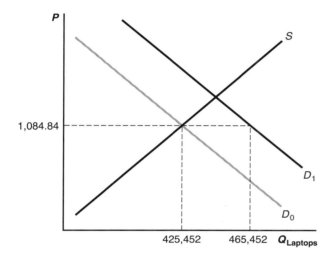

$$P = 1,084.84 \text{ (remember they are sticky}$$
$$\text{and do not change)}$$
$$Q_d = 300 - 10P + 40Y + 30P_{DT}$$
$$Q_d = 300 - 10P + 440,000 + 36,000$$
$$Q_d = 476,300 - 10(1,084.84)$$
$$Q = 465,452$$

g. What would the laptop market outcomes be if prices were flexible and income rose to 11,000? Show these outcomes on a laptop diagram as you did in part e. What amount of either inflation or deflation occurs in the laptop market?

With flexible prices your calculations will be as they were in part d:

$$300 - 10P + 40Y + 30P_{DT} = 300P + 100P_M$$
$$300 - 10P + 440,000 + 36,000 = 300P + 100,000$$
$$310P = 376,300$$
$$P = 1,213.87$$
$$Q = 464,161 = 300(1,213.87)$$
$$+ 100,000$$

With flexible prices your diagram should now look like this:

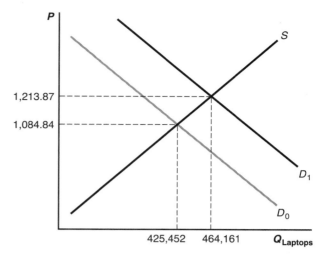

Since the price increases to 1,213.87 from 1,084.84, laptop prices experience inflation of 11.89 percent

$$\left(\frac{1,213.87 - 1,084.84}{1,084.84} = 0.1189 \text{ or } 11.89\% \right).$$

h. Suppose *instead* that desktop prices increase to 1,300 (income remains at 10,000 since we now are changing just the price of the substitute) and that prices in the laptop market are flexible. What will the price and quantity outcomes in the laptop market be under these conditions? Show these results on a separate diagram.

When desktop prices increase the calculations are as follows:

$$300 - 10P + 40Y + 30P_{DT} = 300P + 100P_M$$
$$300 - 10P + 400,000 + 36,000 = 300P + 100,000$$
$$310P = 336,300$$
$$P = 1,094.52$$
$$Q = 421,903 = 300(1,094.52)$$
$$+ 100,000$$

Following an increase in the price of a substitute the diagram would be as follows:

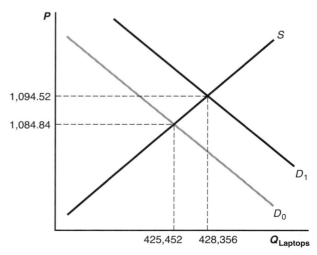

2. This problem gives you an opportunity to practice the skills learned in Problem 1 and in the text. Consider the following two diagrams.

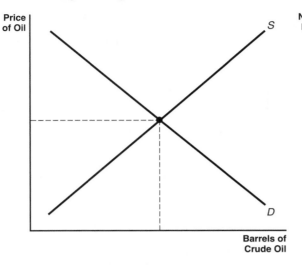

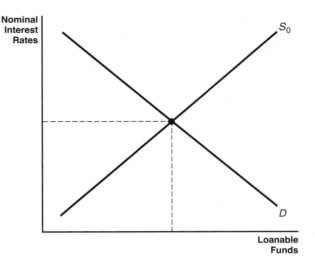

a. What are the endogenous variables in the model of the market for crude oil?

b. What are the endogenous variables in the model of the market for loanable funds?

c. What are two of the exogenous variables in the market for oil found in part a? Name at least one for supply and one for demand.

d. What are two of the exogenous variables in the market for loanable funds found in part b? Name at least one for supply and one for demand.

e. Describe and show on the diagram from part a what happens when the exogenous demand variable you chose for part c increases.

f. Describe, and show on the diagram from part b, what happens when the exogenous supply variable you chose for part d increases.

CHAPTER 1 SOLUTIONS

True/False Questions

1. True. Modern macroeconomics is built upon microeconomic foundations, or individual behavior.

2. True. Macroeconomic issues affect some aspect of the whole economy, generally related to the standard of living.

3. False. See Figure 1.1. The United Kingdom exceeded the United States in the late 1800s.

4. False. See Figure 1.4. Since the mid-1980s, the United States has experienced a downward trend in its unemployment rate.

5. False. See Figure 1.5. Budget deficits were significantly reduced during the 1990s.

6. True. See Figure 1.6. Parameters and exogenous variables come together to provide an outcome or solution for an economic model.

7. False. See Figure 1.7. GDP growth has averaged about 2 percent since 1870.

8. False. See Section 1.3. News releases about quarterly GDP behavior generally describe short-term fluctuations, not long-run economic growth.

Multiple-Choice Questions

1. e, Modern macroeconomics is built upon both micro- and macroeconomic principles.

2. b, Each of these answers except firm behavior is considered a macroeconomic issue.

3. d, Unemployment for the economy as a whole is not generally addressed as a microeconomic issue. In a specific market for a specific type of labor you may see unemployment for those workers raised as a microeconomic issue.

4. c, Each of these issues except personal income is an issue that impacts the economy as a whole, whereas personal income will vary across individuals and is addressed in the microeconomic issue of income distribution.

5. d, As you can see, some issues such as government intervention come up in both micro- and macroeconomic issues. Stock prices generally fall

under financial asset issues, which are more micro in nature but not without their macro implications.

6. a, Survey analysis is a less frequently used technique for economists in general and, when it is used, surfaces most frequently in microeconomic topics.

7. d, A successful model will accomplish each of the objectives listed in parts a–c.

Exercises

1. Snapshots exercise.
   a. 30. See the top left-hand diagram for Hungary. The data go from 1970 to 2007 on the horizontal axis.
   b. 31.4. The number given in parentheses above each graph identifies the value of the last data point for that series in the diagram.
   c. The number 31.4 means that Hungarian GDP per capita is 31.4 percent of GDP per capita in the United States.
   d. GDP per worker (39.5) is greater than GDP per capita (31.4). This means that GDP per worker in Hungary relative to the United States is 8.1 percentage points greater than is GDP per capita (39.5 – 31.4 = 8.1).
   e. GDP per worker should always be greater than GDP per capita since not everyone in a country is employed.
   f. The GDP growth rate of approximately 5 percent is greater than the average growth rate of 2.21 percent (the dotted green line), but it is not possible to tell precisely from the plot provided.

2. Worked exercise. Answers are given in the exercise.

Problems

1. Worked modeling problem. Answers are given in the problem.

2. Practice with models of markets.
   a. The endogenous variables in this model (found on the axes) are the number of barrels of crude oil and the price of crude oil.
   b. The endogenous variables in this model (found on the axes) are the amount of loanable funds and the interest rate.
   c. Demand variables exogenous to this model would include a number of things, such as the demand for heating oil, gasoline, plastics, and natural gas, since they are either produced from crude oil or, as in the case of natural gas, are a substitute for crude oil. Additionally, fuel efficiency in the transportation industry and insulation in buildings can also influence (shift) the demand for crude oil. Supply variables exogenous to this model would include things such as the depth of the oil well and the quality of the crude oil. Additionally, the taxes (and subsidies) levied by the government will have an impact on the supply curve, causing it to shift either to the left or to the right, as will the price of labor and the level of government regulation over the oil industry. In short, a change in any variable in the crude oil market other than the price of oil or the number of barrels produced or demanded will cause either the demand or the supply curve to shift.
   d. Demand variables exogenous to this model include a number of things, such as the demand for investment capital by firms, the size of federal budget deficits and therefore the government's need to borrow, or just the demand for automobile loans by consumers. Additionally, consumer confidence and attitudes toward debt also can influence (shift) the demand for loanable funds. Supply variables exogenous to this model include things such as banks' attitude toward risk, individuals' willingness to postpone consumption and save instead of spend, and the Federal Reserve interest rate policy. Additionally, the level of expected inflation has an impact on the supply of loanable funds causing it to shift either to the left when it's higher or to the right when it's lower. In short, a change in any variable in the loanable funds market other than the nominal interest rate or the quantity of loans demanded or supplied causes *either* the demand or the supply curve to shift.
   e. When an increase in the demand for gasoline or heating oil occurs, it causes the demand for crude oil to increase from D_0 to D_1, as shown in Figure 1.

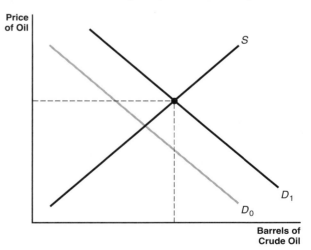

Figure 1

f. When the Fed increases its bond purchases in the open market, it causes the supply of loanable funds to increase from S_0 to S_1, as shown in Figure 2.

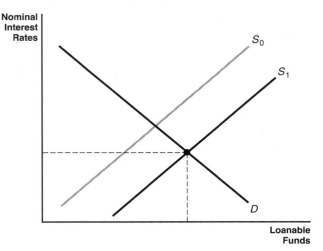

Figure 2

APPENDIX 1
MATH REVIEW

The following review covers several of the different mathematical concepts and skills that economists use in their economic analysis and the model building processes employed in the text. Each problem, including the *challenge problems,* calls on a concept or skill used *some time* in the text and most of the time by the middle of the book. Work through the problems as if you were taking a test; it will help you determine if and where you need to brush up on some skills. Then refer to the solutions at the end of the appendix for the answers and, more important, explanations and instructions about the solution process. If you have trouble completing this section, bring that to the attention of your instructor, who will determine if you need any help brushing up on these skills.

Percentages

1. If the price of DVDs rose from $20 to $22, what amount of inflation did DVDs experience?

2. Suppose you earn $16 an hour and get a 6¼ percent raise. How much will you then make per hour?

3. Suppose you earn $16 an hour and get a raise of $1 per hour. What percentage increase was your raise?

4. If you put $250 in the bank, left it there for a year, and ended up with $265, what interest rate did you earn?

5. If nominal GDP for 2007 *were* $14.5 trillion and for 2008 *were* $15.6 trillion, what would its growth rate have been?

6. What formula does each of problems 1 through 5 have in common?

Graphs

The next two sets of exercises review the relationship between graphing algebraic equations and their economic counterparts.

1. Graph and label the equation $Y_1 = 10 - \frac{1}{2}X$. Be sure to label the axes as well as the intercept and slope.

2. Also graph and similarly label the equation $Y_2 = 2 + \frac{3}{4}X$ on the same diagram.

3. Find the X and Y values for the intersection of Y_1 and Y_2 and label them on the diagram.

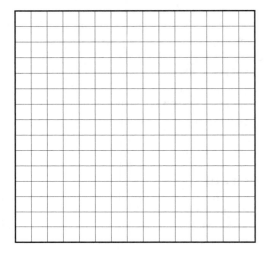

Now suppose that you have two equations: $Q_d = 20 - 2P$ and $Q_s = \frac{8}{3} + \frac{4}{3}P$. Label the vertical axis in this diagram P, for price, and the horizontal axis Q, for quantity.

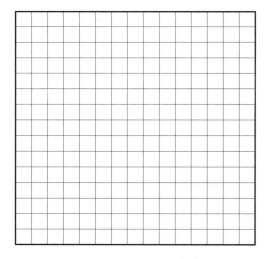

4. Invert the equations Q_d and Q_s; in other words, solve each equation for P. Call the equation with Q_d in it *Demand* and call the equation with Q_s in it *Supply*.

5. Graph both the equation for *Demand* and the equation for *Supply* on the second diagram, labeling them as you did in graphing Problem 1.

6. Find the values for *P* and *Q* at the intersection of *Demand* and *Supply* and label them on the diagram.

7. Suppose that you have the following equation: $C = 50 + \frac{3}{4}Y$, where *C* stands for an individual's consumption and *Y* stands for income.

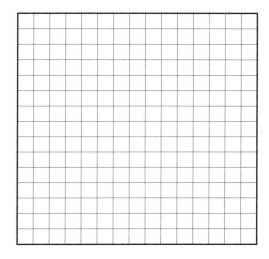

Draw and label this function, including the axes, intercept, and slope, on the diagram above.

8. Provide an economic interpretation for the intercept.

9. Provide an economic interpretation for the slope.

10. Draw and label a second equation representing the income earned on the graph using the equation $Y = Y$.

11. At what level of income will this person's consumption needs be met?

Math Skills

Simplify each of the following, except as noted.

1. $(3x^2 y)(4x)$

2. $(-2xy^3)(-3xy^{-\frac{1}{3}})$

3. $6x^3 + 4x^2 y + 2x^2 z$

4. $3y\{1/2y[2x(3x-1)]+x\}$

5. Factor $y(3y^2 + 7y + 2)$

6. $5x^{-\frac{1}{2}}$

7. $4(2x^a)^2$

8. $5(2x^a)^{\frac{1}{a}}$

9. $(4x^a)(3x^{-\frac{1}{a}})$

10. $\dfrac{a(b+c)}{ab+ac}$

11. $\dfrac{a/b}{c/d}$

12. $\dfrac{a}{a+b}$

13. $2y = 3x + 6$, given $x = \frac{1}{2}y$

14. Solve for *y*: $y = a + by + c + d - ey$

15. For $y = 6x^3$, find $\frac{\partial y}{\partial x}$.

16. For $y = 6x^{\frac{1}{2}}z$, find $\frac{\partial y}{\partial x}$.

Challenge Problems

The following problems resemble those you will encounter in subsequent chapters in the text, but they might seem unfamiliar to you now. Do not worry though; the solution process is explained in the answer section and again in the chapters where you will need to apply these skills. So, for now, work the problems as far as you can; then go to the answers and see how you did or how to complete the problem.

1. For $y_t = x_t^a z_t^b$, what is the growth rate of y_t?

2. For $y_t = 100\dfrac{x_t^a}{z_t^b}$, what is the growth rate of y_t?

3. For $y = 100x^{\frac{1}{2}}z^{\frac{1}{2}}$ show that $100\left(\dfrac{x}{z}\right)^{\frac{1}{2}} = \dfrac{y}{z}$.

4. Solve for *x* when $y = \dfrac{x^3}{27}$.

5. If $a < 1$, what is the solution to $y = 100(1 + a + a^2 + \ldots + a^n)$, for $n = 14$ and $n = \infty$?

6. Suppose you will receive an inheritance of $10,000 in five years and the interest rate is 6 percent. What is the lowest price for which you would sell that inheritance right now?

7. Suppose you were to receive $1,000 today and each year for the next nine years but that the interest rate is only 5 percent. What is the lowest price for which you would sell that inheritance right now?

Math Review Solutions

Percentages

One of the most frequently used mathematical principles in economics is the percentage change of a variable. From inflation to GDP growth, the formula is the same, just the context varies. The percentage change ($\%\Delta X$), or growth rate (g_X), of a variable *X* is $\%\Delta X = \dfrac{X_1 - X_0}{X_0}$ when comparing two values of a variable or $g_X = \dfrac{X_t - X_{t-1}}{X_{t-1}}$ when comparing the current period's value to that from the last period.

1. DVD inflation: $\pi = \dfrac{22 - 20}{20} = \dfrac{2}{20} = \dfrac{1}{10} = 0.1$ or 10%.

2. New wage: $\$16 + \$16(0.0625) = \$16(1 + 0.0625) = \$16(1.0625) = \$17$.

3. Raise: $\dfrac{\$17 - \$16}{\$16} = \dfrac{1}{16} = 0.0625 = 6.25\%$. You should

   take a moment and confirm that $\dfrac{\$17 - \$16}{\$16} = 0.0625$

   and $\$16 + \$16(0.0625) = \$17$, in fact, are equivalent to each other.

4. Interest earnings: $\dfrac{\$265 - \$250}{\$250} = \dfrac{15}{250} = 0.06 = 6\%$.

5. GDP growth: $\dfrac{\text{GDP}_{2008} - \text{GDP}_{2007}}{\text{GDP}_{2007}} = \dfrac{\$15.6 - \$14.5}{\$14.5} =$

   $\dfrac{1.1}{14.5} = 0.075862 \approx 7.6\%$.

6. They each use some version of the percentage change, or growth rate, formula as shown previously. The basic

   form of that formula is $g_X = \dfrac{X_t - X_0}{X_0}$ or $\dfrac{X_t - X_{t-1}}{X_{t-1}}$.

GRAPHS

Supply and demand diagrams are one of economists' primary tools, of course. Problems 1–3 and 4–6 transform the mathematician's use of a graph into an economist's use of a supply and demand diagram.

PROBLEMS 1–3

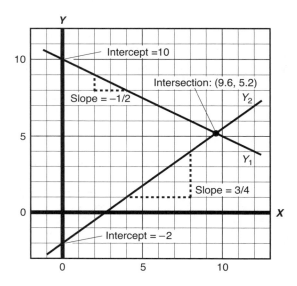

Note: Y_2 has a *positive* slope and represents a *direct* relationship between X and Y. Similarly, Y_1 has a *negative* slope and represents an *indirect,* or *inverse,* relationship between X and Y. To solve for the intersection of Y_1 and Y_2, set the two equations equal to each other and solve for X. Then, substitute X back into either equation to obtain the value for Y, where $Y_1 = Y_2$.

$$10 - \tfrac{1}{2}X = -2 + \tfrac{3}{4}X$$
$$12 = \tfrac{5}{4}X$$
$$X = 12(\tfrac{4}{5}) = \dfrac{48}{5} = 9.6$$
$$Y_1 = 10 - \tfrac{1}{2}(9.6) = 5.2$$
$$Y_2 = -2 + \tfrac{3}{4}(9.6) = 5.2$$
$$(X, Y) = (9.6, 5.2)$$

PROBLEMS 4–6

To invert the Q_s and Q_d equations, solve each of them for P:

$Q_s = \tfrac{8}{3} + \tfrac{4}{3}P$ $\qquad\qquad$ $Q_d = 20 - 2P$

$\tfrac{4}{3}P = -\tfrac{8}{3} + Q_s$ $\qquad\qquad$ $2P = 20 - Q_d$

$P = -\tfrac{3}{4}(\tfrac{8}{3}) + \tfrac{3}{4}Q_s = -2 + \tfrac{3}{4}Q_s$ $\qquad$ $P = 10 - \tfrac{1}{2}Q_d$

The *Supply* equation for graphing purposes becomes $P = -2 + \tfrac{3}{4}Q_s$, the *Demand* equation becomes $P = 10 - \tfrac{1}{2}Q_d$, and the solution process is the same as in Problems 1–3.

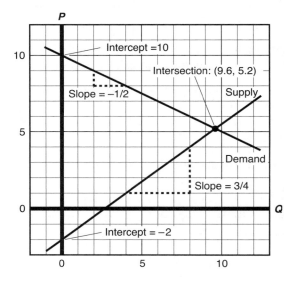

The solution for Problems 4–6, or the market clearing price and quantity, is a price of $\$5.20$ and a quantity of 9.6 units.

As a postscript to problems 1–6, note that in both sets of initial equations X and P are the independent variables and Y and Q are the dependent variables. Economists, however, have a longstanding tradition of placing *Price* on the vertical axis and *Quantity* on the horizontal axis. This dates back to the time of Alfred Marshall, who argued that prices were the outcome of interaction between supply and demand and hence the dependent variable. Leon Walras, however, using the metaphor of an auctioneer, more successfully argued that buyers and sellers responded to prices by adjusting their offers to sell and to buy, hence the formulation of Q_d and Q_s as functions of price.

PROBLEMS 7–11

7 and 10.

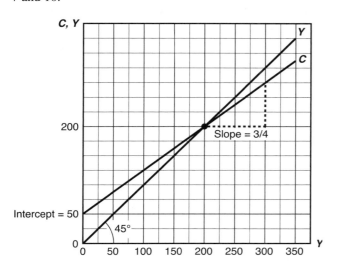

8. We interpret the intercept of 50 as the level of consumption when income equals zero (food, shelter, etc.).

9. The slope represents the change in consumption that results from a change in income. For example, if income in this model increases by 100, consumption increases by 75.

10. The equation $Y = Y$ is represented by the 45° line.

11. As seen in the diagram, consumption equals income at an income level of 200. The solution is as follows:

$$Y = 50 + 0.75Y$$
$$Y - 0.75Y = 50$$
$$Y(1 - 0.75) = 50$$
$$Y = \left(\frac{1}{1-0.75}\right)50 = 4 \times 50 = 200$$

Note that when $Y = C$, no saving takes place, like it does when $Y > C$, nor does any dissaving occur, as it does when $Y < C$.

MATH SKILLS

1. $(3x^2y)(4x) = 12x^3y$

2. $\left(-2xy^3\right)\left(-3xy^{-\frac{1}{3}}\right) = 6x^2y^{\frac{8}{3}}$

3. $6x^3 + 4x^2y + 2x^2z = (2x^2)(3x + 2y + z)$

4.
$$3y\{2y[\tfrac{1}{2}x(3x-1)] + x\} = 3y\{\tfrac{1}{2}y[6x^2 - 2x] + x\}$$
$$= 3y\{3x^2y - xy + x\}$$
$$= 9x^2y^2 - 3xy^2 + 3xy$$
$$= 3xy(3xy - y + 1)$$
$$= 3xy[y(3x-1) + 1]$$

5. Factor $y(3y^2 + 7y + 2) = y(3y + 1)(y + 2)$

6. $5x^{-\frac{1}{2}} = \dfrac{5}{x^{\frac{1}{2}}}$ or $\dfrac{5}{\sqrt{x}}$

7. $4(2x^a)^2 = 4(2^2x^{2a}) = 16x^{2a}$

8. $5\left(2x^a\right)^{\frac{1}{a}} = 5\left(2^{\frac{1}{a}}\right)x$

9. $\left(4x^a\right)\left(3x^{-\frac{1}{a}}\right)^a = 12x^{a-1}$

10. $\dfrac{a(b+c)}{ab+ac} = \dfrac{a(b+c)}{a(b+c)} = 1$

11. $\dfrac{\frac{a}{b}}{\frac{c}{d}} = \dfrac{\frac{a}{b}}{\frac{c}{d}} = \dfrac{a}{b} \times \dfrac{d}{c} = \dfrac{ad}{bc}$

12. $\dfrac{a}{a+b}$ cannot be simplified, although a common error is to try to cancel the a's.

13. $2y = 3x + 6$, given $x = \frac{1}{2}$
$$y2y = 3(\tfrac{1}{2}y) + 6$$
$$2y = \tfrac{3}{2}y + 6$$
$$\tfrac{1}{2}y = 6$$
$$y = 12, \quad x = 6$$

14.
$$y = a + by + c + d - ey \qquad y = a + by + c + d - ey$$
$$y - by + ey = a + c + d$$
$$y(1 - b + e) = a + c + d$$
$$y = \frac{1}{1-b+e}(a + c + d)$$

15. For $y = 6x^3$, find $\dfrac{\partial y}{\partial x}$ $\qquad$ $\dfrac{\partial y}{\partial x} = 18x^2$

16. For $y = 6x^{\frac{1}{2}}z$, find $\dfrac{\partial y}{\partial x}$ $\qquad$ $\dfrac{\partial y}{\partial x} = 3x^{-\frac{1}{2}}z$

Problems 15 and 16 use the derivative rule, where for $y = ax^n$, $\dfrac{\partial y}{\partial x} = nax^{n-1}$. In Problem 15, it is also a total derivative, since y is differentiated with respect to all the independent variables (in this case x is the only one). Problem 16, however, is a partial derivative since no derivative of y with respect to z is taken.

CHALLENGE PROBLEMS

Each of Problems 1 and 2 use two of the three growth rate rules (discussed in Section 3.5), where

$$\text{for } y = x^a, \ g_y = ag_x; \text{ for } y = xz, \ g_y = g_x + g_z;$$
$$\text{and for } y = \frac{x}{z}, \ g_y = g_x - g_z.$$

1. For $y_t = x_t^a z_t^b$, what is the growth rate of y_t?

$$g_y = ag_x + bg_z$$

2. For $y_t = 100\dfrac{x_t^a}{z_t^b}$, what is the growth rate of y_t?

$$g_y = 0 + ag_x - bg_z$$

Since a constant does not change or grow, g_{100} equals zero, just as the derivative of a constant equals zero.

Problem 3 uses a modeling tool of multiplying by a special

form of 1 such as $\dfrac{a}{a}$, or in this case, $\dfrac{z^{\frac{1}{2}}}{z^{\frac{1}{2}}}$.

3. For $y = 100x^{\frac{1}{2}}z^{\frac{1}{2}}$ show that $100\left(\dfrac{x}{z}\right)^{\frac{1}{2}} = \dfrac{y}{z}$:

$$100\left(\frac{x}{z}\right)^{\frac{1}{2}}\frac{z^{\frac{1}{2}}}{z^{\frac{1}{2}}} = \frac{100x^{\frac{1}{2}}z^{\frac{1}{2}}}{z^{\frac{1}{2}}z^{\frac{1}{2}}} = \frac{y}{z}$$

Problem 4 requires taking an *n*th root, in this case a cubed root.

4. Solve for *x* when

$$y = \frac{x^3}{27}$$

$$y = \frac{x^3}{27} \implies y^{\frac{1}{3}} = \left(\frac{x^3}{27}\right)^{\frac{1}{3}} \implies y^{\frac{1}{3}} = \frac{x}{3} \implies x = 3y^{\frac{1}{3}}$$

Problem 5 requires recognition of the term in parentheses as a geometric series. Recall that a series

$$S_n = x + xa + xa^2 + \ldots + xa^n$$

is solved by multiplying both sides of the equation by *a*

$$S_na = xa + xa^2 + xa^3 + \ldots + xa^{n+1},$$

then subtracting S_na from S_n (when subtracting S_na from S_n, note that almost all the *xa* terms on the right-hand side cancel out in this process) to get

$$S_n - S_na = x - xa^{n+1}.$$

Then factor out S_n and *x* and divide both sides by $1 - a$

$$S_n(1-a) = x(1 - a^{n+1}) \implies S_n = x\frac{1 - a^{n+1}}{1-a}.$$

5. If $a < 1$, what is the solution to $y = 100(1 + a + a^2 + \ldots + a^n)$, for $n = 14$ and $n = \infty$?

$$y = 100\frac{1 - a^{15}}{1 - a}$$

$$y = 100\frac{1 - a^{\infty}}{1 - a} = 100\frac{1}{1-a}, \text{ since for } a < 1, \ a^{\infty} = 0$$

Regarding the intuition for the term a^{∞} when *a* is less than 1, think of the examples: $\frac{1}{2}^2 = 0.25$, $\frac{1}{2}^3 = 0.125$, $\frac{1}{2}^4 = 0.0625$, $\frac{1}{2}^4 = 0.03125$, and so on. Note that each successive multiplication of $\frac{1}{2}$ by $\frac{1}{2}$ generates a smaller and smaller result.

6. Suppose you will receive an inheritance of $10,000 in five years and the interest rate is 6 percent. What is the lowest price for which you would sell that inheritance right now? This is a present discounted value problem and asks how much money you would need to save today to have $10,000 in five years:

$$pdv(1 + 0.06)^5 = \$10,000$$

$$pdv = \frac{\$10,000}{(1 + 0.06)^5} = \frac{\$10,000}{1.33823} = \$7,472.58$$

7. Suppose you were to receive $1,000 today and each year for the next nine years but that the interest rate is only 5 percent. What is the lowest price for which you would sell that inheritance right now? This also is a present discounted value problem but of a series of installments and so it is just like the geometric series exercise in Problem 5 combined with the present value exercise in Problem 6. It also is a significant part of Chapter 7 in the text. In this case, $x = \$1,000$ (instead of 100) and $a = \dfrac{1}{1 + 0.05}$, which means that $a < 1$ so the conditions for using the geometric series in Problem 5 are met:

$$pdv = \$1,000\frac{1 - \left(\frac{1}{1.05}\right)^{9+1}}{1 - \frac{1}{1.05}} = \$1,000\frac{1 - (0.95238)^{10}}{1 - 0.95238} =$$

$$\$1,000\frac{0.38609}{0.04762} = \$8,107.82$$

Note: Your calculations may vary slightly due to rounding. There is no rounding in the preceding answer, even though the numbers displayed have been rounded.

CHAPTER 2

Measuring the Macroeconomy

OVERVIEW

Gross domestic product (GDP), the market value of all final goods and services produced in an economy during a calendar year, along with the other national income accounts from which it comes, provides a national pulse that allows us to evaluate the health of our national economy. During the past thirty years, despite a few recessions, the U.S. economy has experienced relatively stable growth, averaging just over 3 percent per year. During that same time period, consumption's share of GDP has grown by about 4 percentage points, while the share of government purchases (but not government spending) declined by about the same amount. While not a perfect measure, GDP per capita does allow us to track the average living standard of people in a country, but it fails to account for household production, people's health, and environmental impact. In the United States, GDP per capita rose an average of 2.3 percent during the last half of the twentieth century. The actual increase in living standards may be higher or lower than the change in GDP per capita would suggest, depending on the contributions of household production, people's health, and environmental changes. Further complicating GDP comparisons over time is the change in relative prices that occurs among different products. Using the Fisher index to update price changes each year through a chain-weighting process produces the most accurate representation of GDP changes over time. Making international comparisons, however, requires additional care. In addition to having to account for the use of different currencies, we also need to account for differences in local currency purchasing power but in different countries. To do this we use a set of common world prices.

KEY CONCEPTS

Economic profits are the earnings experienced by a firm that exceed what is necessary to keep its owners from exiting and shutting the firm down. The owners are at least recovering their opportunity costs.

National income accounting provides a systematic measure of aggregate economic activity. In fact, it provides three ways to produce the same final value for gross domestic product: expenditures, income, and production or value added.

Gross domestic product (GDP) is the key overall measure of economic activity in an economy. It consists of the value of all goods and services produced during a calendar year for which there have been legal market transactions. As a measure of all productive activity, however, it suffers from the omission of household production and underground or black-market activities. It also fails to account for certain health and environmental issues.

Trade balance is another name for net exports. A positive trade balance means that a country's exports exceed its imports, and a negative trade balance means that a country has imported more than it exported.

The *income approach to national income accounting (GDI)* recognizes that every dollar of goods and services produced must also generate a combined dollar's worth of income for each of the factors of a product's production (rent from land and resource usage, wages from labor, interest from capital, and profit from entrepreneurship). A useful application of the income approach is to divide income into two categories: one for labor income (wages and the labor part of profit) and one for the income received by the owners of all other productive resources (rent for land, interest for capital, and the capital part of profit).

The *expenditure approach to national income accounting* assigns all spending to one of four categories: consumption, investment, government purchases, and the foreign sector; and since for accounting purposes firms essentially purchase their unsold inventory each year and then sell it in the following year, the sum of these categories generates total spending or GDP for the year, that is, $GDP = C + I + G + NX$.

The *national income identity, $Y = C + I + G + NX$,* utilizes both the income (*GDI*) and expenditure (*GDP*) approaches to national income accounting by noting that they both measure the same thing in different ways and that they can, therefore, be set equal to each other.

The *production approach to national income accounting* considers the value added by each producer at each stage of production. This method emphasizes the contribution toward GDP of each of the participants in the production process. The sum of "value added" at each stage of production necessarily equals the final value of the product when sold on completion.

Labor's share of GDP, wages and the labor part of profit, has remained relatively stable over time at about two-thirds of total production according to the income approach to national income accounting.

Depreciation occurs when a firm's capital assets (its buildings and equipment and any productive inputs other than the labor and materials that become part of the output produced) experience wear and tear and eventually require replacement.

Real GDP is the concept used to measure the real—physical or actual—production of goods and services in the absence of price changes. It allows us to answer questions about the growth of an economy. For example, did the United States produce more actual goods and services during 2006 than during 2005?

Nominal GDP uses current prices from the year in question and refers to the actual or face value of the total sales generating GDP during that year.

Chain weighting is a method of calculating real GDP that generates a more accurate calculation of growth between years than if we used either of the individual years of the comparison period as the base year. It assumes that price growth for a period is midway between the rates suggested by either of the years in question. Thus, we gradually update the prices used to make comparisons by averaging the results of the prices for each of the adjacent years individually, then repeat the process for each pair of adjacent years in the

entire period (that is, we use the *Fisher index* and average the results of the *Laspeyres index,* beginning year prices, and the *Paasche index,* final year prices, for each pair of prices for the entire GDP series).

GDP deflator represents the price level for the entire goods and services that a country produces each year. It is an index generated from all the prices for all of the goods and services measured by the national income accounts.

The *unemployment rate* tells us the percentage of people formally looking for employment who are unable to find jobs. It is discussed further in Chapter 7.

The *interest rate* is the price you pay for using someone else's resources today. It can take the form of either goods, services, or money and compensates the owner of those resources for waiting to use them themselves while you use them. Interest rates are discussed further in Chapter 8.

The *inflation rate* is the percentage change in the price level and also receives further discussion in Chapter 8.

An *exchange rate* is the price of one country's currency in terms of another country's currency. For example, the price of a dollar might be 7.7 yuan, in which case the exchange rate is 7.7 yuan, per dollar (or 13 cents per yuan). Exchange rates are discussed further in Chapter 19.

International comparisons of GDP present us with the difficulty of comparing two countries that not only have different currencies, but whose currencies also have different degrees of purchasing power even once the exchange rate has been taken into account. Therefore, to make meaningful international comparisons, we must first make the conversion to a common currency, then take into account differences in purchasing power by converting each country's GDP to a common set of prices.

TRUE/FALSE QUESTIONS

1. National income accounting provides useful short-term snapshots of a nation's economic activity that provide meaningful insights into its growth over time but are of relatively little use in making international comparisons.

2. As shares of GDP, its components—consumption, investment, government purchases, and net exports—are ranked here in order of their size.

3. Since before the Great Depression, consumption has played a significant role in the economy, consistently comprising two-thirds of GDP.

4. During World War II, government purchases accounted for more than twice their usual percentage of GDP.

5. Economists use the term "capital" to refer to the money necessary to establish and begin operating a new business venture.

6. Roughly 50 cents from every dollar of sales in the United States goes to the owners of capital.

7. The net operating surplus of a business is just another name for profit.

8. National income accounting data provide support for the claim that corporations are not getting richer at the expense of labor.

9. GDP includes all goods and services produced in an economy during a calendar year.

10. The sale of a used car adds to the value of GDP.

11. GDP comparison between years is best accomplished using nominal GDP.

MULTIPLE-CHOICE QUESTIONS

1. The National Income and Product Accounts provide a systematic method for aggregating all of the following areas of economic activity except
   a. the production of automobiles.
   b. the provision of health care services.
   c. music distributed legally over the Internet.
   d. the distribution of computer software and hardware.
   e. none of the above.

2. When a firm earns "economic profits," we can safely argue that
   a. the firm is breaking even.
   b. the entrepreneurs (Homer and Marge in the text) have partially recovered their opportunity cost.
   c. the entrepreneurs are earning a normal competitive return from their enterprise.
   d. the entrepreneurs are earning an above-normal return from their enterprise.
   e. none of the above.

3. If a firm experiences at least some degree of market power, even if only a little, then
   a. economic profits will be positive.
   b. accounting profits will exceed economic profits.
   c. price will exceed marginal revenue.
   d. price will exceed marginal cost.
   e. both a and d are correct.

4. GDP includes each of the following except
   a. consumption.
   b. government.
   c. foreign exchange.
   d. investment.
   e. none of the above.

5. Consumption expenditures include each of the following categories except
   a. automobiles.
   b. medical care.
   c. entertainment.
   d. new home construction.
   e. food.

6. Government purchases of goods and services at all levels of government in the United States include each of the following except
   a. spending on public schools.
   b. military expenditures.
   c. spending on Medicare.
   d. research by the National Science Foundation.
   e. spending on highway construction.

7. Another name for net exports is
   a. imports minus exports.
   b. exports plus imports.
   c. foreign exchange.
   d. trade balance.
   e. foreign trade.

8. Which of the following does not help explain the recent increase in consumption spending as a share of GDP?
   a. decreased government spending
   b. falling trade balances
   c. increased credit availability
   d. positive technology shock
   e. none of the above; they all help to explain it.

9. Labor's share of national income is approximately
   a. 75 percent.
   b. 67 percent.
   c. 60 percent.
   d. 57 percent.
   e. 50 percent.

10. The production approach to national income accounting uses which of the following methodologies?
    a. expenditures
    b. income
    c. consumption
    d. value added
    e. factors of production

11. Our current measure of GDP, as valuable as it is in measuring the performance of our economy, suffers from several limitations. Which of the following is not one of them?
    a. the exclusion of household production
    b. the presence of an underground economy
    c. the impact of the Clean Air Act on U.S. economic activity
    d. the increased life expectancy of U.S. citizens
    e. the impact of global warming generated by U.S. economic activities

12. What is the appropriate relationship between nominal and real GDP?
    a. real GDP = nominal GDP − price level
    b. nominal GDP = real GDP ÷ price level
    c. nominal GDP = real GDP + price level
    d. real GDP = nominal GDP ÷ price level
    e. real GDP = nominal GDP × price level

13. Which of the following is not one of the difficulties in measuring GDP changes over time?
    a. Quantities produced have changed; prices have not.
    b. Prices have changed; quantities produced have not.
    c. Both prices and quantities produced have changed.
    d. the existence of an underground economy
    e. changes in the quality of the goods produced

14. The most accurate method of portraying the change in real GDP over time uses the
    a. Paasche index.
    b. Laspeyres index.
    c. Fisher index.
    d. an average of the Fisher and Laspeyres indices.
    e. both c and d.

15. Economists generally prefer the chain-weighted procedure employed by the Fisher index because it
    a. reduces distortions caused by high inflation.
    b. provides better comparisons of GDP over longer periods of time.
    c. provides a more accurate portrayal of changes in living standards over time.
    d. provides a more accurate portrayal of real GDP changes over time.
    e. all of the above

16. When determining any particular component's share in GDP, for example, consumption's share in GDP during a given year, it is best to use _____ values.
    a. Paasche
    b. Laspeyres
    c. Fisher
    d. nominal
    e. real

17. When comparing economic performance across countries, key considerations include all of the following except
    a. currency conversion among different countries.
    b. different prices for the same good or service in different countries.
    c. local prices in each country.
    d. unemployment in each country.
    e. real GDP in each country.

18. When comparing economic performance across countries, we observe all of the following except

    a. low-wage countries generally have many goods that sell for lower prices than their high-wage counterparts.
    b. international GDP comparisons based on common prices are less accurate.
    c. local services in poor countries generally cost less than local services in rich countries.
    d. international GDP comparisons based on exchange rates are inferior to common price comparisons.
    e. rich countries generally have higher price levels.

EXERCISES

These exercises will give you practice determining which types of productive activities are included in the calculations that provide GDP estimates.

1. Which of the following are included when estimating GDP?
    a. flour sold to the bakery at the local grocery store
    b. tires sold to General Motors
    c. a purchase of Wal-Mart stock in the stock market
    d. flour sold to a customer at the grocery store
    e. tires sold to the university you attend
    f. household production (laundry, cooking, etc.)
    g. a car purchased from a national rental car agency
    h. the sale of a new home
    i. Temporary Assistance to Needy Families (TANF)
    j. laundry services at the dry cleaner
    k. drug trafficking and other illegal services
    l. sale of an existing home
    m. interest payments on the national debt
    n. haircut in a salon
    o. rental value of owner-occupied housing
    p. an increase in the quality of health care that lengthens life expectancy by two years
    q. the discovery of additional oil reserves in the middle of Nebraska

2. Based on your work in Exercise 1, what inferences can you make regarding the accuracy of current GDP estimates for the United States?

PROBLEMS

Worked Problem

This problem takes you step by step through the process of generating both nominal and real GDP figures for a simple two-good economy. Note as you begin work on it that it is designed to show real GDP growth between the years 2008 and 2009 but no growth in real GDP between the years 2009 and 2010. You will find that nominal GDP therefore behaves differently than real GDP, as expected between

2008 and 2009 but perhaps unexpectedly between 2009 and 2010. This problem also provides additional practice calculating growth rates, and it provides the opportunity to get a feeling for the process involved in generating a chain-weighted GDP series.

1. Consider the following table describing a hypothetical economy that produces only DVDs and TVs. Fill in the missing elements using the growth rate formula,

   $g_x = \left(\dfrac{x_t - x_{t-n}}{x_{t-n}}\right)$, (in this problem $n = 1$) for the

   percentage change in all but the last row, where the formula for growth rates using chained prices is $g_x =$

   $\sqrt{\dfrac{x_t^{'10}}{x_{t-1}^{'10}} \cdot \dfrac{x_t^{'09}}{x_{t-1}^{'09}}} - 1$. Note that in this formula the ratio

   involving the $x^{'09}$ values represents the first year or *Laspeyres index* value and the ratio with the $x^{'10}$ values represents the *Paasche index* value of the *Fisher index* average. The use of the radical sign makes this a geometric average, which is appropriate for determining growth rates because it more accurately allows for different yearly growth rates.

	2008	2009	2010	Percent Change	
				2008–2009	2009–2010
Quantity of DVDs	200	225	225	A	0
Quantity of TVs	10	12	12	20	B
Price of DVDs ($)	20	20	20	0	0
Price of TVs ($)	1,200	1,100	1,000	C	–9
Nominal GDP	D	17,700	16,500	E	F
Real GDP in 2008 prices	16,000	G	18,900	18.13	0
Real GDP in 2009 prices	H	17,700	I	18.00	0
Real GDP in 2010 prices	J	16,500	16,500	17.86	0
Real GDP in chained prices, benchmarked to 2010	K	16,500	16,500	L	0

a. Calculate the value of cell A. This cell calculates the growth in the number of DVDs sold in the year 2009 relative to the year 2008 as follows:

$\left(\dfrac{225 - 200}{200}\right) = 0.125$ or 12.5%.

b. Calculate the value of cell B. This cell calculates the growth in TV sales in the year 2010 relative to the year 2009 as in part a for DVDs:

$\left(\dfrac{12 - 12}{12}\right) = 0$ or 0%.

c. Calculate the value of cell C. This cell calculates the growth or percentage change in the price of TVs between 2008 and 2009:

$\left(\dfrac{1,100 - 1,200}{1,200}\right) = -0.083$ or -8.3%.

d. Calculate the value of cell D. This cell calculates nominal GDP for the year 2008, which is the sum of price × quantity for both DVDs and TVs: $(200 \bullet 20) + (10 \bullet 1,200) = 1,600$.

e. Calculate the value of cell E. This cell calculates the growth or percentage change in nominal GDP between 2008 and 2009:

$\left(\dfrac{17,700 - 16,000}{16,000}\right) = 0.1063$ or 10.63%.

f. Calculate the value of cell F. This cell calculates the growth rate of nominal GDP between the years 2009 and 2010:

$\left(\dfrac{16,500 - 17,700}{17,700}\right) = -0.0678$ or -6.78%.

g. Calculate the value of cell G. This calculates the value of real GDP in 2009 using 2008 prices, that is, using the *Laspeyres* method: $(225 \bullet 20) + (12 \bullet 1,200) = 18,900$.

h. Calculate the value of cell H. This cell calculates the value of real GDP in 2008 using 2009 prices, that is, using the *Paasche* method: $(200 \bullet 20) + (10 \bullet 1,100) = 15,000$.

i. Calculate the value of cell I. This cell calculates the value of real GDP in 2010 using 2009 prices, that is, using the *Laspeyres* method: $(225 \bullet 20) + (12 \bullet 1,100) = 17,700$.

j. Calculate the value of cell J. This cell calculates the value of real GDP in 2008 using 2010 prices, that is, using the *Paasche* method: $(200 \bullet 20) + (10 \bullet 1,000) = 14,000$.

k. Calculate the value of cell K. K is the value of real GDP in year 2008 necessary to generate a real GDP of 16,500 in year 2009 for chained GDP benchmarked to the year 2010. Therefore, it is necessary to work backward and calculate the value for cell L but stop just short of making it a growth rate by subtracting 1. Note that the number you get

for $\sqrt{\dfrac{16,500}{14,000} \cdot \dfrac{17,700}{15,000}}$ is approximately 1.1793.

Hence, dividing 16,500 by 1.1793 reduces its value to 13,992.

l. Calculate the value of cell L. L is the growth rate of the geometric average of changes between 2008 and 2009 using prices from 2009 and 2010. Cell L calculates the growth rate of real GDP between 2008 and 2009 indexed to the year 2010:

$$\sqrt{\frac{16,500}{14,000} \bullet \frac{17,700}{15,000}} - 1 = 0.1793 \text{ or } 17.93\%.$$

m. Explain the difference in behavior between nominal and real GDP in this example?
Real growth exceeds nominal growth because the price of technology (TVs) has fallen. Nominal growth would grossly understate the real level of activity in the economy.

n. What is the relationship between real GDP growth using 2009 and 2010 prices and real GDP growth using the chained prices benchmarked to 2010?
Chained real GDP is an average of real GDP derived using constant prices. Note that 17.93 percent is an average of 18 percent and 17.86 percent.

2. Comparing another country to the United States. Consider Mexico. Mexican GDP in the year 2007 was approximately 11.2 trillion pesos. U.S. GDP that year was approximately $14.1 trillion. The dollar exchanged for 10.92 pesos. Converted to U.S. dollars, the price level in Mexico relative to the price level in the United States was 0.6834.

a. Approximately how much would a dollar's worth of products in the United States cost in Mexico?

b. How large is the Mexican economy relative to the U.S. economy if we just use the exchange rate to make that comparison?

c. Alternatively, how much larger is the U.S. economy than the Mexican economy?

d. How large is the Mexican economy relative to the U.S. economy if we use common prices?

e. Again, using common prices, how much larger is the U.S. economy than the Mexican economy?

f. What can account for the differences between these comparisons?

3. Suppose that an earthen dam breaks, flooding downstream communities, damaging or destroying hundreds of millions of dollars' worth of homes and businesses in addition to any recreational and environmental impact. See en.wikipedia.org/wiki/Teton_Dam for an actual example of such an occurrence. Note that this problem is more about the approach to and methodology of accounting for GDP than about any specific numbers that might be generated.

a. Visit the accompanying Wikipedia entry and determine approximately what measurable impact on GDP the Teton Dam disaster generated. What estimate can you provide?

b. What would the impact on GDP be if the construction costs also were included?

c. Would you want to include only explicit construction costs in this estimate?

d. What welfare impact did the residents of the downstream communities of Rexburg, Wilford, Sugar City, Salem, and Hibbard experience as a result of this increase in GDP?

e. How accurately does the GDP increment from part a reflect the welfare changes experienced in Idaho as a result of this disaster?

CHAPTER 2 SOLUTIONS

True/False Questions

1. False. While the first two elements of the statement (about snapshots and growth) are correct, the third part (about international comparisons) is not. See Section 2.1.

2. False. See both Table 2.1 and Figure 2.2. Government purchases traditionally have been a larger share of GDP than investment.

3. False. See Figure 2.1. "Consistently" is the term that makes this statement false. Consumption has varied from over 80 percent (1931–33) to less than 50 percent (1943–44). In one sense, though, the statement can be true, since consumption averaged 67 percent for the period 1929–2005.

4. True. See Figure 2.1. Government purchases, usually around 20 percent, exceeded 40 percent of GDP during 1942–45.

5. False. See Section 2.2. For economists, "capital" refers to inputs into the production process such as buildings and computers, and often is referred to as *capital stock*. In finance and business, the term "capital" is used to refer to the money or funding used to acquire the things economists designate as capital stock.

6. False. See Section 2.2 and Figure 2.3. Labor's share of GDP is approximately two-thirds and owners of capital receive the other third.

7. True. See Section 2.2.

8. True. See Section 2.2. Note that reaching this conclusion requires splitting up profit or the net operating surplus of business between its labor and capital income components.

9. False. GDP includes all of the *final* goods and services produced in an economy during a calendar year. Including all goods and services would include

intermediate goods and generate a double counting problem. See Section 2.2.

10. True. But not the entire sales price, only the dealer's profit that gets treated as a service. See Section 2.2.

11. False. Real GDP should be used to make between-year comparisons since it adjusts for price level changes over time. See 2.3, "A Simple Example: Where Real GDP Doesn't Change."

Multiple-Choice Questions

1. e, none of the above. National income accounting incorporates each of these activities in its estimates of overall economic activity. See Section 2.1.

2. d, the entrepreneurs are earning an above-normal return. See Section 2.2.

3. e, both a and d are correct. Profit maximization requires MR = MC. In long-run equilibrium for a competitive firm, there is no economic profit. For economic profit to exist, price must exceed marginal cost in the short run. In a competitive industry, the existence of P > MC generally signals the opportunity for entry to other entrepreneurs.

4. c, foreign exchange. Foreign exchange is the market for exchanging currencies between countries. Net exports are the missing component of GDP in this question.

5. d, new home construction. This is a component of investment (residential). See Section 2.2.

6. c, spending on Medicare. This is a transfer payment. See Section 2.2.

7. d, trade balance. Net exports equals exports minus imports, or the *trade balance*. See Section 2.2.

8. e, none of the above. See the end of the expenditure approach in Section 2.2 for a discussion to that end.

9. b, 67 percent. See Section 2.2 and Figure 2.3.

10. d, value added. This approach keeps track of the "value added" at each stage of the production process. See Section 2.2.

11. c, the impact of the Clean Air Act on U.S. economic activity. These costs will be reflected in firms' cost of doing business, and, therefore, their influence will be felt on the value of GDP.

12. d, real GDP = nominal GDP ÷ price level. Recall that the nominal GDP = price level × real GDP. See Section 2.3.

13. a, quantities produced have changed; prices have not. If prices never changed, comparing production between years would be much simpler because we would know that any changes derived only from different quantity levels. See Section 2.3.

14. c, the Fisher index, because it averages the Paasche and Laspeyres indices. See Section 2.3.

15. e, all of the above. See Section 2.3.

16. d, nominal values, because all the values being compared will have occurred during the same year. See Section 2.3.

17. d, while important, unemployment is not necessary for the conversion and comparison of GDP figures between countries.

18. b, GDP comparisons based on common prices are *more* accurate. See Section 2.4.

Exercises

1. Answers d, e, h, j, n, and o are correct because each of them is a *final* good or service and does not become part of a product that is subsequently resold.

   The other answers are incorrect for these reasons: a and b are intermediate goods; c is a transfer of ownership, nothing is produced; f contains no market transaction, even though production took place; g, a used car, was counted in GDP when it was acquired by the car rental agency; i is an income transfer, not a market transaction, facilitated purchases will be counted at the time of sale; k are illegal transactions, part of the underground economy, no market transactions are reported; l, a used home, was counted in GDP when it was new; m is an income transfer, not a market transaction, facilitated purchases will be counted at the time of sale. Note that in parts g and l the commissions for both the sale of the used car and the existing home will be counted toward GDP because of the service they provided during the calendar year of the sale. Options p and q present special cases. The health care services rendered will be counted but the longer life expectancy will not. Nor will the additional reserves be counted until they are actually extracted and sold, but the research, exploration, and discovery activities will be counted as part of GDP.

2. At a minimum, we must conclude that official GDP estimates understate the level of production occurring in the United States, both for legal and illegal reasons. Specifically, in the legal realm, neither household production nor bartered transactions are included, while none of the illegal production is included.

Problems

1. Worked Problem. Answers are given in the problem.

2. a. Using the conversion factor of the Mexican to U.S. price level, we know that a dollar's worth of products in the United States would cost approximately 61¢, or 5.7 pesos (0.6079 × 9.46) in Mexico.
    b. The Mexican economy in the year 2000 was 5.92 percent of the U.S. economy. First, convert the pesos to dollars then make the ratio between Mexico and the United States:

$$\left(\frac{11.2 \text{ tr pesos}\big/14.1}{14.1 \text{ tr dollars}}\right) = \frac{0.79433}{14.1} = 0.05634 \text{ or } 5.63\%$$

    c. Inverting the fraction of the U.S. economy that Mexico is generates the order of magnitude that the United States is larger than Mexico. In other words, the U.S. economy is almost 18 times larger than the Mexican economy: $\left(\frac{1}{0.0563} = 17.8\right)$.
    d. Using common prices to further adjust the peso to dollar conversion, the Mexican economy in the year 2007 was 8.2 percent the size of the U.S. economy:

$$\left(\frac{\dfrac{11.2 \text{ tr pesos}\big/14.1}{0.6834}}{14.1 \text{ tr dollars}}\right) = \frac{1.16232}{14.1} = 0.082434 \text{ or } 8.2\%$$

    e. Using common prices, the U.S. economy is at least 10 times larger than the Mexican economy:

$$\left(\frac{1}{0.082434} = 12.13092\right) \text{ or } 12.13.$$

    f. The difference in local purchasing power of each nation's currency accounts for the difference between 18 in part c and 12 in part e.

3. a. The Wikipedia website indicates that approximately $300 million worth of claims were paid by the federal government. If we make the assumption that all the payments actually went to replacing and rebuilding previous possessions and structures, then we could argue that GDP increased by the amount of the payments made by the federal government.
    b. Including the explicit construction costs would raise the estimated impact on GDP to $400 million.
    c. No. If we consider the subsequent expenditures on goods and services caused by the increased earnings directly attributable to the construction and later to the reparations of the Teton Dam, then the impact on GDP could be considerably larger. But, even then, we would not have accounted for the many hours of unpaid labor (a form of household production) that both the people who directly suffered losses and the thousands of people who volunteered in the cleanup efforts contributed to producing the output of flood cleanup. We can see that including only explicit construction costs significantly understates the impact on GDP that would occur if all the market and non-market impact were accounted for.
    d. A numerical solution to this question also is quite difficult to generate. Initially, we might estimate the value of their losses and subtract it from the increment in GDP and determine whether or not the difference was positive or negative. This, however, would not account for the entire impact on their welfare. Were they healthier afterward compared to before the disaster? How was the quality of their environment affected? How much was their welfare affected by the losses that were irreplaceable?
    e. While we can generate a figure for new goods and services produced to replace the losses associated with the Teton Dam disaster, we must concede that this value significantly understates the total impact of the event.

| An Overview of Long-Run Economic Growth

OVERVIEW

Economic-growth and standard-of-living increases in the United States and other industrialized nations during the past century have been unparalleled in the history of the world. Some countries, China and India among them, have stronger growth records in the recent past, but many countries, like Ethiopia and Bangladesh, have not experienced anywhere near the same kind of economic growth. This chapter's primary purpose is to become familiar with this basic behavior and the basic tools used to analyze growth over time, such as the growth-rate formula itself, ratios scales, growth-rate properties, and a basic production function.

KEY CONCEPTS

Economic growth generally is measured as the increase in the per capita level of goods and services (GDP) produced in a country from year to year. More precisely, economic growth is measured with a *growth rate,* or the percentage change, of per capita GDP on an annual basis.

A *growth rate* for any variable is the percentage change in that variable from period to period and is calculated as

$\dfrac{x_{t+1} - x_t}{x_t}$ or $\dfrac{x_t - x_{t-1}}{x_{t-1}}$. The difference is that $\dfrac{x_{t+1} - x_t}{x_t}$

calculates the growth between the current and the next

period, while $\dfrac{x_t - x_{t-1}}{x_{t-1}}$ calculates the growth between

the previous period and the current period. The process is the same in either case.

A *ratio scale* is a way of graphically presenting data that grow over time and emphasizes what is happening with the growth rate of a variable rather than the variable's value. It is particularly useful in determining the behavior of average growth. If the average growth rate is constant, as in Figure 1, the variable will appear to grow along a straight line. If the variable's growth rate increases, then later observations will lie above a straight line extending from the earlier observations, as in Figure 2. Likewise, if its growth rate decreases over time, later observations lie below such a line, as in Figure 3. We create a *ratio scale* diagram by using a scale that exhibits a constant ratio on the vertical axis, such as 1, 2, 4, 8, . . . (each number doubles), or 10, 100, 1,000, 10,000, . . . (each number is 10 times larger). In a spreadsheet, using a logarithmic scale accomplishes the same thing.

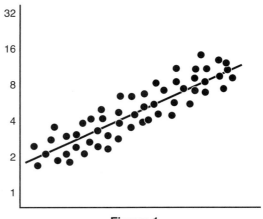

Figure 1

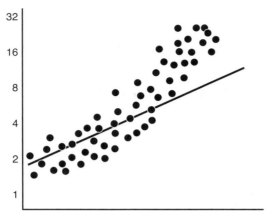

Figure 2

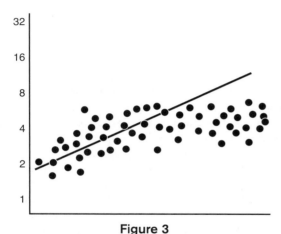

Figure 3

The *Rule of 70* states that any variable growing at a
constant rate of growth, $\bar{g}$, as in $y_t = y_0(1 + \bar{g})^t$, doubles
in approximately the number of years equal to 70
divided by that constant growth rate; and it does not
matter with what beginning value that variable starts.
For example, if your savings grow at 3 percent per
year, it will double in approximately 70/3 or 23.33
years; or if your interest rate is 5 percent, then it will
double in approximately 70/5 or approximately 14
years.

Convergence occurs when two or more countries come to
experience approximately the same level of GDP per
capita and simultaneously experience the same growth
rate, so that, on a ratio scale diagram such as Figure
3.6 in the text, their GDP per capita paths lie on top of
each other.

The Great Divergence refers to the income differential
trends that have been occurring during the past four
centuries. Prior to the year 1500, high-income

countries enjoyed living standards that were at most
two or three times higher than in low-income countries.
Per capita GDP differentials between rich and poor
countries today of five to 10 times in magnitude are not
uncommon. In some extreme cases, the magnitude of
difference reaches 45.

The following are a few *critical math principles* governing
the use of growth rates:

1. The average growth rate for *t* number of periods:

$$\bar{g} = \left(\frac{y_t}{y_0}\right)^{1/t} - 1$$

2. The rules for computing the growth rates of
products, ratios, and exponents:
   a. Products: If $z = xy$, then $g_z = g_x + g_y$
   b. Ratios: If $z = x/y$, then $g_z = g_x - g_y$
   c. Exponents: If $z = x^a$, then $g_z = ag_x$

See multiple-choice questions 5, 16, and 17;
Exercise 3; and Problem 4 for practice using the
mathematics of growth rates.

TRUE/FALSE QUESTIONS

1. Changes in GDP per capita measure changes in
economic well-being over time.

2. By the end of the twentieth century, per capita GDP in
the United States was approximately twice that of
Japan and the United Kingdom.

3. Modern economic growth in countries like the United
States, the United Kingdom, and Japan has been relatively consistent since the late 1800s.

4. Per capita GDP in the United States has increased more
than 500 percent during the past century.

5. In spite of significant economic growth worldwide, living standards still vary drastically among countries.

6. The time it would take for a country to double its GDP
depends only on its growth rate and not on how much
GDP it currently produces.

7. Per capita GDP in China so far in the twenty-first
century has grown at a rate approximately equal to that
of the United States.

8. Relative to the United States, the world's population
today experiences three to four times the GDP per
capita than it did just half a century ago.

MULTIPLE-CHOICE QUESTIONS

1. In a country experiencing economic growth we would expect to see each of the following except an increase in a country's
   a. standard of living.
   b. level of GDP.
   c. level of household production.
   d. life expectancy.
   e. level of education.

2. Per capita GDP for each of the following countries is less than it is in the United States. In which country is it least similar to the United States?
   a. United Kingdom
   b. China
   c. Brazil
   d. Ethiopia
   e. Japan

3. Given the pace of modern economic growth in recent decades, today's college graduates can expect to earn approximately _____ amount of lifetime income as their parents when measured in constant prices.
   a. one-half the
   b. one-third the
   c. twice the
   d. three times the
   e. the same

4. To economists, the phrase "economic growth" has a relatively precise meaning. Which of the following statements best conveys that meaning?
   a. an increase in living standards
   b. an increase in average income
   c. the rate of change in GDP
   d. the rate of change in per capita GDP
   e. the rate of change in personal income

5. When calculating economic growth, which of the following are accurate representations of that process when $\bar{g}$ equals a constant growth rate?
   a. $y_t - y_{t-1} = \bar{g} \times y_{t-1}$

   b. $\bar{g} = \dfrac{y_{t+1} - y_t}{y_t}$

   c. $y_{t+1} = y_t(1 + \bar{g})$

   d. $\bar{g} = \dfrac{y_t}{y_{t-1}} - 1$

   e. all of the above
   f. only b and d

6. The purpose of using a ratio scale when graphing economic variables over time is to
   a. allow the comparison of one country relative to another.

   b. determine if the growth rate of a variable is increasing, decreasing, or constant.
   c. determine if a country's growth rate is positive, negative, or constant.
   d. make growth rate changes more readily observable on a graph.
   e. all of the above

7. Approximately how fast would a country have to grow in order for its income to double in 20 years?
   a. 2.5 percent
   b. 3.5 percent
   c. 4 percent
   d. 5 percent

8. Ratio-scaled graphs compress the scale of _____ axis(es).
   a. both
   b. the horizontal
   c. the vertical
   d. neither

9. During the past 140 years, per capita GDP in the United States has doubled how many times?
   a. one
   b. two
   c. three
   d. four
   e. five

10. During the past 40 years, which country has been out of the pack regarding its growth rate of GDP per capita?
    a. United States
    b. United Kingdom
    c. China
    d. Japan
    e. Germany

11. During the past 30 years, which country has experienced the highest growth rate of GDP per capita?
    a. United States
    b. Japan
    c. United Kingdom
    d. China
    e. Germany

12. Which of the following countries had the highest average GDP growth per capita during 1960 to 2007?
    a. United States
    b. Luxembourg
    c. Japan
    d. Taiwan
    e. Hong Kong

13. In 1960, two-thirds of the world's population lived in what the text calls "abject poverty," that is, less than 5 percent of the per capita GDP of citizens in the United States. By the year 2000, the amount of the world's population living in abject poverty
    a. is still two-thirds.
    b. has fallen to one-half.
    c. has fallen to one-third.
    d. is less than 12 percent.
    e. is only 1 percent.

14. The dramatic reduction in world poverty experienced during the last half of the twentieth century was due primarily to
    a. foreign aid to Third World countries from the United States and other industrialized nations.
    b. the reduction of AIDS incidence in African countries.
    c. the increased use of technology in production processes around the world.
    d. increased growth rates in China and India.
    e. reduced trade barriers in less-developed nations.

15. Which of the following is not a benefit of economic growth?
    a. higher incomes
    b. increased life expectancy
    c. increased income inequality
    d. reductions in physical labor requirements
    e. increased availability of goods and services

16. Which of the following is not a property of growth rates?
    a. If $z = x/y$, then $g_z = g_x - g_y$.
    b. If $z = 2xy$, then $g_z = 2(g_x + g_y)$.
    c. If $z = \left(x/y\right)^2$, then $g_z = 2(g_x - g_y)$.
    d. If $z = x^a$, then $g_z = ag_x$.
    e. If $z = xy$, then $g_z = g_x + g_y$.

17. Which of the following illustrates the proper use of the properties regarding growth rates for the equation $Y = AK^aL^b$?
    a. $g_Y = g_A + g_K + g_L$
    b. $g_Y = abg_A + ag_K + bg_L$
    c. $g_Y = ab(g_A + g_K + g_L)$
    d. $g_Y = g_A + ag_K + bg_L$
    e. $g_Y = g_A + ab(g_K + g_L)$

EXERCISES

Exercises 1 and 2 provide practical examples of the application and use of growth rate formulas. Exercise 3 provides an opportunity to practice using the growth rate rules found in the chapter material.

1. You have been hired to forecast future population levels for a small country. You know that this country currently has 5 million citizens and for several decades the population growth has been extremely stable at 1.25 percent.
   a. What will be the population one year from now?
   b. What will be the population 50 years from now?
   c. Suppose that the population growth surges suddenly and grows instead at a rate of 2 percent. How will your answers to parts a and b change?

2. You have $1,500 in your account at the bank. If you leave it there undisturbed and let the interest accumulate, at an interest rate of 4 percent, how much money will you have in
   a. six months?
   b. one year?
   c. five years?
   d. Why is the answer in part c not simply $(1 + 0.04) \cdot \$1,500 \cdot 5 = \$1,800$?

3. Let the variable z be defined as follows and let the variables x and y grow at the rates of 3 and 5 percent, respectively. By how much will z grow in each of the following cases?
   a. $z = xy$
   b. $z = x^2y^{-1/2}$
   c. $z = x/y$
   d. $z = 3xy$

PROBLEMS

These problems provide further opportunity to practice your growth rate skills. Problem 2 provides step-by-step guidance through the process of creating a ratio scale diagram using a spreadsheet program. The context for that process utilizes a savings account where interest is compounded annually. The graphing process is identical to that of producing a ratio scale diagram for any other variable, for example, GDP.

1. Assume you are still working for the same country as in Exercise 1. This time, however, the country wishes to achieve a population level of 10 million, twice the current population, 50 years from now.
   a. What (constant) population growth rate must it maintain in order to accomplish this goal?
   b. What if this country chose a goal of 8 million people? What population growth rate would that require?

Worked Problem

2. You wish to create a ratio scale diagram that shows the growth of $10 put in a savings account that earns 5 percent interest per year between the years 2000 and 2050.

a. Suppose the first number on your vertical axis is $5 and you use a constant ratio of 5 to construct your ratio scale diagram. What would be the values for your vertical axis labels?

Increasing by a factor of 5 over each interval on a ratio scale diagram, the vertical axis labels would be 5, 25, 125, 625, . . . or $5^1, 5^2, 5^3, 5^4, ...$

b. How many years would it take before you would have $20? Using the Rule of 70, it would take $14 \left(= \frac{70}{5} \right)$ years for the $10 to double to $20.

c. What if you began with $20, how many years would it take before you had $40?

It would also take 14 years, calculated the same way as in part b. Remember that the amount of money, or starting level of a variable, does not play a role in determining how long it takes for a variable to double in value. Section 3.3.3 explains that only the interest rate matters.

d. Create a spreadsheet showing the growth of your $10 as described in the instructions to this problem. The following template will get you started. If you utilize the cells B1 and B2 as shown, you can experiment with different interest rates and starting values and see the impact of changing them on the behavior of the "Savings" variable.

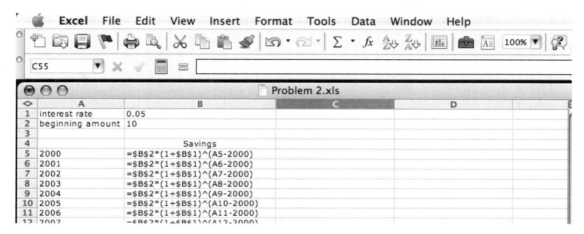

If you use the graphing techniques illustrated in Chapter 1, it should look like this when you get finished:

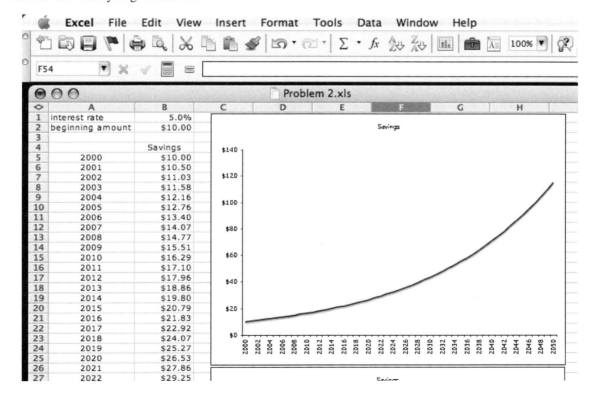

e. Convert your diagram into a ratio scale diagram showing that the series you created in part d actually does grow at a constant rate. To convert this diagram into a ratio scale diagram, first click on the vertical axis and then click on the "Format" pull-down menu and click on "Selected Axis," as shown next.

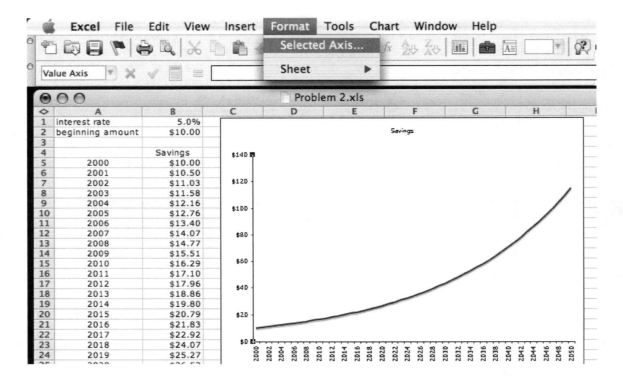

By clicking on "Scale," you will be presented with the following menu of options. The general default setting is for each of the first five boxes to be checked and the last three to be unchecked. Check the one identified as "Logarithmic," as shown.

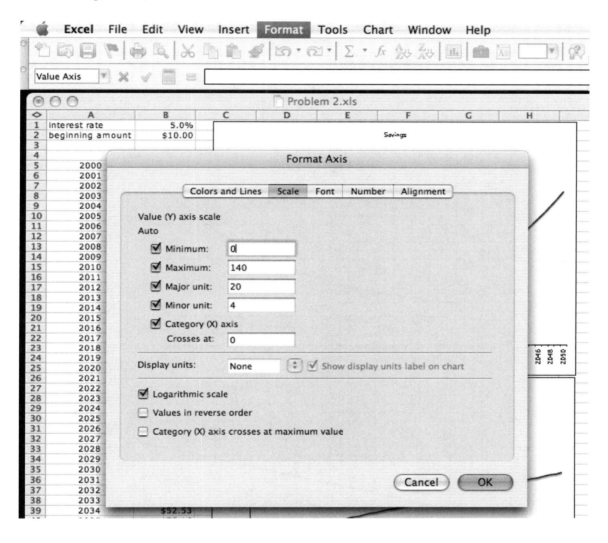

Click on "OK," and your diagram should then appear as the second diagram in the picture that follows:

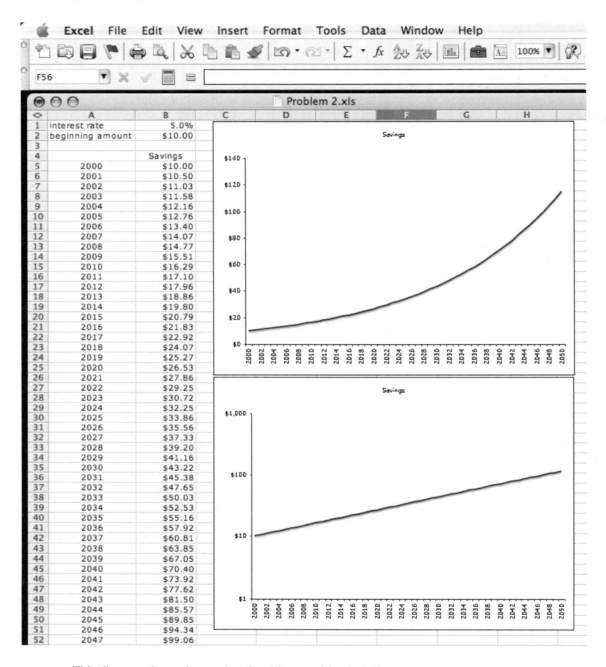

This diagram shows the results of making two identical diagrams and letting one remain unchanged while displaying the second one as a ratio (or logarithmic) scale diagram. Now take a minute to verify your answers from parts b and c, using the diagrams you just created.

3. You have $10,000 to put into a financial instrument. What interest rate must you negotiate in order to have $15,000
   a. five years from now?
   b. eight years from now?
   c. 10 years from now?

4. In 1960 real GDP was $2.8 trillion and in 2009 it was $13 trillion. Population was 180.7 million and 307.2 million, respectively. Determine if the growth rate of GDP per capita has kept up with the population growth rate since *1960*.
   a. What is the average population growth rate between 1960 and 2009?
   b. What is the growth rate of GDP between 1960 and 2009?
   c. Which is greater?
   d. What is the growth rate of GDP per capita between 1960 and 2009?
   e. What are two ways you can calculate your answer in part d?

CHAPTER 3 SOLUTIONS

True/False Questions

1. True. While not a perfect measure, changes in GDP per capita broadly reflect changes in the standard of living for citizens of a nation. See Section 3.2.

2. False. U.S. GDP per capita was only about one and a third to one and a half times as large as that of the United Kingdom and Japan. See Figure 3.1.

3. False. Great Britain and the United States began their period of sustained growth significantly earlier than Japan. See Section 3.2.

4. True. See Figure 3.2. Between the years 1900 and 2000, per capita GDP grew from about 5,000 to almost 35,000.

5. Both true and false. It is true that they currently do vary drastically, especially between countries like the United States and Ethiopia, but prior to the year 1500, the use of the word "drastically," for many economists, would make the statement false. See Section 3.2.

6. True. This is an implication from the Rule of 70. See Section 3.3.

7. False. By observing Figure 3.6, we can see that the line representing Chinese growth in the twenty-first century is significantly steeper than the one for the United States.

8. True. Figure 3.8 illustrates this improvement in the distribution of world population by per capita GDP.

Multiple-Choice Questions

1. c, level of household production. As a country grows and people's standard of living grows, one reason for this growth is that people specialize more in order to become more productive and end up using the market for many of the things they used to do for themselves.

2. d, Ethiopia's per capita income is only 1/64 that of the United States. All the other countries have a per capita income of at least one-tenth that of the United States. See Section 3.4.

3. c, See Section 3.3.

4. d, See Section 3.3.

5. e, See Section 3.3. Practice manipulating each answer into one of the other forms.

6. e, See Section 3.3 and Figures 3.4, 3.5, and 3.6.

7. b, See Section 3.3. $20 = {70}/{x} \Rightarrow x = {70}/{20} = 3.5$ or 3.5 percent.

8. c, See Section 3.3 and Figure 3.5.

9. d, See Section 3.3 and Figure 3.5 and begin at 1870.

10. c, See Section 3.3 and Figure 3.6. Note that since 1970 the slope of China's GDP per capita line in Figure 3.6 is significantly steeper than any of the other pictured countries.

11. d, See Section 3.4 and Figure 3.6. Note the steepness (or higher growth rate) of China's per capita GDP curve after 1980.

12. d, See Section 3.4 and Figure 3.7. Note that this figure uses a ratio scale on the horizontal axis of the diagram.

13. d, See Section 3.4, Figure 3.8, and the case study, "People versus Countries."

14. d, increased growth in China and India. See the case study, "People versus Countries."

15. c, See Section 3.6. Increased income inequality is a cost of economic growth.

16. b, The number 2 affects only the level of z, not its growth rate. See Section 3.5 and Table 3.1. Note, too, that for $z = 2xy$, $g_z = g_2 + g_x + g_y$ and since $g_2 = 0$, $g_z = 0 + g_x + g_y$ and $g_z = g_x + g_y$, or the growth rate of z is only a function of the growth rates of x and y.

17. d, Each exponent applies only to the variable for which it is an exponent. See the case study in Section 3.5 on using growth rules in a famous example.

Exercises

1. a. $5{,}062{,}500 = 5{,}000{,}000 \times (1 + 0.0125)^1$
    b. $9{,}305{,}112 = 5{,}000{,}000 \times (1 + 0.0125)^{50}$
    c. $5{,}100{,}000 = 5{,}000{,}000 \times (1 + 0.02)^1$
    $13{,}457{,}940 = 5{,}000{,}000 \times (1 + 0.02)^{50}$

2. a. $\$1{,}529.71 = 1{,}500 \times (1 + 0.04)^{0.5}$
    b. $\$1{,}560.00 = 1{,}500 \times (1 + 0.04)^1$
    c. $\$1{,}824.98 = 1{,}500 \times (1 + 0.04)^5$
    d. The difference between \$1,824.98 and \$1,800.00 occurs because the calculation in part c accounts for leaving the principle in the bank and earning compounded interest, that is, interest on the interest earnings, during each subsequent year, whereas the \$1,800 accounts for only simple interest earned only on the principle each year.

3. a. $g_z \approx g_x + g_y$ $\qquad$ $g_z \approx 3\% + 5\%$ $\qquad$ $= 8\%$
    b. $g_z \approx 2g_x - .5g_y$ $\qquad$ $g_z \approx 6\% - 2.5\%$ $\qquad$ $= 3.5\%$
    c. $g_z \approx g_x - g_y$ $\qquad$ $g_z \approx 3\% - 5\%$ $\qquad$ $= -2\%$
    d. $g_z \approx g_3 + g_x + g_y$ $\qquad$ $g_z \approx 0\% + 3\% + 5\%$ $\qquad$ $= 8\%$
    See Table 3.1.

Problems

1. a. 1.396 percent

    $$5{,}000{,}000(1 + \bar{g})^{50} = 10{,}000{,}000$$
    $$(1 + \bar{g})^{50} = \frac{10{,}000{,}000}{5{,}000{,}000} = 2$$
    $$\bar{g} = 2^{\frac{1}{50}} - 1 = 0.01395948 \approx 1.4\%$$

    Alternatively, one can also use the Rule of 70:

    $$\frac{70}{\bar{g}} \approx 50 \text{ or } \frac{70}{50} \approx \bar{g} \approx 0.014 \text{ or } 1.4 \text{ percent.}$$

    b. 0.944 percent

    $$5{,}000{,}000(1 + \bar{g})^{50} = 8{,}000{,}000$$
    $$(1 + \bar{g})^{50} = \frac{8{,}000{,}000}{5{,}000{,}000} = 1.6$$
    $$\bar{g} = 1.6^{\frac{1}{50}} - 1 = 0.009444392 \approx 0.94\%$$

2. Worked problem. The answers are in the text.

3. a. 8.447 percent.

    $$10{,}000(1 + \bar{g})^5 = 15{,}000$$
    $$(1 + \bar{g})^5 = \frac{15{,}000}{10{,}000} = 1.5$$
    $$\bar{g} = 1.5^{\frac{1}{5}} - 1 = 0.084471771 \approx 8.4\%$$

    b. 5.199 percent.

    $$10{,}000(1 + \bar{g})^8 = 15{,}000$$
    $$(1 + \bar{g})^8 = \frac{15{,}000}{10{,}000} = 1.5$$
    $$\bar{g} = 1.5^{\frac{1}{8}} - 1 = 0.051989506 \approx 5.2\%$$

    c. 4.138 percent.

    $$10{,}000(1 + \bar{g})^{10} = 15{,}000$$
    $$(1 + \bar{g})^{10} = \frac{15{,}000}{10{,}000} = 1.5$$
    $$\bar{g} = 1.5^{\frac{1}{10}} - 1 = 0.041379744 \approx 4.1\%$$

4. a. $\left(\dfrac{307.2}{180.7}\right)^{\frac{1}{49}} - 1 = 0.01089$, or 1.09 percent

    b. $\left(\dfrac{13}{2.8}\right)^{\frac{1}{49}} - 1 = 0.03183$, or 3.37 percent

    c. GDP growth, $0.03183 > 3.18$ percent

    d. GDP per capita in 1960

    $$= \frac{2.8 \text{ trillion}}{180.7 \text{ million}} = \$15{,}495.30$$

    GDP per capita in 2009

    $$= \frac{13 \text{ trillion}}{307.2 \text{ million}} = \$42{,}317.71$$

    Average per capita GDP growth between 1960 and 2009 was

    $$\left(\frac{\$42{,}317.71}{\$15{,}495.30}\right)^{\frac{1}{49}} - 1 = 0.02072, \text{ or approximately}$$

    2.072 percent

    e. First, as shown in part d; second, use $z = y/x$ and the approximation of $g_z \approx g_y - g_x$ and get $3.18\% - 1.09\% = 2.07\%$. Note that the 2.07 percent calculated here is approximately equal to the 2.072 percent obtained in part d.

CHAPTER 4 | A Model of Production

OVERVIEW

An economic model consists of a set of equations that represent the essential elements of the economy relevant to the issue at hand. Solving a model requires determining the solution for each of the model's endogenous variables, beginning with the values for each of the exogenous variables. If all countries were identical, we could use the same production function for each of them. Since they are not, we explore how we can compensate for these differences to make comparisons among countries. In this process, we conclude that, while both total factor productivity and capital stock per worker matter, total factor productivity contributes a lot more to the explanation of per capita GDP differences between countries than the amount of capital stock per worker. We also distinguish between the total scale of an operation, where returns to scale have relevance for the firm, and diminishing returns, where returns to a single input matter to the producer.

KEY CONCEPTS

Macroeconomic models, like all economic models, make simplifying assumptions to describe the essential or salient features of the economy. For the model in this chapter, that means explaining the determination of output per worker and why it varies across countries. Once defined, a model is tested against the data to determine its ability to explain real-world observations. Modifications and further tests take place and the model's refinement continues.

A *production function* is a mathematical equation that describes the relationship between the output, or product, being produced and the inputs into the production of that product. The general form of a production function is $Q = F(K, L, \ldots)$, where Q is the output or product being produced, K (capital) and L (labor) are the two primary inputs, and the ellipsis represents all other additional inputs into the production process.

The *Cobb-Douglas production function*, $Y = \bar{A}K^aL^b$, is a specific form, or type, of production function used extensively in economics. Since the Cobb-Douglas production function exhibits several very desirable properties, it is particularly useful in macroeconomics and growth theory. It has the ability, depending on the sum of $a + b$, to reflect either constant ($a + b = 1$), increasing ($a + b > 1$), or decreasing ($a + b < 1$) returns to scale; it is linear in its log form, which is very useful when performing empirical work; and it works well when modeling the substitutability in aggregate production relationships between capital and labor in most countries around the world.

Constant returns to scale (CRTS) occur when the rate at which all the inputs in a production process are increased yields the same rate of increase in the output of that production process. For example, with CRTS, a doubling of all of the inputs generates twice the level of output and the parameters a and b represent the output shares, respectively, that capital and labor receive.

Increasing returns to scale (IRTS) occur when the rate at which all of the inputs in a production process are increased yields an even greater increase in the output of that production process. For example, with IRTS, a doubling of all of the inputs generates more than twice the level of output.

Decreasing returns to scale (DRTS) occur when the rate at which all of the inputs in a production process are increased yields a smaller rate of increase in the output of that production process. For example, with DRTS, a doubling of all of the inputs generates less than twice the level of output.

The *standard replication argument* refers to the possibility of expanding, or more precisely, of doubling, output by doubling all the inputs in a production process and works only when the production process exhibits constant returns to scale.

Profit maximization involves the firm's choice regarding its level of production given all its constraints. It involves choosing the mix of capital and labor usage in the production process as well as the price to charge for output once it is produced. Profit maximization relies on the general economic principle of operating where the marginal benefits of pursuing an activity just equal the marginal costs of continuing it. For a firm's product that means marginal revenue equals marginal cost. For its inputs, it means marginal product equals marginal cost; for example, the marginal product of labor equals the real wage for a profit-maximizing firm.

A *numéraire* is the good to which the prices of all other goods are related. In the U.S. economy, we use the dollar bill. In the story in the text, it's ice cream; in general, it's simply "output" itself.

Marginal products occur for each input to the production process when all other inputs are held constant. For example, in the function $Q = F(X, Y, Z)$, the marginal product of input X, MP_x ($\Delta Q/\Delta X$ or $\partial Q/\partial X$, the partial derivative of Q with respect to X), is the change in output (∂Q) that occurs for a marginal change in the level of an input ($\partial X = 1$) when all other inputs to the production process remain unchanged. Marginal products can be positive ($\partial Q/\partial X > 0$) or negative ($\partial Q/\partial X < 0$), depending on the signs of the production function's first derivative with respect to the particular input. Profit-maximizing firms do not produce in regions where their marginal product is negative and maximize profit where their marginal products decrease with additional input usage. Economists call this characteristic a *diminishing marginal product*. Mathematically, a profit-maximizing firm will produce in the region where the production function itself increases at a decreasing rate, as determined by a negative second derivative of the production function with respect to the particular input in question ($\partial^2 Q/\partial X^2 < 0$). In other words, firms definitely hire the next worker when the marginal product of labor (MP_L) produced by that worker increases and will continue to do so even when the MP_L decreases, as long as the MP_L exceeds the wage. Once the MP_L equals the wage, the firm stops hiring workers.

General equilibrium analysis occurs when all the factor and product markets in a model are required to clear simultaneously. In contrast, *partial equilibrium* analysis occurs when the focus of investigation concerns an equilibrium condition in only a single factor or product market.

A *factor share* is the amount of the earnings from production that each input (factor of production) receives from the sale of the output produced. If the *numéraire* is that output, then the term "share" takes on even more significance because it becomes the amount of production that each factor gets to take home, its share.

Development accounting uses comparable measures of the capital stock and labor force for different countries and the general equilibrium model developed in this chapter to account for differences in incomes between these countries.

Total factor productivity refers to the efficiency of a country's use of its capital and labor stocks in the production of GDP. Empirically, it is the measure of production that cannot be directly attributed to either capital or labor in the production process. In the Cobb-Douglas production function, $Y = \bar{A}K^aL^b$, total factor productivity is represented by the parameter $\bar{A}$.

Human capital is the stock of skills that individuals accumulate to make them more productive. Such skills can be general and therefore useful throughout society and across all firms in general. Basic primary, secondary, and college educations fit into this category of human capital. Economists often ask what the *returns to education* are by asking how much higher average wages are for those who have various levels, or years, of education. Some human capital is more specific to a particular firm or type of production process and may be of less use to another, different, type of firm but of extreme value to the particular firm in question. In general, greater accumulation of human capital leads to higher income on the part of the individual.

Technology refers in the most general sense to the type of production process used by an individual, firm, industry, or country. In a less general sense, it refers to both the type of machinery and capital stock used in the production process and the way in which both capital and labor are combined.

An *institution* is an organization that may be social, political, or economic in nature. Institutions serve to define and guarantee property rights, govern social interaction, and facilitate economic transactions. Collectively, they provide the context for and define the way in which a country operates, from the basics of individual household production to the most sophisticated international trade negotiations and treaties.

A *misallocation* occurs when productive resources are distributed and/or employed in such a way that productive efficiency is reduced along with the total output of an economy.

TRUE/FALSE QUESTIONS

1. The best economic models use simple equations to shed light on some of the most fundamental questions in economics.

2. Because the Cobb-Douglas production function exhibits constant returns to scale in K and L, it must, of necessity, exhibit decreasing returns to scale in L alone.

3. In the Cobb-Douglas production function, $Y = \bar{A}K^aL^b$, the factor of proportionality indicates that labor's share of output is equal to a.

4. From the production model, we learn that the deciding factor determining the total amount of output in a country (and thus what makes it rich or poor) is the amount of capital stock possessed by the country.

5. Doubling the amount of capital stock per worker in a country would not make each worker twice as productive.

6. A nation's capital stock consists of all of its factories, tractors, computers, machine tools, monetary resources, and other capital goods.

7. Capital's share of income over time, both in the United States and throughout the world, is fairly close to one-third.

MULTIPLE-CHOICE QUESTIONS

1. A basic characterization of modern macroeconomics includes each of the following except
   a. the documentation of a set of macroeconomic facts that needs to be explained.
   b. building a model to understand the set of macro - economic facts needing explanation.
   c. testing any model constructed to evaluate the said set of macroeconomic facts.
   d. distinguishing between competing models for the one most consistent with the facts.
   e. none of the above; they are all part of modern macroeconomics.

2. Suppose you encounter a Cobb-Douglas production function of the form $Y = \bar{A}K^aL^{1-a}$, for all $a > 0$. This production function will exhibit _____ returns to scale.
   a. marginal
   b. increasing

c. decreasing
d. constant
e. no

3. Suppose you are working with a Cobb-Douglas production function, for all $a > 0$ and $b > 0$. Which of the following equations exhibits increasing returns to scale?
   a. $Y = \bar{A}K^aL^{1+a}$
   b. $Y = \bar{A}K^aL^b$
   c. $Y = \bar{A}K^{1-a}L^a$
   d. $Y = \bar{A}K^aL^{1-a}$
   e. $Y = \bar{A}K^aL^{1-b}$

4. The standard replication argument maintains that
   a. repeated uses of the same production process generate replication efficiencies.
   b. replicating the same production process is the most efficient method of increasing output.
   c. doubling all inputs in a production process most efficiently doubles the level of output.
   d. exactly doubling all the inputs exactly doubles the level of output.
   e. All of the above are correct.

5. For the production function $Y = \bar{A}K^aL^{1-a}$, the marginal product of capital is
   a. $(1 - a)\bar{A}K^{a-1}L^{1-a}$.
   b. $a\bar{A}K^aL^{-a}$.
   c. $a\bar{A}K^{a-1}L^{1-a}$.
   d. $(1 - a)\bar{A}K^aL^{-a}$.
   e. $(1 - a)\bar{A}K^{a-1}L^{-a}$.

6. For the production function $Y = AK^aL^{1-a}$, the marginal product of labor is
   a. $(1 - a)\bar{A}K^aL^{1-a}$.
   b. $a\bar{A}K^aL^{1-a}$.
   c. $a\bar{A}K^{a-1}L^{-a}$.
   d. $(1 - a)\bar{A}K^aL^{-a}$.
   e. $(1 - a)\bar{A}K^{a-1}L^{-a}$.

7. For an a equal to one-third in the production function $Y = \bar{A}K^aL^{1-a}$, the marginal product of labor is
   a. $\dfrac{3}{2} \bullet \dfrac{Y}{L}$.
   b. $\dfrac{2}{3} \bullet \dfrac{Y}{L}$.
   c. $\dfrac{2}{3} \bullet \dfrac{L}{Y}$.
   d. $\dfrac{3}{2} \bullet \dfrac{L}{Y}$.
   e. $\dfrac{2}{3} \bullet (Y + L)$.

8. For an *a* equal to one-third in the production function $Y = \bar{A}K^aL^{1-a}$, the marginal product of capital is

   a. $\dfrac{3}{1} \cdot \dfrac{Y}{K}$.

   b. $\dfrac{1}{3} \cdot \dfrac{K}{Y}$.

   c. $\dfrac{3}{1} \cdot \dfrac{K}{Y}$.

   d. $\dfrac{1}{3} \cdot \dfrac{Y}{K}$.

   e. $\dfrac{1}{3} \cdot \dfrac{K}{L}$.

9. The solution for the five equation model presented in Chapter 4 produces five equilibrium values and is referred to as a
   a. partial equilibrium because there are more than five variables in the economy.
   b. multiple equilibrium because there are multiple variables in the solution.
   c. general equilibrium because the solutions for more than one variable are found.
   d. simple equilibrium because there are only five variables in the model.
   e. approximate equilibrium because the variable values are only estimates.

10. Which of the following statements about the solution of the production model is not correct?
    a. The sum of the payments to capital and labor exhaust output.
    b. Economic profits are equal to zero.
    c. Total income equals total production.
    d. Production and income both equal spending.
    e. None of the above; they are all correct.

11. Which of the following equations does not accurately represent output per capita in a country exhibiting constant returns to scale?

    a. $y = \dfrac{\bar{A}K^aL^{1-a}}{L}$

    b. $y = \dfrac{\bar{A}K^a}{L^a}$

    c. $y = \bar{A}k^a$

    d. $y = \dfrac{\bar{A}K^{1+a}L^{1-a}}{KL}$

    e. None of the above; they all do.

12. In the equilibrium solution for the production model $y^* = \bar{A}\bar{k}^{1/3}$, which of the following does not increase per capita GDP?
    a. Increase the size of the productivity parameter.

    b. Decrease the number of workers.
    c. Increase the size of the capital stock.
    d. Reduce capital's factor of proportionality.
    e. none of the above

13. Which of the following arguments are economists least likely to use to justify one of their models?
    a. The model provides useful insights about how the world works despite its simplifying assumptions.
    b. The model works well when confronted with the data.
    c. The model is mathematically elegant, yet simple.
    d. The model has been successfully tested for a number of years.
    e. The model is robust across data from several countries.

14. According to the data presented in the text's discussion of the empirical fit of the production model, which of the following countries most closely resembles the United States in terms of per capita GDP in the year 2007?
    a. Italy
    b. Japan
    c. Spain
    d. Switzerland
    e. United Kingdom

15. In the absence of productivity differences, which country's per capita GDP should most closely resemble that of the United States on the basis of its observed capital stock per person in the year 2007?
    a. Italy
    b. Japan
    c. Spain
    d. Switzerland
    e. United Kingdom

16. Which of the following descriptions does not apply to the parameter $\bar{A}$ in the production model $Y = \bar{A}K^aL^b$?
    a. $\bar{A}$ represents a measure of efficiency.
    b. $\bar{A}$ represents a measure of productivity.
    c. $\bar{A}$ measures how well a country utilizes its factor inputs (K and L).
    d. $\bar{A}$ measures research and development in a country.
    e. $\bar{A}$ measures total factor productivity.

17. Which country has an implied total factor productivity closest to that of the United States?
    a. Italy
    b. Japan
    c. Spain
    d. Switzerland
    e. United Kingdom

18. As a result of development accounting, economists seeking to explain the differences in income between countries have found that
    a. capital per person explains only a quarter of the differences.
    b. total factor productivity explains about half of the differences.
    c. total factor productivity explains about two-thirds of the differences.
    d. capital per person explains about two-thirds of the differences.
    e. capital per person and total factor productivity together still leave about 20 percent of the differences unexplained.

19. Total factor productivity differences likely stem from each of the following except
    a. education levels.
    b. human capital.
    c. a country's legal system.
    d. institutions.
    e. none of the above.

20. The returns to a college education are likely to be the highest in which of the following countries?
    a. Burundi
    b. Japan
    c. Brazil
    d. China
    e. Spain

21. Total factor productivity is likely to explain more growth in countries with each of the following except
    a. greater accumulation of human capital.
    b. more advanced technology.
    c. well-defined and protected property rights.
    d. the separation of governmental powers.
    e. none of the above.

22. Economists point to several key institutional features that help explain the differences in income levels between countries. Which of the following is not one of those differences?
    a. well-established property rights
    b. contract enforcement
    c. separation of powers (executive, legislative, and judicial)
    d. price controls
    e. well-defined legal system

23. Economists argue that the effects of resource misallocation include each of the following outcomes except
    a. marginal products of labor that are too high.
    b. marginal products of capital that are too low.
    c. unrealized total factor productivity.
    d. increased firm and industry profitability.
    e. none of the above.

EXERCISES

1. Determine whether each of the following production functions exhibits constant, increasing, or decreasing returns to scale in capital and labor and show why.
    a. $Y = AK^{3/4}L^{3/4}$
    b. $Y = AK^{1/4}L^{3/4}$
    c. $Y = AK^{1/4}L^{1/4}$
    d. $Y = A + K^{3/4}L^{3/4}$
    e. $Y = L + K^{3/4}L^{1/4}$

2. Create two per-worker versions for each of the following production functions, one for the value of $A = 1$ and one for the value of $A = 5$. Then produce two diagrams, one for part a and one for part b, that include the diagrams for both values of A.
    a. $Y = AL + K$
    b. $Y = AK^{1/4}L^{3/4}$.

PROBLEMS

Worked Problem

This problem takes you step by step through the general equilibrium solution process for the complete production model with all five equations and five unknowns.

1. Suppose that our sample economy is both competitive in nature and appropriately modeled by a Cobb-Douglas production function exhibiting constant returns to scale with a factor of proportionality for labor equal to one-half. As in the text, assume that the supplies of capital and labor are fixed at $\bar{K}$ and $\bar{L}$ and that $A = \bar{A}$.
    a. What does the production function for this economy look like?
        Provide both a specific mathematical function and draw the corresponding diagram. Use the standard Cobb-Douglas form: $Y = AK^a L^b$. Since constant returns to scale are required, the coefficient $b = (1 - a)$ and the production function becomes $Y = AK^a L^{(1-a)}$; and because labor's exponent $(1 - a)$ becomes the factor of proportionality in the marginal product of labor, we can determine that $a = 1/2$ and the final form of the production function for this problem is $Y = AK^{1/2}L^{1/2}$. The graph of the production function, therefore, takes on the usual shape of a square root function, as seen in the following diagram.

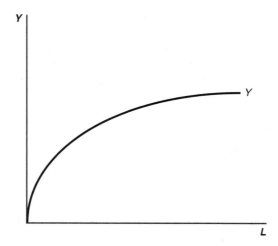

b. Derive the profit-maximizing conditions that determine how much capital and labor will be employed in this economy?

Recall that profit (Π) is the difference between total revenue and total costs. Total revenue in this instance is PY, where P represents the price level and becomes the *numéraire* for this problem. Total costs are $rK + wL$. Profit maximization occurs in the capital market when $MP_K = r$ and in the labor market when $MP_L = w$. To derive these conditions, begin with the following maximization problem:

$$\max_{K,L} \Pi = AK^{1/2}L^{1/2} - rK - wL.$$ Then, to maximize

profit, take derivatives of Π with respect to both K and L, set them equal to zero and solve for r and w, respectively as follows:

$$\frac{\partial \Pi}{\partial K} = \frac{1}{2}AK^{-1/2}L^{1/2} - r \qquad \frac{\partial \Pi}{\partial L} = \frac{1}{2}AK^{1/2}L^{-1/2} - w$$

$$\frac{1}{2}AK^{-1/2}L^{1/2} - r = 0 \qquad \frac{1}{2}AK^{1/2}L^{-1/2} - w = 0$$

$$\frac{1}{2}AK^{-1/2}L^{1/2} = \frac{1}{2}A\left(\frac{L}{K}\right)^{1/2} = r \qquad \frac{1}{2}AK^{1/2}L^{-1/2} = \frac{1}{2}A\left(\frac{K}{L}\right)^{1/2} = w$$

Note that the left-hand side of each of these solutions is the marginal product of capital and labor,

respectively; that is, $MP_K = \frac{1}{2}A\left(\frac{L}{K}\right)^{1/2} = r$ and

$MP_L = \frac{1}{2}A\left(\frac{K}{L}\right)^{1/2} = w$. Note, first, in review, the

inverse relationship between L and w and between K and r. The demand for capital is found by solving

$$\frac{1}{2}A\left(\frac{L}{K}\right)^{1/2} = r \text{ for } K, \text{ and the demand for labor is}$$

found by solving $\frac{1}{2}A\left(\frac{K}{L}\right)^{1/2} = w$ for L. Note, too,

that both solutions can be manipulated easily to yield the form of marginal product given in equation (4.4) and Table 4.1 in the text. We simply multiply by a special form of 1, as follows.
Note that

$$\left(\frac{K}{K}\right)^{1/2} = \left(\frac{L}{L}\right)^{1/2} = 1$$

$$\frac{1}{2}A\left(\frac{L}{K}\right)^{1/2} = r \qquad \frac{1}{2}A\left(\frac{K}{L}\right)^{1/2} = w$$

$$\frac{1}{2}A\left(\frac{L}{K}\right)^{1/2}\left(\frac{K}{K}\right)^{1/2} = r \qquad \frac{1}{2}A\left(\frac{K}{L}\right)^{1/2}\left(\frac{L}{L}\right)^{1/2} = w$$

$$\frac{1}{2}\frac{A}{K^{1/2}}\frac{L^{1/2}}{K^{1/2}}\frac{K^{1/2}}{} = r \qquad \frac{1}{2}\frac{A}{L^{1/2}}\frac{K^{1/2}}{L^{1/2}}\frac{L^{1/2}}{} = w$$

$$\frac{1}{2}\frac{Y}{K} = r \qquad \frac{1}{2}\frac{Y}{L} = w$$

c. Use the results from part b and the conditions given in the instructions to define and draw the equilibrium conditions in both the capital and labor markets of this economy.

The equilibrium conditions in each market are derived by setting demand equal to supply. Since, from the instructions, we know the supplies of both capital and labor are fixed at $\bar{K}$ and $\bar{L}$, respectively, and that $A = \bar{A}$, we can simply substitute those values accordingly and generate the capital and labor market solutions as shown. We also assume that the other market is simultaneously in equilibrium, since we are working our way toward a general equilibrium solution. Therefore, the solutions for the capital and labor markets are

$$\frac{1}{2}\bar{A}\left(\frac{\bar{L}}{\bar{K}}\right)^{1/2} = r^* \text{ and } \frac{1}{2}\bar{A}\left(\frac{\bar{K}}{\bar{L}}\right)^{1/2} = w^*$$

Their graphs look like this:

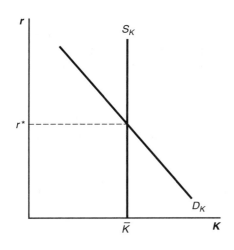

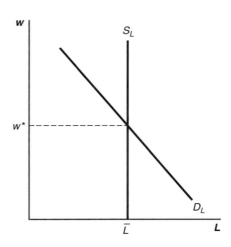

d. Create a table displaying all five equations and all five unknowns in the complete production model of this economy equivalent to Table 4.1 in the text.

The Production Model:
Five Equations and Five Unknowns

Unknowns/endogenous variables: Y, K, L, r, w

The production function: $Y = AK^{\frac{1}{2}}L^{\frac{1}{2}}$

Rule for hiring capital: $\dfrac{1}{2} \cdot \dfrac{Y}{K} = r$

Rule for hiring labor: $\dfrac{1}{2} \cdot \dfrac{Y}{L} = w$

Demand = Supply for capital: $K = \bar{K}$

Demand = Supply for labor: $L = \bar{L}$

Parameters/exogenous variables: $\bar{A}, \bar{K}, \bar{L}$

---

e. Solve this new production model. Account for each step and display the results in a table similar to Table 4.2.

Begin this process by first noting that the equilibrium values for K^* and L^* already are known as $\bar{K}$ and $\bar{L}$. Then, use the known values of $\bar{K}$ and $\bar{L}$ to

generate the equilibrium values of r* and w* and do the same thing for the equilibrium value of output, Y^*. The solution of the model can then be shown as:

The Solution of the Production Model

Capital: $K^* = \bar{K}$

Labor: $L^* = \bar{L}$

Rental rate: $r^* = \dfrac{1}{2} \cdot \dfrac{Y^*}{K^*} = \dfrac{1}{2} \cdot \bar{A} \cdot \left(\dfrac{\bar{L}}{\bar{K}}\right)^{\frac{1}{2}}$

Wage: $w^* = \dfrac{1}{2} \cdot \dfrac{Y^*}{L^*} = \dfrac{1}{2} \cdot \bar{A} \cdot \left(\dfrac{\bar{K}}{\bar{L}}\right)^{\frac{1}{2}}$

Output: $Y^* = \bar{A}\bar{K}^{\frac{1}{2}}\bar{L}^{\frac{1}{2}}$

---

2. Continue using the model developed in Problem 1. Remember that this generated a Cobb-Douglas production function of the form $Y = AK^{\frac{1}{2}}L^{\frac{1}{2}}$.
   a. Determine what the capital and labor shares of output are and show that they sum to 1.
   b. Convert this production function to a per-worker version.
   c. Determine the equilibrium value of capital stock per worker and output per worker for $\bar{A}, \bar{K},$ and $\bar{L}$.

3. Complete the following table for the year 2008.

	In 2005 dollars		Relative to the U.S. values (US = 1)			
Country	(1) Capital per Person	(2) GDP per Capita	(3) Capital per Person	(4) GDP per Capita	(5) Predicted y^*	(6) Implied TFP to Match Data
United States	105,530	42,887	1.0000	1.0000	1.0000	1.0000
Switzerland	135,817	37,302				
Brazil	14,141	9,646				
India	4,643	3,826				

a. Given the values in columns 1 and 2, fill in columns 3 and 4.

b. Using the production function from Problem 1, $Y = AK^{\frac{1}{2}}L^{\frac{1}{2}}$, compute the predicted values for column 5, assuming no total factor productivity differences between countries ($\bar{A} = 1$).

c. Calculate the implied total factor productivity values for column 6.

CHAPTER 4 SOLUTIONS

True/False Questions

1. True. See Section 4.1.

2. True. Since constant returns to scale exist only for both K and L jointly, doubling only one of them generates less than twice as much output. Section 4.2.

3. False. The factor of proportionality for labor is b. See Section 4.2 near equation (4.5) and Section 4.2 near equation (4.6).

4. False. It is determined by the amount of capital, the amount of labor, and their interaction with each other, or total factor productivity. See Section 4.2.

5. True. This is true because of diminishing returns to capital. See Section 4.3.

6. False. The presence of "monetary resources" in the statement makes it false. Otherwise each of the components are elements of a nation's capital stock. See Section 4.3.

7. True. See the very end of Section 4.3.

Multiple-Choice Questions

1. e, Each answer is a part of modern macroeconomics; even though part d is not discussed in the chapter, the text does indicate that it is a part of modern macroeconomics. See Section 4.1.

2. d, constant. When using a Cobb-Douglas production, function the sum of the exponents (a and b) on each of the inputs (K and L, in this case) must sum to 1 to achieve constant returns to scale. See Section 4.2.

3. a, For this function to exhibit increasing returns to scale, the sum of the exponents on K and L must sum to greater than 1, which they do ($1 + 2a$). See Section 4.2.

4. d, Doubling all inputs doubles output under constant return to scale. Answer c is tempting, but the standard replication argument is just about doubling the level of output, not about how efficiently it is done.

5. c, Recall that the derivative of y with respect to x for $y = ax^n$ is $\partial y / \partial x = nax^{n-1}$. In this case, both the parameter $\bar{A}$ and the variable L in the production function are treated as the constant a. See Section 4.2, equation (4.3), and footnote 2.

6. d, In this case, the parameter $\bar{A}$, and the variable K in the production function are treated as constants in the production function. See Section 4.4, equation (4.4), and footnote 2.

7. b, This is an alternative form of $\frac{2}{3}\bar{A}\left(\frac{K}{L}\right)^{\frac{1}{3}}$, achieved by multiplying by a special form of 1, where $1 = \left(\frac{L}{L}\right)^{\frac{2}{3}}$.

Note that $\frac{2}{3}\bar{A}\left(\frac{K}{L}\right)^{\frac{1}{3}}\left(\frac{L}{L}\right)^{\frac{2}{3}} = \frac{2}{3}\frac{\bar{A}K^{\frac{1}{3}}L^{\frac{2}{3}}}{L^{\frac{1}{3}}L^{\frac{2}{3}}} = \frac{2}{3}\frac{Y}{L}$. See Section 4.2.

8. d, This is an alternative form of $\frac{1}{3}\bar{A}\left(\frac{L}{K}\right)^{\frac{2}{3}}$, achieved by multiplying by a special form of 1, where $1 = \left(\frac{K}{K}\right)^{\frac{1}{3}}$.

Note that $\frac{1}{3}\bar{A}\left(\frac{L}{K}\right)^{\frac{2}{3}}\left(\frac{K}{K}\right)^{\frac{1}{3}} = \frac{1}{3}\frac{\bar{A}L^{\frac{2}{3}}K^{\frac{1}{3}}}{K^{\frac{2}{3}}K^{\frac{1}{3}}} = \frac{1}{3}\frac{Y}{K}$. See Section 4.2.

9. c, general equilibrium. The stated reason is accurate. See Section 4.2.

10. e, None of the above. Each of the statements is correct. See Section 4.2.

11. e, None of the above. Parts a–c are shown in equation (4.8) and, in part d, the K in the denominator cancels a K in the numerator, leaving K^a, and part d is identical to part a.

12. d, Reducing capital's share of output does not increase output per worker, as it eventually will lead to a smaller capital stock and therefore less output per worker. Set $\bar{A}$ equal to 1 and try using one-fifth instead of one-third for the factor of proportionality (the exponent on k) on a few numbers for k, and you will get the idea.

13. c, The other statements are much more probable justifications and much more important. A model may be elegant and simple, but that alone does not make it useful to economists. See Section 4.3.

14. d, Switzerland. Its per capita GDP is 87 percent of the U.S. per capita GDP. See Table 4.3 and Table 4.4.

15. a, Italy. Its capital stock per person is 92.7 percent of the U.S. capital stock per person. The next closest is Spain at 90.8 percent. Italy's predicted per capita GDP

is 97.5 percent of the U.S. per capita GDP, less than a 3 percent difference. The next closest is Spain, with a 3.2 percent difference. See Table 4.3.

16. d, research and development. The other four statements correctly describe $\bar{A}$. See Section 4.3.

17. e, the United Kingdom. See Section 4.3 and Table 4.4.

18. c, total factor productivity explains two thirds of the income differences between countries. See Section 4.3.

19. e, part a is a subset of part b as is part c of part d. See Section 4.4.

20. a, Burundi. Returns to education are often higher where, in general, there is less of it. See Section 4.4.

21. e, Each of these will make it more likely that the explanation of additional growth will accrue to a country's total factor productivity because they all contribute in ways that are not measureable in the same way that units of capital or numbers of worker hours can be measured.

22. d, price controls are an intervention into the economy on the part of the institution of government, not an institution itself. See Section 4.4.

23. d, A few firms may experience increased profitability as the example of the Prime Minister's cousin in the text suggests, but industry profitability as a whole will be less if productive resources are misallocated.

Exercises

1. Recall that, to determine returns to scale, we double each of the inputs, in this case K and L, that is, $F(2K, 2L)$, then determine if doing so yields double the output or more or less than double the output. More than twice the output means increasing returns to scale, and less than twice the output means decreasing returns to scale.

a. This function exhibits increasing returns to scale:

$$A(2K)^{\frac{3}{4}}(2L)^{\frac{3}{4}} = A2^{\frac{3}{4}}K^{\frac{3}{4}}2^{\frac{3}{4}}L^{\frac{3}{4}} = A2^{(\frac{3}{4}+\frac{3}{4})}K^{\frac{3}{4}}L^{\frac{3}{4}} =$$
$$A2^{\frac{3}{2}}K^{\frac{3}{4}}L^{\frac{3}{4}} > 2Y$$

b. This function exhibits constant returns to scale:

$$A(2K)^{\frac{1}{4}}(2L)^{\frac{3}{4}} = A2^{\frac{1}{4}}K^{\frac{1}{4}}2^{\frac{3}{4}}L^{\frac{3}{4}} = A2^{(\frac{1}{4}+\frac{3}{4})}K^{\frac{1}{4}}L^{\frac{3}{4}} =$$
$$A2^{1}K^{\frac{1}{4}}L^{\frac{3}{4}} = 2Y$$

c. This function exhibits decreasing returns to scale:

$$A(2K)^{\frac{1}{4}}(2L)^{\frac{1}{4}} = A2^{\frac{1}{4}}K^{\frac{1}{4}}2^{\frac{1}{4}}L^{\frac{1}{4}} = A2^{(\frac{1}{4}+\frac{1}{4})}K^{\frac{1}{4}}L^{\frac{1}{4}} =$$
$$A2^{\frac{1}{2}}K^{\frac{1}{4}}L^{\frac{1}{4}} < 2Y$$

d. This function exhibits decreasing returns to scale:

$$A+(2K)^{\frac{1}{4}}(2L)^{\frac{3}{4}} = A+2^{\frac{1}{4}}K^{\frac{1}{4}}2^{\frac{3}{4}}L^{\frac{3}{4}} =$$
$$A+2^{(\frac{1}{4}+\frac{3}{4})}K^{\frac{1}{4}}L^{\frac{3}{4}} = A+2K^{\frac{1}{4}}L^{\frac{3}{4}} < 2Y$$

Note that

$$2Y = 2\left(A + K^{\frac{1}{4}}L^{\frac{3}{4}}\right) = 2A + 2K^{\frac{1}{4}}L^{\frac{3}{4}} > A + 2K^{\frac{1}{4}}L^{\frac{3}{4}};$$

therefore, we have decreasing returns to scale.

e. This function exhibits constant returns to scale:

$$2L+(2K)^{\frac{3}{4}}(2L)^{\frac{1}{4}} = 2L+2^{(\frac{3}{4}+\frac{1}{4})}K^{\frac{3}{4}}L^{\frac{1}{4}} =$$
$$2L+2K^{\frac{3}{4}}L^{\frac{1}{4}} = 2\left(L + K^{\frac{3}{4}}L^{\frac{1}{4}}\right) = 2Y$$

2. Recall that, to convert a standard production function in levels into a per-worker production function, it is necessary to divide both sides by the number of workers, or L, and that $Y/L = y$ and $K/L = k$.

a. $Y = AL + K \implies \dfrac{Y}{L} = \dfrac{AL}{L} + \dfrac{K}{L} \implies y = A + k.$

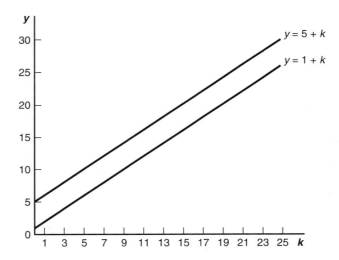

b. $Y = AK^{1/4}L^{3/4} \Rightarrow \dfrac{Y}{L} = AK^{1/4}\dfrac{L^{3/4}}{L} = AK^{1/4}L^{-1/4} =$

$A\left(\dfrac{K}{L}\right)^{1/4} \Rightarrow y = Ak^{1/4}.$

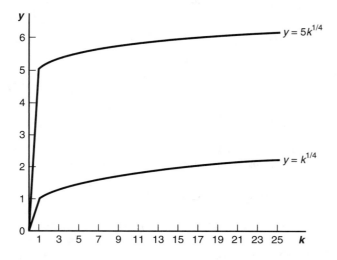

Problems

1. Worked Problem. The problem is worked in the text.

2. a. Payments to labor and capital are w^*L^* and r^*K^*.
   Note that they also exhaust output $w^*L^* + r^*K^* = Y$.

   As shares of output, we have $\dfrac{w^*L^*}{Y^*} + \dfrac{r^*K^*}{Y^*} = 1.$

   Recall that $r^* = \dfrac{1}{2}\bar{A}\left(\dfrac{\bar{L}}{\bar{K}}\right)^{1/2}$, $w^* = \dfrac{1}{2}\bar{A}\left(\dfrac{\bar{K}}{\bar{L}}\right)^{1/2}$,

   $K^* = \bar{K}$, and $L^* = \bar{L}$, then begin with the output shares:

   $$\dfrac{\frac{1}{2}\bar{A}\left(\frac{\bar{K}}{\bar{L}}\right)^{1/2}\bar{L}}{Y^*} + \dfrac{\frac{1}{2}\bar{A}\left(\frac{\bar{L}}{\bar{K}}\right)^{1/2}\bar{K}}{Y^*} = \dfrac{\frac{1}{2}\bar{A}\bar{K}^{1/2}\bar{L}^{1/2}}{Y^*} + \dfrac{\frac{1}{2}\bar{A}\bar{L}^{1/2}\bar{K}^{1/2}}{Y^*}$$

   $$\dfrac{\frac{1}{2}Y^*}{Y^*} + \dfrac{\frac{1}{2}Y^*}{Y^*} = \dfrac{1}{2} + \dfrac{1}{2} = 1$$

   b. $Y = AK^{1/2}L^{1/2} \Rightarrow \dfrac{Y}{L} = \dfrac{AK^{1/2}L^{1/2}}{L} \Rightarrow y = \dfrac{AK^{1/2}}{L^{1/2}} =$

   $A\left(\dfrac{K}{L}\right)^{1/2} = Ak^{1/2}.$

   c. $y^* = \dfrac{Y^*}{L^*} = \dfrac{\bar{A}\bar{K}^{1/2}\bar{L}^{1/2}}{\bar{L}} = \bar{A}\left(\dfrac{\bar{K}}{\bar{L}}\right)^{1/2} = \bar{A}\bar{k}^{1/2}.$

3. The completed table is as follows:

| | In 2005 dollars | | Relative to the U.S. values (US = 1) | | | |
Country	(1) Capital per Person	(2) GDP per Capita	(3) Capital per Person	(4) GDP per Capita	(5) Predicted y^*	(6) Implied TFP to Match Data
United States	105,530	42,887	1.0000	1.0000	1.0000	1.0000
Switzerland	135,817	37,302	1.2870	0.8698	1.1345	0.7667
Brazil	14,141	9,646	0.1340	0.2249	0.3661	0.6144
India	4,643	3,826	0.0440	0.0892	0.2098	0.4253

a. The formula is $\dfrac{\text{country } X}{\text{U.S.}}$ for both columns 3 and 4.

b. First derive the per-worker version of $Y = AK^{1/2}L^{1/2}$, which is $y = k^{1/2}$, then calculate for Switzerland, for example, $y^* = (1.2870)^{1/2}$ (since TFP or $\bar{A} = 1$ for both countries).

c. Implied TFP $(\bar{A})$ for a country comes from

$$y = \bar{A}k^{1/2} \Rightarrow \dfrac{y}{k^{1/2}} = \dfrac{\bar{A}k^{1/2}}{k^{1/2}} \Rightarrow \bar{A} = \dfrac{y}{k^{1/2}}. \text{ For}$$

Switzerland, for example, $\bar{A} = \dfrac{0.8698}{(1.2870)^{1/2}}.$

CHAPTER 5 | The Solow Growth Model

OVERVIEW

The Solow growth model is one of the most important models used by macroeconomists in the world today because it provides us significant insight into the capital accumulation process. Building on the basic production model from Chapter 4, the Solow growth model endogenizes the accumulation of capital stock and helps explain why countries with high investment rates have high capital-output ratios. Through the principle of transition dynamics, it also provides an explanation for differences in growth rates across countries; namely, that countries further away from a steady-state level of capital stock and production have faster growth rates. However, even with these contributions, the limits placed on the model by its reliance on the process of capital accumulation leave the Solow growth model unable to explain a significant portion of the short-term growth experienced by countries in transition and unable to explain the long-term growth experienced by the majority of countries having reached steady states.

KEY CONCEPTS

When increasing its capital stock, a country faces a *resource constraint* of $Y = C + I$ and can only put new capital stock in place to the extent that it does not consume all that it produces, that is, $I = Y - C$.

The *capital accumulation equation* distinguishes the production model in Chapter 4 from the Solow growth model in Chapter 5. It incorporates a dynamic element describing how capital evolves over time. Formally, the capital accumulation equation, $K_{t+1} = K_t + I_t - \bar{d}K_t$, tells us that tomorrow's capital stock (K_{t+1}) depends

on today's existing capital stock (K_t) plus today's investment, or new capital stock (I_t), less any capital stock usage, or *depreciation* ($\bar{d}K_t$), where $\bar{d}$ is the rate of depreciation.

In the context of growth over time, *stocks* are the quantities that survive or remain the same from period to period. By contrast, *flows* last for only a single period but occur repeatedly and can vary from previous occurrences each time they take place. For example, all the tools, machines, computers, buildings, and so forth, that make up a nation's capital *stock* began as investment, or a *flow,* into the nation's capital *stock* and all will *flow* out of it in the form of depreciation as they wear out and get discarded or replaced.

The *real interest rate* is the increase in purchasing power, or additional real resources, that a borrower must return to a lender at the end of the loan period.

Saving occurs when people consume less than they earn or produce. For example, since income can be either consumed or saved, $Y = C + S$, then saving will occur when $S = Y - C$ and $Y - C > 0$.

Net investment occurs when the flows into the nation's capital stock differ from the flows out of it. While depreciation generally occurs at a fairly constant rate, investment does not. Net investment, therefore, can be either positive, when investment exceeds depreciation, or negative, when investment fails to exceed depreciation.

The *Solow diagram* (Figure 5.1 in the text) measures capital (K) on the horizontal axis and investment ($\bar{s}Y$) and depreciation ($\bar{d}K$) on the vertical axis. It consists of two curves, both functions of capital, that together describe the process of an economy's transition to a steady state. The first curve, new investment ($\bar{s}Y$), exhibits diminishing returns to capital because new investment is a portion ($\bar{s}$) of output (Y) and thus inherits its properties as a result. The second (linear) curve represents depreciation ($\bar{d}K$) or the constant proportion of the capital stock that is used up each period. The vertical difference between these two curves, or the change in the capital stock each period, depicts net investment. As seen in Figure 5.2 in the text, the production function itself also can be added to the Solow diagram to reflect the level of output corresponding to the levels of investment and depreciation at a given level of capital stock.

A *steady state* occurs in the absence of change. In the Solow model and the Solow diagram, a steady state refers to the behavior of investment relative to depreciation and simultaneously to both the level of capital stock and the level of production in an economy. More formally, it refers to the point where investment equals depreciation ($\bar{s}Y = \bar{d}K$) and corresponds to a specific level of capital stock (K^*) and output (Y^*). See Figure 5.2 in the text.

The *capital-output ratio, K/Y,* represents the amount of capital a country has relative to its level of output produced by that capital stock. It is determined both by a country's saving and depreciation rates and helps to determine that country's level of output production.

The *principle of transition dynamics* is the general principle that states that, the further away an economy is from its steady state (in percentage terms), the greater its immediate growth rate will be as it moves toward that steady state. The closer an economy is to its steady state, the slower it will grow. Positive growth occurs when the economy is below its steady state, and growth is negative when the economy is above its steady state. In the case of the Solow growth model explored in this chapter, such growth is driven by a nation's capital accumulation process, specifically, the speed at which it accumulates or depletes its capital stock.

Diminishing returns occur in all productive processes when one or more of the factor inputs remain constant, such as the amount of labor when more and more additional capital is put into place. In the production model used here, this means that, as more and more capital stock gets put into place, output still increases, as does investment, since it is a function of output, but by less and less with each increment of capital.

TRUE/FALSE QUESTIONS

1. The Solow growth model is simply another, more formal title for the same production model developed in Chapter 4.

2. The Solow growth model relies on the accumulation of capital as its primary explanation for growth.

3. A nation's current capital stock is the accumulation of all past investment activity.

4. Accounting for the role of capital stock accumulation in the economy, the Solow model reduces the importance attributed to the role of total factor productivity (TFP) in the production model developed in Chapter 4.

5. The Solow growth model falls short of being able to explain the widespread phenomenon of economic growth for most countries over extended periods of time.

6. The Solow growth model provides further support for the conclusion that, in the short run, differences in growth rates across countries derive primarily from transition dynamics.

7. Most poor countries in the world today would benefit from large capital infusions to help them move more rapidly to their steady states.

8. The Solow growth model provides a robust explanation of long-run economic growth.

MULTIPLE-CHOICE QUESTIONS

1. Which one of the following equations is not a part of the formal Solow growth model developed in Chapter 5?
   a. $Y_t = \bar{A}K_t^{1/3}L_t^{2/3}$
   b. $C_t + I_t = Y_t$
   c. $K_{t+1} = K_t + I_t - \bar{d}K$
   d. $K_t = \bar{K}$
   e. $I_t = \bar{s}Y_t$

2. Which one of the five equations used in the Solow model makes it dynamic?
   a. $Y_t = \bar{A}K_t^{1/3}L_t^{2/3}$
   b. $K_{t+1} = K_t + I_t - \bar{d}K$
   c. $L_t = \bar{L}$
   d. $C_t + I_t = Y_t$
   e. $I_t = \bar{s}Y_t$

3. The Solow model in Chapter 5 differs from the production model in Chapter 4 in several ways. Which of the following is one of those ways?
   a. Profit maximization in the labor market no longer applies.
   b. The capital market plays no role.
   c. Output is allocated between consumption and investment.
   d. Production is a function of capital, labor, and total factor productivity.
   e. Investment is a function of income.

4. Which of the following reasons best explains the absence of the equation for consumption, $C_t = (1 - \bar{s})Y_t$, from the Solow model?
   a. Consumption is not part of the model.
   b. It would make the model unsolvable.
   c. The model's primary concern is investment.
   d. Including an equation for consumption would be redundant.
   e. It makes counting the equations and the unknowns too difficult.

5. Which of the following statements about stocks and flows is not correct?
   a. A stock survives over time.
   b. A flow lasts only a short period of time.
   c. Flows satisfy an accumulation equation.
   d. A change in the capital stock of a nation is a flow of investment.
   e. None of the above, they are all correct.

6. Which of the following statements about investment is incorrect?
   a. $i_t = \bar{s}y_t$
   b. $I_t = Y_t + C_t$
   c. $I_t = \bar{s}\bar{A}K_t^a L_t^b$
   d. $I_t = \Delta K_t + \bar{d}K_t$
   e. $I_t = \bar{s}Y_t$

7. Which point in Figure 1 represents the steady-state level of output?

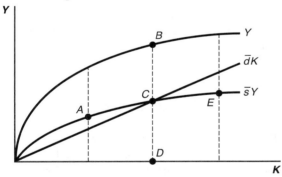

Figure 1

   a. Point *A*
   b. Point *B*
   c. Point *C*
   d. Point *D*
   e. Point *E*

8. Which point in Figure 1 determines the steady-state level of capital stock?
   a. Point *A*
   b. Point *B*
   c. Point *C*
   d. Point *D*
   e. Point *E*

9. Which of the following statements defines a steady state in the Solow model?
   a. $\Delta K_t = 0$
   b. $K_{t+1} = K_t$
   c. $\bar{s}Y = \bar{d}K$
   d. $K_t - K_{t-1} = 0$
   e. all of the above

10. Under which of the following conditions will the capital stock of a country continue to grow?
    a. $\bar{s}Y > \bar{d}K$
    b. $K^* > K$
    c. $Y > Y^*$
    d. both a and b
    e. both a and c

11. The process of an economy moving toward its steady state is called
    a. equilibrium dynamics.
    b. an equilibrium process.
    c. a steady-state approach.
    d. transition dynamics.
    e. transitioning the economy.

12. Which of the following statements regarding the nature of K^* is untrue?
    a. A higher rate of investment leads to a larger K^*.
    b. The speed at which capital depreciates determines the level of K^*.
    c. A higher level of total factor productivity increases the level of K^*.
    d. The size of the labor force determines the level of K^*.
    e. None of the above, they all are true.

13. An increase in output per worker can result from all of the following except
    a. an increase in total factor productivity.
    b. an increase in the labor force.
    c. better machine maintenance and care of other productive equipment.
    d. an increased savings rate.
    e. a more productive capital stock.

14. Data regarding capital-output ratios and investment rates presented in Chapter 5 tend to confirm the theoretical result of _____ correlation between the two variables.
    a. a positive
    b. a negative
    c. an asymmetric
    d. a symmetric
    e. no

15. The underlying economic principle behind the Solow model's convergence to a steady state is
    a. profit maximization.
    b. constant returns to scale.
    c. capital accumulation.
    d. diminishing returns.
    e. continual depreciation.

16. The steady-state solution in the Solow growth model is characterized by all the following conditions except
    a. $c^* = (1 - \bar{s})y^*$.
    b. $y^* \equiv \dfrac{Y^*}{L}$.
    c. $K_{t+1} = K_t$.
    d. $g_Y > 0$.
    e. $g_Y = g_K$.

17. In the Solow growth model, increase in the investment rate ($\bar{s}$) causes the steady-state level of a country's capital stock to
    a. rise.
    b. fall.
    c. stay the same.
    d. not enough information to tell
    e. first rise and then return to its steady-state level.

18. Which of the following would not cause the steady-state level of output to increase?
    a. an increase in the investment rate
    b. an increase in the depreciation rate
    c. an increase in total factor productivity
    d. an increase in the labor force
    e. an increase in capital's share of output

19. Which of the following would cause the steady-state level of a nation's capital stock to increase?
    a. a decrease in the labor force
    b. a decrease in the investment rate
    c. a decrease in the depreciation rate
    d. a decrease in total factor productivity
    e. a decrease in capital's share of output

20. Which of the following statements is inconsistent with the principle of transition dynamics as it applies to the Solow growth model?
    a. If an economy is above its steady state, its growth rate will be negative.
    b. As an economy approaches its steady state, its growth rate declines.
    c. The further an economy is below its steady state, the faster it will grow.
    d. An economy falling slightly short of its steady-state level of capital stock will still grow but very slowly.
    e. Once an economy reaches its steady state, it will continue growing at its population growth rate.

21. Data presented in Chapter 5 of the text suggest that, when considering relatively rich countries, we can expect
    a. no correlation between their level of GDP per capita and their growth rate.
    b. a positive correlation between their level of GDP per capita and their growth rate.
    c. a negative correlation between their level of GDP per capita and their growth rate.
    d. very slow growth in per capita GDP, because they already are so rich.
    e. higher growth rates in per capita GDP, because it takes money to make money.

22. Data presented in Chapter 5 of the text suggest that, when considering the world as a whole, we can expect
    a. no correlation between a country's level of GDP per capita and its growth rate.
    b. a positive correlation between a country's level of GDP per capita and its growth rate.
    c. a negative correlation between a country's level of GDP per capita and its growth rate.
    d. very slow growth in per capita GDP, because most of the world is relatively poor.
    e. moderate growth rates in per capita GDP, because they are a historical regularity.

EXERCISES

1. The following table illustrates the process of capital accumulation. Using the capital accumulation and allocation of resources equations from the Solow model (see Table 5.2 in the chapter), complete the empty cells in the following table. Assume a growth rate of 3 percent for investment and a depreciation rate of 7 percent. Challenge yourself by filling out the table before you look at the process hints in parts a–d in the solutions to this exercise.

(1) Time, t	(2) Capital, K_t	(3) Investment, I_t	(4) Depreciation, $\bar{d}K_t$	(5) Change in Capital, ΔK_t
0	2,000	300		
1				
2				
3				
4				
5				

2. Show why an equation for consumption, such as $C_t = (1 - \bar{s})Y_t$, would introduce a redundant equation into the Solow growth model.
   a. Begin with the resource constraint ($C_t + I_t = Y_t$), substitute into it the equation for the allocation of resources ($I_t = \bar{s}Y_t$), and solve for C_t.
   b. Explain why the result you find in part a is redundant.

PROBLEMS

1. Consider the economy represented by the accompanying Solow growth model:

$$Y_t = \bar{A}K_t^{\frac{1}{3}}\left(\bar{L}_t\right)^{\frac{2}{3}}$$

$$\Delta K_t = I_t - \bar{d}K_t$$

$$Y_t = C_t + I_t$$

$$I_t = \bar{s}Y_t$$

$$L_t = \bar{L}$$

In this problem we look at the adjustment process, or the transition dynamics, surrounding a return or movement to a steady-state solution for a country. Begin by drawing the steady-state solution for the country described by this model on a Solow diagram.
   a. Now suppose a natural disaster occurs, such as Hurricane Katrina. Assume that half of the country's capital stock is destroyed and draw the impact of this event on your diagram.
   b. Work through the transition dynamics following this event for at least two periods and carefully draw them on your diagram, explaining the process involved.
   c. Discuss the behavior of income, consumption, and investment during this process.
   d. Draw an appropriate ratio scale diagram showing the behavior of output over time for the events of this problem.
   e. Show the new steady-state solution on both of your diagrams.

2. Now consider another country identical to the one in Problem 1. Assume that it, too, begins in its steady state and draw another Solow diagram for it.
   a. Now assume that, in this economy, there is a sudden change that causes total factor productivity to improve by 50 percent and draw the impact of this event on your diagram.
   b. Work through the transition dynamics following this event for at least two periods and carefully draw them on your diagram, explaining the process involved.
   c. Discuss the behavior of income, consumption, and investment during this process.
   d. Draw the appropriate ratio scale diagram showing the behavior of output over time for this event.
   e. Show the new steady-state solution on both of your diagrams.

Worked Problem

3. Consider the economy represented by the accompanying Solow growth model:

$$Y_t = K_t^{\frac{1}{3}}\left(\bar{L}_t\right)^{\frac{2}{3}}$$
$$\Delta K_t = I_t - 0.07K_t$$
$$Y_t = C_t + I_t$$
$$I_t = 0.2Y_t$$
$$L_t = 125$$

In this problem, let $\bar{s} = 0.2$, $\bar{d} = 0.07$, $\bar{A} = 1$, and $\bar{L} = 6,000$. Having these values allows you to calculate specific values for the steady-state values of capital and output as well as the steps involved in the transition dynamics. Assume also that the economy begins in its steady state and draw another Solow diagram for it.

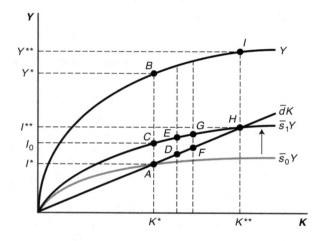

a. What are the steady-state values for capital, output, investment, and consumption? Label these on your diagram. First, notice that, by solving for the variables in the order listed, each variable is ready to feed into another for the subsequent solution. That

said, solve for the steady-state level of the capital stock. Recall that the steady state occurs when $\Delta K = 0$ and, in Section 5.4, K^* is shown to be a function of only the four parameter values given in the instructions to this problem:

$$\Delta K = 0 = I_t - 0.07K_t^*$$
$$I_t = 0.07K_t^*, \text{ using } I_t = 0.2Y_t^*$$
$$0.2Y_t^* = 0.07K_t^*, \text{ recall that } Y_t^* = K_t^{*\frac{1}{3}}6,000^{\frac{2}{3}}$$
$$0.2K_t^{*\frac{1}{3}}6,000^{\frac{2}{3}} = 0.07K_t^*$$
$$\frac{0.2K_t^{*\frac{1}{3}}6,000^{\frac{2}{3}}}{K_t^{*\frac{1}{3}}} = \frac{0.07K_t^*}{K_t^{*\frac{1}{3}}}$$
$$0.2 \bullet 6,000^{\frac{2}{3}} = 0.07K_t^{*\frac{2}{3}}$$
$$\left[\left(\frac{0.2}{0.07}\right)6,000^{\frac{2}{3}}\right]^{\frac{3}{2}} = \left(K_t^{*\frac{2}{3}}\right)^{\frac{3}{2}}$$

$$K_t^* = \left(\frac{0.2}{0.07}\right)^{\frac{3}{2}}6,000 = 28,976.7173$$

$$Y_t^* = 28,976.7173^{\frac{1}{3}}6,000^{\frac{2}{3}} = 10,141.85106$$
$$I_t^* = 0.2 \bullet 10,141.85106 = 2,028.37021$$
$$C_t^* = (1-0.2)10,141.85106 = 8,113.48085$$
$$\text{or } \left(Y_t^* - I_t^*\right)$$

b. Now assume that this economy suddenly increases its saving or investment rate by 50 percent and draw the impact of this event on your diagram. See the diagram. Note that $\bar{s}Y$ shifts up and Y does not.

c. In the period of this initial change, what happens to consumption, investment, and output? Consumption falls from $Y^* - I^*$ to $Y^* - I_0$, I^* increases to I_0, and nothing happens to output.

d. Calculate and show the relationship (mathematically) between the values of capital stock, income, investment, depreciation, and consumption for the first two periods following this change. Also show these outcomes on your diagram.

| | $A_1 = 1$ | | | | $L = 6,000$ | |
| | $s_1 = 0.2$ | | $s_2 = 0.3$ | | $d = 0.07$ | |
	Capital Stock K	Income $Y = AK^{1/3}L^{2/3}$	Consumption $C = (1-s)Y$	Investment $I = sY$	Depreciation dK	Net Investment $\Delta K = I - dK$
Steady state	28,976.72	10,141.85	8,113.48	2,028.37	2,028.37	0.00
Period 1	28,976.72	10,141.85	7,099.30	3,042.56	2,028.37	1,014.19
Period 2	29,990.90	10,258.82	7,181.17	3,077.65	2,099.36	978.28
Period 3	30,969.18	10,369.17	7,258.42	3,110.75	2,167.84	942.91

Period 1 on the diagram is the initial steady-state period at K^*. Period 2 on the diagram is the first dashed line to the right of K^*, or $K^* + C–A$. Period 3 on the diagram is the next dashed line to the right, or $K^* + C–A + E–D$. In period 2, K_2 equals $28,976.72 + 1,014.19$; Y, C, I, and $\bar{d}k$ then are calculated from left to right using the appropriate values just generated, as shown in the equations in the fourth row of the table. Likewise in period 3, K_3 equals $K_2 + \Delta K$ and the other variables are calculated as they were for period 2.

e. Calculate the new steady-state values for capital, output, investment, and consumption due to the increase in $\bar{s}$ from 0.2 to 0.3 and show them on your diagram:

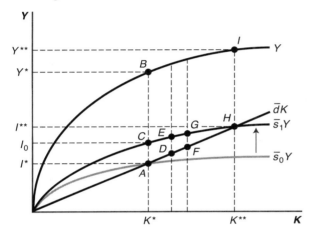

$$K_t^{**} = \left(\frac{0.3}{0.07}\right)^{3/2} 6,000 = 53,233.62886$$

$$Y_t^{**} = 53,233.62886^{1/3}6,000^{2/3} = 12,421.18007$$

$$I_t^{**} = 0.3 \bullet 12,421.18007 = 3,726.35402$$

$$C_t^{**} = (1 - 0.2)12,421.18007$$
$$= 8,694.826007 \text{ or } \left(Y_t^* - I_t^*\right)$$

f. Draw the appropriate ratio scale diagram showing the behavior and label the values of output over time for this event. Begin with the initial period and end with the final steady state:

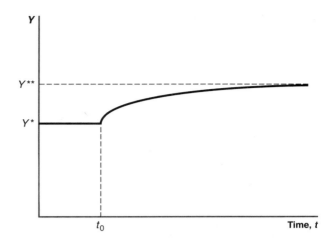

CHAPTER 5 SOLUTIONS

True/False Questions

1. False. The two models are distinguished by the endogenous nature of the capital stock in the Solow growth model. See Section 5.1.

2. True. See Section 5.1, and after working through the whole chapter, also see Section 5.9.

3. False. It doesn't include the depreciation and discarding of capital stock. See the description of K_{t+1} in Section 5.2.

4. False. Just the opposite, TFP becomes even more important. Mathematically this is seen through the larger exponent on $\bar{A}$. See Section 5.4.

5. True. While it can explain short-term growth to some extent, it predicts no growth in the steady state. See Section 5.6.

6. True. See Section 5.8.

7. False. Most countries already are at their steady states. Such infusions would lead to only temporary growth and a transition back to their earlier steady state unless the determinants of their steady state also change. See Section 5.9.

8. False. It actually fails to do this by predicting zero growth once a country reaches its steady state.

Multiple-Choice Questions

1. d, $K_t = \bar{K}$. This, in fact, is the feature of the model from Chapter 4 that the Solow model replaces with the capital accumulation equation. See Section 5.2.

2. b, $K_{t+1} = K_t + I_t - \bar{d}K_t$. It is the only equation that spans two time periods, t and $t + 1$.

3. c, Output is allocated between consumption and investment. Parts a and b, present in the production model, still function in the background of the Solow growth model. Parts d and e are explicit equations in the Solow growth model. See Section 5.2 and Table 5.2.

4. d, it would be redundant. See the case study "Some Questions about the Solow Model."

5. c, *stocks* satisfy an accumulation equation. See the case study "Some Questions about the Solow Model."

6. b, $I_t = Y_t + C_t$ would be correct were it $I_t = Y_t - C_t$. See the case study "Some Questions about the Solow Model."

7. b, Point *B*. It is the point on the production/output function determined by the steady-state level of capital stock. See Section 5.4 and Figure 5.2.

8. d, Point *D*. It is the level of capital stock where $\bar{s}Y = \bar{d}K$. See Section 5.4 and Figure 5.2.

9. e, all of the above. Each defines the steady-state level of capital stock in some way. See Section 5.4.

10. d, both a and b. Both these points are to the left of K^*. See Section 5.4 and Figure 5.2.

11. d, transition dynamics. See Section 5.4.

12. e, none of the above. See Section 5.4.

13. b, an increase in the labor force. Note that, for Y/L, an increase in L causes output per worker to decrease. See Section 5.4.

14. a, a positive. See Section 5.5 and Figure 5.3.

15. d, diminishing returns. See Section 5.6.

16. d, $g_Y > 0$ is untrue. In the steady state, $g_Y = 0$. See Section 5.7.

17. a, rise. See Section 5.8 and Figures 5.4 and 5.5.

18. b, an increase in the depreciation rate. See Section 5.8 and Figure 5.8.

19. c, a decrease in the depreciation rate. See Section 5.8 and Figure 5.6.

20. e, in the Solow growth model, the steady-state growth rate for any country is zero. See Section 5.9.

21. c, a negative correlation. See Section 5.9. and Figure 5.8.

22. a, no correlation. See Section 5.9 and Figure 5.9.

Exercises

1. The completed table is as follows:

(1) Time, t	(2) Capital, K_t	(3) Investment, I_t	(4) Depreciation, $\bar{d}K_t$	(5) Change in Capital, ΔK_t
0	2,000.00	300.00	140.00	160.00
1	2,160.00	309.00	151.20	157.80
2	2,317.80	318.27	162.25	156.02
3	2,473.82	327.82	173.17	154.65
4	2,628.47	337.65	183.99	153.66
5	2,782.13	347.78	194.75	153.03

Hints:

a. Fill in column 3 by letting investment grow by 3 percent each period.

b. Calculate depreciation ($\bar{d}K_t$) for period 0 and fill in the first cell in column 4.

c. Calculate the value for the change in capital ($\Delta K_t = I_t - \bar{d}K_t$) and fill in the value for the first cell in column 5.

d. Calculate the value for capital in period 1 (K_1) by adding the change in capital in period 0 (ΔK_0) to the level of capital in period 0 (ΔK_0) so that $K_{t+1} = K_t + \Delta K_t$.

e. Repeat the process in parts b, c, and d for the remaining five periods of the table.

2. a. resource constraint, ($C_t + I_t = Y_t$); allocation of resources, ($I_t = \bar{s}Y_t$); substituting and solving for C_t, we get

$$C_t + \bar{s}Y_t = Y_t$$
$$C_t = Y_t - \bar{s}Y_t$$
$$C_t = (1 - \bar{s})Y_t$$

b. The equation $C_t = (1 - \bar{s})Y_t$ is redundant because it can be derived from information already available in the model. It contributes nothing new to the model.

Problems

1. The accompanying diagram shows the initial steady-state levels of capital stock and output, K^*, and Y^*, before the destruction. They correspond to points A and B.

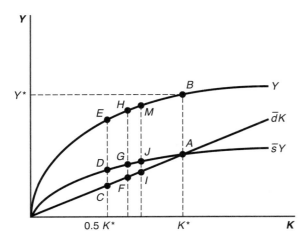

a. The term $0.5K^*$ designates the destruction of one half of K^*.

b. In the first period following the disaster, the amount of capital $D–C$ (net investment, or ΔK) is added to $0.5K^*$. In the second period following the capital stock decrease, the amount $G–F$ is added to $(0.5K^* + D–C)$. And so forth, so that in the third

period (not shown), we would have a value for $K = 0.5K^* + D–C + G–F + J–I$.

c. Income, consumption, and investment all fall as a result of the decrease in the level of capital stock. Note that, just as E is less than B and D less than A, so is $E–D$ less than $B–A$. Note, too, that income, consumption, and investment all grow as the economy returns to its steady state.

d. See the following diagram, where the destruction of capital stock occurs at time period t_0, output initially falls and then gradually returns to its steady-state level.

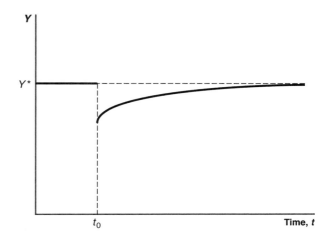

e. The economy returns to K^* and Y^* as in the initial steady state.

2. The accompanying diagram shows the initial steady-state levels of capital stock and output, K^* and Y^*, prior to the increase in total factor productivity. They correspond to points A and B.

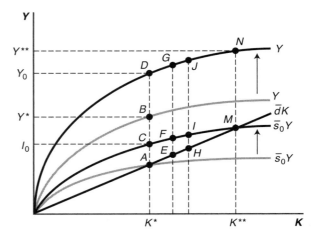

a. The increase in TFP is reflected by the upward shifts of Y and $\bar{s}Y$ and immediately yield the levels of output, Y_0, and investment, I_0.

b. In the first period following the change in TFP, the amount of capital $C–A$ is added to K^*. In the second period, the amount $F–E$ is added to $(K^* + C–A)$. And so forth, so that, in the third period (not shown), we have a value for $K = K^* + C–A + F–E + I–H$.

c. Due to the improved TFP, income, consumption, and investment all increase as the economy in this problem moves to a new and higher steady-state level of economic activity.

d. See accompanying diagram where at time period t_0, total factor productivity, $\bar{A}$, increases. Note that output increases immediately, but not all the way to Y^{**}, and then gradually increases the rest of the way over time.

e. The economy moves to the new steady state of K^{**} and Y^{**}.

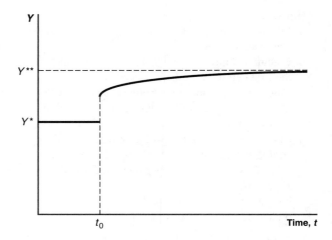

3. Worked Problem. The problem is worked in the text.

CHAPTER 6 | Growth and Ideas

OVERVIEW

As a subsequent development to the Solow growth model, the Romer growth model expands macroeconomists' ability to address one of the most important questions about an economy's growth experience; namely, how an economy can sustain growth over an extended period of time. This ability comes from including in the model a variable that accounts for the role of knowledge, both the level of existing knowledge and the development of new ideas. This variable allows the model to explain sustained growth over long periods of time. A crucial insight into understanding this innovation comes from recognizing that knowledge and ideas do not wear out like machines and, while machines cannot be used in two places at once, knowledge and ideas can. Also crucial is the understanding that, if doubling capital and labor leads to twice as much output, doubling capital and labor and at the same time increasing the knowledge base of a country will more than double the amount of output it produces. We also must understand that ideas do not just fall from the sky. Firms require incentives to pursue research and development, especially when the process costs a lot and comes with no guarantee of success. This recognition and the fact that many research pursuits do not work out requires that firms depart from the competitive model and earn economic profit on those projects that turn out successfully. Finally, the combination of both the Solow and Romer growth models presented at the conclusion of this chapter provides a more complete understanding of an economy's ability to exhibit sustained growth for long periods of time, an explanation for differing growth rates across countries, as well as different levels of sustained growth.

KEY CONCEPTS

The *idea diagram* describes the chapter's discussion of the economics of ideas as a progression from the distinction between ideas and objects, to nonrivalry in the use of ideas, to their role in generating increasing returns, to the problems they create for using a model of pure competition to describe a country's economy.

Ideas are the ingredient in a production process that makes sustained economic growth possible. More formally, they are the instructions for arranging the raw materials of the universe in ways that transform them into useful products. While ideas often can be represented by something tangible, they begin as something unseen by the human eye and intangible to the human hand. Once shared, they fail the exclusion test for a private good, because they are nonrivalrous in use. As we see later, their use, whether in public or private goods or both, still leaves them available for additional uses with no diminished usefulness.

Objects are the *raw materials* of the universe that ideas operate on and transform into useful products. On a practical level, objects include both inputs into and outputs from the production process. We generally think of them as something tangible that can be seen, touched, picked up, and possessed; something that passes the exclusion test for a private good. We also treat workers' labor as an object, or input, into the production process that ideas can direct to one use or another.

Rivalry in use or consumption occurs when one person's use of an object prohibits another person's use of the same object. We see this characteristic most frequently with the use of private goods, where the *excludability*

61

principle applies and the owner of that good or resource has the legal right to restrict its use. At the input level of the production process rivalry underlies the principle of scarcity. Once an object is used in a production process, even of a public good, its use is no longer available for any other simultaneous purpose.

Nonrivalry in use or consumption stands in contrast to rivalrous situations, because one person's use or consumption of a good or, in the context of this chapter, an idea does not prevent another person's use of the same idea. A familiar example of this concept in the context of public goods employs a streetlight that everyone in its reach can use without prohibiting anyone else's use. However, public goods still require resources (objects) that, once used for the public good, are no longer available for alternative uses. Ideas differ from objects in this regard. Their use in both public and private goods still leaves them available for additional uses at the same time. Once generated, they experience no scarcity.

Increasing returns were introduced in Chapter 4 as *increasing returns to scale*, which occur when doubling all of the inputs in a production process generates more than double the output from that production process. This concept is important in this chapter, because a process that exhibits constant returns to scale in capital and labor will exhibit increasing returns to scale when, in addition to capital and labor, ideas also are increased.

Pareto optimality means that an allocation of resources, or goods and services, is such that there is no way to re - allocate it in an attempt to make one person better off without making someone else worse off.

Problems with perfect competition arise with the requirements of perfect information and marginal cost pricing found in perfectly competitive models. These problems have particular significance in increasing returns to scale in industries that involve large fixed costs to start up production but require relatively small marginal costs to continue producing. The incentive to commit significant resources to researching and developing new ideas and products disappears if a firm can set its prices equal only to low marginal costs and has no chance to recover large fixed costs.

Fixed costs present a firm with no opportunity for change, at least in the short run. The lease on a firm's building or the payment on its capital stock remains fixed from period to period but over time may be renegotiated. Once made, however, expenditures for researching and developing new products and ideas become sunk costs and cannot be renegotiated. They remain fixed.

The Romer model incorporates three critical elements: objects, ideas, and increasing returns to scale. It pro-duces both output, which is either consumed or invested, and ideas. Ideas accumulate in a way that capital does not, because they do not depreciate. They also provide a channel for sustained growth in this model that the Solow model does not have. In the simplest form of the Romer model, inputs consist only of labor (objects) and ideas. It exhibits constant returns to scale in labor and increasing returns to scale in both labor and ideas. It has no steady state in the long run but rather a balanced growth path that allows it to explain the persistent economic growth observed in the world over time.

The combined Solow-Romer model (found in the appendix to Chapter 6) relaxes the assumption of labor as the only object input and includes capital as well. It exhibits constant returns to scale in capital and labor and increasing returns to scale in capital, labor, and ideas. It, too, has no long-run steady state but, like the Romer model, converges to a balanced growth path in the long run. It includes the principle of transition dynamics, which provides an explanation for understanding differences in growth rates across countries, and behavioral parameters, that explain different growth rates between countries over long periods of time.

A *balanced growth path* exists when all the endogenous variables in the model grow at a constant rate. In the Solow model, a balanced growth path cannot exist, because in its steady state, capital and labor do not grow ($g_Y = g_K = 0$). In the Romer model, however, the two endogenous variables end up growing at the same constant rate ($g_Y = g_A$) along a balanced growth path.

Growth effects occur when the productive nature, or ability, of inputs to a production process increase. They occur between the initial and ending balanced growth paths and are particularly strong when the degree of increasing returns to scale is larger. Growth effects also can result from changes in the behavioral parameters of the model, such as the fraction of workers employed on the development of new ideas or the rate at which new ideas are produced.

Level effects refer to the difference between old and new balanced growth paths that result from increases in the amount, or level, of inputs used in the production process.

The *principle of transition dynamics* in the context of the Romer model parallels the general principle introduced in Chapter 5 with the Solow growth model. For the Romer model, it states that the further an economy is below its balanced growth path (in percentage terms), the faster it will grow as it moves toward that balanced growth path. The closer an economy is to its balanced growth path, the slower it will grow. Similarly, the further an economy is above its balanced growth path, the slower the growth it will experience.

Growth accounting helps us understand, or account for, the sources of growth an economy experiences. Beginning with a general Cobb-Douglas production function, $Y_t = A_t K_t^{1/3} L_t^{2/3}$, exhibiting constant returns to scale in capital and labor and a provision for the influence of ideas or, more generally, for the level of total factor productivity, A_t, we are able to measure each variable except total factor productivity and use those measurements in regression analysis to determine the contribution of each variable toward the growth of output. That portion of growth left unaccounted for by capital and labor then is attributed to total factor productivity.

The *productivity slowdown* refers to a period of time between 1973 and 1995, when output per hour grew by less than half of what it had grown during the previous 25 years. Several explanations are explored in the chapter, including oil shocks, less research and development (fewer new ideas), and changes in sectoral composition (the mix between manufacturing and services).

The *new economy* refers to the dramatic increase in growth experienced between 1995 and 2008, when output grew again at an annual rate similar to the 25 years prior to the productivity slowdown. Researchers credit the growth equally to capital stock accumulation and improvements in total factor productivity.

TRUE/FALSE QUESTIONS

1. The Romer growth model focuses on capital accumulation as one of the possible engines of sustained economic growth.

2. The economics of ideas underlies Adam Smith's invisible hand conclusions about the virtues of perfectly competitive markets.

3. Sustained economic growth occurs only with the discovery of new ideas.

4. Altruists violate the principle of self-interest.

5. Economists have found that, in general, unregulated markets tend to provide an optimal level of product and marketplace innovation.

6. The total stock of ideas, rather than ideas per capita, solely determines the sustainability of a country's long-term growth.

7. The standard replication argument that underlies constant returns to the production of objects also supports increasing returns to objects and ideas when taken together.

8. Many economists argue that the role of institutions that protect property rights and guarantee contractual agreements may be greatly undervalued with respect to their ability to promote knowledge transmittal and growth in a country.

9. The Solow growth model's major limitation is its inability to explain the positive growth observed in an economy over long periods of time.

MULTIPLE-CHOICE QUESTIONS

1. Which of the following are not examples of "ideas" as discussed in the text?
   a. just-in-time inventory
   b. turning sand into computer chips
   c. turning the roots of potato plants into snack food
   d. turning crude oil into plastic
   e. none of the above; they all are.

2. The modern theory of economic growth that distinguishes between ideas and objects applies readily to which area of economics?
   a. international trade
   b. economic development
   c. intellectual property economics
   d. antitrust economics
   e. all of the above

3. What is the correct thought process for the idea diagram presented in the text?
   a. Problems with pure competition → Increasing returns → Nonrivalry → Ideas
   b. Nonrivalry → Ideas → Increasing returns → Problems with pure competition
   c. Problems with pure competition → Ideas → Nonrivalry → Increasing returns
   d. Ideas → Nonrivalry → Increasing returns → Problems with pure competition
   e. Increasing returns → Problems with pure competition → Ideas → Nonrivalry

4. Which of the following would not be considered an object in Romer's new growth theory?
   a. a molecule of oxygen
   b. the theory of relativity
   c. an antibiotic
   d. an hour of labor
   e. a silicon chip

5. In terms of Romer's work on growth theory, new ideas are best described as
   a. thoughts no one has entertained before.
   b. words in a book no one has read before.
   c. instructions for new economically useful products.
   d. all of the above.
   e. none of the above.

6. Which of the following best embodies the principle of nonrivalry?
   a. the concept of scarcity
   b. increasing returns to scale
   c. the formulas in a spreadsheet
   d. a cell phone
   e. a specific spreadsheet program

7. Objects generally are rivalrous
   a. because most inputs can be used only once.
   b. because of the principle of scarcity.
   c. if one person's use inhibits another person's use.
   d. because they can be used only in one place at a time.
   e. all of the above

8. Which of the following does not exhibit the characteristic of nonrivalry?
   a. the quadratic formula
   b. news about last year's Super Bowl winner
   c. a cake recipe
   d. a flu vaccination
   e. none of the above

9. Which of the following production functions does not exhibit increasing returns to scale?
   a. $Y_t = A_t^b K_t^a L_t^{1-a}$, $b = 0$
   b. $Y_t = A_t^b K_t^a L_t^{1-a}$, $b = 1$
   c. $Y_t = A_t^{1/b} K_t^a L_t^{1-a}$, $b = 2$
   d. $Y_t = A_t^b K_t^a L_t^{1-a}$, $0.5 < b < 1$
   e. $Y_t = A_t^b K_t^a L_t^{1-a}$, $b > 2$

10. The production function $Y_t = A_t K_t^a L_t^{1-a}$ exhibits each of the following properties except
    a. constant returns to scale in capital and labor.
    b. increasing returns to scale in all inputs.
    c. constant returns to scale in ideas.
    d. constant returns to scale in capital, labor, and ideas.
    e. diminishing marginal products of capital and labor.

11. Which of the following statements is not relevant to the problems with pure competition when growth models include a knowledge base and the generation of new ideas?
    a. The nonrivalry characteristic of new ideas generates increasing returns.
    b. Consumers often resist new technology because of its cost.
    c. Perfect competition requires price to equal marginal costs.
    d. Firms require economic profits to undertake research and development.
    e. Fixed costs are the legacy of original research.

12. Which of the following has not been or is not used by governments to provide firms additional incentives to pursue original research and development?
    a. patents
    b. copyrights
    c. trade secrets
    d. direct funding
    e. government subsidies

13. The Romer growth model contains each of the following elements except
    a. a beginning stock of ideas.
    b. the use of an "object" as an input.
    c. the creation of an object as an output.
    d. the presence of increasing returns to scale in labor.
    e. the presence of nonrivalry that leads to sustained growth over time.

14. The equation $L_{yt} + L_{at} = \bar{N}$ in the Romer model
    a. defines the allocation of labor.
    b. acts as a resource constraint.
    c. has no purpose, as it is a redundant equation.
    d. is one of five equations and is important because it contains two unknowns.
    e. allows the model to be solved for output per worker.

15. Which of the following will not increase the level of output per worker in the Romer growth model?
    a. an increase in the stock of knowledge
    b. greater productivity in the production of new ideas
    c. an increase in the labor allocated to producing new ideas
    d. a reduction in the size of the population
    e. the passage of time

16. The Romer growth model explains long-run growth in an economy for each of the following reasons except
    a. the reliance of per capita output on the stock of ideas.
    b. the absence of diminishing returns to the existing stock of ideas.
    c. increasing returns to ideas and objects together.
    d. the nonrivalry of objects in the production process.
    e. none of the above; they all explain long-run growth.

17. A balanced growth path can be described in several ways. Which of the following does not describe it accurately?
    a. All endogenous growth rates are constant.
    b. All endogenous growth rates are equal.
    c. All growth rates neither rise nor fall.
    d. All endogenous growth rates are positive.
    e. None of the above; they are all correct.

18. Which of the circles in Figure 1 indicates the effect that would arise from an increase in the number of researchers relative to the number of producers of output?

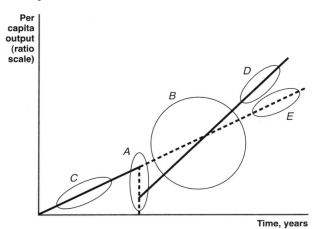

Figure 1

    a. *A*
    b. *B*
    c. *C*
    d. *D*
    e. *E*

19. Which of the circles in Figure 1 indicates the effect that would arise from an increase in the productivity of researchers working on idea production?
    a. *A*
    b. *B*
    c. *C*
    d. *D*
    e. *E*

20. The combined Solow-Romer growth model supports each of the following elements from the individual models except
    a. the invention of ideas as the key to sustained long-run growth.
    b. the nonrivalry of ideas that enables sustainable long-run growth.
    c. transition dynamics that can explain different growth rates in different countries.
    d. the provision of a theory of capital accumulation.
    e. none of the above; it supports them all.

21. The Cobb-Douglas production function provides a very useful growth accounting formula that supports the combined Solow-Romer growth model with the interpretation of total factor productivity as reflecting a country's stock of knowledge. Which of the following equations is the Solow growth accounting formula?

    a. $g_{Yt} = \frac{1}{3} g_{Kt} + \frac{2}{3} g_{Lyt} + g_{At}$

    b. $g_{Yt} = \frac{1}{3} g_{At} + \frac{1}{3} g_{Kt} + \frac{1}{3} g_{Lyt}$

    c. $g_{Yt} = \frac{2}{3} g_{Kt} + \frac{2}{3} g_{Lyt} - \frac{1}{3} g_{At}$

    d. $g_{Yt} = \frac{1}{3} g_{Kt} + \frac{2}{3} g_{Lyt} - g_{At}$

    e. $g_{Yt} = g_{At} - \frac{1}{3} g_{Kt} - \frac{2}{3} g_{Lyt}$

22. The episode in U.S. economic history referred to as the *productivity slowdown* took place during
    a. 1948–2002.
    b. 1948–73.
    c. 1973–2002.
    d. 1973–95.
    e. 1995–2002.

23. Economists rely on which of the following elements to explain the productivity slowdown in the U.S. economy?
    a. oil price shocks
    b. decreased spending on research and development
    c. a shift from manufacturing to services
    d. political unrest and lack of leadership
    e. None of these specifically; the exact causes remain elusive.

24. Economists rely on which of the following elements to explain the period of time in the United States now called the *new economy?*
    a. increased labor productivity
    b. increased capital accumulation
    c. increased total factor productivity
    d. both a and c
    e. both b and c

25. In the combined Solow-Romer growth model, long-run growth is even faster than in the Romer model alone. Which of the following statements provides an explanation for this observation?
    a. Capital accumulation makes workers more productive.
    b. More productive workers require more capital.
    c. Knowledge growth increases output, and output growth increases the capital stock.
    d. all of the above
    e. only a and b

26. When combining the Solow and Romer models, we will observe each of the following characteristics except
    a. new ideas develop continuously over time.
    b. a stagnant knowledge base.
    c. a constant rate of growth in output per capita.
    d. a steady-state level of capital stock consistent with a balanced growth path.
    e. both b and d.

27. In the combined Solow-Romer growth model, we found that output grew at a faster rate than it did in the Romer model alone, even though it did not grow at all in the steady-state solution of the Solow model. We can appeal to several reasons to explain this finding. Which of the following is not one of them?
    a. the inclusion of capital accumulation in the Romer model
    b. productivity increases that derive from the use of capital
    c. increased capital demand due to higher productivity
    d. the direct effect of knowledge growth on output growth
    e. none of the above

28. On a balanced growth path in the combined Solow-Romer growth model, each of the following would generate a higher level of output per capita except
    a. a higher investment, or savings, rate.
    b. a greater share of workers producing objects.
    c. a larger body of knowledge.
    d. a higher rate of capital stock depletion.
    e. a smaller populace.

29. The principle of transition dynamics still applies in the Solow-Romer growth model because
    a. capital stock still achieves a steady state.
    b. the economy has to be able to move from one balanced growth path to another.
    c. the further below its balanced growth path an economy is, the faster it will grow.
    d. the production function still exhibits diminishing returns to capital.
    e. the production function still exhibits constant returns to scale in capital and labor.

30. Which of the following statements does not apply to the combined Solow-Romer growth model?
    a. The principle of transition dynamics can explain differing growth rates across countries.
    b. The discovery of new ideas explains sustained long-run growth.
    c. Government policies can cause differences in long-term growth rates across countries.
    d. Total factor productivity explains a significant part of differing growth rates across countries.
    e. none of the above

EXERCISES

1. Explain whether the following goods are rivalrous or nonrivalrous.
   a. a sandwich from the local sandwich shop
   b. a song sold by iTunes
   c. a song played on the radio
   d. a new computer software program
   e. a USB flash drive

2. This exercise provides practice using a ratio scale diagram while working with growth rates and balanced growth paths. Use Figure 2 and Table 6.1 below to work the problems in this exercise. You may also want to review the growth rate rules from Chapter 3.
   a. Which balanced growth path, *A, B,* or *C,* has the fastest per capita output growth rate, and what is it?
   b. What are the growth rates for the other two balanced growth paths?
   c. If lines *A* and *B* represent the initial and ending growth paths for the same country as described by the Romer growth model found in Table 6.1, what changes in that country could explain the behavioral outcomes illustrated by the change from *A* to *B?*
   d. Identify the level effect found in Figure 2 and explain which balanced growth path experienced it and what could have caused it.
   e. Continuing on with part d, how long does it take this country to "recover" in terms of per capita GDP? Explain how you can tell.
   f. Working with the same country, how long does it take for per capita GDP to double once the change you identified in part d takes place?

Table 6.1   The Romer Growth Model

Endogenous variables: Y_t, A_t, L_{yt}, L_{at}

$$Y_t = A_t L_{yt}$$

$$\Delta A_t = \bar{z} A_t L_{at}$$

$$L_{yt} + L_{at} = \bar{N}$$

$$L_{at} = \bar{l}\bar{N}$$

Parameters: $\bar{z}, \bar{N}, \bar{l}, \bar{A}_0$

Recall that $A_t = \bar{A}_0 (1+\bar{g})^t$

3. Again use Figure 2 and Table 6.1 to work this exercise. Suppose that the initial stock of knowledge for the country represented by balanced growth path *A* were to double. Describe in detail what would happen to balanced growth path *A.* Be sure to include a discussion of both level and growth effects.

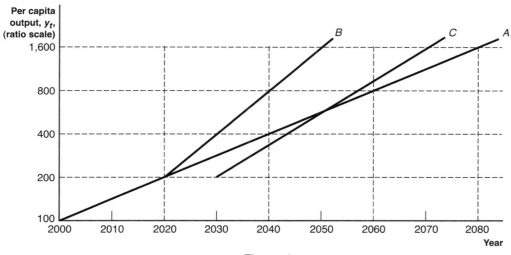

Figure 2

PROBLEMS

Worked Problem

Note: Exercise 6 in the text also is a worked problem and bears some similarity to this problem.

1. This problem provides an opportunity to become more familiar with the Romer growth model and how to work with it. Consider again the model in Table 6.1 and assume parameter values of

$$\bar{A}_0 = 250, \bar{l} = 0.08, \bar{z} = 1/4{,}000, \text{ and } \bar{N} = 2{,}000.$$

a. Show algebraically how to solve for the growth rate of per capita output in this economy.

Step 1. Solve for output per worker by substituting the labor allocation equation into the resource constraint, then the resource constraint into the production function, as follows:

$$L_{yt} + \bar{l}\bar{N} = \bar{N}$$

$$L_{yt} = \bar{N} - \bar{l}\bar{N} = \left(1 - \bar{l}\right)\bar{N}, \text{ substitute } L_{yt} \text{ into } Y_t$$

$$Y_t = A_t L_{yt}$$

$$Y_t = A_t \left(1 - \bar{l}\right)\bar{N}$$

$$y_t = \frac{Y_t}{\bar{N}} = A_t \left(1 - \bar{l}\right)$$

Note that $\bar{N}$ equals population and Y_t equals output so that $Y_t/\bar{N}$ equals output per capita.

Step 2. Note that y_t grows at the rate that A_t grows and solve for the growth rate of A_t using the idea production function:

$$\Delta A_t = \bar{z} A_t L_{at}$$

$$\frac{\Delta A_t}{A_t} = \bar{z} L_{at} = \bar{z}\bar{l}\bar{N}$$

$$\bar{g} = \bar{z}\bar{l}\bar{N} \Rightarrow A_t = A_0 \left(1 + \bar{g}\right)^t$$

Step 3. Substitute A_t into y_t, so that $y_t = A_0(1 + \bar{g})^t(1 - \bar{l})$, and note that y_t grows at the rate $\bar{g} = \bar{z}\bar{l}\bar{N}$.

b. Using the given parameter values, what is the initial growth rate of per capita output in this economy?

$$\bar{g} = \bar{z}\bar{l}\bar{N} = \frac{1}{4{,}000} \times 0.08 \times 2{,}000 = 0.04 \text{ or } 4\%$$

c. What is the value of per capita output in year 0? How much greater will per capita output be in year 50? What will its value be then?

In year 0, output per capita is $y_t = 250(1 + 0.04)^0(1 - 0.08) = 230$. Since per capita output grows at the same rate as the stock of ideas, we to need calculate only the growth in the knowledge base to determine the growth of per capita output: $(1 + 0.04)^{50} \approx 7.11$. Per capita output increases by approximately 711 percent, or a little over seven times in 50 years for a country with an annual per capita output growth rate of 4 percent. In 50 years, the level of per capita output will be $y_t = 250(1 + 0.04)^{50}(1 - 0.08) \approx 1{,}634.54$.

d. Suppose that, in year 10, a new technology allows workers to become twice as productive at generating new ideas. What will the new growth rate be? Since

$$2\bar{z} = \frac{2}{4,000}, \bar{g} = \bar{z}\bar{l}\,\bar{N} = \frac{1}{2,000} \times 0.08 \times 2,000 =$$

0.08 or 8% = 2(4%)

e. What impact will this have on per capita output in period 50? That is, what will the new per capita level of output be for this country? How much greater is it than the answer you found in part c?

   This answer has two parts to it. First, determine the value of A_{10} and y_{50} given A_{10}. The value for $A_{10} = 250(1 + 0.04)^{10} = 370.06$. With a growth rate of 8 percent rather than 4 percent, output per capita 40 years later will be $y_{50} = 370.06(1 + 0.08)^{40}(1 - 0.08) \approx 7,396.25$, over 4.5 times greater than 1,634.54.

2. This problem continues with the Romer growth model in Table 6.1 and uses the same starting parameter values of $\bar{A}_0 = 250, \bar{l} = .08, \bar{z} = 1/4,000$, and $\bar{N} = 2,000$ as in Problem 1.

   a. Suppose now that, in year 0, this country decides to allocate twice as much of its workforce to the production of new ideas. What impact will this have on per capita output in period 10? That is, how will it change from the value that would have occurred in the absence of this change?

   b. How can you explain the difference you found in part a?

   c. With this change in labor allocation, how will the value for output in year 50 compare to what it would have been without the change?

   d. In Problem 1, the productivity of idea researchers was doubled. In this problem, the number of idea researchers was doubled. How can you explain the difference you found between these two approaches?

3. This problem provides practice using the *growth accounting formula* initially developed by Robert Solow and still used to analyze economic growth. Recall from the text that it utilizes the basic Cobb-Douglas production function, $Y_t = A_t K_t^a L_t^{1-a}$, with the value for a set equal to 1/3.

   a. Challenge yourself by working through the process of turning the Cobb-Douglas production function into the following growth accounting formula without referring back to the text:

   $$g_{Yt} - g_{Lt} = \frac{1}{3}\left(g_{Kt} - g_{Lt}\right) + \frac{2}{3}\left(g_{Lyt} - g_{Lt}\right) + g_{A}.$$

   b. Continue that challenge by explaining what the terms on the left-hand side of the equal sign represent as well as what each of the three groups of terms on the right-hand side of the equal sign mean.

   c. Complete the following table:

	$g_{(Y/L)}(\%)$ (%)	$g_{(K/L)}$ (%)	$g_{\left(L_{yt}/L\right)}$ (%)	TFP (%)
The U.S. economy		4	1.50	1.20
A European economy	2.53	3		0.86
A Latin American economy	2		2	0.33
An Asian economy	6	15	0.45	

4. This problem brings together the elements of both the Solow and the Romer growth models. Use Table 6.2 to work through each part of this problem. Note that the exponents on capital and output producing labor are different from those used in the text. Before beginning, think for a minute about the differences these changes are likely to evoke.

Table 6.2   The Combined Solow-Romer Growth Model

Endogenous variables: $Y_t, K_t, A_t, L_{yt}, L_{at}$

$$Y_t = A_t K_t^{1/5} L_{yt}^{4/5}$$
$$\Delta K_t = \bar{s} Y_t - \bar{d} K_t$$
$$\Delta A_t = \bar{z} A_t L_{at}$$
$$L_{yt} + L_{at} = \bar{N}$$
$$L_{at} = \bar{l} \bar{N}$$

Parameters: $\bar{d}, \bar{s}, \bar{z}, \bar{N}, \bar{l}, \bar{A}_0$

Recall that $A_t = \bar{A}_0 (1 + \bar{g})^t$

a. What would you be able to say about this country and its balanced growth path if you knew that the growth rate of output per worker ($g_{(Y/L)}$) was equal to the growth rate of the capital stock per worker ($g_{(K/L)}$)?

b. What would you be able to say if you knew that capital stock per worker was growing at a faster rate than output per worker? Show what you are describing on a balanced growth path diagram similar to Figure 6.6 in the text.

c. Using the model in Table 6.2, show algebraically how to solve for the growth rate of output along the balanced growth path.

d. Continue using this model to show algebraically how to solve for the growth rate of output per worker along the balanced growth path.

e. Finally, how does this model differ from the one in the text? What difference did it make to change the coefficients on capital and output producing labor?

CHAPTER 6 SOLUTIONS

True/False Questions

1. False. This statement is about the Solow growth model. See Section 6.1.

2. False. The economics of objects not ideas is what underlies Adam Smith's conclusions. See Section 6.2.

3. True. See Section 6.2.

4. False. Their self-interest simply ranks some things higher than income. See the case study "Open Source Software and Altruism."

5. False. Romer and others actually concluded just the opposite. See Sections 6.2 and 6.3, in particular footnotes 9 and 10.

6. False. Sustained knowledge growth, not just the stock of knowledge, determines sustainable growth. See Section 6.3.

7. True. If the standard replication argument yields constant returns to scale, then by necessity, increasing ideas in addition to objects in the production process will yield increasing returns to output. See Section 6.3.

8. True. See Section 6.6.

9. True. The model did allow for "exogenous technological progress" but only as an assumption, not as an explanation provided by the model. See Section 6.7.

Multiple-Choice Questions

1. e, they all are. See Section 6.1.

2. e, all of the above. See Section 6.1.

3. d, see section 6.2.

4. b, the theory of relativity. It is an idea, all the others are objects. See Sections 6.2 and 6.3.

5. c, the instructions. See Section 6.2.

6. c, the formulas in a spreadsheet. See Section 6.2.

7. e, all of the above. See Section 6.2.

8. d, the flu vaccination. Once it has been injected, no one else can be injected with it. There is a nonrivalrous dimension of a flu vaccination, however, when those people who work and live with the vaccinated person avoid exposure to someone with the flu. See Section 6.2.

9. a, if $b = 1$, $A^b = 0$, and there are constant returns to scale. See Section 6.2.

10. d, constant returns to scale in capital, labor, and ideas. See Section 6.2.

11. b, resisting new technology would be a problem with demand, not with perfect competition. For practice, explain to yourself to what problem each of the other answers alludes. See Section 6.2.

12. c, trade secrets. These are not offered by the government but protected by the firm. See Section 6.2.

13. d, increasing returns to labor. Returns to labor are constant, returns to labor and ideas are increasing. See Section 6.3.

14. b, acts as a resource constraint. See Section 6.3 and equation (6.4).

15. c, increasing the portion of workers in ideas production, at least initially, will lead to less output per worker as fewer workers produce objects. See Section 6.3, Experiment #2, and Figure 6.4.

16. d, the nonrivalry of objects. Ideas are nonrivalrous, not objects. See Sections 6.2 and 6.3.

17. b, all growth rates are not required to be equal, just constant.

18. a, level effects result in changes in the level of output per worker because fewer workers are used to produce output. See Figure 6.4.

19. b, growth effects are seen through the change in the slopes of the two lines. See Figure 6.4.

20. e, the combined Solow-Romer growth model supports all of the conclusions of both of the individual models. See Section 6.4.

21. a, this is identical to equation (6.11) in the text, except that the TFP term is placed at the end instead of the beginning of the equation. See Section 6.5.

22. d, see Section 6.5 and Table 6.2.

23. e, see Section 6.5 and footnote 20.

24. e, see Section 6.5 and footnote 21.

25. d, all of the above. See Section 6.9.

26. e, both b and d. The knowledge base grows as does capital; there is no steady state in the combined model. See Section 6.9.

27. e, none of the above. See Section 6.9.

28. d, higher capital stock usage, or depreciation. See Section 6.9 and equation (6.23).

29. d, diminishing returns to capital. See Section 6.9.

30. e, none of the above. See Sections 6.5 and 6.9.

Exercises

1. Recall that rivalry occurs when one person's use of an object inhibits the usefulness of that object to another person. See Section 6.2.
   a. A sandwich, rivalrous; once eaten by one person, no one else can eat it.
   b. A song sold by iTunes, both; rivalrous when listened to on headphones and because it can be played only on authorized computers; nonrivalrous because additional copies are available for purchase by other consumers and because it can be listened to by many people at the same time, depending on the sound system in use.
   c. A song played on the radio, nonrivalrous; because anyone with a radio in the listening area can listen to the song.
   d. A new computer software program, nonrivalrous; because with appropriate licensing, it can be used on an unlimited number of computers.
   e. A USB flash drive, rivalrous; because if one person is using it or has it in a backpack, no one else can use it.

2. This exercise uses the Rule of 70. See Section 3.3.
   a. Country B, it has the steepest balanced growth path and a growth rate of 7 percent ($70/10 \approx 7\%$).
   b. Country A, ($70/20 \approx 3.5\%$); Country C, ($70/13\frac{1}{3} \approx 5.25\%$). Note that Figure 2 clearly shows that output doubles three times in 40 years only for Country C. Knowing this, we know that output doubles in $3\overline{)40} = 13\frac{1}{3}$ years.
   c. In the Romer growth model, a higher growth rate can occur because of an increase in either the efficiency of idea producers ($\bar{z}$) or the size of the population ($\bar{N}$).
   d. The level effect is found in the year 2030 where Country A's balanced growth path gets steeper and becomes what is shown as Country C. A possible cause could come from an increase in the portion of the workforce employed in the development of new ideas. Such a change would cause output to fall initially, as fewer workers produce objects, but to grow faster as the country develops a greater knowledge base.
   e. It takes this country 20 years to achieve the same level of GDP per capita as it would have with its previous labor force allocation.
   f. Thirteen and one-third years: $70/5.25 \approx 13\frac{1}{3}$. Recall from part b that the growth rate along balanced growth path C is 5.25 percent.

3. A doubling of the stock of knowledge would cause balanced growth path *A* to experience a level effect and shift upward from its current intercept of 100 to an intercept of 200. This country would experience no growth effect as a consequence and continue to grow at the same rate as before, since neither $\bar{z}$, $\bar{l}$, nor $\bar{N}$ changed. See Section 6.3.4.

Problems

1. Worked problem. The problem is worked in the text.

2. Begin with the same solution for per capita output:
   $y_t = A_0(1 + \bar{g})^t(1 - \bar{l})$, where $\bar{g} = \bar{z}\bar{l}\bar{N}$.
   a. With $\bar{l} = 0.08$, $y_t = 250(1 + 0.04)^{10}(1 - 0.08) \approx$
      340.46.
      With $\bar{l} = 0.16$, $y_t = 250(1 + 0.08)^{10}(1 - 0.16) \approx$
      453.37.
   b. Output per worker falls initially from 230 to 210
      because fewer workers are producing it (you can
      confirm this for year 0 as was shown in Problem 1),
      but because more ideas are being produced, there is
      a higher growth rate and output now exceeds where
      it would have been with fewer workers producing
      ideas. Figure 2 in Exercise 2 illustrates this result.
   c. With $\bar{l} = 0.08$, $y_t = 250(1 + 0.04)^{50}(1 - 0.08) \approx$
      1,634.54.
      With $\bar{l} = 0.16$, $y_t = 250(1 + 0.08)^{50}(1 - 0.16) \approx$
      9,849.34.
   d. First we need to make the problems identical by
      making the change of both $\bar{z}$ and $\bar{l}$ apply in period 0
      and then compare the results to the no-change
      scenerio.
      - No change:
        $y_t = 250(1 + .04)^{50}(1 - .08) \approx 1,634.54$
      - $\bar{z}$ doubles in period 0:
        $y_t = 250(1 + .08)^{50}(1 - .08) \approx 10,787.37$
      - $\bar{l}$ doubles in period 0:
        $y_t = 250(1 + .08)^{50}(1 - .16) \approx 9,849.34$

      More output per worker was produced when the
      productivity of researchers was doubled relative to
      doubling the number of researchers. Note that the
      growth rate of ideas, and hence output per capita,
      increased to 8 percent in both cases. Therefore, the
      explanation must rely on the larger number of
      workers still in place producing output.

3. Begin with the Cobb-Douglas production function:
   $Y_t = A_t K_t^{1/3} L_t^{2/3}$. See Section 6.5.
   a. Apply the growth rate properties for multiplication
      and exponents from Chapter 3, Section 3.5 to get
      $g_{Yt} = g_{At} + \dfrac{1}{3}g_{Kt} + \dfrac{2}{3}g_{Lt}$, then subtract g_{Lt} from
      both sides while applying one-third of it to the
      growth rate of capital and two-thirds of it to the
      growth rate of workers producing output to get
      $g_{Yt} - g_{Lt} = g_{At} + \dfrac{1}{3}\left(g_{Kt} - g_{Lt}\right) + \dfrac{2}{3}\left(g_{Lyt} - g_{Lt}\right)$. Then,
      simply move the g_{At} term to the end of the right-hand
      side: $g_{Yt} - g_{Lt} = \dfrac{1}{3}\left(g_{Kt} - g_{Lt}\right) + \dfrac{2}{3}\left(g_{Lyt} - g_{Lt}\right) + g_{At}$
   b. $g_{Yt} - g_{Lt}$ is the growth rate of output per worker.
      $\dfrac{1}{3}\left(g_{Kt} - g_{Lt}\right)$ is the contribution of capital stock per
      worker toward the growth rate of output per worker.
      $\dfrac{2}{3}\left(g_{Lyt} - g_{Lt}\right)$ represents the composition of the
      labor force and its contribution to the growth rate of
      output per worker. The last term, g_{At}, represents the
      growth in total factor productivity.
   c. The completed table is

   Note that $g_{(Y/L)} = g_{Yt} - g_L$.

	$g_{\left(Y/L\right)}$ (%)	$g_{\left(K/L\right)}$ (%)	$g_{\left(L_{yt}/L\right)}$ (%)	TFP (%)
The U.S. economy	3.53	4	1.50	1.20
A European economy	2.53	3	1	0.86
A Latin American economy	2	1	2	0.33
An Asian economy	6	15	0.45	0.70

*Depending on rounding you may get 1.01% solving for each of these cells. For practice, try working the calculation just on the right-hand side of the output per worker growth accounting formula to get the value in the output per worker column.

4. The combined Solow-Romer model.

   a. Using the capital accumulation equation and dividing both sides by K_t, we know that

   $$g_{Kt} = \frac{\Delta K_t}{K_t} = \bar{s}\frac{Y_t}{K_t} - \bar{d}.$$ We also know that, on a

   balanced growth path, g_{Kt} is constant. For it to be constant, we can determine that $g^*_K = g^*_Y$. Hence, we know that, if $g_{(Y/L)} = g_{(K/L)}$, $g_Y = g_K$, since g_L is the same for both of them. Therefore, we can state that the country described in part a of this problem is on its balanced growth path.

   b. In this case the country would be experiencing accelerated, or faster, growth than it could indefinitely maintain, shown inside the circle in the diagram below, as it approached its new balanced growth path. See Section 6.9 and Figure 6.6 in the text.

   c. Recall from part a that $g^*_K = g^*_Y$ on a balanced growth path. This, along with the production function $Y_t = A_t K_t^{\frac{1}{5}} L_{yt}^{\frac{4}{5}}$, the growth rate for the production of ideas, $g^*_{At} = \bar{g} = \bar{z}\bar{l}\bar{N}$, and the growth rate rules allows us to solve for g^*_Y:

   $$g^*_{Yt} = g^*_{At} + \frac{1}{5}g^*_{Kt} + \frac{4}{5}g^*_{Lyt}$$

   $$g^*_{Yt} = \bar{g} + \frac{1}{5}g^*_{Yt} + \frac{4}{5}(0)$$

   $$\frac{4}{5}g^*_{Yt} = \bar{g}$$

   $$g^*_{Yt} = \frac{5}{4}\bar{g} = \frac{5}{4}\bar{z}\bar{l}\bar{N}$$

   d. Solve first for the level of output along the balanced growth path, $Y_t^* = A_t^* K_t^{*\frac{1}{5}} L_{yt}^{*\frac{4}{5}}$ by substituting the balanced growth path value for each of the endogenous variables. We know from the production function for new ideas and the labor allocation equation that the value of A_t^* grows over time:

   $$\Delta A_t = \bar{z}A_t L_{at}$$

   $$\frac{\Delta A_t}{A_t} = \bar{z}L_{at} = \bar{z}\bar{l}\bar{N}$$

   $$\bar{g} = \bar{z}\bar{l}\bar{N} \implies A_t^* = A_0(1+\bar{g})^t$$

   We also know from the capital accumulation equation that K_t^* equals

   $$\Delta K_t = \bar{s}Y_t - \bar{d}K_t$$

   $$g_{Kt} = \frac{\Delta K_t}{K_t} = \bar{s}\frac{Y_t}{K_t} - \bar{d}, \text{ since } g^*_Y = g^*_K$$

   on a balanced growth path

   $$g^*_Y = \bar{s}\frac{Y_t^*}{K_t^*} - \bar{d}, \text{ adding } \bar{d} \text{ and dividing by } \bar{s}$$

   $$\frac{g^*_Y + \bar{d}}{\bar{s}} = \frac{Y_t^*}{K_t^*}, \text{ inverting both sides}$$

   $$\frac{K_t^*}{Y_t^*} = \frac{\bar{s}}{g^*_Y + \bar{d}}, \text{ multiplying by } Y_t^*$$

   $$K_t^* = \frac{\bar{s}}{g^*_Y + \bar{d}}Y_t^*$$

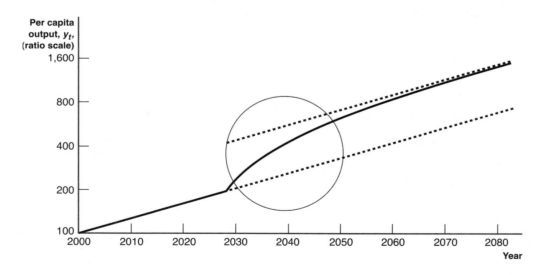

Finally, the resource constraint and the labor allocation equations provide the value of L_{yt}^* :

$$L_{at} = \bar{l}\,\bar{N}$$

$$L_{yt} + L_{at} = \bar{N}, \text{ substitute for } L_{at}$$

$$L_{yt} + \bar{l}\,\bar{N} = \bar{N}$$

$$L_{yt}^* = \bar{N} - \bar{l}\,\bar{N} = \left(1 - \bar{l}\right)\bar{N}$$

Now, substitute the balanced growth values for each of the endogenous variables in $Y_t^* = A_t^* K_t^{*\,1/5} L_{yt}^{*\,4/5}$:

$$Y_t^* = A_t^* K_t^{*\,1/5} L_{yt}^{*\,4/5}$$

$$Y_t^* = A_t^* \left(\frac{\bar{s}}{g_Y^* + \bar{d}}\,Y_t^*\right)^{1/5} \left[\left(1 - \bar{l}\right)\bar{N}\right]^{4/5},$$

raise both sides to the 5/4 power

$$Y_t^{*\,5/4} = \left\{ A_t^* \left(\frac{\bar{s}}{g_Y^* + \bar{d}}\,Y_t^*\right)^{1/5} \left[\left(1 - \bar{l}\right)\bar{N}\right]^{4/5} \right\}^{5/4}$$

$$Y_t^{*\,5/4} = A_t^{*\,5/4} \left(\frac{\bar{s}}{g_Y^* + \bar{d}}\,Y_t^*\right)^{1/4} \left(1 - \bar{l}\right)\bar{N},$$

separate $\dfrac{\bar{s}}{g_Y^* + \bar{d}}$ from Y_t^*

$$Y_t^{*\,5/4} = A_t^{*\,5/4} \left(\frac{\bar{s}}{g_Y^* + \bar{d}}\right)^{1/4} Y_t^{*\,1/4} \left(1 - \bar{l}\right)\bar{N}, \text{ and divide by } Y_t^{*\,1/4}$$

$$Y_t^* = A_t^{*\,5/4} \left(\frac{\bar{s}}{g_Y^* + \bar{d}}\right)^{1/4} \left(1 - \bar{l}\right)\bar{N}, \text{ divide by } \bar{N} \text{ to get } y_t^*$$

$$y_t^* = A_t^{*\,5/4} \left(\frac{\bar{s}}{g_Y^* + \bar{d}}\right)^{1/4} \left(1 - \bar{l}\right), \text{ substitute } g_Y^* = \tfrac{5}{4}\bar{z}\bar{l}\,\bar{N}$$

$$y_t^* = A_t^{*\,5/4} \left(\frac{\bar{s}}{\tfrac{5}{4}\bar{z}\bar{l}\,\bar{N} + \bar{d}}\right)^{1/4} \left(1 - \bar{l}\right)$$

$$y_t^* = \left[A_0 \left(1 + \bar{g}\right)^t\right]^{5/4} \left(\frac{\bar{s}}{\tfrac{5}{4}\bar{z}\bar{l}\,\bar{N} + \bar{d}}\right)^{1/4} \left(1 - \bar{l}\right)$$

$$y_t^* = A_0^{5/4} \left(1 + \bar{z}\bar{l}\,\bar{N}\right)^{5t/4} \left(\frac{\bar{s}}{\tfrac{5}{4}\bar{z}\bar{l}\,\bar{N} + \bar{d}}\right)^{1/4} \left(1 - \bar{l}\right)$$

e. For comparison purposes, the equivalent solution for the model in the text would be

$$y_t^* = A_t^{3/2} \left(\frac{\bar{s}}{g_Y^* + \bar{d}}\right)^{1/2} \left(1 - \bar{l}\right), \text{ substitute } g_Y^* = \tfrac{3}{2}\bar{z}\bar{l}\,\bar{N}$$

$$y_t^* = A_t^{3/2} \left(\frac{\bar{s}}{\tfrac{3}{2}\bar{z}\bar{l}\,\bar{N} + \bar{d}}\right)^{1/2} \left(1 - \bar{l}\right)$$

$$y_t^* = \left[A_0 \left(1 + \bar{g}\right)^t\right]^{3/2} \left(\frac{\bar{s}}{\tfrac{3}{2}\bar{z}\bar{l}\,\bar{N} + \bar{d}}\right)^{1/2} \left(1 - \bar{l}\right)$$

$$y_t^* = A_0^{3/2} \left(1 + \bar{z}\bar{l}\,\bar{N}\right)^{3t/2} \left(\frac{\bar{s}}{\tfrac{3}{2}\bar{z}\bar{l}\,\bar{N} + \bar{d}}\right)^{1/2} \left(1 - \bar{l}\right)$$

Decreasing capital's share of output in the Cobb-Douglas production function from one-third to one-fifth reduces its return and the incentive to put additional capital in place. It also reduces both the direct and indirect effects related to capital accumulation discussed in Section 6.5. Therefore, a lesser role for capital stock will do less to augment the underlying role of growth in knowledge found in the combined Solow-Romer growth model.

CHAPTER 7

The Labor Market, Wages, and Unemployment

OVERVIEW

Labor markets constitute the most important market most individuals ever encounter. In recent years, labor force participation has grown significantly to encompass well over 60 percent of the United States population. As part of a longer-run perspective of the economy, this chapter explores workers' labor supply decisions, the incentives that drive them, firms' demand for labor, and the influence of factors ranging from resource markets to the role played by government. It also distinguishes between frictional unemployment, as the economy transitions, and structural unemployment, where parts of the economy seem to stagnate indefinitely. In this context, structural differences between countries in the industrialized world, particularly with respect to social safety nets such as unemployment insurance, offer informative insights into the behavior of persistent unemployment. This chapter explores influences on the natural rate of unemployment and introduces present discounted values and methods for calculating potential lifetime earnings. It also provides insight into understanding recent U.S. productivity growth and similar increases in the value of postsecondary education.

KEY CONCEPTS

The *employment-population ratio* tells us what percent of the population has a job. It consists of the number of employed people divided by the entire population of a country.

The *labor force* is the number of people in a country both holding and seeking employment. In the United States, one must be at least 16 years of age to become a member of the labor force. Note that, if you do not hold a

job and are not looking for a job, you are not in the labor force.

The *unemployment rate* tells us what percent of the labor force has no job. It consists of the number of people in the labor force without a job divided by the number of people in the labor force.

Job creation is the process of generating new jobs, either in existing or new employment venues, and can occur either in the private or the public sector. It generally coincides with the demand for workers in new and emerging industries and sectors of the economy in the process of adopting new technologies.

Job destruction consists of job losses that will no longer exist regardless of the state of the economy. It generally occurs in the private sector as the result of evolving production techniques, typically associated with technological change, when newer technologies and production techniques displace older practices.

Wage rigidity refers to the tendency of wages to remain fixed in the face of labor market disequilibria, particularly the tendency of wages to remain fixed, and therefore too high, in the presence of rising unemployment. This failure of wages to fall during decreases in the demand for labor leads to larger than necessary labor market fluctuations.

The *natural rate of unemployment* combines both the structural and frictional components of unemployment and occurs when an economy experiences neither expansions nor contractions. It allows for a growing economy and a growing labor force, where the percentage of the labor force entering unemployment exactly equals the percentage of the labor force finding employment.

Cyclical unemployment occurs during recessions, when the actual unemployment rate exceeds the natural rate of unemployment. Cyclically unemployed workers expect to return to work as soon as the state of the economy improves and the demand for their skills returns to its normal level.

Structural unemployment persists regardless of the state of the economy. It results from plant closings, structural changes in production, or other events that produce displaced workers, who either no longer have marketable skills or do not live in an area where a market for their skills exists. Because of these reasons, structural unemployment provides the greatest cause for concern, since structurally unemployed workers experience the longest periods of joblessness and consequently greater economic losses.

Frictional unemployment results from an inevitably dynamic economy, where people either lose jobs as a consequence of change of behavior or because they voluntarily leave employment to search for better work somewhere else. Periods of frictional unemployment typically last for a relatively short period of time and, under voluntary circumstances, generally lead to improved employment conditions.

The *Bathtub Model of Unemployment* helps explain the natural rate of unemployment by focusing on the number of people leaving, or flowing out of, a position of employment into a state of unemployment and on the number of people entering, or flowing into, a position of employment from a state of unemployment. The level of unemployment is like water in a bathtub without a plug, whereby the level of water in the bathtub only remains constant or at a steady state when the flows out of and into the bathtub equal each other. Similarly, unemployment only remains constant, or at a steady state, when the number of people losing jobs exactly matches the number of people finding jobs.

The *finding rate* is the percentage of unemployed workers who leave the ranks of the unemployed by finding jobs and the *separation rate* is the percentage of employed workers who lose their jobs during a given period.

A *present discounted value*, sometimes referred to as the *time value of money,* provides a current value for a future sum of money or a series of payments received over the course of several years. It requires the assumption of an interest rate that could be earned on the present value of that money during the period of time in question were the money received in the present and held in an interest-bearing account until the end of that time period.

Skill-biased technical change occurs when workers become more productive and therefore more in demand by firms because of their proficiency with new technological developments, such as computers, the Internet, and new kinds of computer software. This change seems to affect highly skilled professions particularly, contributing to increased wage premiums for additional education.

The opening up of international trade, particularly in the inputs to production, that has become known simply as *globalization* can also have a positive impact on the wage permium that college-educated workers receive as demand for increased levels of human capital increases faster than students can become college educated

TRUE/FALSE QUESTIONS

1. Labor market discussions provide a long-run context for short-run unemployment problems.

2. In the face of increased labor demand, wage rigidities lead to larger fluctuations in unemployment.

3. Americans work substantially more hours per week than Europeans.

4. A substantial part of the explanation for lower GDP per worker in Europe than in the United States comes from a much larger European labor force.

5. The fact that Europeans have more leisure in their workweek is a good thing.

6. The recipient of a four-year scholarship paying out $10,000 each year toward tuition from a prestigious university did not really get a scholarship worth $40,000.

MULTIPLE-CHOICE QUESTIONS

1. Average wages in the United States have grown at an average of _____ percent per year for the last century.
   a. 1
   b. 2
   c. 3
   d. 4
   e. 5

2. Since the early 1960s, the employment-population ratio in the United States
   a. has remained relatively constant.
   b. has consistently risen.
   c. rose at first, but has generally been relatively constant.
   d. has trended upward with short periods of decline.
   e. has generally fallen.

3. Beginning in the mid-1960s, the employment-population ratio's trend behavior has been driven primarily by
   a. men leaving the labor force in greater numbers.
   b. men joining the labor force in greater numbers.
   c. women leaving the labor force in greater numbers.
   d. women joining the labor force in greater numbers.
   e. both a and d.

4. Which of the following is not true of a person classified as unemployed?
   a. She does not have a job.
   b. She is at least 16 years old.
   c. She is not in the labor force.
   d. She is currently available to work.
   e. She has looked for work in the last four weeks.

5. Each of the following describes unemployment in the United States except
   a. the most frequent experience with unemployment lasts less than three months.
   b. 4 percent of the unemployed have been so in excess of six months.
   c. the median length of unemployment is between eight and 10 weeks in normal times.
   d. the job-finding rate spikes upward shortly after 26 weeks of unemployment.
   e. the average unemployment payment is approximately $750 per month.

6. In the long run, the employment-population ratio and the unemployment rate are determined by each of the following except
   a. profit maximization on the part of the firm.
   b. the diminishing marginal product of labor.
   c. the price of leisure.
   d. the size of the population.
   e. the minimum wage.

7. Which of the following effects will an increase in income tax rates not bring about?
   a. a reduction in the employment-population ratio
   b. a downward shift to the right of the labor supply curve
   c. an increase in wages paid by the firm
   d. a decrease in the supply of labor
   e. none of the above; they all will occur.

8. A decrease in the demand for labor could be caused by any of the following except
   a. an increase in corporate income taxes.
   b. an increase in the price of crude oil.
   c. the cost of hiring and training workers.
   d. the cost of terminating employment of existing workers.
   e. higher wage demands on the part of workers.

9. The bulge, or increase and then decline, in the natural rate of unemployment experienced during the 1960s, 1970s, and 1980s is best explained by
   a. the entry of larger numbers of women into the labor force.
   b. the impact of ending the Vietnam War and fighting the Cold War.
   c. changing social norms and reduced discrimination from the equal rights movement.
   d. the entry of the baby boom generation into the labor force.
   e. none of the above.

10. The natural rate of unemployment encompasses which of the following types of unemployment?
    a. frictional, structural, and cyclical
    b. structural and cyclical
    c. structural and discouraged workers
    d. frictional and structural
    e. frictional and cyclical

11. Higher structural unemployment in European countries can be explained by all of the following except
    a. worldwide productivity slowdowns.
    b. high oil prices.
    c. relatively generous welfare benefits.
    d. more efficient labor market institutions.
    e. higher unemployment compensation than in other countries.

12. Which of the following does not present a problem for the unemployment rate as an accurate measure of labor market performance?
    a. discouraged workers
    b. part-time workers
    c. generous unemployment benefits
    d. frictional unemployment
    e. wage rigidities

13. Which of the following is the correct form of the present discounted value (pdv) equation, where fv equals the future value and R equals the interest rate?
    a. $\text{pdv} = fv(1 + R)^n$
    b. $\text{pdv} = fv + (1 + R)^n$
    c. $\text{pdv} = fv - (1 + R)^n$
    d. $\text{pdv} = fv/(1 + R)^n$
    e. $\text{pdv} = (1 + R)^n/fv$

14. Each of the following factors helps explain the recent rise in the cost of a college education except
    a. a greater number of students pursuing higher education.
    b. staffing costs associated with providing additional educational opportunities.
    c. increasing wage premiums for college-educated workers.
    d. reduced state and federal funding support.
    e. new capital expenditures to keep universities technologically current.

15. How can we best explain increasingly higher wages for college graduates when the supply of them is growing so rapidly?
    a. The labor market does not function the same way as the market for other goods.
    b. The increase in the supply of college graduates is greatly exaggerated.
    c. The demand for college graduates has increased relative to supply.
    d. The demand for college graduates has decreased.
    e. The supply of college graduates has increased relative to demand.

16. Which of the following explanations do not work to support a sustained increase in the demand for highly educated workers?
    a. Technological innovations that require more highly skilled workers.
    b. Information-based technologies have the greatest impact when used by more educated workers.
    c. Shortages of highly skilled workers elsewhere in the world leave the United States with a relative shortage as well.
    d. Globalization and the opening of international labor markets for highly educated workers.
    e. Outsourcing that allows the international flow of highly educated workers.

EXERCISES

1. The case study in the text discusses three developments that affected labor markets in terms of female labor force participation: changing social norms (more acceptable for women to work outside the home), technological progress in managing fertility (better birth control), and reduced discrimination (better pay).
    a. Challenge yourself by illustrating these effects on a labor market diagram before referring back to the text.
    b. Show how your diagram is consistent with the increased employment-population ratio presented in Figure 7.1 in the text.
    c. For women's wages to have risen during this time period, what must be true about the relative sizes of these shifts?

2. In a present discounted value problem, we represent a stream of 20 $1,000 annual payments starting today as

$$\text{pdv} = \$1,000 \times \left(1 + \frac{1}{(1+R)} + \frac{1}{(1+R)^2} + \dots + \frac{1}{(1+R)^{19}}\right).$$ Since each term inside the parentheses after the first 1 is less than one, the sum of those terms qualifies as a geometric series where

$$1 + \frac{1}{(1+R)} + \frac{1}{(1+R)^2} + \dots + \frac{1}{(1+R)^n} = \frac{1 - \left(\frac{1}{1+R}\right)^{n+1}}{1 - \frac{1}{1+R}}$$

    a. In addition to the formula saying "$n + 1$," explain why the exponent in the present discounted value

$$\text{problem, pdv} = \$1,000 \times \frac{1 - \left(\frac{1}{1+R}\right)^{20}}{1 - \frac{1}{1+R}}, \text{ is 20 when}$$

    $n = 19$.
    b. Suppose that the interest rate in this problem is 5 percent. Using the formula, what is the present discounted value of this series of payments?

3. *Challenge Exercise.* Exercise 2 assumed that each payment in an income stream is received at the beginning of each year. Using the same formula as in Exercise 2, show how this problem would change if the payment were received at the end of each year. How much more or less would the present discounted value be in this case?

PROBLEMS

1. Suppose that this month an economy has 150 million employed workers and 15 million unemployed workers. Use the Bathtub Model of Unemployment and assume that the separation rate in this economy is 1.5 percent per month and that the finding rate is 22 percent per month.
    a. What is the current unemployment rate?
    b. How many people will be unemployed next month?
    c. What will the unemployment rate be next month?
    d. At what unemployment rate would the number of unemployed remain the same from one month to the next?
    e. If the labor force remains constant, how many workers will be unemployed in the steady-state level of unemployment?

2. Many people argue that government support or funding of college scholarships creates a more egalitarian society. Others argue that scholarships benefit only those able to attend college. Suppose, for simplicity, that the labor market naturally decomposes into two segments: skilled and unskilled. Those who attend college belong to the skilled segment and those who do not fall into the unskilled segment, and skilled workers earn more than unskilled workers.
    a. Draw a pair of diagrams illustrating this scenario. In particular, be sure to indicate the wage premium experienced by skilled workers.
    b. Now suppose the government introduces a scholarship program that persuades a significant number of

unskilled workers to attend college and become skilled workers. Illustrate the impact of this program on your diagrams; in particular, be sure to indicate the impact on the wage premium now experienced by skilled workers.

c. Now reconcile your finding with the wage premium experience of skilled workers in the United States since 1980.

Worked Problem

3. Suppose that some parents decide to begin saving for their young child's college education. They currently have 15 years until their child will begin college. Current tuition, room, and board cost $10,000 per year. Assume, unrealistically, for this problem, that these costs will remain constant over the next 20 years and interest rates are 5 percent. Also assume that their child will finish college in four years.

a. How much would these parents need to set aside today to have the entire cost of their child's college education set aside in 15 years?

Four years of college, $40,000, discounted by 5 percent for 15 years would be

$$\text{pdv} = \frac{\$40,000}{(1+0.05)^{15}} = \$19,240.68$$

b. What if interest rates were 10 percent instead?

This time, $40,000 discounted by 10 percent for 15 years would be

$$\text{pdv} = \frac{\$40,000}{(1+0.1)^{15}} = \$9,575.68$$

c. Calculate, instead, how much they would need to save at the beginning of each year to have saved the entire cost of their child's college education in 15 years if interest rates were 5 percent.

The present value of these savings would still be $19,240.68, so since we know the present value, we need to calculate just the payments to savings, or the payment stream, necessary to generate a total of $40,000 in 15 years:

$$\$19,240.68 = \text{pymt} \times \frac{1-\left(\frac{1}{1+0.05}\right)^{15}}{1-\frac{1}{1+0.05}}$$

$$\text{for a pymt} = \frac{\$19,240.68}{10.898441} = \$1,765.42$$

d. What if interest rates were 10 percent instead? The present value of the savings in this case is $9,575.68, so we again make a similar calculation:

$$\$9,575.68 = \text{pymt} \times \frac{1-\left(\frac{1}{1+0.1}\right)^{15}}{1-\frac{1}{1+0.1}}$$

$$\text{for a pymt} = \frac{\$9,575.68}{8.366687} = \$1,144.50$$

4. More realistically now, continue on with Problem 2 but assume that college costs will increase steadily at 7 percent per year for the next 20 years.

a. Calculate the costs for tuition, room, and board for these parents' child 16, 17, 18, and 19 years from now.

b. How much would these parents now need to set aside today to have the entire cost of their child's college education saved in 15 years? Assume an interest rate of 5 percent.

c. How much would they now need to save each year to have saved the entire cost of their child's college education in 15 years if interest rates were 5 percent?

CHAPTER 7 SOLUTIONS

True/False Questions

1. True. See Section 7.1.

2. False. Unlike workers' unwillingness to accept lower wages when labor demand decreases, workers readily accept higher wages when labor demand increases. See Section 7.3 and Figure 7.6.

3. True, today. Thirty-five years ago this was not the case. See Section 7.5.

4. False. European GDP per worker is lower because European workers each work fewer hours. See Section 7.5.

5. True, if the choice is voluntary. False if that leisure comes about as the result of labor market distortions. See Section 7.5.

6. True. For an interest rate greater than zero, the

$$\text{pdv} = \frac{\$10,000}{(1+R)^0} + \frac{\$10,000}{(1+R)^1} + \frac{\$10,000}{(1+R)^2} + \frac{\$10,000}{(1+R)^3} < \$40,000$$

See Section 7.6.

Multiple-Choice Questions

1. b, 2 percent. See Section 7.2.

2. d, trended upward with short periods of decline. See Figure 7.1.

3. e, both a and d. See Section 7.2.

4. c, see Section 7.2.

5. e, the average is closer to $275 per week or $1,100 per month. See Section 7.2.

6. e, the minimum wage. See Section 7.3.

7. b, a downward shift to the right of the labor supply curve is an increase in the supply of labor. See Section 7.3 and Figure 7.4.

8. e, higher wage demands on the part of workers. This would be a movement along the labor demand curve, not a shift or decrease in demand. See Section 7.3 and Figure 7.5

9. d, the baby boom entrance into the labor force. See the case study "Supply and Demand Shocks in the U.S. Labor Market."

10. d, frictional and structural. See Section 7.3.

11. d, more efficient labor market institutions; it is just the opposite. See Section 7.5.

12. d, frictional unemployment. Each of the others introduces either an inefficiency or leads to an understatement of the problem. See Sections 7.3 and 7.5.

13. d, $pdv = fv/(1 + R)^n$. See Section 7.6.

14. d, reduced state and federal funding do not increase the cost of a college education, just the portion paid by people other than the state and federal governments. See Section 7.7.

15. c, demand has increased relative to supply. See Section 7.7.

16. e, this would lead to firms using lesser-paid workers. See Section 7.7.

Exercises

1. changing social norms → increased supply, fertility management → increased supply, reduced discrimination → increased demand
   a. The three rightward shifts are shown above.

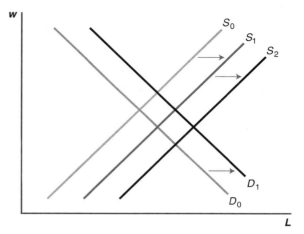

   b. The increased employment-population ratio is shown by the increase from L_0 to L_1 once we consider the population to be relatively stable in comparison to the number of people working.

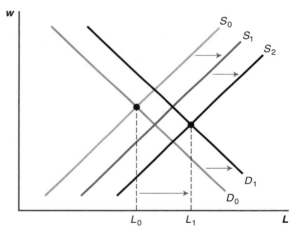

   c. For wages to have risen during the past 25 years, the increase in labor demand must have dominated the increases in labor supply.

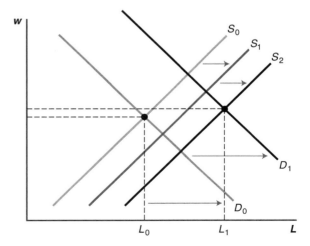

2. a. It involves the solution process for a fixed number of terms in a geometric series. In this case, the number of terms is 20, but since the numbering actually starts with 0, the last exponent in the series carries the number 19. Note that $1/(1 + R)^0 = 1$, or the first term in the series, and that the second term $1/(1 + R)$ is actually $1/(1 + R)^1$. Intuitively, there are 20 payments, but since the present value of a payment received today is the value of that payment, there is no reason to discount it. Only $19(n)$ payments need to be discounted.

b. For an interest rate of 5 percent,

$$pdv = \$1,000 \times \frac{1 - \left(\dfrac{1}{1+0.05}\right)^{20}}{1 - \dfrac{1}{1+0.05}} = \$13,085.32$$

3. Financial calculators, or the function formulas in a spreadsheet, have a programming option for whether the payment is received at the beginning or end of the period, and most of them set the default option to the end of the period. To calculate the present value for a stream of 20 payments received at the end of each period using the formula rather than a calculator, simply treat the series as a sum of 21 payments received at the first of the period minus the first payment:

$$pdv = \$1,000 \times \left[\frac{1 - \left(\dfrac{1}{1+0.05}\right)^{21}}{1 - \dfrac{1}{1+0.05}} - 1 \right] = \$12,462.21$$

The difference is $\$13,085.32 - \$12.462.21 = \$623.11$, which amounts to the "lost interest" from not getting the money at the beginning of each period.

Problems

1. Answer to problem #1:

a. $\dfrac{U_t}{\bar{L}} = \dfrac{15}{150+15} = \dfrac{15}{165} = 0.0909 \approx 9.1\%$

b. $15 + (0.015 \times 150) - (0.22 \times 15) = 13.95$ million

c. $\dfrac{U_t}{\bar{L}} = \dfrac{13.95}{150+15} = \dfrac{13.95}{165} = 0.0845 \approx 8.5\%$

d. $\dfrac{s}{s+f} = \dfrac{0.015}{0.015+0.22} = \dfrac{0.015}{0.235} = 0.0638 \approx 6.4\%$

e. $U^* = \dfrac{s}{s+f} \times \bar{L} = \dfrac{0.015}{0.015+0.22} \times 165 = 0.064 \times 16 = 10.56 \approx 10.6$ million

2. a. The initial wage differential is

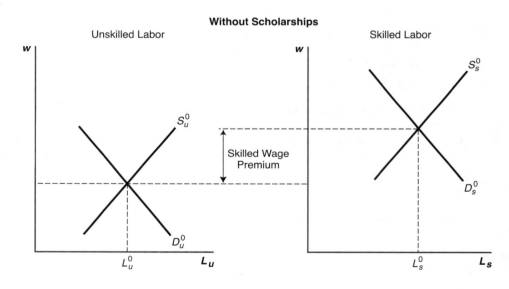

Without Scholarships

b. After the scholarship program, unskilled workers
become skilled workers and the skilled wage
premium shrinks.

With Scholarships

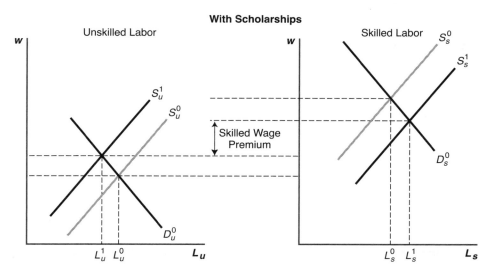

c. One way to reconcile an increasing skilled wage
premium is for there to be an increase in the supply
of unskilled workers that more than offsets the
portion of workers becoming skilled.

3. Worked Problem. The problem is worked in the text.

4. The calculations for this problem are as follows:
   a. Since the $10,000 tuition, room, and board costs
   grow at a rate of 7 percent,

$$\$10,000 \times (1+0.07)^{16} = \$29,522$$

$$\$10,000 \times (1+0.07)^{17} = \$31,588$$

$$\$10,000 \times (1+0.07)^{18} = \$33,799$$

$$\$10,000 \times (1+0.07)^{19} = \$36,165$$

b. To have the entire amount in hand in 15 years
requires the sum of four separate present value
calculations:

$$\text{pdv} = \frac{\$29,522}{(1+0.05)^{16}} = \$13,524$$

$$\text{pdv} = \frac{\$31,588}{(1+0.05)^{17}} = \$13,782$$

$$\text{pdv} = \frac{\$33,799}{(1+0.05)^{18}} = \$14,044$$

$$\text{pdv} = \frac{\$36,165}{(1+0.05)^{19}} = \$14,312$$

$$\$13,524 + \$13,782 + \$14,044 + \$14,312 = \$55,662$$

c. This is the same calculation as in Problem 2, parts c
and d:

$$\$55,662 = \text{pymt} \times \frac{1-\left(\dfrac{1}{1+0.05}\right)^{15}}{1-\dfrac{1}{1+0.05}}$$

$$\text{for a pymt} = \frac{\$55,662}{10.898441} = \$5,107$$

CHAPTER 8 | Inflation

OVERVIEW

Inflation is the annual percentage increase, or growth, of the economy's price level, and is generally measured by the Consumer Price Index (CPI) and the GDP Deflator. Inflation imposes costs throughout an economy. When inflation is higher than expected, it does so through involuntary redistributions of wealth from lenders to borrowers as well as other forms of economic distortions. Even when inflation occurs as expected, it imposes economic costs through both shoe leather and menu costs, for example, as well as purchasing power losses for all nominal non-interest-bearing assets. The Fisher equation describes how nominal interest rates account for both real interest rates and inflation. The quantity theory of money, combined with the classical dichotomy, teaches us that the balance between money supply and GDP growth determines long-run inflation. If money grows at a faster rate than GDP, inflation occurs; when money grows at a slower rate than GDP, deflation occurs. While money supply growth in excess of GDP growth always causes inflation in the long run, a government that spends money faster than it generates tax revenues and simply issues money to pay for those excess expenditures also fuels increased inflation rates in the long run. Unchecked, such behavior produces hyperinflation, as in the recent cases of Argentina, Brazil, and Russia.

KEY CONCEPTS

Inflation is the positive growth rate, or the annual percentage increase, of the price level. *Deflation,* on the other hand, is the negative growth rate, or annual percentage decrease, of the price level. Using the CPI, until 2009 the United States has experienced inflation every year since 1955. Prior to that (1775–1955), the United States experienced almost as many years of deflation (42 percent) as it did years of inflation (58 percent).

Reserves consist primarily of the private bank deposits held by the nation's central bank (the Federal Reserve System in the United States). These deposits earn no interest and can be redeemed for currency at will by the private banks that own them. The central bank requires banks to hold reserves to ensure sufficient resources to meet depositor demands.

The *monetary base* includes the currency in circulation and the reserves of the banking system. As will be shown in Chapter 11, the Federal Reserve System adjusts the monetary base through its open market operations as it implements monetary policy in the United States.

The *quantity theory of money,* by utilizing the quantity equation, or equation of exchange, $M_t V_t = P_t Y_t$, states that nominal GDP ($P_t Y_t$) equals the effective amount of money ($M_t V_t$) used to purchase it. Alternatively, the quantity theory of money also defines *the velocity of money,* $V_t = P_t Y_t / M_t$, or the number of times the money supply changes hands to generate GDP.

The *classical dichotomy* describes the long-run distinction between the nominal and real sides of the economy. In the long run, real GDP derives solely from real considerations, such as the rate of investment, research and development, and total factor productivity. In the long run, nominal considerations, like the money supply and how much of it exists, do not determine the level of production, only the price level.

The *neutrality of money* states that changes in the money supply have no long-term real effects on the economy and result in changes only in the price level and the rate of inflation.

Nominal interest rates are the stated interest rates on savings accounts, credit card statements, or other loan negotiations. They determine the number of dollars earned on interest-bearing assets or paid on interest-bearing liabilities.

Real interest rates equal the marginal product of capital in the long run and equate to the net earnings that result from the purchase, use, and disposal of a piece of capital. From consumers standpoint, the real interest rate is the increase in purchasing power, or the return in real goods as a reward for postponed consumption, received for letting someone else use their money. As will be shown in Chapters 9–14, in the short run, real interest rates can vary from the marginal product of capital.

The *Fisher equation*, $i_t = r_t + \pi_t$, defines the relationship between nominal and real interest rates as the sum of the real interest rate and inflation. Since real interest rates are not directly observable, unless inflation equals zero, economists use the Fisher equation to calculate real interest rates as: $r_t = i_t - \pi_t$.

Indexing a variable, a contract, and so forth to inflation means adjusting nominal values to reflect any changes in inflation, so that only changes in the real activity effect changes in behavior.

Hyperinflation describes a condition of rapidly increasing inflation, often in excess of 500 to 1,000 percent, that can both start and end very rapidly when the right conditions come together. Generally, a government's inability to continue borrowing funds and its willingness to print new paper money to pay its debts are sufficient conditions to set the stage for a period of hyperinflation.

The government budget constraint consists of the uses (government expenditures) and three types of revenue sources (taxes, borrowings, and money supply increases) for the government, such that

$$\underbrace{G}_{\text{uses}} = \underbrace{T + \Delta B + \Delta M}_{\text{sources of funds}}.$$

Seignorage refers to the revenue generated for the government through its printing and issuing of money in the economy. Thus, as the government acquires goods and services, or makes debt payments, without raising any revenue directly from the public, it causes all nominal assets held by the public to lose some of their purchasing power. (For some interesting modern examples, like the U.S. "Fifty State" series of quarters, look up *seignorage* in Wikipedia on the Internet.)

The inflation tax is the more literally descriptive name given to this modern form of *seignorage*. Recall that with the assumption of a constant velocity, $\pi = \%\Delta\bar{M} - \%\Delta\bar{Y}$. Since issuing additional currency at a growth rate faster than that of GDP causes the price level to increase, real asset holders are left unaffected and the burden of an inflation tax falls directly on nominal asset holders.

Central Bank Independence, established through the separation of power between fiscal and monetary authorities, is a key element in the avoidance of an inflation tax.

TRUE/FALSE QUESTIONS

1. Milton Friedman argues that inflation is a monetary phenomenon.

2. Thomas Sargent argues that inflation is a monetary phenomenon.

3. Throughout its history, the United States has managed to avoid experiencing periods of hyperinflation.

4. The Consumer Price Index and the GDP deflator provide two significantly different measures of inflation.

5. Empirical measures of velocity using M2 make the assumption of a constant velocity tenuous at best.

6. Evidence from around the world supports a positive correlation between inflation and growth of the money supply.

7. The classical dichotomy explains the inability of monetary policy to have any real impact on the level of economic activity in an economy.

8. While the relationship between inflation and money supply growth holds for industrialized countries like the United States and the United Kingdom, it does not hold for countries around the world in general.

9. When inflation exists, the real interest rate always is lower than the nominal interest rate.

10. Higher-than-expected inflation harms both bankers and savers.

11. Unexpectedly high inflation transfers wealth from borrowers to lenders.

12. Inflation causes relative prices to become distorted.

13. Inflation taxes occur only in periods of high or hyperinflation.

MULTIPLE-CHOICE QUESTIONS

1. Which of the following measures most accurately reflects changes in the cost of living experienced by members of the United States' economy?
   a. CPI inflation
   b. GDP inflation
   c. the unskilled wage
   d. the relative share of GDP
   e. They all convey approximately the same picture over the long run.

2. Each of the following items has been used for money except
   a. seashells.
   b. gold and silver.
   c. cigarettes.
   d. rocks.
   e. none of the above; they have all been used for money.

3. Currency in the United States is
   a. called *fiat money.*
   b. money because the government says it is.
   c. valued because other people also value it.
   d. not backed by anything.
   e. all of the above.

4. The nation's monetary base includes which of the following?
   a. currency
   b. checking deposits
   c. private bank reserves
   d. gold reserves in the New York Fed
   e. both a and c

5. Most of the money in the world today consists of
   a. currency.
   b. checks.
   c. bonds.
   d. electronic impulses.
   e. credit cards.

6. The quantity theory of money utilizes the quantity equation or equation of exchange. Which of the following relationships is it?
   a. $M_t V_t = P_t Y_t$
   b. $M_t P_t = V_t Y_t$
   c. $M_t P_t = V_t Y_t$
   d. $M_t Y_t = P_t V_t$
   e. $M_t V_t = P_t Y_t$

7. For the quantity equation to become a complete quantity theory of money, how many more equations are necessary?
   a. one
   b. two
   c. three
   d. four
   e. five

8. The long-run theory of output determination depends on each of the following except
   a. the investment rate.
   b. research and development.
   c. the allocation of labor resources.
   d. the money supply.
   e. total factor productivity.

9. The distinction between the nominal and real sides of the economy is called the
   a. neutrality of money.
   b. Fisher relationship.
   c. classical dichotomy.
   d. neoclassical distinction.
   e. Sargent rule.

10. According to the quantity theory of money, which of the following statements is incorrect?
    a. $M_t V_t = P_t Y_t$
    b. $g_M + g_V = g_P + g_Y$
    c. $\%\Delta M = \%\Delta P + \%\Delta Y - \%\Delta V$
    d. $\pi = \%\Delta M - \%\Delta V$
    e. $\%\Delta P = \%\Delta M - \%\Delta Y$

11. To link the level of inflation to growth in the money supply, as shown in the text, all of the following are necessary except
    a. the quantity theory of money.
    b. the classical dichotomy.
    c. a constant velocity of money.
    d. a central bank that targets inflation.
    e. a central bank that determines the money supply.

12. Which of the following is not a feature of money neutrality?
    a. Relative prices remain unchanged.
    b. Changes in the money supply cause no real economic effects in the long run.
    c. Changes in the money supply cause no real economic effects in the short run.
    d. All nominal prices respond immediately and fully.
    e. The classical dichotomy holds.

13. All of the following are characteristics of the real interest rate except
    a. the real interest rate is equal to the marginal product of capital in the long run.
    b. the real interest rate is the interest rate earned on deposits in a savings account.
    c. the real interest rate describes the return in goods on borrowed money.
    d. the real interest rate sometimes can be negative.
    e. the real interest rate is the lender's percentage change in purchasing power when a loan gets repaid.

14. In the United States, the highest nominal interest rates were experienced in the
    a. 1960s.
    b. 1970s.
    c. 1980s.
    d. 1990s.
    e. 2000s.

15. Which of the following is not a cost of inflation when it is anticipated?
    a. erosion of fixed incomes such as pensions
    b. deterioration of fixed-interest assets for banks
    c. the distortion of relative prices
    d. the distortion of investment decisions
    e. redistribution of wealth

16. Which of the following statements about higher-than-expected inflation is correct?
    a. Higher-than-expected inflation has similar impacts on both borrowers and lenders.
    b. Higher-than-expected inflation transfers wealth from borrowers to lenders.
    c. Higher-than-expected inflation transfers wealth from lenders to borrowers.
    d. Higher-than-expected inflation impacts only those who are unable to plan for it.
    e. both c and d

17. Which of the following is not a source of funds for federal government spending?
    a. income taxes
    b. additional debt
    c. property taxes
    d. gasoline taxes
    e. increased money supply

18. An inflation tax is levied primarily on
    a. business owners.
    b. land owners.
    c. nominal asset holders.
    d. consumers.
    e. debtors.

19. An inflation tax occurs when
    a. the government tells the Treasury to print more money in order to finance government spending.
    b. the government raises taxes to pay for higher priced goods and services it requires.
    c. the Federal Reserve issues additional currency that the governent uses to finance its spending.
    d. the government issues additional debt (Treasury bonds) in order to finance government spending that now costs more.
    e. none of the above; the majority of government revenues are raised through taxing income, not inflation.

20. Since the early 1970s, which of the following countries has not experienced an inflation tax?
    a. Mexico
    b. Russia
    c. Nigeria
    d. the United States
    e. none of the above

21. Since the early 1970s, which of the following countries has not experienced an inflation tax associated with hyperinflation?
    a. Russia
    b. Brazil
    c. Nigeria
    d. Argentina
    e. none of the above

EXERCISES

1. Using the quantity theory and the equation of exchange, $M_t V_t = P_t Y_t$, assume that velocity remains constant with each dollar changing hands four times per year, inflation equals 3 percent, and GDP growth is 3.5 percent. How much will the money supply need to increase to keep inflation and GDP growth at their current levels?

Worked Exercise

2. Suppose that you just turned 21, inflation during your lifetime has averaged 3 percent, and it is expected to continue at 3 percent for the next 30 years.
    a. If the sneakers you just bought cost $125 today, how much would they have cost the year you were born?

       We are looking for the value of X that satisfies the equation: $X(1 + 0.03)^{21} = \$125$. This essentially is a present discounted value problem, except that the "present" value in this case is the value of X 21 years ago: $X = \$125/(1 + 0.03)^{21} = \$67.19$.
    b. If the CPI were equal to 100 in the year you were born, what would it be today?

       With an inflation rate of 3 percent and an index, or price level, value of 100, the CPI would increase to 186 over the course of 21 years: $100(1 + 0.03)^{21} = 186$.
    c. How much inflation would have occurred in your lifetime?

       Since inflation is the percentage increase in the price level (usually, but not necessarily, on an annual basis), we would calculate it as
       $$\pi = \frac{186 - 100}{100} = 0.86, \text{ or } 86\%.$$

d. What if the CPI instead had been 107.6 the year you were born, what would it be today?

Similarly, $107.6(1 + 0.03)^{21} = 200.17$.

e. Calculate inflation using the CPI values from part d. Now, how much inflation occurred during your lifetime?

Also similarly,

$$\pi = \frac{200.17 - 107.6}{107.6} = 0.86, \text{ or } 86\%$$

f. Explain any differences or similarities between your answers to parts c and e.

The answers to both parts c and e are 86 percent because each of the index numbers grew at the same rate of 3 percent for 21 years. Inflation, in other words, is independent of the index value assigned to the price level.

3. Go to the Internet and do a search for the *Economic Report of the President* (ERP). You should get a URL hit of www.gpoaccess.gov/eop/ that will let you access the latest edition of the ERP. You will find two links: one for downloading the entire ERP and one for a list of links to spreadsheet files for each of the tables. You probably will find the link to the spreadsheet files much easier to navigate if you are interested in just data. If you choose to either download or view the PDF file of the entire ERP in your browser, when you open it you will find several chapters (10 in the 2010 ERP) and two appendices, Appendix A and the statistical tables (or Appendix B). The B-tables contain thousands of macroeconomic data series. Go to the section titled "Prices." If, instead, you choose to look only at the spreadsheet files, click on the "List of Statistical Tables" link and scroll down to the "Prices" heading.

a. Find *Consumer price indexes for major expenditure classes, 1965–2009 [For all urban consumers; 1982–84 = 100, except as noted]* and download the spreadsheet for these data. (In the 2007 ERP, this was Table B-60; the numbering sometimes changes from year to year.) Create a spreadsheet with years in the first column and the CPI data in the second column.

b. Calculate inflation for each year of each decade (fast on a spreadsheet), then find the average inflation rate during the 1960s, 1970s, 1980s, 1990s, and the 2000s.

c. Which years had the highest and lowest inflation rates?

d. Return to the ERP tables, go to the section titled "Money Stock, Credit, and Finance" and find "Bond yields and interest rates, 1929–2009" (Table B-73 in the 2010 ERP), copy the values for the three-month Treasury Securities, and paste them into your spreadsheet on the appropriate rows for each year, next to where you calculated inflation.

e. Using the Fisher equation, calculate real interest rates for each year and then calculate averages for each decade.

f. Which years had the highest and lowest real interest rates?

g. Which two decades had the most years with negative real interest rates?

h. How were the causes of these negative real rates either similar or dissimilar?

PROBLEMS

Worked Problem

1. Assume that the velocity of money in a country is constant and real GDP growth equals 3 percent per year, the money stock grows by 6 percent per year, and the nominal interest rate is 5 percent.

a. What is the value of the real interest rate?

From the equation of exchange, $M_tV_t = P_tY_t$, we get $g_M + g_V = g_P + g_Y$. Recall that $g_P = \pi$ and make the following substitutions: $6\% + 0\% = \pi + 3\%$, and calculate inflation as $\pi = 3\%$. Using the Fisher equation, $i = r + \pi$, and filling in the values we know, we get $r = 5 - 3$ or 2%.

b. Provide an economic interpretation of the real interest rate.

The real interest rate is the increase in purchasing power, or the return in real goods as a reward for the postponed consumption, that you receive for letting someone else use your money. Firms and entrepreneurs know this as the marginal product of capital.

2. Suppose the desired level of return on capital is 3.5 percent and capital depreciates at the rate of 5 percent per year. Assume also that inflation is expected to run at 2.5 percent for the next several years. What is the maximum interest rate a firm would be willing to pay?

3. Assume that the change in the monetary base (currency plus bank reserves) reflects a reasonable measure of seignorage in the United States. Use the *Economic Report of the President*'s statistical tables for the monetary base (Table B-71 in the 2010 ERP) and deficits (Table B-78 in the 2010 ERP) to complete this problem. The ERP also has nominal GDP data, but it is published too soon to have an annual figure for the most recent year. So, for nominal GDP data, go to the Bureau of Economic Analysis (www.bea.gov/national/index.htm#gdp) and click on the link "Current-dollar and real GDP." This file will give you the same data as the ERP but will include the annual figure for the

missing last year of the ERP series. (See Exercise 3 for the location of the ERP.)

   a. How much did the monetary base change in each year of the twenty-first century?

   b. What was the average seignorage as a percent of GDP for these years?

   c. What were deficits during these years of the twenty-first century?

   d. Does it appear that seignorage was a major source of revenue during these years?

4. Suppose that inflation over the next five years ends up averaging twice the level that everyone currently expects. Explain how each of the following individuals will be benefited or harmed.

   a. a student with an automobile loan

   b. a banker holding automobile loans

   c. a homeowner with a fixed-rate mortgage

   d. a banker holding fixed-rate mortgages

   e. parents saving for a child's college education

   f. an investor holding assets generating capital income that grows at the same rate as inflation

   g. individuals relying on relative prices to make efficient allocation decisions

   h. What conclusions can you draw about the effects of unanticipated inflation?

5. How well does inflation reflect increases in workers' cost of living? What else would you have to know before you could provide an accurate answer to this question?

CHAPTER 8 SOLUTIONS

True/False Questions

1. True. See his quote preceding Section 8.1 and his explanation regarding the root of inflation toward the end of Section 8.5.

2. False. See his quote preceding Section 8.1 and his explanation of the responsibility that fiscal policy bears for generating excessive inflation toward the end of Section 8.5.

3. False. See Section 8.1 for a description of two U.S. experiences with extremely high inflation.

4. False. See the Section 8.1 case study "How Much Is That?" The methods are different, but the pictures are similar.

5. False. They actually validate it. See Section 8.2.

6. True. See Figures 8.2 and 8.3.

7. False. The classical dichotomy deals with the long run. It does not argue that money cannot affect the economy in the short run. See Section 8.2.

8. False. This relationship holds around the world, particularly in countries with higher rates of money growth. See Section 8.2 and Figure 8.3.

9. True. See equation (8.6) and Figure 8.3.

10. True. Savers have less purchasing power in the money they have saved and bankers have higher interest expenses on their deposit liabilities. See Section 8.4.

11. False. When payments are fixed in nominal terms, higher-than-expected inflation rates mean that borrowers return less purchasing power to lenders with each payment, thus transferring wealth from lenders to borrowers. See Section 8.4.

12. True. Since different prices inflate at different rates, relative prices change, requiring constant recalibration on the part of economic decision makers. See Section 8.4.

13. False. Whenever the government obtains additional revenue from increasing the monetary base and the money supply, an inflation tax occurs, even if the level of inflation is low. See Section 8.5.

Multiple-Choice Questions

1. e, they all give a similar picture. See the Section 8.1 case study "How Much Is That?"

2. e, none of the above. See Section 8.2.

3. e, all of the above. See Section 8.2.

4. e, both a and c. See Section 8.2.

5. d, electronic impulses. See the Section 8.2 Case Study: "Digital Cash."

6. e, $M_t V_t = P_t Y_t$. See Section 8.2.

7. c, three. See Section 8.2.

8. d, the money supply. See Section 8.2.

9. c, classical dichotomy. See Section 8.2.

10. d, $\pi = \%\Delta M - \%\Delta V$. It should be $\pi = \%\Delta M - \%\Delta Y$. See Section 8.2.

11. d, a central bank that targets inflation. The balance between money supply growth and GDP growth determines long-run inflation. Faster (slower) money growth than GDP growth generates inflation (deflation). See Section 8.2.

12. c, money neutrality does not apply in the short run. See Section 8.2.

13. b, savings accounts earn a nominal interest rate. See Section 8.3.

14. c, the 1980s, specifically 1981. See Figure 8.4.

15. e, the redistribution of wealth. See Section 8.4.

16. e, since it is unexpected, people will be unable to plan for it. See Section 8.4.

17. c, property taxes are used at the local level. See Section 8.5.

18. c, nominal asset holders, which includes all lending institutions and anyone who owns bonds, savings accounts, or debt of any type. See Section 8.5.

19. c, Congress has the Federal Reserve charged with responsibility for regulating the nation's money supply, which includes the issue of new currency. See Section 8.5.

20. e, none of the above. See the Section 8.5 Case Study: "Episodes of High Inflation."

21. c, Nigeria. See the Section 8.5 Case Study: "Episodes of High Inflation" and Figure 8.5.

Exercises

1. 6.5 percent. From the equation of exchange, $M_t V_t = P_t Y_t$, we get $g_M + g_V = g_P + g_Y$ or 6.5 % + 0% = 3% + 3.5%.

2. Worked Problem. The problem is worked in the text.

3. a. See Table 1, Year and CPI.
   b. See Table 1, Inflation and the first Average per Decade.
   c. Lowest inflation was in 2009 at –0.36 percent. Highest inflation was in 1980 at 13.5 percent.
   d. See Table 1, 3 mo. T-Bill Rate.
   e. See Table 1, Real Interest Rate and the second Average per Decade.

Table 1

Year	CPI	Inflation	Average per Decade	3 mo. T-Bill Rate	Real Interest Rate	Average per Decade	Year	CPI	Inflation	Average per Decade	3 mo. T-Bill Rate	Real Interest Rate	Average per Decade
1965	31.5			3.95%			1988	118.3	4.14%		6.69%	2.55%	
1966	32.4	2.86%		4.88%	2.02%		1989	124.0	4.82%	5.55%	8.12%	3.30%	3.29%
1967	33.4	3.09%		4.32%	1.23%								
1968	34.8	4.19%		5.34%	1.15%		1990	130.7	5.40%		7.51%	2.11%	
1969	36.7	5.46%	3.90%	6.68%	1.22%	1.41%	1991	136.2	4.21%		5.42%	1.21%	
							1992	140.3	3.01%		3.45%	0.44%	
1970	38.8	5.72%		6.43%	0.74%		1993	144.5	2.99%		3.02%	0.03%	
1971	40.5	4.38%		4.35%	–0.03%		1994	148.2	2.56%		4.29%	1.73%	
1972	41.8	3.21%		4.07%	0.86%		1995	152.4	2.83%		5.51%	2.68%	
1973	44.4	6.22%		7.04%	0.82%		1996	156.9	2.95%		5.02%	2.07%	
1974	49.3	11.04%		7.89%	–3.15%		1997	160.5	2.29%		5.07%	2.78%	
1975	53.8	9.13%		5.84%	–3.29%		1998	163.0	1.56%		4.81%	3.25%	
1976	56.9	5.76%		4.99%	–0.77%		1999	166.6	2.21%	3.00%	4.66%	2.45%	1.87%
1977	60.6	6.50%		5.27%	–1.24%								
1978	65.2	7.59%		7.22%	–0.37%		2000	172.2	3.36%		5.85%	2.49%	
1979	72.6	11.35%	7.09%	10.05%	–1.31%	–0.78%	2001	177.1	2.85%		3.44%	0.60%	
							2002	179.9	1.58%		1.62%	0.04%	
1980	82.4	13.50%		11.51%	–1.99%		2003	184.0	2.28%		1.01%	–1.26%	
1981	90.9	10.32%		14.03%	3.71%		2004	188.9	2.66%		1.38%	–1.28%	
1982	96.5	6.16%		10.69%	4.53%		2005	195.3	3.39%		3.16%	–0.23%	
1983	99.6	3.21%		8.63%	5.42%		2006	201.6	3.23%		4.73%	1.50%	
1984	103.9	4.32%		9.53%	5.26%		2007	207.3	2.85%		4.41%	1.56%	
1985	107.6	3.56%		7.47%	3.92%		2008	215.3	3.84%		1.48%	–2.36%	
1986	109.6	1.86%		5.98%	4.12%		2009	214.5	–0.36%	2.57%	0.16%	0.52%	0.16%
1987	113.6	3.65%		5.82%	2.17%								

f. Lowest real interest rate was in 1975 at −3.29 percent. Highest real interest rate was in 1983 at 5.42 percent.

g. The 1970s had the most, with seven years; the 2000s were next, with four.

h. The negative real interest rates in the 1970s came more from inflation, while the negative real interest rates in the 2000s came from very low nominal interest rates.

Problems

1. Worked Problem. The problem is worked in the text.

2. 11 percent. Given 5 percent depreciation and 2.5 percent inflation, to earn at least 3.5 percent the firm's nominal return, $i = r + d + \pi$, must be at least 3.5% + 5% + 2.5%, or 11%.

3. a. See Table 2, Change in the MB.
   b. See Table 2, Change in MB as % of GDP.
   c. See Table 2, Deficits.
   d. The data in Table 2 seem to suggest that very little seignorage has occurred in the United States in the past (recall that money supply growth generates inflation when it is in excess of output growth) and that seignorage has not been used as a major funding source to finance deficits in the United States. As deficits rose dramatically at the end of the decade in 2008 and 2009, the increase in the monetary base exhibited many times more growth than has been customary in the United States, suggesting the possibility of increased seignorage.

4. a and c. The students and homeowners both benefit from this higher-than-expected inflation, since their fixed payments now are made with cheaper dollars.
   b and d. Bankers holding fixed-rate home and auto loans are harmed because they receive less value in payment than they extended when they issued the loans.
   e. Parents saving for college also are harmed because the purchasing power of their savings decreases.
   f. The investor is not harmed or helped by the rise in inflation, since the income's purchasing power remains unchanged.
   g. Individuals find allocation decisions less efficient to make when all prices do not rise at the same rate, which they usually do not.
   h. Unexpected inflation transfers wealth from lenders to borrowers and decreases the purchasing power of nominal assets at a faster rate than anticipated. It also distorts decision processes made on the basis of relative prices. See Section 8.4.

5. Inflation works well as a proxy for standard of living changes only if wages remain unchanged in the process. To provide an accurate response, the relative changes in wages also must be known. For example, if $\%\Delta W = \pi$, then the standard of living remains unchanged.

Table 2

Year	Monetary Base (billions of $)	Change in the MB (billions of $)	Nominal GDP (billions of $)	Change in MB as % of GDP	Deficits (billions of $)
1999	593.74		9,353.5		125.6
2000	584.98	−8.76	9,951.5	−0.09	236.2
2001	635.57	50.58	10,286.2	0.49	128.2
2002	681.65	46.08	10,642.3	0.43	−157.8
2003	720.39	38.74	11,142.1	0.35	−377.6
2004	759.38	38.99	11,867.8	0.33	−412.7
2005	787.58	28.20	12,638.4	0.22	−318.3
2006	812.41	24.83	13,398.9	0.19	−248.2
2007	824.37	11.96	14,077.6	0.08	−160.7
2008	1,654.07	829.70	14,441.4	5.75	−458.6
2009	2,017.70	363.63	14,256.3	2.55	−1,412.7

CHAPTER 9 | An Introduction to the Short Run

OVERVIEW

The short-run model developed in Chapters 9–14 focuses on the economy's performance during a specific short period of time, frequently in the present, but also on past and expected future performance. Of particular interest is the economy's response to aggregate supply-and-demand shocks that cause fluctuations in the level of economic activity. Shocks can generate either costs or benefits to the economy. The costs of economic fluctuations occur in several forms, including lost wages and production during recessions and inflation costs during booms. Benefits include improved productivity, lower inflation, and increased living standards, among other things. Inflation costs rise during booms and fall during recessions; they also receive particular attention because of the role monetary policy plays in keeping them under control. This chapter briefly introduces important underpinnings of the short-run model developed more fully in subsequent chapters.

KEY CONCEPTS

The short run and the long run first appeared as key concepts in Chapter 1. Those definitions are repeated here for convenience and expanded on.

Short-run economic analysis occurs when one or more of the factors of production in the economic process cannot be changed in response to changes or disturbances in the economy. For example, in the short run, workers in a factory might have to work overtime to meet an increase in demand until the factory itself can be expanded.

Long-run economic analysis occurs when there has been sufficient time for all factors of production to adjust to changes or disturbances in the economy. For example, in the long run, the size of a factory can be expanded to meet an increase in demand due to an increase in population.

In the context of the short-run model developed in this and subsequent chapters, *short-run fluctuations* account for what often seem like much more pressing issues, such as the recent financial crisis and the recession that began in 2007. Economists designate the period of time that actual output deviates from potential output (typically two years or so) as the *short run*.

By contrast, the *long run*, again in the context of the short-run model and from the broader macroeconomic perspective, is taken as given because it has already been determined in the long-run model. The long run incorporates potential output and its trend over time as well as a long-run rate of inflation and treats each of these as exogenous to short-run economic activity.

Potential output refers to the level of economic activity, or output, that an economy can continuously produce on a long-term basis if all inputs to the production process are employed at a sustainable level. In the absence of shocks, an economy operating at its potential level of output will experience no change in inflation. Potential output, however, is not observable and therefore must be estimated by economists.

An *annualized rate of change* is an estimate of a variable's annual growth rate derived from the current quarterly or monthly growth rate by multiplying by four or 12 accordingly.

Shocks occur unexpectedly from a long-term perspective and can originate on the demand or supply side of the economy, or both. Supply-side shocks include such occurrences as oil price disturbances and changes in worker productivity, while demand-side shocks include such things as sudden decreases in the demand for housing, increases in military expenditures, or changes in the tax code. Some shocks, like the recent financial crisis, impact both the supply and the demand sides of the economy.

Long-run trends reflect the underlying growth of an economy's potential output. In the context of the combined Solow-Romer growth model, an economy's long-run trend can be related to its balanced growth path.

Short-run fluctuations in output occur when economic activity departs from its long-run trend for a period of time. Economists refer to these fluctuations as *booms* and *recessions* and consider them normal parts of the business cycle.

A *boom* takes place when production levels in an economy exceed its long-run trend for a period of time. Booms generate additional income and output production but also bring concerns of increased inflation with them.

In contrast, a *recession* occurs when production levels in an economy fall short of its long-run trend for a period of time. Recessions impose significant costs on an economy, both in terms of lost wages and lost production.

Short-run output, $\tilde{Y}_t$ refers to the term that measures percentage fluctuations in GDP around its long-run trend, or $\tilde{Y}_t = \dfrac{Y_t - \bar{Y}_t}{\bar{Y}_t}$. Economists also often refer to this term as *detrended output* and as a *percentage GDP gap*. A positive short-run output denotes a booming economy, whereas a negative short-run output indicates a recession for that economy.

The *Great Depression* is the name given to the period of time, beginning in 1929, when the entire world suffered a prolonged and severe recession. Opinions vary about when it ended, but many argue that it lasted until World War II. During the depths of the Great Depression in the United States, unemployment was 25 percent and short-run output was a negative 25 percent to 30 percent, depending on measurement methods.

The *Phillips curve* describes the dynamic relationship between short-run output $\left(\dfrac{Y_t - \bar{Y}_t}{\bar{Y}_t}\right)$ and changes in inflation ($\Delta\pi_t$ or $\pi_t - \pi_{t-1}$). Positive short-run output (a booming economy) generates increases in inflation, while negative short-run output (associated with an economy in recession) causes inflation to fall.

Okun's law defines the relationship between short-run output fluctuations $\left(\dfrac{Y_t - \bar{Y}_t}{\bar{Y}_t}\right)$ and changes in the unemployment gap ($u_t - \bar{u}$). During booms, when short-run output is positive, actual unemployment (u_t) falls short of the natural rate of unemployment ($\bar{u}$). During recessions, the opposite occurs, and negative short-run output produces actual unemployment in excess of the natural rate of unemployment. For every 2-percentage-point increase in short-run output, unemployment falls by 1 percentage point, and vice versa.

The *IS curve*, fully developed in Chapter 11, characterizes the inverse relationship between real interest rates and short-run output. Higher real interest rates depress short-run output, while lower real interest rates stimulate short-run output. This relationship also serves, in Chapter 12, as the relationship underlying Federal Reserve policy decisions as it seeks to influence the level of economic activity.

TRUE/FALSE QUESTIONS

1. Shocks to the economy are completely unanticipated.

2. In macroeconomic analysis, a period of less than two years defines the *short run*.

3. Current output consists of two components: long-run trend and short-run output.

4. In a recession, short-run output is negative.

5. Prices reflect scarcity.

6. Okun's law provides economists with a connection between short-run output and changes in unemployment.

MULTIPLE-CHOICE QUESTIONS

1. Examples of shocks to the economy include all of the following except
   a. sudden changes in oil prices.
   b. changes in government spending.
   c. the development of new technology.
   d. an increase in inflation.
   e. a natural disaster.

2. Which of the following shocks to the economy would cause inflation to increase?
   a. an increase in productivity
   b. an increase in disposable income
   c. improved computer technology
   d. the discovery of new oil reserves
   e. an increase in the unemployment rate

3. Underlying the short-run model is each of the following characteristics except
   a. the exogeneity of potential output.
   b. the predetermination of the long-run inflation rate.
   c. the predetermination of the current inflation rate.
   d. the deviation of actual from potential output.
   e. none of the above; they all characterize the short-run model.

4. Which of the following accurately describes short-run output?

   a. $\tilde{Y}_t = \dfrac{Y_t - \bar{Y}_t}{\bar{Y}_t}$

   b. $\bar{Y}_t = \dfrac{Y_t - \tilde{Y}_{tt}}{\tilde{Y}_{tt}}$

   c. $Y_t = \dfrac{\tilde{Y}_t - \bar{Y}_t}{\bar{Y}_t}$

   d. $\tilde{Y}_t = \dfrac{\bar{Y}_t - Y_t}{\bar{Y}_t}$

   e. $\tilde{Y}_t = \dfrac{\bar{Y}_t - Y_t}{Y_t}$

5. Which of the following statements regarding short-run output is incorrect?
   a. It represents a percentage deviation from the long run trend.
   b. It is a percentage GDP gap.
   c. It is a detrended representation of current economic activity.
   d. It is positive during booms and negative during recessions.
   e. None of the above; they are all correct.

6. Which of the following statements regarding a recession is not correct?
   a. Short-run output is negative.
   b. A recession ends when short-run output becomes positive.
   c. A recession ends when short-run output begins to rise.
   d. A typical recession lasts about two years.
   e. A recession generally begins when short-run output declines and becomes negative.

7. When determining the life span of a recession, the Business Cycle Dating Committee would most likely consider each of the following except
   a. wholesale sales figures.
   b. retail sales figures.
   c. manufacturing output.
   d. GDP.
   e. inflation.

8. The typical length of a recession is approximately _____ months.
   a. 6
   b. 12
   c. 18
   d. 24
   e. 30

9. A typical recession leads to losses of approximately _____ percent of GDP.
   a. 4
   b. 5
   c. 6
   d. 7
   e. 8

10. The costs of a recession can be observed in several ways. Which of the following is most difficult?
    a. the number of jobs lost
    b. the amount of purchasing power lost by nominal assets
    c. the amount of income lost per family of four
    d. the reduction in GDP
    e. business failures

11. The beginning of modern macroeconomics is most closely associated with which of the following events?
    a. the establishment of the Federal Reserve System
    b. the Great Depression
    c. the publishing of *The General Theory of Employment, Interest, and Money* by John Maynard Keynes
    d. the Great Society
    e. FDR's public works projects

12. When studying potential GDP, economists
    a. begin with current GDP then adjust for cyclical unemployment.
    b. make an estimate based on current capital stock and any excess capacity.
    c. analyze the trend passing through quarterly GDP observations.
    d. pick a year of full-employment then let GDP grow constantly at the average GDP growth rate for the past 25 years.
    e. determine years of full-employment for each decade and calculate balanced growth paths between those years.

13. The short-run model has its foundation in several basic premises. Which of the following is not one of them?
    a. An economy experiences a constant barrage of shocks.
    b. Fiscal policy tools can influence economic activity in the economy.
    c. Fiscal and monetary policy can work together to maintain full employment.
    d. Monetary policy can change the level of output in the economy.
    e. Government can use its policy-making ability to maximize GDP.

14. The Phillips curve describes
    a. how inflation increases during boom times.
    b. the impact recessions have on inflation.
    c. the impact current output has on inflation.
    d. the change in inflation attributable to positive and negative GDP gaps.
    e. all of the above.

15. The Federal Reserve is credited with intentionally causing which of the following recessions in order to fight inflation?
    a. 1960
    b. 1970
    c. 1980
    d. 1991
    e. 2001

16. In the United States, a positive short-run output of 3 percent, on average, causes inflation to
    a. decrease by a percent and a half.
    b. remain unchanged if GDP grows by 3 percent.
    c. increase by 1 percent.
    d. increase by a percent and a half.
    e. decrease by 1 percent.

17. In the United States, a short-run output of negative 2 percent means that unemployment will be _____ the natural rate of unemployment.
    a. 1 percent above
    b. 1 percent below
    c. a percent and a half above
    d. a percent and a half below
    e. 2 percent above

18. The IS curve describes the relationship between the real interest rate and economic activity as _____ related because _____.
    a. positively, higher real interest rates generate more investment
    b. negatively, lower real interest rates generate more investment
    c. cyclically, of the normal ups and downs of the business cycle
    d. countercyclically, higher real interest rates stimulate investment
    e. countercyclically, lower real interest rates stimulate investment

EXERCISES

1. Using the Phillips curve presented in Chapter 9, $\Delta\pi = 1/2\tilde{Y}$, what can be inferred from each of the following scenarios?
   a. Short-run output equals 2 percent.
   b. Inflation decreases by 2 percent.
   c. Short-run output increases by 2 percentage points.
   d. Inflation is steady at 3 percent.

2. Using Okun's law, $u - \bar{u} = -1/2\tilde{Y}$, what do we know about unemployment or output in each of the following situations? Assume $\bar{u} = 5\%$.
   a. Short-run output equals 2 percent.
   b. Unemployment increases by 1 percent.
   c. Short-run output decreases by 2 percentage points.
   d. Unemployment is steady at 5 percent.

3. Using the IS curve briefly described at the end of Chapter 9, explain what happens to economic activity when the central bank lowers real interest rates.

PROBLEMS

Worked Problem

1. Use the following table to complete parts a through d. Assume that Current Output has been adjusted for inflation so that it represents real GDP:

	Current Output	Potential Output	Output Gap	Short-Run Output
2012	16.97			
2013	17.90			
2014	18.25			
2015	19.10			
2016	20.00			
2017	19.90			
2018	20.00			
2019	20.75			
2020	21.50			
2021	22.50			

a. Assume that $Y_t = \bar{Y}_t$ in 2014 and has grown and will continue to grow at a constant rate of 3 percent, then fill in the Potential Output column:

$\bar{Y}_t = 18.25(1+0.03)^{t-2014}$ for each year in the table; for example,

$\bar{Y}_{2014} = 18.25(1+0.03)^{2014-2014} =$
$18.25(1+0.03)^0 = 18.25$ and
$\bar{Y}_{2018} = 18.25(1+0.03)^{2018-2014} =$
$18.25(1+0.03)^4 = 18.25(1.12551) =$
$20.540558 \approx 20.54$.

For years before 2014, the process is the same. For example, the calculation for 2012 is

$$\bar{Y}_t = 18.25(1+0.03)^{2012-2014} =$$
$$18.25(1+0.03)^{-2} = \frac{18.25}{(1+0.03)^2} =$$
$$\frac{18.25}{1.0609} = 17.20238 \approx 17.20$$

See the table in part c for all the calculations.

b. Calculate $Y_t - \bar{Y}_t$ and fill in the Output Gap column. Subtract Potential Output ($\bar{Y}$) from Current Output (Y) for each year. See the table in part c for these calculations.

c. Calculate $\bar{Y}_t$ by dividing the Output Gap by Potential Output and fill in the Short-Run Output column. The following table includes the results from the calculations in parts a–c:

	Current Output	Potential Output (a)	Output Gap (b)	Short-Run Output (c)
2012	16.97	17.20	−0.23	−1.35%
2013	17.90	17.72	0.18	1.02%
2014	18.25	18.25	0.00	0.00%
2015	19.10	18.80	0.30	1.61%
2016	20.50	19.36	1.14	5.88%
2017	20.00	19.94	0.06	0.29%
2018	20.20	20.54	−0.34	−1.66%
2019	20.75	21.16	−0.41	−1.92%
2020	21.50	21.79	−0.29	−1.34%
2021	22.50	22.45	0.05	0.24%

d. How many years of boom and recession are there during this decade? Expansions, years with a positive GDP gap, generate positive values for Short-Run Output, $\dfrac{Y_t - \bar{Y}_t}{\bar{Y}_t} > 0$, and occur in 5 of the years during this decade. Recessions, in contrast, occur with negative GDP gaps and generate negative values for Short-Run Output, $\dfrac{Y_t - \bar{Y}_t}{\bar{Y}_t} > 0$. This decade has four recession years. Note that this country experiences neither an expansion nor a recession in the year 2014, as Short-Run Output equals zero.

2. Continue with the table from Problem 1, use the same data for Potential and Short-Run Output, but now include a column for GDP growth:

	Current Output	GDP Growth	Potential Output	Short-Run Output
2012	16.97			
2013	17.90			
2014	18.25			
2015	19.10			
2016	20.00			
2017	19.90			
2018	20.00			
2019	20.75			
2020	21.50			
2021	22.50			

a. Calculate the growth rate of Current Output and fill in the GDP Growth column along with the other corresponding values from your work in Problem 1. *Hint:* Doing these problems on a spreadsheet saves a lot of time and makes drawing the graph in the next part of this problem much easier.

b. Construct a diagram showing Current and Potential Output for each year during this decade.

c. Using the preceding table and the diagram, determine in how many years output increased and decreased.

d. How can the answers from Problem 1 part d and Problem 2 part c be reconciled?

3. Continue with the table from Problem 1, use the same data for Potential and Short-Run Output, but now include a column for unemployment. Assume that the natural rate of unemployment is 5 percent.

	Current Output	Potential Output	Short-Run Output	Unemployment
2012	16.97			
2013	17.90			
2014	18.25			
2015	19.10			
2016	20.00			
2017	19.90			
2018	20.00			
2019	20.75			
2020	21.50			
2021	22.50			

a. Calculate the level of unemployment experienced by this economy and fill in the unemployment column.
b. What can be said about GDP growth, short-run output, and unemployment? Will they always all give the same impression about the state of the economy?

4. Continue with the table from Problem 1, use the same data for Potential and Short-Run Output, but now include a column for Inflation:

	Current Output	Potential Output	Short-Run Output	$\Delta\pi$	Inflation
2012	16.97				
2013	17.90				
2014	18.25				
2015	19.10				
2016	20.00				
2017	19.90				
2018	20.00				
2019	20.75				
2020	21.50				
2021	22.25				

a. Assume that, in 2011, this economy experienced an inflation rate of 2.25 percent. Calculate the change and level of inflation and fill in their respective columns.

b. From the data in this table, what regularity might monetary authorities take note of in their fight against inflation?

5. Examine the table provided at the end of the solutions for this chapter. It contains all the data from each of Problems 1–4 and shows the interrelationships among all four problems.

CHAPTER 9 SOLUTIONS

True/False Questions

1. False. Changes in taxes and government spending never are completely unanticipated due to the legislative process. See Section 9.2.

2. False. The short run is the length of a deviation from potential output. It may last less than, or sometimes longer than, two years. See Section 9.2.

3. False. Current output is a combination of long-run trend and short-run fluctuations. Short-run output has been detrended. See Section 9.2.

4. True. See Section 9.2.

5. True. See Section 9.3.

6. False. Okun's law provides economists with the connection between short-run output and the unemployment gap, that is, $u - \bar{u}$. See Section 9.4.

Multiple-Choice Questions

1. d, an increase in inflation. Shocks cause either the aggregate demand or supply curve to shift; inflation then responds over time. See Section 9.2.

2. b, an increase in disposable income. It comes from a change in tax policy. See Section 9.2.

3. c, the predetermination of the current inflation rate. Current inflation is determined by the short-run model. See Section 9.2.

4. a, $\tilde{Y}_t = \dfrac{Y_t - \bar{Y}_t}{\bar{Y}_t}$. See Section 9.2.

5. e, none of the above. See Section 9.2.

6. b, when short-run output becomes positive. Rather, a recession ends when short-run output begins to rise or become less negative. See Section 9.2.

7. e, inflation. Inflation measures the behavior of prices. The Business Cycle Dating Committee considers measures of real activity, such as sales or production. See Section 9.2.

8. d, 24. See Section 9.2.

9. a, 4. See Section 9.2.

10. b, the amount of purchasing power lost by nominal assets. Typically, a recession slows the advance of inflation, which also slows the loss of nominal asset purchasing power. See Section 9.2.

11. b, the Great Depression. See the case study "The Great Depression."

12. c, analyze the trend passing through quarterly GDP observations. See Section 9.2.

13. e, government can use its policy-making ability to maximize GDP. Precisely not. Policy makers must operate under the constraint of the Phillips curve. See Section 9.3.

14. e, all of the above. See Section 9.3.

15. c, 1980. See Section 9.3.

16. d, increase by a percent and a half, according to the Phillips curve. See Section 9.3 and Figure 9.7.

17. a, 1 percent above. See Section 9.4 and Figure 9.8.

18. b, negatively, lower real interest rates generate more investment. See Section 9.5.

Exercises

1. a. Inflation increases by $\Delta\pi = 1/2\tilde{Y} = 1/2(2\%) = 1\%$.
   b. Short-run output was -4%, $-2\% = 1/2\tilde{Y} = 1/2(-4\%)$ or $\tilde{Y} = 2(-2\%)$.
   c. Inflation increases by 1 percent more than it otherwise would have increased. Note, however, that we know only the change in $\tilde{Y}$, not its value. Therefore, we cannot say how much inflation will go up overall, just that it will increase 1 percent more than it otherwise would have.
   d. A steady rate of inflation implies $\Delta\pi = 0$, which means that $\tilde{Y} = 0$.

2. a. Unemployment is 1 percent below its natural rate, that is, $u = 5\% - 1/2(2\%) = 4\%$.
   b. Short-run output has decreased by 2 percentage points, but we know neither the level of unemployment nor the value for short-run output.
   c. Unemployment increases by 1 percent, but again, we know neither the level of unemployment nor the value for short-run output.
   d. The economy is at full employment with a short-run output of zero.

3. Lower real interest rates will stimulate interest-sensitive spending by firms and consumers. For example, at lower interest rates, mortgages are cheaper and more people can afford to buy and finance new housing. That spending in turn stimulates overall economic activity and the short-run output increases.

Problems

1. Worked Problem. The problem is worked in the text.

2. a. Recall that $g_{Y_t} = \dfrac{Y_t - Y_{t-1}}{Y_{t-1}}$. Therefore, it is not possible to calculate a growth rate for the year 2012, since no value for current output in 2011 is available. The values for this table are

	Current Output	GDP Growth	Potential Output	Short-Run Output
2012	16.97		17.20	−1.35%
2013	17.90	5.48%	17.72	1.02%
2014	18.25	1.96%	18.25	0.00%
2015	19.10	4.66%	18.80	1.61%
2016	20.50	7.33%	19.36	5.88%
2017	20.00	−2.44%	19.94	0.29%
2018	20.20	1.00%	20.54	−1.66%
2019	20.75	2.72%	21.16	−1.92%
2020	21.50	3.61%	21.79	−1.34%
2021	22.50	4.65%	22.45	0.24%

b.

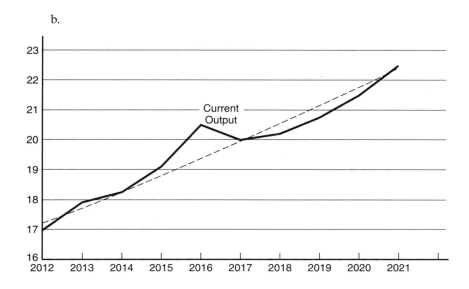

c. Output increased in eight years of this decade and decreased in one (2017).

d. Note that booms (years of positive short-run output) and recessions (years of negative short-run output) do not necessarily correspond to years of positive GDP, or current output, growth. It is quite possible for output to grow during periods of negative short-run output (as in the years 2018, 2019, and 2020) and to decline during boom periods (as in the year 2017).

3. a. Use Okun's law, $u_t - \bar{u} = -1/2\tilde{Y}_t$ and the assumption that $\bar{u} = 0.05$ to calculate unemployment by solving for $u_t = 0.05 - 1/2\tilde{Y}_t$. The values for this table are

	Current Output	Potential Output	Short-Run Output %	Unemployment %
2012	16.97	17.20	−1.35	6.68
2013	17.90	17.72	1.02	5.49
2014	18.25	18.25	0.00	6.00
2015	19.10	18.80	1.61	5.20
2016	20.50	19.36	5.88	3.06
2017	20.00	19.94	0.29	5.86
2018	20.20	20.54	−1.66	6.83
2019	20.75	21.16	−1.92	6.96
2020	21.50	21.79	−1.34	6.67
2021	22.50	22.45	0.24	5.88

b. Note that the possibility exists for unemployment to rise during boom years (as in years 2014 and 2017) and fall during periods of negative short-run output. The United States, in fact, experienced rising unemployment during the years of GDP growth that occurred immediately following the 1991 and 2001 recessions. Thus, without careful attention to surrounding activity, improper inferences can be made from GDP growth, short-run output, and unemployment data.

4. a. The change in inflation, $\Delta\pi$, comes directly from the Phillips curve, $\Delta\pi = 1/2\tilde{Y}$, and since $\Delta\pi = \pi_t - \pi_{t-1}$, knowing inflation from the previous year can generate current inflation, $\pi = \pi_{t-1} + 1/2\tilde{Y}$. The values for this table are

	Current Output	Potential Output	Short-Run Output %	Change in Inflation %	Inflation %
2012	16.97	17.20	−1.35	−5.73	0.27
2013	17.90	17.72	1.02	0.51	0.78
2014	18.25	18.25	0.00	0.00	0.78
2015	19.10	18.80	1.61	0.80	1.59
2016	20.50	19.36	5.88	2.94	4.53
2017	20.00	19.94	0.29	0.14	4.67
2018	20.20	20.54	−1.66	−0.83	3.85
2019	20.75	21.16	−1.92	−0.96	2.88
2020	21.50	21.79	−1.34	−0.67	2.22
2021	22.50	22.45	0.24	0.12	2.34

b. Monetary authorities might note the regularity with which a positive short-run output causes inflation to rise and a negative short-run output causes inflation to fall.

5. This table shows all the interrelationships found in Problems 1–4:

	Current Output	Potential Output	Output Gap	Short-Run Output %	Growth Rate 3% GDP Growth %	Natural Rate of Unemployment 6% Unemployment %	Unemployment Gap %	Change in Inflation %	Inflation 2011 0.95% Inflation %
2012	16.97	17.20	−0.23	−1.35	7.75	6.68	0.68	−0.68	0.27
2013	17.90	17.72	0.18	1.02	5.48	5.49	−0.51	0.51	0.78
2014	18.25	18.25	0.00	0.00	1.96	6.00	0.00	0.00	0.78
2015	19.10	18.80	0.30	1.61	4.66	5.20	−0.80	0.80	1.59
2016	20.50	19.36	1.14	5.88	7.33	3.06	−2.94	2.94	4.53
2017	20.00	19.94	0.06	0.29	−2.44	5.86	−0.14	0.14	4.67
2018	20.20	20.54	−0.34	−1.66	1.00	6.83	0.83	−0.83	3.85
2019	20.75	21.16	−0.41	−1.92	2.72	6.96	0.96	−0.96	2.88
2020	21.50	21.79	−0.29	−1.34	3.61	6.67	0.67	−0.67	2.22
2021	22.50	22.45	0.05	0.24	4.65	5.88	−0.12	0.12	2.34

CHAPTER 10 | The Great Recession: A First Look

OVERVIEW

The financial crisis of 2007 to 2009 and its accompanying recession, referred to now as "the Great Recession," call our attention to the short run in which we live. The crisis had its seeds in many areas but first caught the country's attention in general when the housing bubble burst in late 2006 and early 2007. Increased global saving rates contributed to the run up of prices in housing and other asset markets. Securitization of financial assets, deteriorating lending standards, and excess leverage helped fuel a liquidity crisis in which financial market activity slowed significantly and both the United States and most of the world were faced with the worst recession since the Great Depression. This chapter also covers basic financial institution concepts, such as balance sheets, leverage, and insolvency; how those aspects came into play during the financial crisis; and how the problems of systemic risk led to unprecedented government involvement in response to existing and anticipated economic conditions.

KEY CONCEPTS

The worst recession since World War II began in December 2007 following events that came to a head with the bursting of the housing bubble in 2006. *The Great Recession,* as its come to be known, peaked in late 2009 with an unemployment rate of 10.1 percent. At this printing, some economists think that it's over, but the debate still lingers.

In early 2005 Federal Reserve Board Chairman Ben Bernanke spoke of a *global saving glut* that arose out of increased saving in developing countries in response to a number of financial crises that caused them to rethink their behavior, while at the same time developed countries began borrowing these funds for their own consumption and investment activities.

The *Taylor rule* (discussed more thoroughly in Chapter 13) both describes and prescribes a relationship between percentage GDP gaps and inflation gaps that stipulates how much the central bank should raise, or lower, interest rates in response to current economic conditions. If GDP gaps and/or inflation gaps are positive then the central bank should raise interest rates and, of course, lower them if they are negative.

Asset *securitization* is the process of bundling together a large number of similar assets—such as mortgages, a few of which might have a high probability of default—into a single debt instrument that is viewed as much safer because the great majority of its components have very low default probability and as a group make for a safer asset for the entity that holds it. The resulting security can also be split up again into riskier and safer portions and sold off to various entities desiring such instruments.

An institution is illiquid when it does not have enough cash on hand to meet its immediate cash requirements, even if it has other assets that simply cannot be converted into cash at that moment in time. Without special arrangements, as in the cases of Fannie Mae and Freddie Mac, such an entity becomes insolvent, or is forced to go bankrupt, as was the case with Lehman Brothers. During our recent financial crisis, when this happened to several institutions simultaneously, we experienced a *liquidity crisis.*

Short-run output, $\tilde{Y}_t$, is defined as the percentage difference between actual output and potential output. It is also known as a percentage GDP gap where

$$\tilde{Y}_t = \frac{Y_t - \bar{Y}_t}{\bar{Y}_t},$$ where Y_t represents actual output, or GDP

itself, and $\bar{Y}_t$ represents potential output, or potential GDP.

A *balance sheet* is an accounting representation of an institution's assets and liabilities that is generally organized into two halves with several categories that equal each other. One half consists of *assets,* things of value that the institution owns, and the other half consists of *liabilities,* things of value that the institution owes to other entities.

Within a balance sheet, one category consists of items owed to the institution's owners whether they are individuals or shareholders. This category represents the *equity*, *net worth*, or *capital* that belongs to the institution's owners once all of the liabilities to other individuals are subtracted from the institution's assets and is the category that makes the balance sheet balance.

In the banking industry, banks face a *reserve requirement* that binds them by law to keep a certain percentage of their deposits in a special reserve account for the purpose of meeting their depositor's business requirements. Similarly, bank owners are required to have a certain amount of their own money, or capital, involved in the institution. That *capital requirement* binds them to have the institution's net worth be at least a certain percentage of total assets.

Leverage is the number of times that total assets are larger than the net worth of an institution. For example, if total assets are $1,000 and net worth is $100, the leverage of that institution is ten.

When the net worth of an institution (total assets minus the liabilities that the institution owes to others) falls below zero, that is, becomes negative, that institution becomes *insolvent* and is declared *bankrupt*.

A *bank run* occurs when enough of a bank's depositors all want to withdraw their deposits but the bank is unable to meet their demands given its current state of affairs. The danger of a bank run is that an otherwise healthy institution can be forced into bankruptcy on the basis of an unwarranted panic. The Federal Deposit Insurance Corporation (FDIC) eliminates this risk on the part of smaller depositors (currently those with less than $250,000).

Systemic risk becomes a problem when economic conditions threaten a sufficient number of key financial institutions with insolvency that as a result of their involvement with still other financial institutions the entire financial system as a whole becomes threatened with failure or collapse.

TRUE/FALSE QUESTIONS

1. Too much saving and not enough spending precipitated the global financial crisis.

2. Securitization cannot insulate investors from aggregate risk.

3. Short-run output, $\tilde{Y}_t$, fell more than three times as much during the Great Recession as it did during the previous recession in 2001.

4. During the Great Recession, unemployment peaked at just over 11 percent.

5. The Great Recession affected the United States more severely than other industrialized nations.

6. Leverage is the ratio of total liabilities to total assets.

7. If banks could avoid bank runs, insolvency would no longer be a concern.

8. With the establishment of the FDIC, the possibility of systemic risk has been largely averted.

MULTIPLE-CHOICE QUESTIONS

1. During the financial crisis of 2007–09, each of the following financial powerhouses failed except
   a. Lehman Brothers.
   b. Bear Stearns.
   c. Washington Mutual.
   d. Goldman Sachs.
   e. None of the above; they all failed.

2. During the Great Recession housing prices fell by _____ percent.
   a. less than 10
   b. approximately 15
   c. about 20
   d. roughly 25
   e. over 30

3. During the Great Recession the Federal Reserve lowered the federal funds rate to _____ percent.
   a. 4
   b. 3
   c. 2
   d. 1
   e. 0

4. Prior to the Great Recession the average spread between the LIBOR rate and the three-month U.S. Treasury Bill was _____ percentage points. During the recession it increased to approximately _____ percent.
   a. 0.25; 3.5
   b. 0.50; 3.5
   c. 0.25; 2
   d. 0.50; 2
   e. 1; 3.5

5. During the Great Recession the Real S&P Stock Index fell more steeply than it had in the past _____ decades.
   a. 3
   b. 4
   c. 5
   d. 6
   e. 7

6. Which of the following is not a type of securitized asset?
   a. mortgage-backed security
   b. asset-backed commercial paper
   c. Treasury-security instrument
   d. collateralized debt obligation
   e. credit card–backed security

7. Several events contributed to the economic downturn that has become known as the Great Recession. Which of the following was not one of them?
   a. a significant decline in housing prices
   b. a global saving glut
   c. interest rate hikes on the part of the Federal Reserve
   d. large increases in the price of crude oil
   e. They all played a role.

8. Much of the way through 2007 a concern in the banking sector over an increasingly large number of bad mortgages caused banks to quit lending to each other and hold more Treasury securities instead. Economists call this a
   a. bank run.
   b. period of insolvency.
   c. liquidity crisis.
   d. bankruptcy.
   e. decrease in bank reserves.

9. The primary holders of mortgage-backed securities were
   a. credit unions.
   b. life insurance companies.
   c. small community and regional banks.
   d. large commercial and investment banks.
   e. pension funds.

10. Each of these variables reflected significant losses during the Great Recession except
    a. U.S. short-run output ($\tilde{Y}_t$).
    b. total nonfarm employment.
    c. the real S&P 500 Stock Price Index.
    d. the price of oil.
    e. none of the above; they all did.

11. During the Great Recession each of the components of GDP fell except
    a. consumption.
    b. investment.
    c. government purchases.
    d. exports.
    e. imports.

12. During the Great Recession employment in the United States fell by approximately _____ percent.
    a. 3
    b. 4
    c. 5
    d. 6
    e. 7

13. As a result of the Great Depression, inflation, as measured by the CPI, _____ for the first time in six decades.
    a. increased
    b. decreased
    c. became negative
    d. exhibited tendencies of hyperinflation
    e. was of no concern to policy makers

14. Which of the following countries was hit the hardest by the Great Recession?
    a. Asian NICs
    b. Euro area
    c. Japan
    d. United Kingdom
    e. United States

15. Which of the following was not a component of a bank's balance sheet?
    a. assets
    b. liabilities
    c. net worth
    d. capital requirement
    e. required reserves

16. Which of the following is not a relationship between components of a bank's balance sheet?
    a. reserve requirement
    b. capital requirement
    c. leverage
    d. equity
    e. long-term debt

EXERCISES

Hypothetical Bank A			
Cash	$500,000	Deposits	$5,000,000
Reserves		Short-term debt	$3,000,000
Loans	$1,000,000	Long-term debt	$3,000,000
Investments	$10,000,000	**Total Liabilities**	
		Equity	
Total Assets		**Total Liabilities & Equity**	

1. Use the accompanying balance sheet for Hypothetical Bank A to complete each of the following parts of this problem.
   a. What are reserves for this bank if they are held on deposits only, the bank holds $1 million in excess reserves, and the reserve requirement is 10 percent?
   b. What are total assets, total liabilities,and net worth?
   c. Does this balance sheet balance? Why?

Hypothetical Bank B			
Cash	$500,000	Deposits	$7,000,000
Reserves	$700,000	Short-term debt	$3,000,000
Loans	$6,800,000	Long-term debt	$3,000,000
Investments	$7,000,000	**Total Liabilities**	$13,000,000
		Equity	$2,000,000
Total Assets	$15,000,000	**Total Liabilities & Equity**	$15,000,000

2. Use the accompanying balance sheet for Hypothetical Bank B to complete each of the following parts of this problem.
   a. If this bank is just meeting its capital requirement, what is it?
   b. How leveraged is this bank? What danger does that present?
   c. Suppose the bank's customers wanted to withdraw $3 million worth of deposits due to rumors of an in-house accounting scandal. Will the bank be able to honor their requests?
   d. What situation is the bank now facing, and what four options could it pursue?

PROBLEMS

Worked Problems

1. This problem takes you through the steps of recreating figures from the text as suggested in exercise 1 at the end of the chapter. We begin by choosing Figure 10.10 that compares 12-month inflation rates using the CPI with all items and the CPI excluding food and energy and reproducing it.

   a. Access the FRED® database: http://research.stlouisfed.org/fred2/

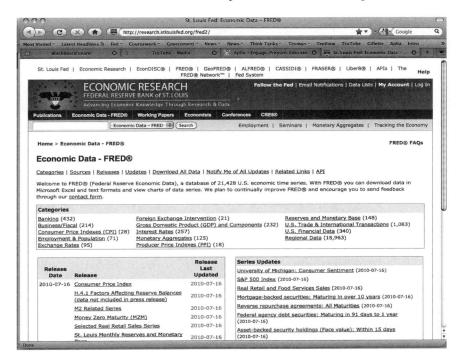

   b. Click on **Consumer Price Indexes (CPI)**

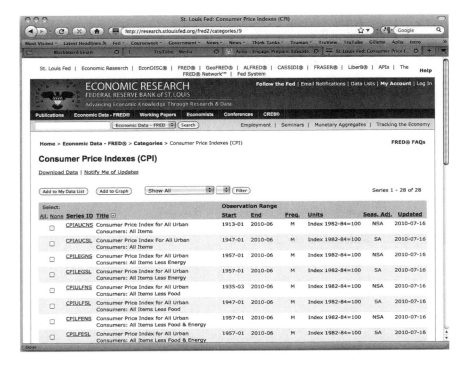

c. Choose **CPIAUCSL Consumer Price Index For All Urban Consumers: All Items**

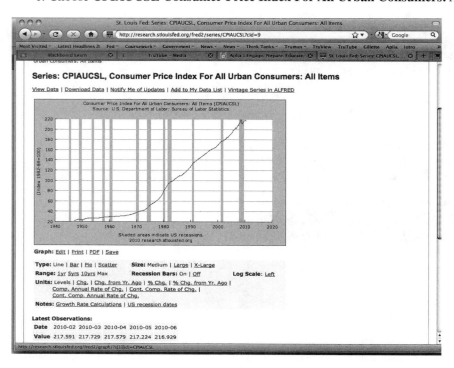

d. Look below the graph and click on X-Large.

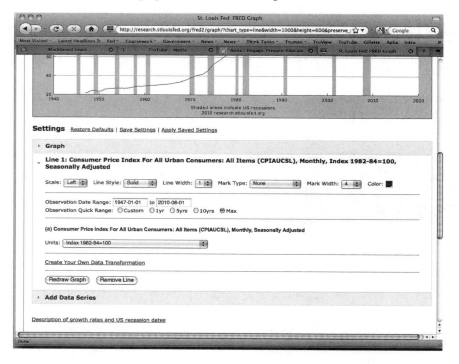

e. Now look below the graph for a pop-up menu with choices for Units: (you should find it saying Index 1982–84 = 100) and select **Percent Change from Year Ago**. Now click on the **Redraw Graph**.

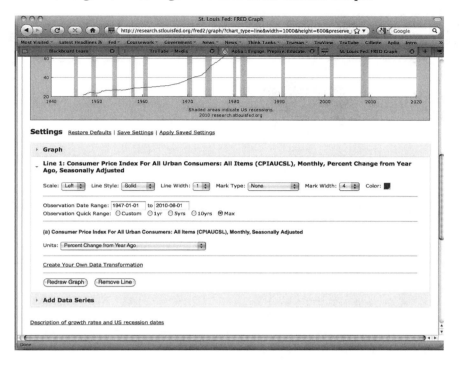

f. Now click on **Add Data Series** and then on **Browse**.

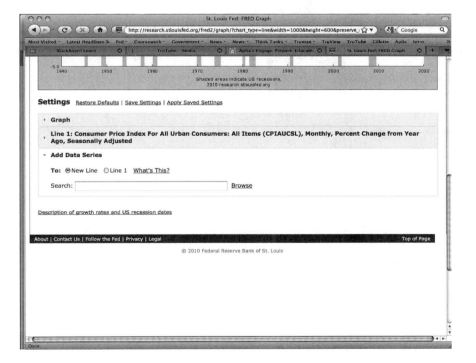

g. Click on **Consumer Price Indexes (CPI)** and scroll down and click on **CPILFESL, Consumer Price Index for All Urban Consumers: All Items Less Food & Energy**, and the graph should automatically refresh with both series displayed.

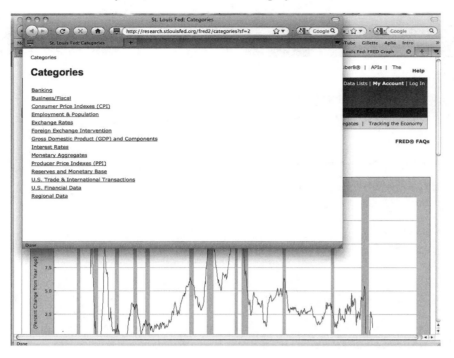

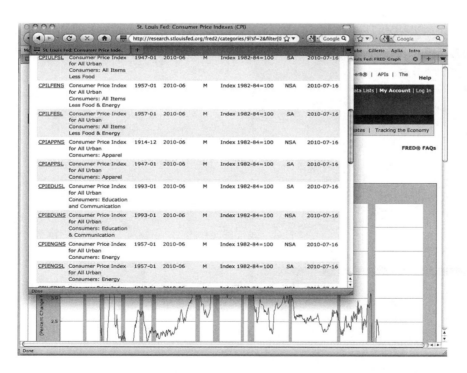

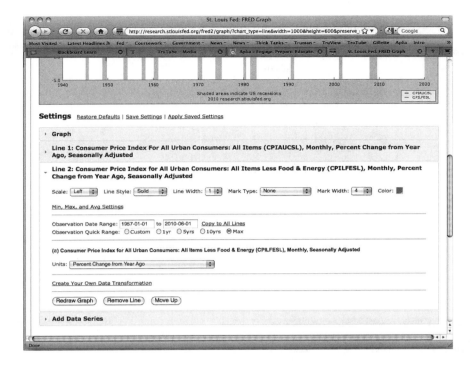

h. Just one step left. Now adjust the **Observation Date Range** to display only the observations since the beginning of 1990. To do this, click on the first date cell. A calendar will pop up; change the year to 1990 and click on **Close**, then on **Copy to All Lines** and finally on the **Redraw Graph** button.

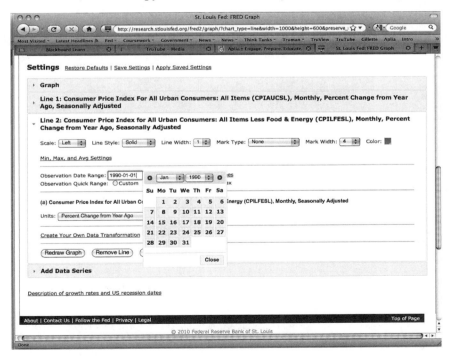

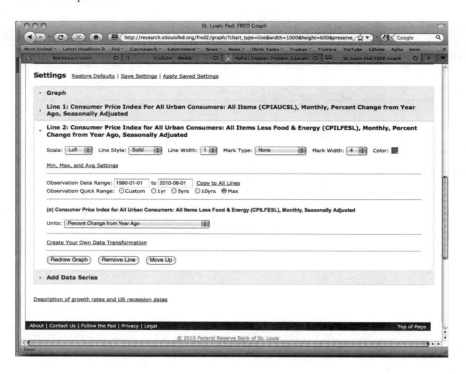

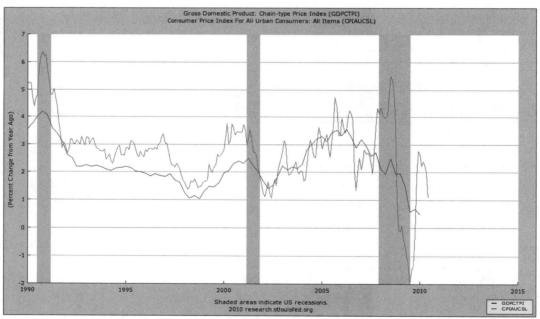

i. What observations can you make about the behavior of the **All Items** CPI relative to the **All Items Less Food & Energy** version of the CPI?

The **All Items** series is much more volatile than the one without food and energy. Still, we all buy both food and energy so in some cases it may well be the more relevant series.

j. What has happened to these variables since the beginning of 2010 when Figure 10.10 in the text was published?

In the first six months of 2010 each series continued to fall. *The rest is up to you.*

2. This problem continues in the spirit of Problem 1 but draws on earlier material from Chapter 2 by using a broader measure of consumption than the CPI and then by comparing CPI inflation with inflation as derived from the GDP deflator.

a. Access the FRED® database: http://research.stlouisfed.org/fred2/

b. Click on **Gross Domestic Product (GDP)** and components.

c. Click on **Price Indexes & Deflators**

d. Choose **PCEPI, Personal Consumption Expenditures: Chain-type Price Index**, and create an extra-large figure just as you did in Problem 1. (Don't forget to change the units to **Percentage Change from Year Ago**.)

e. Now add **PCEPILFE, Personal Consumption Expenditures: Chain-Type Price Index Less Food and Energy**, and restrict the sample to begin in 1990 just as you did in Problem 1.

f. Compare this graph to the one generated in Problem 1 and describe the similarities and differences between the two.

g. Now repeat this process again using the **CPI All Items** series from Problem 1 and the GDP Deflator (**GDPCTPI, Gross Domestic Product: Chain-type Price Index**) found at http://research.stlouisfed.org/fred2/categories/19.

h. Describe the similarities and differences that you find between the CPI inflation rate and the GDP Deflator inflation rate.

3. In this problem we want to examine the balance sheets of two major financial institutions (Goldman Sachs and Discover Financial Services) and walk through issues of leverage, debt finance, and bankruptcy for each of them.

a. Go to:
http://finance.yahoo.com/q/bs?s=GS&annual and
http://finance.yahoo.com/q/bs?s=DFS+Balance+Sheet&annual
and get the balance sheets for Goldman Sachs and Discover Financial Services.

b. Calculate the leverage ratio for each of these companies.

c. How can you use the leverage ratio to calculate how much of their total assets each of these companies has financed with equity versus with debt?

d. How much (in percentage terms) could the value of each company's total assets fall before it would become insolvent?

CHAPTER 10 SOLUTIONS

True/False Questions

1. False. It was a combination of too much saving in some countries and too much spending and borrowing in other countries. See Section 10.2.

2. True. This is exactly what failed to happen in the financial crisis. See Section 10.2.

3. True. See Section 10.3, Figure 10.7.

4. False. It was just over 10 percent. See Section 10.3, Figure 10.8.

5. False. During 2009 the Euro area, the U.K., and Japan all suffered greater percentage losses than did the U.S. See Section 10.3, Table 10.3.

6. False. It's total liabilities to net worth. See Section 10.4.

7. False. Banks can become insolvent just through changes in asset values. See Section 10.4.

8. False. The systemic risk faced during the financial crisis of 2007–2009 occurred in spite of coverage increasing from $100,000 to $250,000. See Section 10.4.

Multiple-Choice Questions

1. d, Goldman Sachs did not fail; it converted to a bank holding company. See Section 10.1.

2. e, over 30 (33.5) percent. See Section 10.2, Figure 10.1.

3. e, zero, (technically it was a range from 0.0–0.25%. See Section 10.2, Figure 10.2.

4. a, 0.25 and 3.5, respectively. See Section 10.2, Figure 10.3.

5. e, seven, it fell further quicker than any time since the Great Depression. See Section 10.2, Figure 10.4.

6. c, each of the others is. See Section 10.2. (See also *securitization* in Wikipedia for references to other types of asset-backed securities including credit cards.)

7. e, they all played a role. See Section 10.2.

8. c, a liquidity crisis. See Section 10.2, The Financial Turmoil of 2007–2009.

9. d, large commercial and investment banks. See Section 10.2, The Financial Turmoil of 2007–2009.

10. e, each variable fell as a result of the Great Recession. See Section 10.3.

11. c, government purchases. See Section 10.3, Table 10.1.

12. d, 6 percent. See Section 10.3, Figure 10.9.

13. c, became negative. See Section 10.3, Figure 10.10.

14. c, Japan. See Section 10.3, Table 10.3.

15. d, capital requirement. This is a relationship between elements of the bank's balance sheet. See Section 10.4.

16. e, long-term debt. Reserve and capital requirements are percentages of other elements, leverage is a multiple, and equity is a residual. See Section 10.4.

Exercises

1. The completed balance sheet for this problem should look like this:

Hypothetical Bank B

Cash	$500,000	Deposits	$5,000,000
Reserves	$1,500,000	Short-term debt	$3,000,000
Loans	$1,000,000	Long-term debt	$3,000,000
Investments	$10,000,000	**Total Liabilities**	$11.000,000
		Equity	$2,000,000
Total Assets	$13,000,000	**Total Liabilities & Equity**	$13,000,000

   a. Required reserves are $500,000 making total reserves $1,500,000.
   b. Total assets sum to $13,000,000, total liabilities to $11,000,000 and equity, the difference between the two, is $2,000,000.
   c. Yes, it does balance because the net worth of $2,000,000 is the difference between total assets and total liabilities.

2. For convenience we repeat the balance sheet for Hypothetical Bank B.

Hypothetical Bank B

Cash	$500,000	Deposits	$7,000,000
Reserves	$700,000	Short-term debt	$3,000,000
Loans	$6,800,000	Long-term debt	$3,000,000
Investments	$7,000,000	**Total Liabilities**	$13.000,000
		Equity	$2,000,000
Total Assets	$15,000,000	**Total Liabilities & Equity**	$15,000,000

   a. Net worth as a percent of total assets is:

   $$\frac{2,000,000}{15,000,000} = 0.1333 \text{ or } 13.33\%$$

   b. Leverage for this bank is $\frac{13,000,000}{2,000,000} = 6.5$.

   This means that for every 7.5 dollars of assets the bank holds, 6.5 of them are borrowed. To see this, divide both total assets and equity by 2,000,000. You'll get 7.5 for total assets and 1 for equity. Then subtract 1 from 7.5 to get 6.5—the number of dollars borrowed for each dollar of equity. This becomes dangerous when the bank experiences enough withdrawals that it becomes illiquid, or unable to meet its immediate cash requirements.

   c. In this case the bank will not be able to meet its depositors' requests because it does not have sufficient cash or reserves on hand to meet the demand for withdrawals.
   d. The bank is now illiquid and has four options at its disposal:
      i.   It can call in some of its loans.
      ii. It can sell some of its investments.
      iii. It can acquire additional equity.
      iv. It can take out bankruptcy.
   Other options are also potentially available, but these are the main candidates.

Problems

1. Worked Problem. The problem is worked in the text.

2. Parts a–e should generate a figure like this:

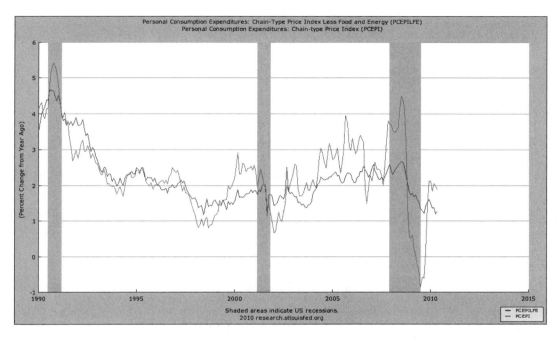

f. Both figures look very similar with respect to the
   series' behavior, but two obvious differences include
   the maximum and minimum values on the y-axis.
   Using the CPI, range is between 7 and –2 whereas
   for the Personal Consumption Expenditures from the
   broader-based GDP component that range is only
   between 6 and –1.

g. Using both the CPI and the GDP inflation series
   gives us the following diagram:

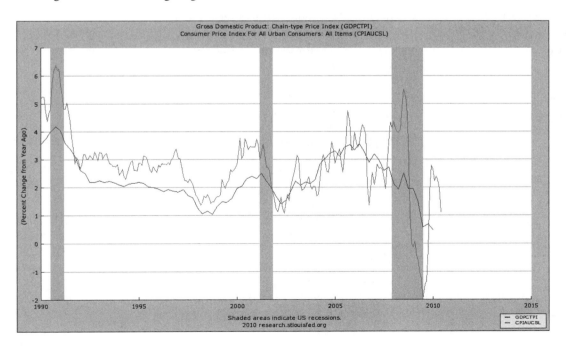

h. Prior to the 2001 recession the CPI generated a higher level of inflation than did the GDP Deflator. Since that time the CPI inflation has centered more on the level of inflation using the GDP Deflator, but with much greater volatility. During the last recession, for example, the CPI inflation fluctuated over a range three times as great as that of the GDP Deflator.

3. a. For the year 2009 the balance sheets were as follows:

The Goldman Sachs Group, Inc.		Discover Financial Services	
Period Ending	**31-Dec-09**	Period Ending	**30-Nov-09**
Assets		**Assets**	
Current Assets		Current Assets	
Cash And Cash Equivalents	219,233,000	Cash And Cash Equivalents	18,056,016
Short-Term Investments		Short-Term Investments	1,350,000
Net Receivables	67,900,000	Net Receivables	
Inventory		Inventory	
Other Current Assets		Other Current Assets	
Total Current Assets		**Total Current Assets**	
Long-Term Investments	532,341,000	Long-Term Investments	29,237,844
Property Plant and Equipment		Property Plant and Equipment	499,303
Goodwill		Goodwill	255,421
Intangible Assets		Intangible Assets	195,636
Accumulated Amortization		Accumulated Amortization	
Other Assets	29,468,000	Other Assets	1,462,064
Deferred Long-Term Asset Charges		Deferred Long-Term Asset Charges	
Total Assets	**848,942,000**	**Total Assets**	**46,020,987**
Liabilities		**Liabilities**	
Current Liabilities		Current Liabilities	
Accounts Payable	366,026,000	Accounts Payable	3,064,327
Short/Current Long-Term Debt	165,876,000	Short/Current Long-Term Debt	
Other Current Liabilities	39,418,000	Other Current Liabilities	32,093,012
Total Current Liabilities		**Total Current Liabilities**	
Long-Term Debt	338,238,000	Long-Term Debt	
Other Liabilities	49,062,000	Other Liabilities	
Deferred Long-Term Liability Changes		Deferred Long-Term Liability Changes	
Minority Interest		Minority Interest	
Negative Goodwill		Negative Goodwill	
Total Liabilities	**778,228,000**	**Total Liabilities**	**37,585,440**
Stockholders' Equity		**Stockholders' Equity**	
Misc. Stocks Options Warrants		Misc. Stocks Options Warrants	
Redeemable Preferred Stock		Redeemable Preferred Stock	
Preferred Stock	6,957,000	Preferred Stock	1,158,066
Common Stock	8,000	Common Stock	5,448
Retained Earnings	50,252,000	Retained Earnings	3,873,262
Treasury Stock	(32,156,000)	Treasury Stock	(19,642)
Capital Surplus	39,770,000	Capital Surplus	3,573,231
Other Stockholder Equity	5,883,000	Other Stockholder Equity	(154,818)
Total Stockholder Equity	**70,714,000**	**Total Stockholder Equity**	**8,435,547**
Net Tangible Assets	**$70,714,000**	**Net Tangible Assets**	**$7,984,490**

b. Goldman Sachs: $\dfrac{778,228,000}{70,714,000} = 11.005$

   Discover: $\dfrac{37,585,440}{8,435,547} = 4.456$

c. Recall from Exercise 2 that you can simply subtract one from the leverage ratio. Goldman Sachs has financed $10 of assets with debt for each dollar of its own equity, whereas Discover Financial Services has only financed $3.45.

d. Goldman Sachs: $\dfrac{70,714,000}{848,942,000} = 8.33\%$

   Discover: $\dfrac{8,435,547}{46,020,987} = 18.33\%$

CHAPTER 11 | The IS Curve

OVERVIEW

The IS curve, or goods market, makes up a major portion of the short-run model through its description of aggregate demand. Lower real interest rates stimulate economic activity in the markets for goods and services in an economy, and higher real interest rates restrict that activity. This understanding sets the stage for studying the conduct of monetary policy in the next chapter. Shocks to aggregate demand increase or decrease economic activity, regardless of interest rate levels. Knowing this allows policy makers to design better responses with the monetary and fiscal policy tools developed in Chapters 12–15. Similarly, understanding the behavior of consumers and firms helps explain most of a country's nongovernment economic activity. Higher real interest rates cause consumers' investment activity in housing markets and firms' purchases of buildings and equipment to decrease significantly. Consequently, both the level of aggregate demand and short-run output decrease. Consumer preferences for smooth, rather than variable, consumption also contribute to a better understanding of the nature of aggregate demand and how to influence it appropriately when necessary.

KEY CONCEPTS

The *IS curve* begins with the national income identity and describes the relationship between real interest rates and short-run output. Note that the national income identity also defines an equilibrium relationship between current output and aggregate demand. Real interest rates enter primarily through their impact on real investment (housing, buildings, and equipment) but also can influence consumption (see Chapter 11,

Exercise 9, in the text), and later through net exports as we will see in Chapter 19.

The *real interest rate*, R_t, is the effective rate at which firms and individuals can borrow or save. Recall from the Fisher equation that $R_t = i_t - \pi_t$. Higher/lower real interest rates reduce/increase investment and other interest-sensitive spending and increase/decrease savings. The relationship between the real interest rate and the marginal product of capital forms a critical element of the IS curve and drives interest-sensitive spending, such as investment. (Note, for the purposes of Chapter 11, R_t is considered an exogenous variable, but in general it is one of the endogenous variables in our short-run model.)

The *marginal product of capital*, $\bar{r}$, is the amount of additional output generated from investing in an additional unit of capital stock. The return on capital, determined by the workings of the long-run economy, is measured in percentage terms and remains constant along the economy's balanced growth path. In contrast to R_t and the other endogenous variables, it therefore requires no time subscript.

Aggregate demand shocks come from changes in the parameter $\bar{a}$, derived from the demand for goods and services from each of the economy's four spending components: consumption, investment, government, and net exports. Shocks constitute departures from past "normal" behavior ($\bar{a} = 0$) and cause $\bar{a}$ to become either positive or negative according to the nature of the shock.

The *Permanent Income Model of consumption* assumes that people base their consumption decisions on an average of their expected income each period rather than on their current income at any particular point in time. Smoothing consumption out in this way, rather than consuming much larger amounts in some periods and smaller amounts in others, adheres to the principle of diminishing marginal utility on a micro level but also allows for periods of borrowing and saving on a more macro level.

The *Life Cycle Model of consumption* also assumes a smooth stream of consumption over three general periods of a person's lifetime: early borrowing or transfers while young; consuming and saving during working years, and living from savings during retirement. Consumption decisions are based on an average lifetime income rather than income at any particular point in time.

Permanent income is the constant (average) income stream that has the same present discounted value as the fluctuating income stream actually experienced by an individual over time.

Multiplier effects occur when initial shocks to an economy have secondary impacts that exacerbate the initial disturbance. These effects occur through the consumption, income, and investment channels that feel the impact of the initial shock.

A firm's *cash flow* is determined by the amount of internal funding it can pull together after paying all of its expenses. It also helps determine the amount of investment a firm can make without entering the loanable funds market.

Adverse selection means that, when there is an avenue of escape or the possibility of avoiding responsibility, such as insurance or bankruptcy, the riskiest customers will be first in line to participate in an activity.

Moral hazard means that firms or individuals undertake riskier behavior when the possibility of evading responsibility through something like insurance or bankruptcy exists.

Automatic stabilizers include such programs as unemployment compensation, welfare, Social Security, and Medicaid. The government uses these programs to mitigate the effects of rising and falling income caused by fluctuations in the business cycle or movement between life-cycle periods.

The *"no-free-lunch principle"* simply means we cannot get something for nothing. Increased government spending will require either additional taxes today or less spending or more taxes in the future.

Ricardian equivalence argues that consumers understand the no-free-lunch principle and they adjust their con-

sumption behavior according to the present value of their tax liabilities, regardless of when the taxation actually occurs. In other words, they adjust their current consumption expenditures when future tax liabilities increase.

TRUE/FALSE QUESTIONS

1. The term "IS" in the IS curve stands for "investment equals savings."

2. Investment is one of the key channels through which interest rates affect output.

3. The real interest rate, along with $\bar{a}_i$, determines the amount of investment an economy undertakes.

4. An increase in potential output will cause the IS curve to shift to the right.

5. An increase in potential output causes current output to increase by an equal amount.

6. An increase in potential output causes consumption, investment, and government spending, as well as spending on imports and exports, to increase.

7. In the short-run model, the behavior of specific individuals bears little significance.

8. The IS curve is flatter as a result of multiplier effects.

9. Adverse selection occurs when firms make poor investment decisions.

10. Moral hazard describes the problem of firms engaging in riskier behavior than they would if they bore all the risks of the venture.

11. An increase in $\bar{a}_{im}$ causes the IS curve to shift to the right, causing an increase in the short-run output.

12. Spending increases caused by higher interest rates are stronger as they work their way through the economy because of multiplier effects.

MULTIPLE-CHOICE QUESTIONS

1. The IS curve represents the relationship between the short-run output and
   a. inflation.
   b. unemployment.
   c. aggregate demand.
   d. real interest rates.
   e. nominal interest rates.

2. Which of the following is not an element of aggregate demand as described by the setup of the IS curve?
   a. consumption
   b. taxes
   c. government
   d. investment
   e. net exports

3. Modeling consumption as a constant fraction of potential output ($C_t = \bar{a}_c \bar{Y}_t$) makes sense for each of the following reasons except that
   a. consumption expenditures average roughly two-thirds of GDP.
   b. potential output fluctuates less than actual output.
   c. the Permanent Income Hypothesis supports this formulation.
   d. individuals generally prefer smoother consumption paths.
   e. None of the above is correct.

4. Which of the following aggregate demand components generally is *not* modeled as a portion of potential output?
   a. consumption
   b. investment
   c. government
   d. exports
   e. imports

5. If the real interest rate is 8 percent, which of the following investment projects will earn a firm a profit of 10 percent?
   a. $\bar{r} = 10\%$
   b. $\bar{r} = 7.2\%$
   c. $\bar{r} = 18\%$
   d. $\bar{r} = 2\%$
   e. $\bar{r} = 8.8\%$

6. In the short run, which of the following statements is correct?
   a. The real interest rate equals the marginal product of capital.
   b. The real interest rate exceeds the marginal product of capital.
   c. The marginal product of capital exceeds the real interest rate.
   d. The real interest rate does not change.
   e. The real interest rate can rise above or fall below the marginal product of capital.

7. Which of the following chain of events accurately describes the intuition underlying the IS curve?
   a. $R_t \uparrow \rightarrow$ opportunity cost of $I_t \uparrow \rightarrow I_t \downarrow \rightarrow Y_t \uparrow$
   b. $R_t \uparrow \rightarrow$ opportunity cost of $I_t \uparrow \rightarrow I_t \downarrow \rightarrow Y_t \downarrow$
   c. $R_t \uparrow \rightarrow$ opportunity cost of $I_t \downarrow \rightarrow I_t \downarrow \rightarrow Y_t \downarrow$
   d. $R_t \uparrow \rightarrow$ opportunity cost of $I_t \downarrow \rightarrow I_t \downarrow \rightarrow Y_t \uparrow$
   e. $R_t \uparrow \rightarrow$ opportunity cost of $I_t \uparrow \rightarrow I_t \uparrow \rightarrow Y_t \uparrow$

8. Which of the following is not true about the IS curve in the long run?
   a. $\bar{a}_c + \bar{a}_i + \bar{a}_g + \bar{a}_{ex} - \bar{a}_{im} = 1$
   b. $\bar{a} = 0$
   c. $Y_t = \bar{Y}_t$
   d. $\tilde{Y}_t = \bar{Y}_t$
   e. $\tilde{Y}_t = 0$

9. Which of the following conditions between investment and savings is correct?
   a. $I = Y - C - G + IM - EX$
   b. $I = (Y - T - C) + (T - G) + (IM - EX)$
   c. $I = (Y - T - C) + (T - G) + (EX - IM)$
   d. $I = (Y - T - C) + (G - T) + (EX - IM)$
   e. $I = (Y - T - C) + (G - T) + (IM - EX)$

10. In the absence of an aggregate demand shock, a fully employed economy's IS curve would exhibit each of the following characteristics except
    a. $\bar{a} = 0$.
    b. $\bar{b} = 0$.
    c. $R_t = \bar{r}$.
    d. $Y_t = \bar{Y}_t$.
    e. $\tilde{Y}_t = 0$.

11. In the IS curve, or the market for goods and services, which of the following will not result from a change in the real interest rate?
    a. a change in investment spending
    b. a change in the short-run output
    c. a change in consumption
    d. a shift of the IS curve
    e. None of the above; all will take place.

12. Which of the following would not cause the IS curve to shift?
    a. a change in $\bar{a}_i$
    b. a change in $\bar{a}_c$
    c. a change in $\bar{a}_g$
    d. a change in R_t
    e. a change in $\bar{r}$

13. One of the following events will cause movement along the IS curve. Which is it?
    a. a change in firms' responsiveness to changes in the real interest rate
    b. an increase in the share of output going to consumers
    c. decreased interest in American exports
    d. an increase in government spending
    e. a change in interest rates by the Fed

14. A technological improvement that increases potential output will have each of the following impacts on the economy except
    a. an increase in the marginal product of capital.
    b. an increase in $\bar{a}_i$ by firms.
    c. a shift of the IS curve.
    d. a stimulus of the economy.
    e. an increase in real interest rates.

15. Which of the following causes the IS curve in the United States to shift to the left?
    a. an increase in Canadian unemployment
    b. lower interest rates
    c. an increase in the demand for American exports
    d. an increase in investment tax credits
    e. an increase in unemployment in the United States

16. The permanent-income hypothesis holds that people
    a. prefer a smooth consumption path to a volatile one.
    b. base their consumption on average income over time rather than current income.
    c. seek to smooth their consumption due to diminishing marginal utility.
    d. experience periods of borrowing, saving, and dissaving during their lifetime.
    e. do all of the above.

17. Multiplier effects affecting short-run output occur in response to economic shocks originating in the _____ sector.
    a. consumption
    b. investment
    c. exports
    d. all of the above
    e. only a and b

18. Multiplier effects caused by an increase in taxes might include each of the following except
    a. increased unemployment.
    b. higher interest rates.
    c. lower short-run output.
    d. reduced consumption.
    e. less investment.

19. Which of the following is a firm's main determinant of investment?
    a. the nominal interest rate
    b. the real interest rate
    c. the marginal product of capital
    d. the gap between the real interest rate and the marginal product of capital
    e. depreciation allowances

20. Government purchases can play each of the following roles except
    a. transferring resources between individuals.
    b. determining real interest rates.
    c. causing short-run fluctuations.
    d. offsetting short-run fluctuations.
    e. facilitating welfare improvements.

21. Which of the following is not an automatic stabilizer?
    a. Social Security transfers
    b. Medicaid payments
    c. educational tax credits
    d. Temporary Assistance to Needy Families
    e. Medicare payments

22. The *no-free-lunch principle* applies to which of the following considerations involved in the development of appropriate fiscal policy?
    a. the problem of timing lags
    b. the use of automatic stabilizers
    c. the use of discretionary fiscal policy
    d. the principle of Ricardian equivalence
    e. none of the above

23. According to Ricardian equivalence, current consumption would change in the case of
    a. earlier taxation rather than later.
    b. later taxation rather than earlier.
    c. increased deficit spending.
    d. all of the above.
    e. none of the above.

24. The text argues that _____ constitute(s) the most famous use of discretionary fiscal policy in the history of the United States.
    a. Roosevelt's New Deal Program
    b. Johnson's War on Poverty
    c. the Kennedy tax cuts
    d. the 2001 Bush tax cuts
    e. the Reagan tax cuts

EXERCISES

1. Suppose you oversee an economy described by the IS curve. Recall that $\bar{a} = 0$ and assume that $\bar{b} = 1/4$ and $\bar{r} = 2.5\%$. Using a diagram, draw and label what you should expect to happen to either R_t or $\tilde{Y}$ in each of the following cases?
    a. Real interest rates settle in at 2.5 percent.
    b. Real interest rates rise to 3.5 percent.
    c. Real interest rates equal 2.5 percent and $\bar{a} = 1\%$.
    d. Real interest rates rise by 4 percent and $\bar{a}_g = 1\%$.
    e. Short-run output ends up at zero, but $\bar{a} = 1\%$.

2. Suppose you are an economic advisor to a high-ranking government official in charge of interpreting economic activity. Given that the economy conforms to the IS curve where $\bar{a} = 0$, $\bar{b} = 2/5$, and $\bar{r} = 0.03$, draw and label a diagram showing the behavior of short-run output or real interest rates in each of the following instances. Assume that the situations are independent of each other and R_t initially equals $\bar{r}$.
   a. Consumer confidence plunges and consumers reduce spending ($\bar{a}_c$) by 1 percent.
   b. The Federal Reserve lowers real interest rates by 1 percent.
   c. A natural disaster destroys 8 percent of the nation's capital stock and thus lowers potential output by 5 percent. Assume that investment ($\bar{a}_i$) consequently increases by 2 percent during the first year following the shock. We ignore other years for now.

3. What does Ricardian equivalence suggest about the behavior of consumption ($\bar{a}_c$) and, by implication, the behavior of aggregate demand ($\bar{a}$) in response to an increase in government spending ($\bar{a}_g$)?

PROBLEMS

Worked Problem

1. Beginning with the national income identity, $Y_t = C_t + I_t + G_t + EX_t - IM_t$, and the following equations for each of the five sectors—$C_t = \bar{a}_c \bar{Y}_t$, $G_t = \bar{a}_g \bar{Y}_t$, $EX_t = \bar{a}_{ex} \bar{Y}_t$, $IM_t = \bar{a}_{im} \bar{Y}_t$, and $I_t/\bar{Y}_t = \bar{a}_i - \bar{b}(R_t - \bar{r})$—derive and graph an IS curve for the economy described by these equations. Begin this process by substituting the equations for each of the sectors except investment into the national income identity as follows:

$$Y_t = C_t + I_t + G_t + EX_t - IM_t$$
$$Y_t = \bar{a}_c \bar{Y}_t + I_t + \bar{a}_g \bar{Y}_t + \bar{a}_{ex} \bar{Y}_t - \bar{a}_{im} \bar{Y}_t$$

Divide both sides by $\bar{Y}_t$:

$$\frac{Y_t}{\bar{Y}_t} = \bar{a}_c + \frac{I_t}{\bar{Y}_t} + \bar{a}_g + \bar{a}_{ex} - \bar{a}_{im}$$

Substitute for $I_t/\bar{Y}_t$:

$$\frac{Y_t}{\bar{Y}_t} = \bar{a}_c + \bar{a}_i - \bar{b}(R_t - \bar{r}) + \bar{a}_g + \bar{a}_{ex} - \bar{a}_{im}$$

Gather the $\bar{a}$ terms and subtract 1 from both sides:

$$\frac{Y_t}{\bar{Y}_t} - 1 = \bar{a}_c + \bar{a}_i + \bar{a}_g + \bar{a}_{ex} - \bar{a}_{im} - 1 - \bar{b}(R_t - \bar{r})$$

Noting that $\frac{Y_t}{\bar{Y}_t} - 1 = \frac{Y_t - \bar{Y}_t}{\bar{Y}_t} = \tilde{Y}$ and $\bar{a}_c + \bar{a}_i + \bar{a}_g + \bar{a}_{ex} - \bar{a}_{im} - 1 = \bar{a}$, we simplify and get:

$$\tilde{Y}_t = \bar{a} - \bar{b}(R_t - \bar{r}).$$

To graph the IS curve, we need to solve for R_t:

$$\tilde{Y}_t = \bar{a} - \bar{b}(R_t - \bar{r})$$
$$\bar{b}(R_t - \bar{r}) = \bar{a} - \tilde{Y}_t$$
$$(R_t - \bar{r}) = \frac{\bar{a}}{\bar{b}} - \frac{1}{\bar{b}}\tilde{Y}_t$$
$$R_t = \bar{r} + \frac{\bar{a}}{\bar{b}} - \frac{1}{\bar{b}}\tilde{Y}_t$$

Note that, when the economy is fully employed, $\bar{a} = 0$, $\tilde{Y}_t = 0$, and $R_t = \bar{r}$. Note, too, that the slope of the IS curve is simply $1/\bar{b}$.

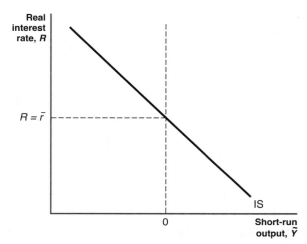

2. Assume that you are working with the same model as in Problem 1 but consumption and investment now take on the following forms: $C_t = (\bar{a}_c + \bar{x}_c \tilde{Y}_t)\bar{Y}_t$ and

$$\frac{I_t}{\bar{Y}_t} = \bar{a}_i - \bar{b}(R_t - \bar{r}) + \bar{x}_i \tilde{Y}_t.$$

   a. Derive and graph the IS curve for the economy described by these forms of consumption and investment.
   b. What is the multiplier for this economy?
   c. What is its slope?
   d. Graphically compare the results between a 1 percent increase in real interest rates for the model in Problem 1 and for the model developed here in Problem 2.
   e. Explain the intuition behind the multiplier effects in this model.

3. Assume a standard IS curve such that $Y_t = C_t + I_t + G_t + EX_t - IM_t$, and each of the five sectors are modeled as follows: $C_t = \bar{a}_c \bar{Y}_t$, $G_t = \bar{a}_g \bar{Y}_t$, $EX_t = \bar{a}_{ex} \bar{Y}_t$, $IM_t = \bar{a}_{im} \bar{Y}_t$, and $I_t/\bar{Y}_t = \bar{a}_i - \bar{b}(R_t - \bar{r})$.
   a. Suppose that the government raises taxes on everyone to balance the budget. Using a diagram, explain what happens both to short-run output and to real interest rates.
   b. Suppose, instead, that government increases spending but, at the same time, increases taxes sufficiently that no change in the budget deficit occurs. Explain what happens both to short-run output and real interest rates in this case.

CHAPTER 11 SOLUTIONS

True/False Questions

1. True. See Section 11.1 and the case study "Why Is It Called the 'IS curve'?"

2. False. Investment is *the* key channel. See Section 11.2.

3. False. It is the *gap* between R_t and $\bar{r}$ rather than just R_t that determines investment. See Section 11.2.

4. False. Changes in $\bar{Y}_t$ do not affect short-run output. See Section 11.4.

5. True. Since each element of aggregate demand is modeled, at least in part, as proportional to potential output (the *a* terms that all sum to 1), current output must change when potential output changes and by the same amount as the change in potential output. See Section 11.4.

6. True. Each is a function of potential output (the *a* terms again). See Sections 11.2 and 11.4.

7. True. The aggregation of millions of individuals makes the behavior of any single individual relatively insignificant by comparison. See Section 11.5.

8. True. Solving the IS curve for R_t reveals that the slope of the IS curve is $1/b$. See Section 11.5.

9. False. Adverse selection deals with firms' service to customers with nondisclosed risks. See Section 11.5.

10. True. See Section 11.5.

11. False. An increase in $\bar{a}_{im}$ means more imports and less domestic production, or a leftward shift of the IS curve. See Section 11.5.

12. False. Higher interest rates cause spending reductions. However, multiplier effects do cause stronger responses to policy initiatives. See Sections 11.5 and 11.6.

Multiple-Choice Questions

1. d, real interest rates. See Section 11.1.

2. b, taxes. Aggregate demand is the total of all forms of spending on goods and services. Taxes reduce the income available for private spending and are counted as government spending when expended by the government. See Section 11.2.

3. e, none of the above is correct. See Section 11.2.

4. b, investment. Investment generally is modeled as a function of the interest rate. See Section 11.2.

5. c, 18 percent, since $(R_t = 18\%) - (\bar{r} = 8\%) = 10\%$. See Section 11.2.

6. e, the real interest rate can be above or below the marginal product of capital. See Section 11.2.

7. b, $R_t \uparrow \rightarrow$ opportunity cost of $I_t \uparrow \rightarrow I_t \downarrow \rightarrow Y_t \downarrow$. See Section 11.3.

8. d, $\tilde{Y}_t = \bar{Y}_t$. See Section 11.3.

9. b, $I = (Y - T - C) + (T - G) + (IM - EX)$. See the case study "Why Is It Called the 'IS Curve'?"

10. b, $\bar{b} = 0$. This would generate a vertical rather than a downward sloping IS curve. See Section 11.4 and solve $\tilde{Y} = \bar{a} - \bar{b}(R_t - \bar{r})$ for R_t.

11. d, a shift of the IS curve. A change in real interest rates causes a movement along the IS curve. A change in consumption is tempting because it is possible for short-run output to affect consumption under relatively believable conditions, such as shown regarding multiplier effects. See Section 11.4 and 11.5.

12. d, a change in R_t. A change in $\bar{r}$ is tempting, but $\bar{r}$ is a constant and not on one of the axes. See Section 11.4.

13. e, a change in interest rates by the Fed. All the other options shift the IS curve. See Section 11.4.

14. e, an increase in real interest rates. See Section 11.4.

15. a, an increase in Canadian unemployment. See Section 11.4.

16. e, do all of the above. See Section 11.5.

17. d, all the above. See Section 11.5.

18. b, higher interest rates. A leftward shift of the IS curve brought on by higher taxes causes interest rates to fall. See Section 11.5.

19. d, the gap between real interest rates and the marginal product of capital. All the others are part of the investment decision in the model but not one of the main determinants. The other main determinant is cash flow. See Section 11.5.

20. b, determining real interest rates. See Section 11.5.

21. c, educational tax credits. These are based on the number and age of child dependents, not on the state of the economy or one's income. See Section 11.5.

22. c, the use of discretionary fiscal policy. See Section 11.5.

23. c, increased deficit spending. The whole point of Ricardian equivalence is that the timing of taxation does not matter, just the present discounted value of lifetime income. See Section 11.5.

24. a, the New Deal Program. See the case study "Fiscal Policy and Depressions."

Exercises

1. For the equation $\tilde{Y} = 0 - \frac{1}{4}(R_t - 0.025)$, parts a and b are shown in Figure 1 and parts c, d, and e are shown in Figure 2.
   a. Short-run output equals zero and real interest rates equal 2.5 percent.
   b. Short-run output equals $-\frac{1}{4}$ percent and real interest rates equal 3.5 percent.

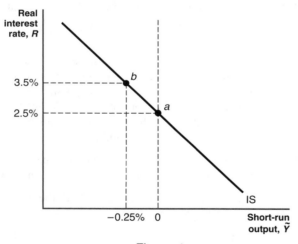

Figure 1

c. Short-run output equals 1 percent and real interest rates equal 2.5 percent.
d. Short-run output equals zero and real interest rates equal 6.5 percent.
   Note that $\tilde{Y} = 0.01 - \frac{1}{4}(0.065 - 0.025)$ requires $\tilde{Y} = 0$.
e. This problem, although differently expressed, generates the same solution as in part d.

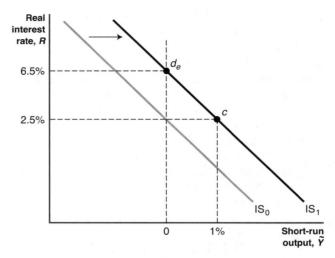

Figure 2

2. Parts a and b are shown in Figure 3 and part c is shown in Figure 4.

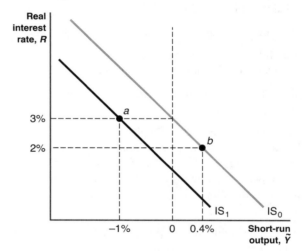

Figure 3

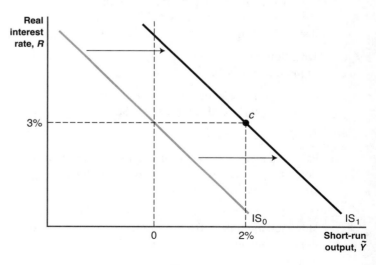

Figure 4

a. Falling consumer confidence causes the IS curve to shift to the left as $\bar{a}_c$ gets smaller. Short-run output equals –1 percent and real interest rates remain constant at 3 percent in the short run.

b. Lower real interest rates of 2 percent rather than 3 percent stimulate investment spending and raise short-run output to 0.4 percent on IS_0. Note that $\tilde{Y} = 0 - {}^2/_5(0.02 - 0.03) = 0.004$ or 0.4%.

c. Lower production capabilities cause potential output ($\bar{Y}$) to decrease but less potential also lowers current output by the same amount, so that the IS curve does not shift from the capital stock destruction. However, as firms experience a higher marginal product of capital and seek to replace the destroyed capital stock, investment increases, so that current output rises relative to potential. Short-run output thus rises to 2 percent and real interest rates still equal 3 percent in the short run.

3. An increase in government spending causes $\bar{a}_g$ as well as $\bar{a}$ to increase. According to Ricardian equivalence, consumers recognize that their future tax liabilities have increased and the present value of their disposable income consequently has decreased. Therefore they reduce their consumption accordingly and $\bar{a}_c$ falls by the same amount as $\bar{a}_g$ increased, leaving current and short-run output unchanged. By implication, the value of $\bar{a}$ also remains unchanged at $\bar{a} = 0$.

Problems

1. Worked Problem. The problem is worked in the text.

2. a. Begin this time as well by substituting the equations for each of the sectors except investment into the national income identity as follows:

$$Y_t = C_t + I_t + G_t + EX_t - IM_t$$

$$Y_t = \left(\bar{a}_c + \bar{x}_c\tilde{Y}_t\right)\bar{Y}_t + I_t + \bar{a}_g\bar{Y}_t + \bar{a}_{ex}\bar{Y}_t - \bar{a}_{im}\bar{Y}_t$$

Divide both sides by $\bar{Y}_t$:

$$\frac{Y_t}{\bar{Y}_t} = \bar{a}_c + \bar{x}_c\tilde{Y}_t + \frac{I_t}{\bar{Y}_t} + \bar{a}_g + \bar{a}_{ex} - \bar{a}_{im}$$

Substitute for $I_t/\bar{Y}_t$:

$$\frac{Y_t}{\bar{Y}_t} = \bar{a}_c + \bar{x}_c\tilde{Y}_t + \bar{a}_i - \bar{b}\left(R_t - \bar{r}\right) + \bar{x}_i\tilde{Y}_t + \bar{a}_g + \bar{a}_{ex} - \bar{a}_{im}$$

Gather the $\bar{a}$ and the $\tilde{Y}_t$ terms and subtract 1 from both sides:

$$\frac{Y_t}{\bar{Y}_t} - 1 = \bar{a}_c + \bar{a}_i + \bar{a}_g + \bar{a}_{ex} - \bar{a}_{im} - 1 + \bar{x}_c\tilde{Y}_t + \bar{x}_i\tilde{Y}_t - \bar{b}\left(R_t - \bar{r}\right)$$

Noting that $\dfrac{Y_t}{\bar{Y}_t} - 1 = \dfrac{Y_t - \bar{Y}_t}{\bar{Y}_t} = \tilde{Y}_t$ and $\bar{a}_c + \bar{a}_i + \bar{a}_g + \bar{a}_{ex} - \bar{a}_{im} - 1 = \bar{a}$, we simplify and get:

$$\tilde{Y}_t = \bar{a} + \left(\bar{x}_c + \bar{x}_i\right)\tilde{Y}_t - \bar{b}\left(R_t - \bar{r}\right).$$

Gather and solve for the $\tilde{Y}_t$ terms:

$$\tilde{Y}_t - \left(\bar{x}_c + \bar{x}_i\right)\tilde{Y}_t = \bar{a} - \bar{b}\left(R_t - \bar{r}\right)$$

$$\left(1 - \bar{x}_c - \bar{x}_i\right)\tilde{Y}_t = \bar{a} - \bar{b}\left(R_t - \bar{r}\right)$$

$$\tilde{Y}_t = \frac{1}{1 - \bar{x}_c - \bar{x}_i}\left[\bar{a} - \bar{b}\left(R_t - \bar{r}\right)\right]$$

To graph this new IS curve, we need to solve for R_t, just as we did in Problem 1:

$$\tilde{Y}_t = \frac{1}{1 - \bar{x}_c - \bar{x}_i}\left[\bar{a} - \bar{b}\left(R_t - \bar{r}\right)\right]$$

Split up $\bar{a}$ and $\bar{b}\left(R_t - \bar{r}\right)$:

$$\tilde{Y}_t = \frac{\bar{a}}{1 - \bar{x}_c - \bar{x}_i} - \frac{\bar{b}}{1 - \bar{x}_c - \bar{x}_i}\left(R_t - \bar{r}\right)$$

$$\frac{\bar{b}}{1 - \bar{x}_c - \bar{x}_i}\left(R_t - \bar{r}\right) = \frac{\bar{a}}{1 - \bar{x}_c - \bar{x}_i} - \tilde{Y}_t$$

invert $\bar{b}/(1 - x_c - x_i)$ and multiply both sides by $(1 - x_c - x_i)/\bar{b}$:

$$\left(R_t - \bar{r}\right) = \frac{\bar{a}}{\bar{b}} - \frac{1 - \bar{x}_c - \bar{x}_i}{\bar{b}}\tilde{Y}_t$$

$$R_t = \bar{r} + \frac{\bar{a}}{\bar{b}} - \frac{1 - \bar{x}_c - \bar{x}_i}{\bar{b}}\tilde{Y}_t$$

Note that, when the economy is fully employed, $\bar{a} = 0$, $\tilde{Y}_t = 0$, and $R_t = \bar{r}$. Figure 5 shows the resulting graph.

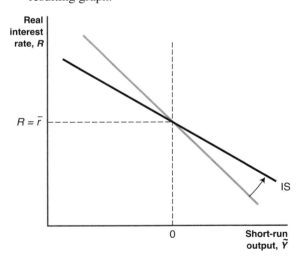

Figure 5

b. The multiplier for this economy is $1/(1 - \bar{x}_c - \bar{x}_i)$. Note that, for values of $\bar{x}_c$ and $\bar{x}_i$ that sum to less than 1 this multiplier always is positive and greater than 1. Values of $\bar{x}_c$ and $\bar{x}_i$ that sum to more than 1 produce a negative multiplier and negative output, which does not make any sense, so we can infer that such values are unrealistic.

c. The slope is $-(1 - \bar{x}_c - \bar{x}_i)/\bar{b}$, which is less than $-1/\bar{b}$ and flatter than without the multiplier effects.

d. In Figure 6, as the bold IS curve and dotted lines illustrate, we see that accounting for multiplier effects generates a greater impact on short-run output than it otherwise would with the same increase in interest rates. In other words, when interest rates increase from $\bar{r}$ to R, the dashed IS curve generates a much smaller decrease in short-run output than the solid IS curve.

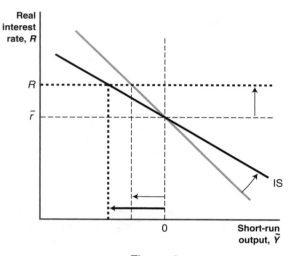

Figure 6

e. The additional spending effects by consumers and firms in response to changes in short-run output, $\bar{x}_c \tilde{Y}_t$ and $\bar{x}_i \tilde{Y}_t$, cause any shock or disturbance to the economy to be magnified beyond its initial impact.

3. a. Raising taxes reduces the amount of income available to consumers for purchases and hence the demand for output. Short-run output falls, corresponding to the change between points a and b, while interest rates remain unchanged.

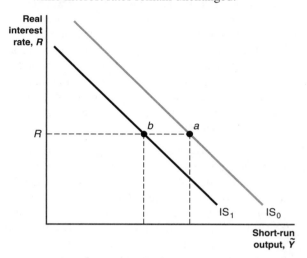

Figure 7

b. If government spending increases are matched by tax increases, then decreased consumption simply offsets increased government spending and the IS curve remains unchanged.

| # Monetary Policy and the Phillips Curve

OVERVIEW

With the addition of the monetary policy (the MP curve) to the IS curve, we have a complete description of the demand side of the economy in the short-run model. Add the Phillips curve, and the short-run model is complete. The MP curve represents the policy intentions of the central bank regarding the level of real interest rates it determines appropriate for the economy. The short-run model also shows how those real interest rates interact with the markets for goods and services to influence the level of aggregate demand. The Phillips curve adds the dynamics of inflation relative to short-run output, which then interact with aggregate demand and determine the level of overall economic activity. Finally, the complete short-run model allows economists to address the impact of shocks to both aggregate supply and aggregate demand and to explore the impact of the policy tools used to address them.

KEY CONCEPTS

The *monetary policy,* or MP, *curve* interacts with the IS curve and represents the real interest rate chosen for an economy by its central bank. It exploits the fact that, due to sticky inflation, the nominal and real rates of interest move very closely together in the short run.

The *IS-MP diagram* consists of an IS curve and an MP curve graphed together with the real interest rate on the vertical axis and short-run output on the horizontal axis. When $\bar{a} = \tilde{Y}_t = 0$, the MP curve should be set so that $R_t = \bar{r}$. See Figure 12.3 in the text for the first use of the IS-MP diagram.

The *federal funds rate* is the interest rate paid by one bank to another for the overnight use of excess reserves. The Federal Reserve controls the federal funds rate by determining the level of reserves in the banking system through its purchase and sale of U.S. Treasury securities. Through the term structure of interest rates and its control of the federal funds rate, the Fed is able to influence all other interest rates in the economy.

The *Fisher equation*, first introduced in Chapter 8, describes the approximate relationship between nominal and real interest rates and inflation: $i_t = R_t + \pi_t$. Together with sticky inflation, the Fisher equation lets us see how nominal and real interest rates move together in the very short run.

The *sticky inflation assumption* derives from observing that, in the short run, prices change more slowly than the money supply. Several explanations help us to understand the justification behind this assumption, including imperfect information and costly computations in the price-setting process, Fed actions themselves and money market conditions, price and wage contracts and the bargaining costs associated with renegotiation, as well as social norms and money illusion. (Money illusion occurs when people focus on the face, or nominal, value of money rather than on its purchasing power, or *real* value.)

Long and variable lags refers to the time involved in collecting data, determining the nature and severity of a shock, deciding on and implementing the appropriate interest rate changes, then waiting for those changes to affect investment demand and, ultimately, output. Economists point out that it generally takes anywhere from six to 18 months before economic activity experiences any significant impact from interest rate changes.

The *term structure of interest rates* describes the relationship between long- and short-term interest rates. Risk considerations aside, individuals should be indifferent between holding several short-term bonds and a single longer-term bond over the same time period. If the longer-term interest rate is an average of the short-term rates, then expected increases/decreases of any of the short-term rates will cause the long-term rate to rise/fall as well.

The *Phillips curve* describes the positive, or direct, relationship between changes in inflation and short-run output, $\Delta\pi_t = \bar{v}\tilde{Y}_t$, or its graphical equivalent, $\pi_t = \pi_{t-1} + \bar{v}\tilde{Y}_t$. It states that positive short-run output causes inflation to increase because of increased resource demand. Likewise, negative short-run output leads to decreases in inflation for similar but opposite reasons.

Expected inflation is an important component of firms' price-setting behavior. Firms begin with what they expect inflation to be, then make adjustments based on current market conditions. How individuals form their inflation expectations generates a lot of interest and two primary methods are addressed: adaptive expectations in this chapter and rational expectations in Chapter 13.

Adaptive expectations occur when individuals simply expect inflation in this period to continue at the same level as last period and are a driving force in the sticky inflation assumption. When inflation changes during the current period, next period's level of expected inflation will change accordingly. Adaptive expectations become a particular problem when trying to combat increasingly high inflation.

Price shocks occur when something causes the Phillips curve to shift either upward or downward. Examples of price shocks include larger-than-expected changes in crude oil prices (either positive or negative), similar changes in the prices of other materials, and union behavior. Formally, they become the $\bar{o}$ in the complete Phillips curve, $\pi_t = \pi_{t-1} + \bar{v}\tilde{Y}_t + \bar{o}$, and again can be either positive or negative.

Demand-pull inflation occurs as a result of economic forces originating in aggregate demand, such as increased consumer demand or government spending. It could also originate from an expansionary monetary policy and be the equivalent of Chapter 8's "too much money chasing too few goods."

Cost-push inflation occurs as a result of economic forces originating in aggregate supply, such as increases in the cost of crude oil or labor.

Disinflation means a reduction of inflation to a lower and more stable inflation rate. Disinflation usually imposes significant costs on an economy, both in terms of unemployment and lost output.

The *Great Inflation* refers to the period of time in the late 1960s and 1970s when the United States experienced its worst bout with inflation since World War II. It occurred in part due to imperfect information about the state of the economy, two oil shocks in the 1970s, and loose monetary policy.

The *opportunity cost* of holding money in today's money markets, either as cash or in a non- or very low-interest-bearing checking account, is the interest that could have been earned had that money been held in a higher-interest-bearing money market or mutual funds account.

Open market operations (OMOs) serve as the primary tool of the Federal Reserve System in its efforts to affect the money supply and thus change interest rates in the economy. OMOs, or the Fed's buying and selling of U.S. Treasury bonds, directly affect the level of reserves in the banking system. Subsequently, changes in the amount of bank reserves traded in the federal funds market cause changes in the corresponding federal funds rate. As previously mentioned, the federal funds rate influences other interest rates in the banking system and ultimately economic activity throughout the entire economy.

A second tool of monetary policy is the *reserve requirements* that the Fed places on banks at the individual level to insure that they have sufficient deposits on hand to meet the daily requirements of their clientele as they write checks and make other financial transactions.

The *reserves* that banks use to meet their reserve requirements are primarily kept on deposit at the central bank and typically earn no interest. An exception to this rule was made during the financial crisis when the Federal Reserve began paying a very low interest rate on the bank reserves it held.

The third tool of monetary policy, the *discount rate,* is the interest rate that banks get charged when they borrow money directly from the Federal Reserve in its role as a *lender of last resort,* a place where banks can turn when they come up short of the reserves necessary to meet their reserve requirements.

TRUE/FALSE QUESTIONS

1. The Federal Reserve cannot "set" the federal funds rate.

2. Central banks have the ability to determine real interest rates in the short run.

3. Because inflation is slow to adjust, an increase in the nominal interest rate will have no effect on the real rate of interest.

4. Cost-push inflation occurs when consumers push firms to produce at higher levels of production in order to meet demand.

5. The Phillips curve relates the level of economic activity to the level of inflation.

6. According to the classical dichotomy, monetary policy has no ability to affect real variables in the economy, only nominal variables.

7. Under the assumption of adaptive expectations, the current period's level of expected inflation is predetermined.

8. Sticky inflation and adaptive expectations make it more difficult for monetary authorities to pursue their policy objectives.

9. The nature of peoples' inflationary expectations makes it necessary to create recessions to reduce expected inflation.

10. If it's your own money you choose to hold, money markets provide one of the few exceptions to the principle of opportunity cost.

MULTIPLE-CHOICE QUESTIONS

1. The mission of the Federal Reserve System includes each of the following except
   a. maintaining a stable price level.
   b. maintaining maximum sustainable output growth.
   c. maintaining maximum sustainable levels of employment.
   d. promoting stability and efficiency within the financial system.
   e. maintaining low and stable inflation.

2. Which of the following is not part of the formal structure of the short-run model?
   a. MP curve
   b. Fisher equation
   c. IS curve
   d. Okun's law
   e. Phillips curve

3. The sticky inflation assumption means that
   a. inflation changes only in periods of time exceeding six months.
   b. inflation does not respond to monetary policy in the very short run.
   c. central banks have the ability to set the real interest rate.
   d. the classical dichotomy does not really hold after all.
   e. inflation is not related to real interest rates.

4. Which of the following is inconsistent with a stable IS-MP outcome where there is no need for change?
   a. $R_t = \bar{r}$
   b. $\tilde{Y}_t = 0$
   c. $Y_t = \bar{Y}_t$
   d. $\bar{a} = 1$
   e. none of the above

5. A sudden decline in housing construction that caused short-run output to decline could be offset by
   a. an increase in government spending.
   b. a decrease in the real interest rate.
   c. a decrease in the federal funds rate.
   d. all of the above.
   e. only a and b.

6. Economists caution against the use of fine-tuning tactics when managing the economy following a disturbance because
   a. it takes time to analyze the data and determine the nature of the shock.
   b. changing interest rates is an imprecise science at best.
   c. it takes time for interest rate changes to have an effect on investment and the economy.
   d. all of the above
   e. only a and c

7. According to the term structure of interest rates, when the interest rate paid on a short-term government bonds goes up,
   a. the interest rate on longer-term government bonds will go down.
   b. other interest rates will remain unchanged.
   c. longer-term interest rates will move in the same direction.
   d. other short-term interest rates will not be affected.
   e. none of the above will occur.

8. Which of the following completely describes the Phillips curve?
   a. $\Delta \pi_t = \bar{v} \tilde{Y}_t$
   b. $u_t - \bar{u} = -1/2 \tilde{Y}_t$
   c. $\pi_t = \pi_{t-1} + \bar{v} \tilde{Y}_t + \bar{o}$
   d. $u_t - u_{t-1} + \bar{v} \tilde{Y}_t + \bar{o}$
   e. $\Delta u_t = \bar{v} \tilde{Y}_t$

9. The Phillips curve consists of two components intuitively described as _____ and _____.
   a. expected inflation, demand conditions
   b. demand, supply conditions
   c. expected inflation, supply conditions
   d. unemployment, demand conditions
   e. unemployment, supply conditions

10. The term π_t^e refers to
    a. adaptive expectations.
    b. rational expectations.
    c. expected inflation.
    d. last period's inflation.
    e. current inflation.

11. Which statement fails to describe the behavior of the
    Phillips curve?
    a. When output is at potential, inflation remains
       constant.
    b. When the economy is booming, inflation
       increases.
    c. When output falls short of its potential, inflation
       decreases.
    d. A steeper Phillips curve causes inflation to
       increase.
    e. Inflation changes are positively correlated with
       short-run output.

12. For short-run output to have no impact on the rate of
    inflation, the slope of the Phillips curve ($\bar{v}$) would need
    to be
    a. very steep.
    b. relatively flat.
    c. horizontal.
    d. vertical.
    e. equal to 1.

13. Which of the following is not a possible source of a
    price shock to the economy?
    a. oil price changes
    b. land price changes
    c. increased regulation
    d. union contracts
    e. interest rate changes

14. The Phillips curve used in the complete short-run
    model of the economy was developed by
    a. A. W. Phillips.
    b. A. W. Phillips and Edmund Phelps.
    c. Milton Friedman and A. W. Phillips.
    d. Paul Samuelson and James Tobin.
    e. Edmund Phelps and Milton Friedman.

15. Which of the following reasons led Paul Volcker to use
    monetary policy to end the Great Inflation?
    a. output losses
    b. congressional mandate
    c. high unemployment

d. excessively loose monetary policy during the
   previous decade
e. large trade deficits

16. Which of the following factors did not contribute to the
    rise in inflation now called the Great Inflation?
    a. the 1973–1974 oil embargo/crisis
    b. the 1979 Iranian/Iraqi oil disruption/crisis
    c. excessive selling of government treasury bonds by
       the Fed
    d. the Fed's open market operations during the produc-
       tivity slowdown of the 1970s
    e. improper reliance on a presumed trade-off between
       inflation and unemployment

17. To fight the inflation of the late 1970s, the Fed raised
    real interest rates high enough to cause
    a. investment to drop substantially.
    b. short-run output to become negative.
    c. the worst recession since World War II.
    d. inflation to fall by half.
    e. all of the above.

18. As a result of ending the Great Inflation, monetary
    authorities caused the economy to experience
    a. lower inflation.
    b. high unemployment.
    c. lost output.
    d. a deep recession.
    e. all of the above.

19. Which of the following does not rely on the sticky
    inflation assumption?
    a. the MP curve
    b. the Phillips curve
    c. expected inflation
    d. adaptive expectations
    e. the classical dichotomy

20. Explanations supporting the assumption of sticky
    inflation include each of the following except
    a. imperfect information on the part of firms and
       individuals.
    b. the cost of evaluating market conditions for more
       frequent price setting.
    c. uncertainty about central bank policy intentions.
    d. wage and material contracts set in nominal terms.
    e. wage indexing pegged to the inflation rate.

21. Explanations supporting the assumption of sticky
    inflation include each of the following except
    a. social norms regarding fairness and equity.
    b. bargaining costs between factors of production,
       firms, and retail outlets.
    c. central bank policy explanations.
    d. individuals' ability to understand the inflation
       process.
    e. money illusion.

22. Which of the following characteristics does not describe nominal interest rates?
    a. the opportunity cost of holding money
    b. the price of borrowing money
    c. inversely related to the demand for money
    d. set by Federal Reserve fiat
    e. None of the above; they all do.

23. Central banks prefer to base monetary policy on interest rate targets rather than monetary aggregates because
    a. the impact of monetary policy occurs through its influence on real interest rates.
    b. money demand experiences many shocks that fuel interest rate volatility.
    c. financial market innovations lead to unforeseeable shifts in money demand.
    d. interest rate volatility destabilizes economic activity in a country.
    e. of all of the above reasons.

24. By targeting interest rates, monetary authorities implicitly adopt policies that
    a. generate greater stability in interest-sensitive sectors of the economy.
    b. automatically increase or decrease the money supply in response to changes in money demand.
    c. insulate output in an economy from money market disturbances.
    d. make central bank behavior more predictable.
    e. accomplish each of the above.

25. The Fed's purchase of bonds in the open market will
    a. cause the supply of bonds to fall.
    b. reduce the size of the monetary base.
    c. lower interest rates.
    d. decrease the money supply.
    e. decrease the size of the national debt.

26. If the Fed wants to raise interest rates, it must
    a. increase money demand.
    b. increase the size of the national debt.
    c. increase the money supply.
    d. sell government bonds.
    e. buy government bonds.

27. Which of the following does the Federal Reserve use as its primary tool for carrying out monetary policy on a daily basis?
    a. open market operations
    b. reserve requirements
    c. the discount rate
    d. credit card regulation
    e. money market operations

EXERCISES

1. Suppose the economy currently is experiencing positive short-run output.
   a. Show this situation on an IS-MP diagram.
   b. Would there be an inflationary threat or a deflationary threat? Use a Phillips curve to support your answer.
   c. Demonstrate what the Fed could do in this situation to resolve the threat you identified in part b.

2. Suppose that the economy is characterized in part by the Phillips curve, $\pi_t = \pi_{t-1} + \bar{v}\tilde{Y}_t + \bar{o}$, and experiences a positive productivity shock so that all workers now produce more for the same work effort.
   a. Show this situation on a Phillips curve diagram.
   b. Explain what is happening to each element of the Phillips curve equation.

3. Suppose that the central bank observed that interest rates in the money market were rising and needed to determine why this was the case.
   a. What would it already know in terms of solving this puzzle, and how would that help? Use a money market diagram to support your explanation.
   b. What would it be able to do in response to restore the previous level of interest rates? Again demonstrate your solution on your money market diagram.

PROBLEMS

Worked Problem

1. Suppose you have just been nominated for the position of chairman of the Federal Reserve System and are testifying before the Senate in your confirmation hearing. The senators have heard of the Fisher equation and know that nominal interest rates are the sum of real interest rates and inflation ($i_t = R_t + \pi_t$). They also are familiar with the IS and Phillips curves but want to know how nominal interest rates can be used successfully to control inflation, when, according to the Fisher equation, they are a function of inflation. Explain.

   To address the answer to their question, break the answer into three parts dealing with the MP curve, the IS curve, and the Phillips curve. Refer to the diagrams they are familiar with in Figure 1.
   a. First, introduce to them the MP curve as representing the level of real interest rates and as indicative of how the Fed can change real interest rates. Explain that, even though the Fed can directly affect the (nominal) federal funds rate only by changing bank reserves through open market operations, in that process it also changes the real rate of interest, because in the very short run (six months or less)

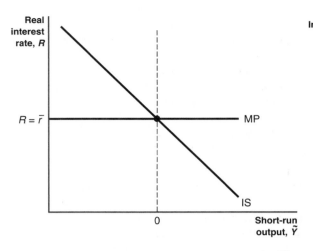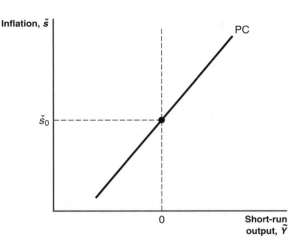

Figure 1

inflation is very slow to adjust. As long as inflation does not change, any change in nominal interest rates effectively changes real interest rates.

b. Second, using the IS curve, explain that real interest rates affect short-run output through its interest-sensitive components. Remind them that, in the simplest cases, investment spending (factories and homes, for example) is the only interest-sensitive spending component but that other consumer spending and activity in the foreign sector also react to interest rate changes. In particular, they react to the difference between real interest rates and the marginal product of capital ($R_t = \bar{r}$). Explain that, when $R_t < \bar{r}$, interest-sensitive spending increases and when $R_t > \bar{r}$, interest-sensitive spending decreases.

c. Third, turn to the Phillips curve and explain how short-run output affects changes in inflation. Indicate that positive short-run output means that firms are producing above their potential, and sustained activity levels of that magnitude produce upward pressure on prices and cause the price level to increase, as firms respond to those pressures. Likewise, when short-run output is negative, some resources remain idle and the same natural competitive pressures cause prices to rise more slowly than if production levels equaled potential output.

d. Together these three curves can explain how nominal interest rates influence the level of inflation experienced in an economy.

2. Suppose you work at a central bank and are given the task of stabilizing output as your primary responsibility.
   a. Using the equation for investment from the IS curve, explain what this goal means for investment spending in your country.
   b. How does your explanation for investment affect the IS curve itself, given that other interest-sensitive spending also exists?

c. What does the goal of output stabilization require of monetary authorities when shocks to the demand for goods and services occur in the IS curve?

d. What policy action would the central bank (the Fed) need to undertake to accomplish the action you identified in part c?

3. In your work at the central bank, output stability remains your central charge. However, you now also are required to maintain a constant level of inflation.
   a. Imagine that a disruption in crude oil supplies causes an inflation shock to occur and $\bar{o}$ to become positive. Use a Phillips curve diagram to demonstrate and explain what must be done to restore inflation to its original level.
   b. Show how this will affect the economy on an IS-MP diagram.
   c. Explain how the central bank can reconcile the two goals of maintaining output stability and constant inflation in the face of an inflation shock.

CHAPTER 12 SOLUTIONS

True/False Questions

1. True. Technically the federal funds rate is a market rate of interest determined by the borrowing and lending activity between banks in the federal funds market. The target federal funds rate is established by the Fed setting a goal for it then standing ready to buy or sell the reserves banks use in the federal funds market, so that the goal for the target rate is met. See Section 12.2 and 12.7.

2. True. Given the assumption, or stylized fact, of sticky inflation. See Section 12.2.

3. False. It will have an effect. Recall that $R_t = i_t - \pi_t$. See Section 12.2.

4. False. This statement describes demand-pull inflation. Cost-push inflation occurs when firms' production costs rise independent of the level of production. See Section 12.3.

5. False. Although Phillips himself first thought this to be true, economic activity actually is related to the *change* in the level of inflation. See the case study "A Brief History of the Phillips Curve."

6. True in the long run after inflation adjustments are made but false in the short run when inflation is sticky. See Section 12.5.

7. True. Adaptive expectations means people expect something that cannot be changed. See Section 12.5.

8. True. See Sections 12.3 and 12.8.

9. False, unless adaptive expectations are the only way people form their inflation expectations. See Section 12.8.

10. False. This statement overlooks the forgone interest of putting your money in an interest-bearing account such as a money market account. See Section 12.6.

Multiple-Choice Questions

1. a, maintaining a stable price level. A stable or constant price level is different from price stability, which can be achieved on a relative basis with low and stable inflation. As you work through this material, note that maintaining a low rate of inflation still allows the price level to rise each period. This question comes from the chapter's introductory quote by Chairman Bernanke.

2. d, Okun's law. While the Fisher equation might seem like an appropriate answer, note that, because of the sticky inflation assumption and the Fisher equation, the MP curve can effect real interest rates by targeting a nominal interest rate, the federal funds rate. See Section 12.1.

3. b, inflation does not respond to monetary policy in the very short run. Part c is tempting but does not exclude the long run, when inflation does change. See Section 12.2.

4. d, $\bar{a} = 1$. The value for $\bar{a}$ instead should be equal to zero. See Section 12.2.

5. d, all of the above. See Section 12.2.

6. e, only a and c. See Section 12.2.

7. c, longer-term interest rates will move in the same direction. See the case study "The Term Structure of Interest Rates."

8. c, $\pi_t = \pi_{t-1} + \bar{v}\tilde{Y}_t + \bar{o}$. Part a is tempting but not complete, the shock still is missing. See Section 12.3.

9. a, expected inflation and demand conditions. See Section 12.3.

10. c, expected inflation. See Section 12.3.

11. d, A steeper Phillips curve . . . A change in the slope of the Phillips curve does not cause it to shift; therefore, inflation remains unchanged. See Section 12.3.

12. c, horizontal. See Section 12.3.

13. e, interest rate changes. See Section 12.3.

14. e, Edmund Phelps and Milton Friedman. See the case study "A Brief History of the Phillips Curve."

15. d, excessively loose monetary policy during the previous decade, which helped cause the double-digit inflation that existed when Volcker took over as chairman. See Section 12.4.

16. c, excessive selling of government treasury bonds by the Fed. See Section 12.4.

17. e, all of the above. See Section 12.4.

18. e, all of the above. See Section 12.4.

19. e, the classical dichotomy. Note that the classical dichotomy holds only in the long run, when inflation is not sticky. See Section 12.5.

20. e, wage indexing pegged to the inflation rate. See Section 12.5.

21. d, individuals ability to understand the inflation process. See Section 12.5.

22. d, set by Federal Reserve fiat. Rather, they are determined by the Fed's control of the monetary base, primarily through open market operations. See Section 12.6, particularly the case study on open market operations.

23. e, of all of the above reasons. Make sure you understand the reasons for each of these statements as given in the text. See Section 12.6.

24. e, accomplish each of the above. Again, make sure you understand the reasons why interest rate targeting accomplishes each of these objectives as given in the text. See Section 12.6.

25. c, lower interest rates. See Section 12.7.

26. d, sell government bonds, which will lower their price, causing the interest rate to increase. Although part e looks like an acceptable answer and actually includes the sale of government bonds, it includes the purchase of government bonds as well and, therefore, is not the best choice. See Section 12.7.

27. a, open market operations, the sale or purchase of government treasury securities in the open market. See Section 12.7.

Exercises

1. In an economy with positive short-run output we have the following situations:

   a. An IS-MP diagram with positive short-run output is shown in Figure 2. Note that, at point *a,* lower real interest rates have generated positive short-run output.

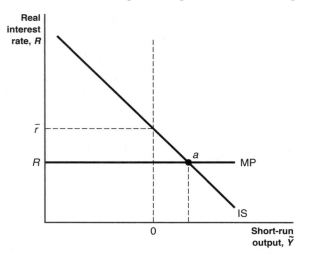

Figure 2

   b. The inflationary threat in this scenario can be seen in a Phillips curve diagram, as shown in Figure 3. Note that, at point *b* (illustrated by all three arrows labeled *b*), positive short-run output has caused inflation to rise to π_1.

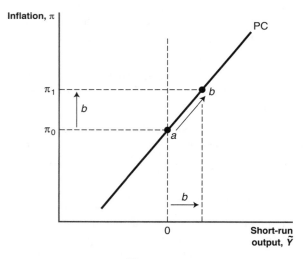

Figure 3

c. By raising real interest rates from R to $\bar{r}$, the Fed can close the positive output gap (illustrated by the movements labeled *c*) and eliminate the inflation threat from part b, as shown in Figure 4.

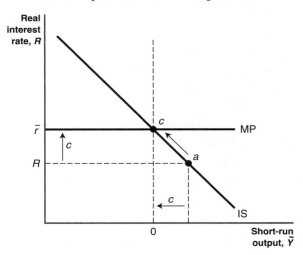

Figure 4

2. a. Since more output is produced with the same level of resources, firms compete through smaller price increases and the positive productivity shock has the effect of shifting the Phillips curve down, lowering inflation from π_0 to π_1, as shown in Figure 5.

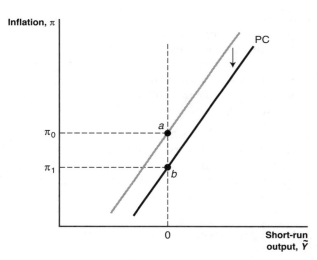

Figure 5

   b. In the Phillips curve itself, $\pi_t = \pi_{t-1} + v\tilde{Y}_t + \bar{o}$, $\pi_t = \pi_1$, $\pi_{t-1} = \pi_0$, $\tilde{Y}_t = 0$, and $\bar{o} = \pi_t - \pi_0$; that is, $\bar{o} < 0$. Note that it is entirely possible, and probable, that both output and potential output are larger as a consequence of the productivity increase, but when both Y_t and $\bar{Y}_t$ increase by the same amount, $\tilde{Y}_t$ remains equal to zero.

3a. In this case, the central bank already would know about its own behavior and have very good information on the activity of commercial banks. The model explicitly implies this by graphing the money supply as a vertical line. Knowing this would help by allowing the central bank to determine that the increase in rates from i^* to i came as a consequence of changes in money demand, as shown in Figure 6, and not from the money supply process.

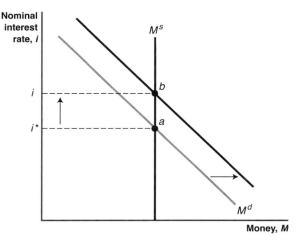

Figure 6

b. In response to an increase in money demand, the central bank could increase the money supply to maintain interest rates constant at i^*, as shown in Figure 7 by points a and b.

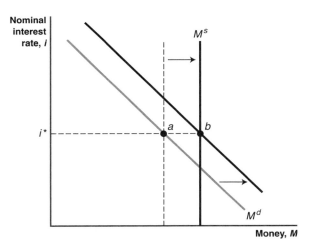

Figure 7

Problems

1. Worked Problem. The problem is worked in the text.
2. a. The equation for investment, $I_t/\bar{Y}_t = \bar{a}_i - \bar{b}(R_t - \bar{r})$, states that any fluctuations of investment from $\bar{a}_i$ arise only when real interest rates do not equal the marginal product of capital.
   b. Investment provides the interest-sensitive component for the IS curve, $\tilde{Y}_t = \bar{a} - \bar{b}(R_t - \bar{r})$. Since $\bar{a}$ equals zero in the absence of shocks to the IS curve, $\tilde{Y}_t = 0$ when $R_t = \bar{r}$. Any fluctuations or instability in short-run output arises only when real interest rates do not equal the marginal product of capital. Including other interest-sensitive spending simply makes the effect of interest rate changes even larger.
   c. In the face of shocks to the IS curve, which cause it to shift either to the left or to the right, output stabilization requires that the central bank raise or lower interest rates in the same direction as the change in short-run output to return output to its potential. Thus, in Figure 8, when there is a positive shock to the IS curve ($\bar{a} > 0$), short-run output becomes positive and must be offset through higher real interest rates, if monetary authorities wish to maintain a stable short-run output equal to zero. Similarly, for $\bar{a} < 0$ and $\tilde{Y}_t < 0$ the central bank must lower real interest rates to stabilize short-run output.

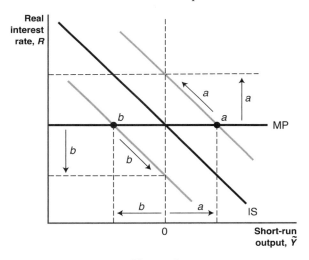

Figure 8

   d. To raise interest rates, the central bank (the Fed) would need to sell bonds; and to lower interest rates, the Fed would need to purchase bonds.
3. a. The crude oil disruption causes the Phillips curve to shift up to PC_1 from PC_0 by the amount $\bar{o} = \pi_1 - \pi_0$. To return inflation back to π_0, the economy must move from point a to point b on PC_1 in Figure 9.

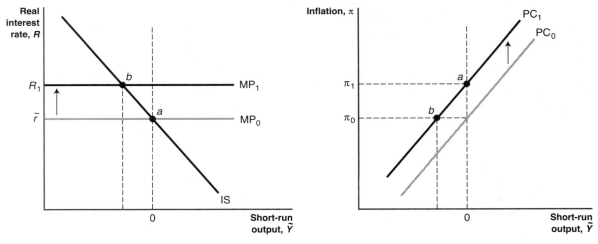

Figure 9

b. On the IS-MP diagram in Figure 9, this also means moving from point *a* to point *b* by raising real interest rates from $\bar{r}$ to R_1, causing short-run output to become negative.

c. Of course, the action in part b is destabilizing in terms of short-run output, but it is also the only proven way to reduce inflation. A trade-off must be made between increased inflation and negative short-run output. Note from Problems 2 and 3 that no such trade-off exists when it comes to shocks to aggregate demand, only with inflation shocks.

CHAPTER 13

Stabilization Policy and the AS/AD Framework

OVERVIEW

Following the study of this chapter, you should think of monetary policy as a systematic approach of addressing shocks that occur in the economy in order to produce at full employment, ensure output stability at potential output, and maintain low and stable inflation. In other words, as a general rule, the central bank fights higher-than-targeted inflation with higher real interest rates and lower-than-targeted inflation with lower real interest rates. Combining this type of monetary policy with the IS curve generates an aggregate demand (AD) curve that relates short-run output to inflation and allows the central bank to determine the appropriate short-run output for the prevailing inflation rate. This interaction of aggregate demand with aggregate supply (AS, the Phillips curve) completely characterizes the short-run model in a single diagram known as the AS/AD framework. Within this framework, we can study the importance of expectations, analyze the debate over rules versus discretion, and evaluate the importance of explicit inflation targets.

KEY CONCEPTS

Systematic monetary policy occurs when a central bank reacts the same way to disturbances in the economy each time they happen. The formalization of a systematic monetary policy generates a monetary policy rule, such as the one explored in this chapter or the Taylor rule explored in Exercises 9 and 11 in the text and Problems 3 and 4 in this study guide.

Monetary policy rules formally define, or prescribe, the central bank's reaction to various states of the

economy. They serve to reduce the uncertainty surrounding central bank responses to various economic disturbances in the decision-making behavior of firms and consumers. To the extent they succeed in reducing such uncertainty, they aid in achieving the goal of economic stability.

Recall from the Solow model, that a *steady state* is a situation where, in the absence of shocks to the economy, the endogenous variables remain constant over time. In this chapter, inflation and short-run output are those variables.

The *aggregate demand* curve, formed from the IS and MP curves, is an inverse relationship between inflation and short-run output that describes how the central bank influences short-run output on the basis of the inflation rate. The AD curve slopes downward because, at higher inflation rates, the central bank increases real interest rates in order to decrease interest-sensitive spending, thus reducing output.

The *aggregate supply* curve, based on the Phillips curve, consists of a positive relationship between inflation and short-run output of the general form $\pi_t = \pi_t^e + \bar{v}\tilde{Y}_t + \bar{o}$, where π_t^e represents expected inflation and may take on different forms, as discussed in the chapter. The AS curve slopes upward, because producing output in excess of potential places additional pressure on firms and requires economywide increases in production costs for all economic activity. Thus, as short-run output increases, so does inflation.

Inflation expectations take on two general forms: adaptive expectations (where π_t^e is a function of actual past values of inflation) and rational expectations (where

π_t^e is a function of what firms and consumers expect inflation to be in light of current developments). In the conduct of monetary policy, inflation expectations play a significant role in the ability of monetary authorities to achieve their goals of full employment, output at potential, and low, stable inflation. They also play a significant role in determining the economic costs of pursuing those goals.

Stagflation occurs with the simultaneous conditions of inflation and stagnation, or negative short-run output, as experienced in the late 1970s, when economies around the world suffered from adverse shocks to aggregate supply.

Real business cycles are the economic fluctuations driven by "real" events in the economy, in contrast to "nominal" events, caused by monetary policy. Economists primarily think of technological innovations in this context.

Inflation-output loops constitute one of the most robust and empirically supported features of the short-run model: the counterclockwise rotation of combinations of inflation and short-run output. For example, following a positive aggregate demand shock, such as a boom to consumer confidence, positive short-run output leads to higher inflation followed by negative short-run output as monetary authorities fight inflation. Negative short-run output then causes inflation to fall, and when inflation falls, monetary authorities again increase short-run output. See Figures 13.14–13.16, and 13.19.

Leading economic indicators include such variables as building permits, initial unemployment claims, new orders for manufactured goods, consumer expectations, etc. These variables suggest the direction that economic activity and its influence on other parts of the economy may take in the near future.

Rules versus discretion refers to the debate regarding the proper conduct of monetary policy. Should monetary authorities be constrained by rules defining the specific systematic policy responses to pursue in response to economic shocks or should they have the discretion of acting as they see fit?

Closely related to the *rules versus discretion* debate is the *time consistency* problem. It occurs when, after the central bank establishes a set of rules, people commit themselves accordingly to the appropriate behavior. The central bank then has the incentive to follow a different course of action than previously announced. Of course, exercising this incentive leads to a loss of credibility rather quickly.

Adaptive expectations occur when individuals simply expect inflation this period to continue at the same level as last period. They are a driving force in the sticky inflation assumption. When inflation changes during the current period, the next period's level of expected inflation then will change accordingly.

Rational expectations differ from adaptive expectations because people use all the information at their disposal to update past inflation values to what they expect in the current period in light of that additional information. Such information may include central bank policy announcements, current and leading indicators, known supply-side disturbances, or other relevant economic data. Inflation may not adjust immediately, however, if the costs of such analysis are too high.

The Lucas critique argues that economic models built on the basis of expectations and behaviors that can change over time present economists with a potential problem. For example, if behavioral parameters, like $\bar{b}$ and $\bar{v}$, are based on expectations involving a particular policy that has since been changed, the behavior forecasted by that model will be inaccurate. Lucas emphasized the importance of correctly estimating current values for such behavioral parameters.

Inflation targets are explicit inflation rates announced by central banks in their pursuit of monetary policy. Arguments in favor of inflation targets include a specific anchor for inflationary expectations on the part of firms and consumers, as well as making it easier to conduct monetary policy if people know what the targets are and are confident of the central bank's commitment to them.

Constrained discretion involves the simultaneous use of commitment to long-term inflation targets and short-term discretion on the part of monetary authorities to respond to shocks as they occur in the economy.

The *Great Moderation* refers to the reduction of inflation in economically advanced countries during the 25 years following the buildup of inflation during the late 1960s and the oil-shock years of the 1970s.

TRUE/FALSE QUESTIONS

1. The Federal Reserve uses a monetary policy rule to establish the federal funds rate based on inflationary conditions in the economy.

2. An aggressive monetary policy that fights inflation with a vengeance generates a flatter aggregate demand curve with greater negative short-run output.

3. A steady state in the AS/AD framework is one in which the economy is not subject to shocks.

4. In the absence of inflation stickiness, inflation targets and thus inflation itself could be reduced without the otherwise necessary output and employment losses.

5. Aggregate demand shocks cause permanently higher levels of inflation.

6. In the late 1990s, Alan Greenspan accurately recognized the productivity shocks of the "new economy" and did not raise interest rates in response to positive short-run output.

7. The nominal federal funds rate is not compatible with a monetary policy rule designed to target real interest rates.

8. Simple monetary rules that depend only on inflation behavior to guide monetary policy are oversimplified and unrealistic because they ignore short-run output.

9. Monetary authorities willing to create large recessions to fight inflation should be most successful at maintaining low inflation.

10. The Lucas critique makes it clear that macroeconomic models where expectations of agents can change over time are inappropriate for use in forecasting economic activity.

11. The Great Moderation refers to the central bank's willingness to retreat from a totally discretionary stance on monetary policy.

MULTIPLE-CHOICE QUESTIONS

1. Which of the following would make a plausible inflation-fighting monetary policy rule?
   a. $R_t = \bar{r} - \bar{m}(\pi_t - \bar{\pi})$
   b. $R_t - \bar{r} = \bar{m}(\bar{\pi} - \pi)$
   c. $R_t = \bar{r} + \bar{m}(\pi_t - \bar{\pi})$
   d. $R_t = \bar{m}(\pi_t - \bar{\pi}) - \bar{r}$
   e. none of the above

2. The slope of the aggregate demand curve is determined by
   a. the sensitivity of the IS curve, or short-run output, to the real interest rate.
   b. the sensitivity of short-run output to the inflation target.
   c. the sensitivity of short-run output to both inflation and the real interest rate.
   d. the sensitivity of short-run output to the real interest rate and central bank sensitivity to inflation.
   e. the sensitivity of short-run output to the inflation rate.

3. Which of the following would not cause the aggregate demand curve to shift?
   a. an increase in government spending
   b. an increase in targeted inflation
   c. an increase in export demand
   d. an increase in inflation
   e. an increase in real interest rates

4. The slope of the aggregate supply curve is controlled by
   a. the stickiness of inflation.
   b. the speed of an inflation shock.
   c. the size of an inflation shock.
   d. the sensitivity of inflation to inflation shocks.
   e. the sensitivity of inflation to short-run output.

5. The aggregate supply curve shifts when
   a. expected inflation changes.
   b. an inflation shock occurs.
   c. last period's inflation changed from the period before.
   d. any of the above occurs.
   e. only b and c

6. Which of the following is not consistent with a steady state in the aggregate supply/aggregate demand framework?
   a. $\pi_t = \pi_{t-1} = \pi^*$
   b. $\bar{\pi} = \pi_{t-1}$
   c. $\tilde{Y} = 0$
   d. $\bar{a} = 0$
   e. $\bar{o} = 0$

7. The aggregate demand curve slopes downward because
   a. inflation reduces the purchasing power of the nation's currency.
   b. consumers spend less when inflation rises.
   c. the central bank raises real interest rates to fight high inflation.
   d. demand curves in general slope downward due to diminishing marginal utility.
   e. none of the above occurs.

8. The aggregate supply curve slopes upward because
   a. production costs increase faster than usual when output exceeds potential.
   b. higher inflation encourages firms to produce more.
   c. consumer demand increases when inflation rises.
   d. both b and c occur.
   e. none of the above occurs.

9. During an inflation shock,
   a. inflation rises.
   b. aggregate supply increases.
   c. aggregate supply decreases.
   d. both a and b occur.
   e. both a and c occur.

10. In the dynamics of the AS/AD framework, the role played by expected inflation during the adjustment process is to determine the
    a. speed of short-run output's return to zero.
    b. slope of the aggregate supply curve.
    c. severity of inflation shocks.
    d. length of an inflation shock.
    e. none of the above

11. According to the principle of transition dynamics, short-run output's return to zero is fastest when
    a. inflation is less sticky.
    b. monetary authorities follow a strict policy rule.
    c. short-run output is farthest away from zero.
    d. inflation is more sticky.
    e. short-run output is closer to zero.

12. A reduction in the central bank's inflation target $(\bar{\pi})$ enters the AS/AD framework through
    a. an increase in aggregate supply.
    b. a decrease in aggregate supply.
    c. an increase in aggregate demand.
    d. a decrease in aggregate demand.
    e. none of the above if expectations are rational.

13. The driving force behind the economy's evolution over time following a shift in aggregate demand is
    a. the value of short-run output.
    b. inflation stickiness.
    c. the adjustment of inflation expectations.
    d. the marginal product of capital.
    e. the real interest rate.

14. Which of the following would not constitute a shock to aggregate demand?
    a. $\bar{a} > 0$
    b. $\bar{a} < 0$
    c. $\bar{\pi} > 0$
    d. $\Delta\bar{\pi} < 0$
    e. none of the above

15. Positive aggregate demand shocks fit each of the following descriptions except that
    a. they are temporary by nature.
    b. they are matched by offsetting recessions.
    c. they raise inflation only temporarily.
    d. they raise the price level permanently.
    e. they generate no costs to the economy.

16. The simple monetary policy rule used throughout most of this chapter responds to inflation but does not respond directly to changes in short-run output. Which of the following would provide a monetary policy rule that directly addressed stabilization for both inflation and short-run output?

    a. $R_t - \bar{r} = \bar{m}(\bar{\pi} - \pi_t) - \bar{n}\tilde{Y}_t$
    b. $R_t - \bar{r} = \bar{m}(\bar{\pi} - \pi_t) + \bar{n}\tilde{Y}_t$
    c. $R_t - \bar{r} = \bar{m}(\pi_t - \bar{\pi}) - \bar{n}\tilde{Y}_t$
    d. $R_t - \bar{r} = \bar{m}(\pi_t - \bar{\pi}) + \bar{n}\tilde{Y}_t$
    e. none of the above

17. Real business cycle models rely primarily on _____ to explain fluctuations in short-run output.
    a. inflation shocks
    b. aggregate demand shocks
    c. government intervention
    d. technology shocks
    e. monetary policy

18. For which period of time did the monetary policy rule illustrated in Figure 13.17 in the text track actual federal funds behavior least well?
    a. 1960–70
    b. 1970–80
    c. 1980–90
    d. 1990–2000
    e. 2000–06

19. The empirical data provide _____ support for the counterclockwise inflation-output loops predicted by the short-run model.
    a. no
    b. weak
    c. some
    d. strong
    e. inconclusive

20. Economic forecasters have the least success in forecasting
    a. continuing expansions.
    b. inflation.
    c. unemployment.
    d. housing conditions.
    e. business cycle turning points.

21. Time consistency problems arise when monetary policy authorities
    a. consistently fight inflation and develop a credible reputation.
    b. clearly state their policy objectives on a regular and timely basis.
    c. fail to consult with price setters before they establish explicit policy rules.
    d. establish new policy objectives after price setters have negotiated their contracts.
    e. encounter shocks to the economy that their policy rules failed to consider.

22. The ultimate goal of monetary policy includes all of the following except
    a. full employment.
    b. short-run output equal to zero.
    c. low, stable inflation.
    d. a stable price level.
    e. output at potential.

23. When price setters use rational expectations to establish new prices, they
    a. use all the information available in the economy.
    b. discount the costs that make inflation sticky.
    c. consider only central bank inflation targets.
    d. place great emphasis on the central bank's willingness to fight inflation.
    e. cause inflation to become more sticky than under adaptive expectations.

24. Suppose price setters operate according to rational expectations and the central bank has extreme credibility concerning its resolve to lower inflation in the economy. Which of the following scenarios is most likely to occur?
    a. Short-run output falls briefly followed by rapid inflation adjustment.
    b. Inflation begins to fall followed by a brief rise and rapid fall of short-run output.
    c. Inflation falls without a rise or fall in short-run output.
    d. Inflation remains constant with no change in short-run output.
    e. Inflation still increases because of inflation inertia but by much less than in the past.

25. Announcing inflation targets by the central bank now is an established practice in each of the following countries except
    a. Australia.
    b. Brazil.
    c. Canada.
    d. Mexico.
    e. the United States.

26. The advantages of explicit inflation targeting include each of the following except
    a. anchoring inflation expectations to the target.
    b. easier output stabilization by the central bank.
    c. more successful short-term stimulus by the central bank.
    d. less need for large declines in short-run output.
    e. none of the above; they are all advantages.

27. The monetary policy approach of *constrained discretion* allows central banks to
    a. avoid the time consistency problem.
    b. retain flexibility in the face of economic shocks.
    c. commit to an inflation target.
    d. all of the above
    e. only b and c

EXERCISES

1. Consider the simple monetary policy rule used throughout most of this chapter: $R_t - \bar{r} = \bar{m}(\pi_t - \bar{\pi})$. Assume that $\bar{r} = 2\%$ and $\bar{m} = \frac{1}{2}$.
   a. What is the slope of this MP curve?
   b. If $R_t = 2\%$ and $\pi_t = 3\%$, what is the central bank's implied target rate of inflation?
   c. Given the assumptions in part b, what is the federal funds rate?

2. Suppose that an inflation shock ($\bar{o} > 0$) occurs in the economy described by the following AD and AS curves: $\tilde{Y}_t = \bar{a} - \bar{b}\bar{m}(\pi_t - \bar{\pi})$ and $\pi_t = \pi_{t-1} + \bar{v}_t \tilde{Y}_t + \bar{o}$.
   a. Use an AS/AD diagram to trace the impact of this shock through the next two periods following its occurrence.
   b. Show what monetary authorities can do to address the shock. What difference does it make if the central bank wants to quickly reduce unemployment rather than inflation?

3. Suppose consumers go on a spending spree and generate concern about rising inflation at the central bank.
   a. Using IS-MP and AS/AD diagrams, show the impact of this consumer behavior.
   b. Show how the central bank's monetary policy rule responds to the inflation affecting the economy.
   c. Show what the central bank can do to offset the inflationary impact of this consumer behavior. Assume that the central bank can respond immediately to the increase in consumer spending and describe the adjustment process.

PROBLEMS

Worked Problem

1. Assume that an economy is characterized by the following IS, MP, and AS curves:

$$\tilde{Y}_t = \bar{a} - \bar{b}(R_t - \bar{r}), \quad R_t - \bar{r} = \bar{m}(\pi_t - \bar{\pi}), \quad \text{and} \quad \pi_t = \pi_{t-1} + \bar{v}\tilde{Y}_t + \bar{o}$$

a. Derive the aggregate demand curve for this economy:

$$\tilde{Y}_t = \bar{a} - \bar{b}[\bar{m}(\pi_t - \bar{\pi})]$$

Substitute the MP curve into the IS curve and simplify:

$$\tilde{Y}_t = \bar{a} - \bar{b}\bar{m}(\pi_t - \bar{\pi})$$

The equation $\tilde{Y}_t = \bar{a} - \bar{b}\bar{m}(\pi_t - \bar{\pi})$ is the AD curve, but it is not yet in the graphing format required in the next part of this problem.

b. When graphed on an AS/AD diagram with inflation on the vertical axis and short-run output on the horizontal axis, what are the slope and intercept of the AD curve? Invert the AD curve derived in part a by solving for inflation in terms of short-run output:

$$\tilde{Y}_t = \bar{a} - \bar{b}\bar{m}\left(\pi_t - \bar{\pi}\right)$$

$$\bar{b}\bar{m}\left(\pi_t - \bar{\pi}\right) = \bar{a} - \tilde{Y}_t$$

$$\pi_t - \bar{\pi} = \frac{\bar{a}}{\bar{b}\bar{m}} - \frac{1}{\bar{b}\bar{m}}\tilde{Y}_t$$

$$\pi_t = \bar{\pi} + \frac{\bar{a}}{\bar{b}\bar{m}} - \frac{1}{\bar{b}\bar{m}}\tilde{Y}_t$$

The slope can now be identified as $-1/\bar{b}\bar{m}$ and the intercept, at the short-run output value of zero, is $\bar{\pi} + \bar{a}/\bar{b}\bar{m}$.

c. What causes the slope of the AD curve to become flatter/steeper? Increases/decreases in the parameter values of $\bar{b}$ and $\bar{m}$ cause the AD curve to become flatter/steeper. In other words, when firms and consumers respond more/less to interest rate changes, short-run output responds more/less and the AD curve is flatter/steeper. Similarly, when monetary authorities respond more/less to inflation changes by changing interest rates, the interest rate changes evoke corresponding changes in short-run output and the AD curve gets flatter/steeper.

d. What kinds of economic events cause the AD curve to shift and how do they show up in the AD curve? Technically, any event that causes a component of the intercept, $\bar{\pi} + \dfrac{\bar{a}}{\bar{b}\bar{m}}$, to change causes the AD curve to shift. Typically, shifts are attributed to changes in any of the components of $\bar{a}$ ($\bar{a}_c$, $\bar{a}_i$, $\bar{a}_g$, $\bar{a}_{ex}$, and $\bar{a}_{im}$) or to a change in $\bar{\pi}$, the central bank's inflation target.

e. Using the AS/AD diagram for this economy, show and label the short-run impacts of an inflation shock and explain who is harmed by it. The shock causes AS_0 to shift to AS_1, moving the economy from point a to point b (Figure 1). Inflation rises to π_1 and short-run output falls to $\tilde{Y}_t$. Inflation harms those living on fixed incomes and those who own

nominal assets. Negative short-run output harms those who lose the benefits from producing output, whether through sales or labor income.

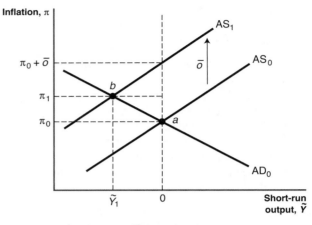

Figure 1

2. Assume that an economy is characterized by the following IS, MP, and AS curves:

$$\tilde{Y}_t = \bar{a} - \bar{b}(R_t - \bar{r}),\ R_t - \bar{r} = \bar{m}(\pi_t - \bar{\pi}),$$
$$\text{and } \pi_t = \pi_{t-1} + \bar{v}\tilde{Y}_t + \bar{o}.$$

Also assume the following parameter values: $\bar{a} = 0$, $\bar{b} = 3/5$, $\bar{r} = 2\%$, $\bar{m} = 1/2$, $\bar{\pi} = 2\%$, and $\bar{v} = 2/3$. Assume further, that a 1% AD shock ($\bar{a} = 1\%$) occurs due to an increase in government spending.

a. Calculate and show on an AS/AD diagram the initial disturbance and two periods of adjustment following the shock; that is, calculate $\tilde{Y}_1$, $\tilde{Y}_2$, and $\tilde{Y}_3$ with the shock in $\tilde{Y}_1$.

b. What could monetary authorities do to offset this shock so that short-run output remained at zero and no inflation occurred?

c. When would this action have to be taken?

3. Assume that an economy is characterized by the following IS, MP, and AS curves:

$$\tilde{Y}_t = \bar{a} - \bar{b}(R_t - \bar{r}),\ R_t - \bar{r} = \bar{m}(\pi_t - \bar{\pi}) + \bar{n}\tilde{Y}_t,$$
$$\text{and } \pi_t = \pi_{t-1} + \bar{v}\tilde{Y}_t + \bar{o}.$$

a. Suppose there are two groups of people in this economy: wage earners and nominal asset holders. Which group of people would align most closely with which component of the MP curve?

b. Derive the AD curve for this economy.

c. What are the slope and intercept of this AD curve?

d. How does the AD curve change if the central bank favors wage earners over nominal asset holders? And vice versa?

e. Explain how the behavior of this economy would vary for each of the scenarios in part d.

4. Assume that an economy is characterized by the following IS, MP, and AS curves:

$$\tilde{Y}_t = \bar{a} - \bar{b}(R_t - \bar{r}), \ R_t - \bar{r} = \bar{m}(\pi_t - \bar{\pi}) + \bar{n}\tilde{Y}_t,$$
$$\text{and } \pi_t = \pi_{t-1} + \bar{v}\tilde{Y}_t + \bar{o}.$$

Assume the following parameter values: $\bar{a} = 0$, $\bar{b} = 3/5$, $\bar{r} = 2\%$, $\bar{m} = 1/2$, $\bar{n} = 1/2$, $\pi = 2\%$, and $\bar{v} = 2/3$. Now assume that an inflation shock of 2% ($\bar{o} = 2\%$) occurs.

   a. Calculate and show on an AS/AD diagram three periods of adjustment following the shock.
   b. Now assume that the central bank favors nominal asset holders to the exclusion of wage earners, that is, $\bar{n} = 0$, and recalculate the inflation shock and two adjustment periods under these conditions.
   c. Suppose you were to observe relatively stable short-run output with wide fluctuations of inflation in an economy. What would you be able to conclude about the source of the disturbances to that economy and about central bank preferences regarding the two groups of people (nominal asset holders and wage earners)?
   d. If you knew that the country had indeed experienced shocks to the economy but you observed neither inflation nor output fluctuations, what conclusions would you then be able to make?

CHAPTER 13 SOLUTIONS

True/False Questions

1. False. The Fed does not officially follow a policy rule. See Sections 13.2 and 13.7.

2. True. Fighting inflation harder requires higher interest rates and greater reductions in interest-sensitive spending. See Section 13.2 and Figure 13.3.

3. False. The economy always is subject to shocks. A steady state is one in which there have been no shocks and the endogenous variables have been constant for some time. See Section 13.4.

4. True. Given a credible central bank and immediate inflation adjustment on the part of price setters. See Section 13.5.

5. False. Inflation rises temporarily; the price level rises permanently. See Section 13.5.

6. True. Most economists now credit him with having made this call correctly. See the case study "Real Business Cycle Models and the 'New Economy.'"

7. False. Recall that $R_t = i_t - \pi_t$ and apply that relationship to the monetary policy rule. See Section 13.6.

8. False. Because they respond to inflation, they implicitly respond to short-run output, as it plays a significant role in determining inflation. See Section 13.7.

9. True. To the extent that price setters raise prices less because of concern over monetary authorities use of policy to create such a recession. See Section 13.7.

10. False. Such models simply need to be reestimated to reflect the changed expectations, otherwise they lead to incorrect predictions. See the case study "Rational Expectations and the Lucas Critique."

11. False. It refers to the decline in inflation during the 25 years since 1980.

Multiple-Choice Questions

1. c, $R_t = \bar{r} + \bar{m}(\pi_t - \bar{\pi})$. It is equivalent to equation (13.1): $R_t - \bar{r} = \bar{m}(\pi_t - \bar{\pi})$. See Section 13.2.

2. d, the sensitivity of short-run output to the real interest rate and central bank sensitivity to inflation. Answer c is tempting but not correct because of the way $\bar{m}$ enters the model only on inflation, in other words, as a monetary policy parameter. See Section 13.2.

3. d, an increase in inflation; it would be a movement along the AD curve. See Section 13.2.

4. e, the sensitivity of inflation to short-run output. See Section 13.3.

5. d, any of the above. See Section 13.3.

6. b, $\bar{\pi} = \pi_{t-1}$. This could be true in the face of any shock. See Section 13.4.

7. c, the central bank raises real interest rates to fight high inflation. See Section 13.4.

8. a, production costs increase faster than usual when output exceeds potential. See Section 13.4.

9. e, inflation increases and aggregate supply decreases. See Section 13.5.

10. a, speed of short-run output's return to zero. See Section 13.5.

11. c, short-run output is furthest away from zero. See Section 13.5.

12. d, a decrease in aggregate demand. See Section 13.5.

13. c, the adjustment of inflation expectations. See Section 13.5.

14. c, $\bar{\pi} > 0$. The value for $\bar{\pi}$ generally is positive. It is changing the value that will generate a shock or cause the AD curve to shift. See Section 13.5.

15. e, generate no costs to the economy. Inflation always has costs, even if only temporary. See Section 13.5.

16. d, $R_t - \bar{r} = \bar{m}(\pi_t - \bar{\pi}) + \bar{n}\tilde{Y}_t$. See Section 13.5.

17. d, technology shocks. See the case study "Real Business Cycle Models and the 'New Economy.'"

18. b, 1970–1980. See Section 13.6 and Figure 13.17.

19. d, strong support. See Section 13.6 and Figure 13.19.

20. e, business cycle turning points. See the case study "Forecasting and the Business Cycle."

21. d, establish policy objectives once price setters are constrained by contracts they have signed. See Section 13.7.

22. d, a stable price level. See Section 13.7.

23. d, place great emphasis on the central bank's willingness to fight inflation. Part a is tempting, but using all information rather than the information at their disposal is too costly. Some information may be too costly to acquire and will not generate significantly different results from what they already have at their disposal. See Section 13.7.

24. c, inflation falls without a rise or fall in short-run output. See Section 13.7 and Figure 13.21.

25. e, the United States. See Section 13.7.

26. e, they are all advantages. See Section 13.7.

27. e, only b and c. The time consistency problem still exists simply because the central bank still can act on a discretionary basis once contracts are set. See Section 13.7.

Exercises

1. a. The slope of this MP curve is zero. It does not respond at all to changes in short-run output. It is as if the equation for the MP curve were $R_t - \bar{r} = \bar{m}(\pi_t - \bar{\pi}) + \bar{n}\tilde{Y}_t$ and the parameter $\bar{n}$ had a value of zero.

   b. Substitute the known values into the MP curve: $2\% - 2\% = \frac{1}{2}(3\% - \bar{\pi})$. Targeted inflation must then be equal to 3 percent.

   c. Rewrite the MP curve, $R_t - \bar{r} = \bar{m}(\pi_t - \bar{\pi})$, in nominal terms, since the federal funds rate is a nominal

rate. Note that $i_t = \bar{r} + \pi_t + \bar{m}(\pi_t - \bar{\pi})$ becomes $i_t = \bar{r} + \pi_t$ when $\pi_t = \bar{\pi}$, and the federal funds rate is $5\% = 2\% + 3\%$. Alternatively, since $R_t = i_t - \pi_t$ from the Fisher equation, $i_t - \pi_t - \bar{r} = \bar{m}(\pi_t - \bar{\pi}) = 0$ when $\pi_t = \bar{\pi}$ and $5\% - 2\% - 3\% = 0$.

2. a. The shock, $\bar{o}$, causes the AS curve to shift upward from AS_0 to AS_1 as shown in Figure 2. Note that AS_1 intersects the 0 value of short-run output at a' and that AS and AD intersect each other at point b in the period of the shock. Short-run output decreases, because when actual inflation rises above the inflation target of π_0, the central bank raises interest rates and reduces interest-sensitive spending and hence aggregate demand. In the next period of adjustment, AS_1 shifts to AS_2. Note that, according to the aggregate supply equation, AS_2 intersects the 0 value of short-run output at π_1 since π_1 is now last period's inflation rate and the new intersection between AS and AD is at point c. In this second period following the inflation shock, current inflation is not so far above the central bank's target so interest rates are lowered a little, some aggregate demand activity restored, and

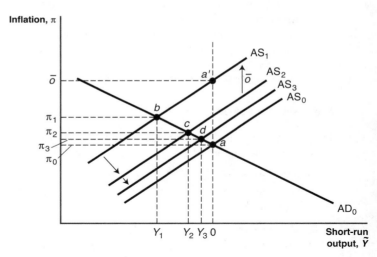

short-run output grows, and so forth in subsequent periods.

Figure 2

   b. Monetary authorities have two choices. The first one, fighting inflation with higher real interest rates, as shown in Figure 2, restores inflation to its original level but brings with it output losses and unemployment. The second choice, lowering interest rates and causing an increase in AD that returns short-run output to zero at the new inflation rate of $\pi_t = \pi_0 + \bar{o}$, reduces unemployment and brings the economy back to full employment but allows inflation to remain at its new higher level of π_1 as shown in Figure 3.

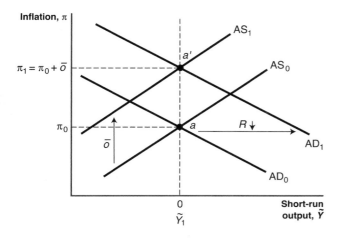

Figure 3

3. a. An increase in consumer spending shifts the IS curve to the right as seen in the top graph in Figure 4 and the AD curve to the right as seen in the bottom graph in Figure 4. In the absence of central bank action or any increase in inflation, the economy will move to point a' with positive short-run output at the level of $\bar{a}$.

   b. Positive short-run output causes inflationary pressure as AD and AS interact. Following the monetary policy rule, the central bank raises real interest rates and the corresponding reduction in interest-sensitive spending in the economy moves it from point a' to point b as shown in Figure 4.

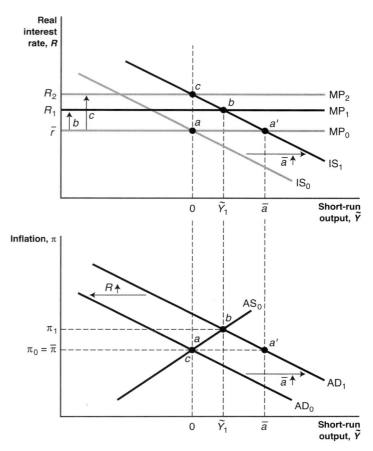

Figure 4

c. If the central bank wishes to avoid the inflation caused by this consumer behavior, it can raise the real interest rate high enough to completely offset the additional consumer spending. With sufficient knowledge, the central bank could, in theory, immediately raise interest rates from $\bar{r}$ to R_2 and cause the AD curve to shift left and offset consumer spending through reductions in interest-sensitive spending, leaving the economy at the points labeled c in Figure 4. Note that the difference here is that, in part c of this problem, there is no increase in the inflation rate. Note as well that, because there is no change in the inflation rate, there will be no shift of the AS curve, as there would have been in part b when just relying on the monetary policy rule to respond to observed changes in the inflation rate.

Problems

1. Worked Problem. The problem is worked in the text.

2. a. First substitute the MP curve into the IS curve to generate an AD curve, then substitute the AS curve into the AD curve:

$$\tilde{Y}_t = \bar{a} - \bar{b}\bar{m}(\pi_t - \bar{\pi}) \qquad \pi_t = \pi_{t-1} + \bar{v}\tilde{Y}_t + \bar{o}$$

$$\tilde{Y}_t = \bar{a} - \bar{b}\bar{m}(\pi_{t-1} + \bar{v}\tilde{Y}_t + \bar{o} - \bar{\pi})$$

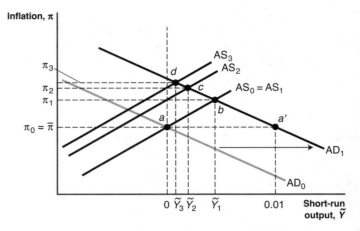

Figure 5

Gather the short-run output terms to the left-hand side of the equation and solve for short-run output:

$$\tilde{Y}_t + \bar{b}\bar{m}\bar{v}\tilde{Y}_t = \bar{a} - \bar{b}\bar{m}(\pi_{t-1} + \bar{o} - \bar{\pi})$$

$$\tilde{Y}_t(1 + \bar{b}\bar{m}\bar{v}) = \bar{a} - \bar{b}\bar{m}(\pi_{t-1} + \bar{o} - \bar{\pi})$$

$$\tilde{Y}_t = \frac{\bar{a}}{1 + \bar{b}\bar{m}\bar{v}} - \frac{\bar{b}\bar{m}}{1 + \bar{b}\bar{m}\bar{v}}(\pi_{t-1} + \bar{o} - \bar{\pi})$$

Substitute all the parameter and starting values into the solution for short-run output and the AS curve:

$$\tilde{Y}_0 = \frac{0}{1 + \tfrac{3}{5}\tfrac{1}{2}\tfrac{2}{3}} - \frac{\tfrac{3}{5}\tfrac{1}{2}}{1 + \tfrac{3}{5}\tfrac{1}{2}\tfrac{2}{3}}(\pi_0 + 0 - 0.02) = 0$$

$$\pi_0 = 0.02 + \tfrac{2}{3}(0) + 0 = 0.02$$

Recall that, prior to the shock, short-run output equals zero. Since $\pi_0 = 0.02$ and $\tilde{Y}_0 = 0$, the economy is at point a before the shock occurs. Now let the shock occur that shifts AD_0 out to AD_1 and, using the solution for short-run output we just derived and the AS curve, make the calculations for three periods and label them as shown in Figure 5:

$$\tilde{Y}_1 = \frac{0.01}{1.2} - 0.250(0.02 - 0.02) = 0.008333$$

$$\pi_1 = 0.02 + \tfrac{2}{3}(0.008333) = 0.025555$$

$$\tilde{Y}_2 = 0.008333 - 0.25(0.025555 - 0.02) = 0.006945$$

$$\pi_2 = 0.025555 + \tfrac{2}{3}(0.006945) = 0.030185$$

$$\tilde{Y}_3 = 0.008333 - 0.25(0.030185 - 0.02) = 0.005787$$

$$\pi_3 = 0.030185 + \tfrac{2}{3}(0.005787) = 0.034043$$

Note that $0.01/1.2 = 0.008333$ remains the same throughout the adjustment process until the value for $\bar{a}$ returns to zero, at some point in the future not specified in this problem.

b. To get the AD curve to shift back to the left the same distance as it shifted to the right in part a, use the IS curve and find the appropriate real interest rate for the central bank to target:

$$\tilde{Y}_t = \bar{a} - \bar{b}(R_t - \bar{r}) \implies 0 = 0.01 - \tfrac{3}{5}(R_t - 0.02)$$

$$\implies R_t = 0.01(\tfrac{5}{3}) + 0.02 = 0.03667$$

In other words, to offset the increased government spending the central bank would need to almost double the real interest rate by raising it to approximately 3.67 percent.

c. This action would need to be taken in period one to avoid the ensuing adjustment process.

3. a. Wage earners would align most closely with the $\bar{n}\tilde{Y}_t$ component because it would keep employment levels closer to full employment. Nominal asset holders would align most closely with $\bar{m}(\pi_t - \bar{\pi})$ because it pays specific attention to changes in inflation. Remember also, that $\bar{n}\tilde{Y}_t$ also indirectly affects inflation through the Phillips (or AS) curve.

b. The derivation follows the same process as in Problem 1, substitute the MP curve into the IS curve and solve for short-run output:

$$\tilde{Y}_t = \bar{a} - \bar{b}(\bar{m}(\pi_t - \bar{\pi}) + \bar{n}\tilde{Y}_t)$$

$$\tilde{Y}_t = \bar{a} - \bar{b}\bar{m}(\pi_t - \bar{\pi}) - \bar{b}\bar{n}\tilde{Y}_t$$

$$\tilde{Y}_t + \bar{b}\bar{n}\tilde{Y}_t = \bar{a} - \bar{b}\bar{m}(\pi_t - \bar{\pi})$$

$$\tilde{Y}_t(1 + \bar{b}\bar{n}) = \bar{a} - \bar{b}\bar{m}(\pi_t - \bar{\pi})$$

$$\tilde{Y}_t = \frac{\bar{a}}{1 + \bar{b}\bar{n}} - \frac{\bar{b}\bar{m}}{1 + \bar{b}\bar{n}}(\pi_t - \bar{\pi})$$

c. To find the slope and intercept for graphing purposes, invert the equation for short-run output derived in part b. (See Problems 4–6 in the math review appendix at the end of Chapter 1 for further explanation about inverting an equation.)

$$\tilde{Y}_t = \frac{\bar{a}}{1+\bar{b}\bar{n}} - \frac{\bar{b}\bar{m}}{1+\bar{b}\bar{n}}(\pi_t - \bar{\pi})$$

$$\frac{\bar{b}\bar{m}}{1+\bar{b}\bar{n}}(\pi_t - \bar{\pi}) = \frac{\bar{a}}{1+\bar{b}\bar{n}} - \tilde{Y}_t$$

Multiply both sides of the equation by the inverse of $\dfrac{\bar{b}\bar{m}}{1+\bar{b}\bar{n}}, \dfrac{1+\bar{b}\bar{n}}{\bar{b}\bar{m}}$, to get:

$$\pi_t - \bar{\pi} = \frac{\bar{a}}{\bar{b}\bar{m}} - \frac{1+\bar{b}\bar{n}}{\bar{b}\bar{m}}\tilde{Y}_t$$

$$\pi_t = \bar{\pi} + \frac{\bar{a}}{\bar{b}\bar{m}} - \frac{1+\bar{b}\bar{n}}{\bar{b}\bar{m}}\tilde{Y}_t$$

The slope is $-\dfrac{1+\bar{b}\bar{n}}{\bar{b}\bar{m}}$, and the intercept is $\bar{\pi} + \dfrac{\bar{a}}{\bar{b}\bar{m}}$.

d. If wage earners are favored over nominal asset holders, $\bar{n}$ becomes larger relative to $\bar{m}$ and the slope of the AD curve becomes steeper. If nominal asset holders are favored over wager earners, the AD curve would become flatter.

e. A steeper/flatter AD curve would generate smaller/larger fluctuations in short-run output in the event of inflation shocks and larger/smaller increases in inflation given AS or AD shocks.

4. a. Before calculating the adjustment process, derive the AD curve, then go through the same derivation process as in Problem 2 to determine the solution

$$\tilde{Y}_t = \frac{\bar{a}}{1+\bar{b}\bar{n}} - \frac{\bar{b}\bar{m}}{1+\bar{b}\bar{n}}(\pi_t - \bar{\pi}) \quad \pi_t = \pi_{t-1} + \bar{v}\tilde{Y}_t + \bar{o}$$

$$\tilde{Y}_t = \frac{\bar{a}}{1+\bar{b}\bar{n}} - \frac{\bar{b}\bar{m}}{1+\bar{b}\bar{n}}(\pi_{t-1} + \bar{v}\tilde{Y}_t + \bar{o} - \bar{\pi})$$

$$\tilde{Y}_t + \frac{\bar{b}\bar{m}\bar{v}}{1+\bar{b}\bar{n}}\tilde{Y}_t = \frac{\bar{a}}{1+\bar{b}\bar{n}} - \frac{\bar{b}\bar{m}}{1+\bar{b}\bar{n}}(\pi_{t-1} + \bar{o} - \bar{\pi})$$

$$\tilde{Y}_t\left(1 + \frac{\bar{b}\bar{m}\bar{v}}{1+\bar{b}\bar{n}}\right) = \frac{\bar{a}}{1+\bar{b}\bar{n}} - \frac{\bar{b}\bar{m}}{1+\bar{b}\bar{n}}(\pi_{t-1} + \bar{o} - \bar{\pi})$$

for short-run output by substituting AS into AD: Note that, to get a common denominator in the term on $\tilde{Y}_t$, use the special form of $1 = \dfrac{1+\bar{b}\bar{n}}{1+\bar{b}\bar{n}}$, then invert the $\dfrac{1+\bar{b}\bar{n}+\bar{b}\bar{m}\bar{v}}{1+\bar{b}\bar{n}}$ term on $\tilde{Y}_t$, and multiply both sides again as in Problem 3 part c:

$$\tilde{Y}_t\left(\frac{1+\bar{b}\bar{n}+\bar{b}\bar{m}\bar{v}}{1+\bar{b}\bar{n}}\right) = \frac{\bar{a}}{1+\bar{b}\bar{n}} - \frac{\bar{b}\bar{m}}{1+\bar{b}\bar{n}}(\pi_{t-1} + \bar{o} - \bar{\pi})$$

$$\tilde{Y}_t = \frac{\bar{a}}{1+\bar{b}\bar{n}+\bar{b}\bar{m}\bar{v}} - \frac{\bar{b}\bar{m}}{1+\bar{b}\bar{n}+\bar{b}\bar{m}\bar{v}}$$
$$(\pi_{t-1} + \bar{o} - \bar{\pi})$$

$$\tilde{Y}_0 = \frac{0}{1 + \frac{3}{5}\frac{1}{2} + \frac{3}{5}\frac{1}{2}\frac{2}{3}} - \frac{\frac{3}{5}\frac{1}{2}}{1 + \frac{3}{5}\frac{1}{2} + \frac{3}{5}\frac{1}{2}\frac{2}{3}}$$
$$(\pi_0 + 0 - 0.02) = 0$$

$$\pi_0 = 0.02 + \frac{2}{3}(0)_t + 0 = 0.02$$

With the solution for $\tilde{Y}_t$ and π_0, the calculations for periods 1–3 can be made and the diagram drawn as shown in Figure 6:

$$\tilde{Y}_1 = \frac{0}{1.5} - 0.2(0.02 + 0.02 - 0.02) = -0.004000$$

$$\pi_1 = 0.02 + \frac{2}{3}(-0.004000) + 0.02 = 0.037333$$

$$\tilde{Y}_2 = 0 - 0.2(0.037333 + 0 - 0.02) = -0.003466$$

$$\pi_2 = 0.037333 + \frac{2}{3}(-0.003466) + 0 = 0.035022$$

$$\tilde{Y}_3 = 0 - 0.2(0.035022 + 0 - 0.02) = -0.003004$$

$$\pi_3 = 0.035022 + \frac{2}{3}(-0.003004) + 0 = 0.033019$$

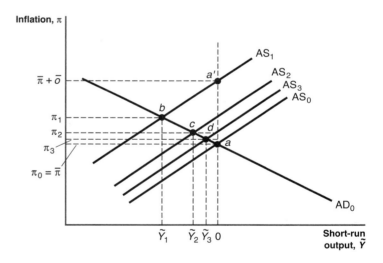

Figure 6

Note that, in contrast to the demand shock in Problem 2, the inflation shock in this problem occurs in period 1 but does not occur again in periods 2 or 3. The inflation shock is a one-time occurrence in period 1 and does not persist in subsequent periods.

b. With $\bar{n} = 0$, the calculations change to the following:

$$\tilde{Y}_1 = \frac{0}{1.2} - 0.25(0.02 + 0.02 - 0.02) = -0.005000$$

$$\pi_1 = 0.02 + \tfrac{2}{3}(-0.005000) + 0.02 = 0.036667$$

$$\tilde{Y}_2 = 0 - 0.25(0.036667 + 0 - 0.02) = -0.004167$$

$$\pi_2 = 0.036667 + \tfrac{2}{3}(-0.004167) + 0 = 0.033889$$

$$\tilde{Y}_3 = 0 - 0.25(0.033889 + 0 - 0.02) = -0.003472$$

$$\pi_3 = 0.033889 + \tfrac{2}{3}(-0.003472) + 0 = 0.031574$$

c. Since AD shocks can be offset with neither output nor inflation fluctuations, one could infer that the disturbances were AS shocks and that the central bank has preferences that favor stable output, or full employment, over the interests of nominal asset holders.

d. As indicated in part c, these conditions would suggest the occurrence of AD shocks.

CHAPTER 14 | The Great Recession and the Short-run Model

OVERVIEW

In Chapter 10 we began our exploration of the Great Recession. In this chapter we continue that exploration in the context of the short-run model and go into more depth regarding the impact of the financial crisis on the economy. After studying this chapter you should be able to show the impact of increased risk premiums in the financial sector on both the IS/MP and AS/AD frameworks. You should also be able to explain the problems that deflation can impose on an economy, as well as discuss the nature of the initial responses to the financial crisis and the onset of the Great Recession both by the Federal Reserve and by the federal government. Finally, you should come away with an understanding of some of the major issues involved in reforming the financial sector in order to reduce the likelihood of the economy repeating this experience.

KEY CONCEPTS

If lenders think that a loan may become problematic for some reason in the future, they will often charge what they call a *risk premium* and ask for a higher-than-normal interest rate. A risk premium may be as mundane as inflation that affects everyone or a more firm and industry-specific effect, such as the probability that a specific borrower will default due to the type of market it's in or due to its own firm management.

A condition known as *deflation* occurs when the price level falls and the rate of inflation becomes negative. This is especially problematic because it causes real interest rates to increase, thus discouraging borrowing for new investment, and as prices and wages fall, it also requires firms and workers to produce more and work longer hours in order to meet fixed nominal debt obligations.

The *zero lower bound* limits how much the Fed and banks can lower their interest rates. Since banks cannot charge people to simply keep their money on deposit without running the risk of massive withdrawals, a zero interest rate, or just slightly above, becomes the lower boundary of what people can earn by keeping their money in the bank.

A *liquidity trap* occurs when deflation removes the incentive for people to borrow money because the cost of paying back loans in deflated dollars is greater than the opportunity for profit, so borrowing stops. More formally, the real rate of interest is too high for their business ventures to remain profitable. It generally means that banks end up sitting on a significant amount of excess reserves because they are unable to issue very many loans and that the Fed's ability to stimulate the economy through its usual tool of interest rate adjustment is also significantly impaired.

When a recession causes prices to fall, inflation to become negative, and real interest rates to increase, interest-sensitive spending is further choked off, worsening the recession and leading to further downward pressure on prices and generating addition deflation. As this process repeats itself, the economy heads into a *deflationary spiral* where this cycle of events occurs over and over again.

Bubbles occur in an economy when prices for a particular asset, such as housing in the events preceding the Great Recession, increase rapidly and exceed their underlying value relative to people's income and the state of the economy. The bursting of this bubble and a fall in housing prices by one-third was one of the main contributors to the final volley of events that culminated in the Great Recession.

The *Fed's balance sheet* is an accounting instrument that outlines the makeup of the Federal Reserve System's assets and liabilities. In the past its assets have consisted primarily of U.S. Treasury obligations (roughly 90 percent). At the end of the Great Recession the Fed had purchased enough other types of assets that U.S. Treasury securities only accounted for a little over 25 percent of its assets. On the other hand, its liabilities that used to include only a very small amount of reserves (a little less than 1 percent) now contain reserve holdings of about 40 percent.

At the beginning of the financial crisis certain mortgage-backed securities whose values had fallen dramatically and no longer had viable secondary market became known as *toxic assets* because they essentially poisoned the balance sheets of those banks who held them.

The federal government responded to the onset of the Great Recession with a *fiscal stimulus package* known as the American Recovery and Reinvestment Act of 2009. It allocated funds for infrastructure projects, education and health care, and transfer payments to state and local governments as well as the unemployed—all designed to reduce the impact of the economic slowdown and put Americans back to work or keep them from becoming unemployed.

One of the problems associated with any type of insurance arrangement that shields an individual or institution from risk is known as a *moral hazard*. when a shielded party does not bear the full responsibility or will not face all of the consequences for its actions, its behavior tends to become riskier than it otherwise would be if that shield were not present. Federally guaranteeing mortgages through institutions such as Fannie Mae and Freddie Mac contribute to the moral hazard problem in the banking industry.

By classifying a number of financial institutions as *too-big-to-fail* during the financial panic, moral hazard problems in the financial sector were increased. Recent regulatory reform has sought to address some moral hazard problems through stricter capital requirements so that more of the institutions own assets are at risk.

TRUE/FALSE QUESTIONS

1. Investment plunged during the Great Recession as firms lost confidence in the Fed's ability to monitor and guide the economy through those turbulent times.

2. Afraid that borrowers would default on their loans in unusually high numbers, lenders increased the risk premium they demanded by several percentage points relative to what it had been just a decade earlier.

3. The Fed has the ability to lower interest rates and stimulate the economy.

4. An increased risk premium affects the economy the same way as an inflation shock.

5. The danger associated with deflation is falling real interest rates.

6. The monetary policy rule from Chapter 13 is a simplified version of the Taylor rule studied in this chapter on the Great Recession and the short-run model.

7. In standard economic models, stock prices represent the estimated profit value of a stock held for one year.

8. The Fed's balance sheet allows observers to gain a better understanding of how far the Fed has strayed from traditional central bank activities since the financial crisis began in 2007.

9. The Troubled Asset Relief Program (TARP) provided funding for state and local governments.

10. Moral hazard involves the possible compromise of financial officials' responsibilities to depositors at federally insured institutions when faced with a trade-off between risk and return versus safety of depositor assets.

11. Macroeconomic forecasting is limited by the inability of its models to account for such fundamental elements of the economy as sticky inflation and limited financial models.

MULTIPLE-CHOICE QUESTIONS

1. Which of the following actions did policy makers not undertake in response to the economic crisis that came to a head in the fall of 2008?
   a. The Fed lowered interest rates (the federal funds rate) all the way to zero.
   b. The Fed purchased mortgage-backed securities and added them to its balance sheet.
   c. The federal government implemented a $700 billion Troubled Asset Relief Program.

d. The federal government passed almost $800 billion worth of stimulus spending.

e. None, they undertook them all.

2. Beginning in 2007, the risk premium on corporate bonds increased dramatically in response to concern over
   a. rising inflation.
   b. falling inflation.
   c. lengthening maturities on corporate bonds.
   d. repayment problems on the part of borrowers.
   e. low interest rates on Treasury bonds.

3. Which of the following is the appropriate representation of the relationship between interest rates and the risk premium?
   a. $R = R^{ff} - \bar{p}$
   b. $R^{ff} = \bar{p} - R$
   c. $R^{ff} = R + \bar{p}$
   d. $\bar{p} = R + R^{ff}$
   e. $R = R^{ff} + \bar{p}$

4. The risk premium enters the short-run model through the
   a. IS curve.
   b. MP rule.
   c. AS curve.
   d. AD curve.
   e. Phillips curve.

5. An increased risk premium will initially be represented in the AS/AD diagram as a
   a. movement along the AD curve.
   b. movement along the AS curve.
   c. shift of the AD curve.
   d. shift of the AS curve.
   e. shift of both the AS and the AD curves.

6. Deflation occurs when
   a. inflation is less than it was last period.
   b. inflation grows at a slower pace.
   c. inflation falls.
   d. inflation turns negative.
   e. inflation is below the Fed's acceptable target range.

7. The economic dangers of deflation include all of the following except
   a. borrowers pay back dollars that are worth more than those that were lent.
   b. lenders get repaid in dollars that are worth less than those that were lent.
   c. rising real interest rates choke off economic activity.
   d. the Fed may not be able to lower interest rates far enough.
   e. nominal interest rates fail to turn negative.

8. In a liquidity trap
   a. banks are unwilling to lend money even though they have excess reserves.
   b. banks are trapped because they have no money to lend to qualified borrowers.
   c. borrowers are trapped because they cannot qualify for loans banks are willing to make.
   d. banks are willing to lend their excess reserves but borrowers are unwilling to commit.
   e. the government imposes a bank holiday preventing any loans from being made.

9. The Taylor rule analysis in the text suggests that each of the following conditions occurred during the financial crisis except
   a. the Fed pursued a relatively expansionary monetary policy.
   b. real interest rates were unusually high despite a low federal funds rate.
   c. the Fed kept real interest rates near zero.
   d. the core inflation rate fell but remained positive.
   e. the GDP gap decreased, becoming more and more negative.

10. Which of the following decades is associated with an asset bubble?
    a. 1910s
    b. 1920s
    c. 1950s
    d. 1970s
    e. 1990s

11. Prior to the financial crisis, which of the following assets constituted the majority of Federal Reserve assets?
    a. loans to nonfinancial corporations
    b. central bank liquidity swaps
    c. mortgage-backed securities
    d. U.S. Treasury securities
    e. commercial paper

12. Which of the following pieces of legislation created a $787 billion fiscal stimulus package?
    a. Troubled Asset Relief Program (TARP)
    b. American Recovery and Reinvestment Act (ARRA)
    c. The Glass-Steagall Act
    d. Gramm-Leach-Bliley Act
    e. Dodd-Frank Wall Street Reform and Consumer Protection Act

13. According to the text, which of the following problems was exacerbated as a result of the way policy makers dealt with the financial crisis?
    a. too big to fail
    b. unemployment
    c. inflation
    d. moral hazard
    e. deflation

14. Which of the following was not one of the financial reform recommendations given by the Squam Lake Group?
    a. create a systemic regulator
    b. enhance capital requirements
    c. link executive compensation to long-term performance
    d. require living wills
    e. increase deposit insurance that banks are required to carry

15. Many critics argue that macroeconomists failed the country both in terms of forecasting and responding to the financial crisis. To what does Federal Reserve Bank of Minneapolis macroeconomist Narayana Kocherlakota give credit as the explanation of this failure?
    a. the limits of technology
    b. too much government intervention
    c. not enough government intervention
    d. lack of regulatory oversight
    e. naive macroeconomic modeling practices

EXERCISES

1. Suppose that you are given the following model that reflects the inclusion of a risk premium due to an increased likelihood of default on the part of the bond issuer.

    The IS curve: $\tilde{Y}_t = \bar{a} - \bar{b}(R_t - \bar{r})$
    The monetary policy rule: $R_t^{ff} - \bar{r} = \bar{m}(\pi_t - \bar{\pi})$
    The risk premium equation: $R_t = R_t^{ff} + \bar{p}$

    Derive the monetary policy rule that reflects the presence of a risk premium consideration as shown above.

2. Using an AS/AD diagram, explain how the presence of a risk, or default, premium might add to the deflationary potential of an economy.

PROBLEMS

Worked Problem

1. Consider the following model of an economy susceptible to aggregate demand shocks in the form of risk premiums on long-term debt instruments.

    The IS curve: $\tilde{Y}_t = \bar{a} - \bar{b}(R_t - \bar{r})$
    The monetary policy rule: $R_t^{ff} - \bar{r} = \bar{m}(\pi_t - \bar{\pi})$
    The risk premium equation: $R_t = R_t^{ff} + \bar{p}$

a. Show mathematically how this change in behavior would enter into the short-run model and the impact it would have on short-run aggregate demand.

   First it would be necessary to derive the aggregate demand curve accordingly. Substitute the risk premium equation into the monetary policy rule by solving it for R_t^{ff} and making the substitution as shown:

$$R_t - \bar{p} - \bar{r} = \bar{m}(\pi_t - \bar{\pi})$$

   Next solve the monetary policy rule for $R_t - \bar{r}$ as usual and make the substitution into the IS curve:

$$\tilde{Y}_t = \bar{a} - \bar{b}(\bar{p} + \bar{m}(\pi_t - \bar{\pi}))$$
$$\tilde{Y}_t = \bar{a} - \bar{b}\bar{p} + \bar{b}\bar{m}(\pi_t - \bar{\pi})$$

   Observe that a positive value of the risk premium, $\bar{p}$, will cause a negative GDP gap if $\bar{a} = 0$ and if inflation is at its target level, that is, $\pi_t = \bar{\pi}$. You should also convince yourself that a positive risk premium will shift the AD curve down and to the left. See the solution to exercise 2(b) if you need to see this worked out.

b. Show mathematically how a risk premium in financial markets would cause aggregate demand curve to shift.

   To see how the impact that a risk premium on aggregate demand will cause the AD curve to shift to the left, we need to invert the AD curve to its graphing format by solving it for π_t as follows:

$$\tilde{Y}_t = \bar{a} - \bar{b}\bar{p} - \bar{b}\bar{m}(\pi_t - \bar{\pi})$$
$$\bar{b}\bar{m}(\pi_t - \bar{\pi}) = \bar{a} - \bar{b}\bar{p} - \tilde{Y}_t$$
$$\pi_t - \bar{\pi} = \frac{\bar{a} - \bar{b}\bar{p}}{\bar{b}\bar{m}} - \frac{1}{\bar{b}\bar{m}}\tilde{Y}_t$$
$$\pi_t = \bar{\pi} + \frac{\bar{a} - \bar{b}\bar{p}}{\bar{b}\bar{m}} - \frac{1}{\bar{b}\bar{m}}\tilde{Y}_t$$

   Since the risk premium term, $\bar{p}$, is now part of the intercept and enters into it with a negative sign, we can see that a positive risk premium will indeed cause the AD curve to shift down and to the left.

c. What would you need to know about financial market behavior concerning risk premiums before this problem could be completed?

   Before completing this problem it would be necessary to have information about the direction of change of the risk premium. Were it to decrease, the AD curve would shift up and to the right, in contrast to the shift to the left if the risk premium increases.

2. Suppose that the economic conditions encountered in Problem 1 are still in effect and that in this case there has been a huge increase in the size of the risk

premium required by lenders. Use the following AS/AD model to address this problem.

The IS curve: $\tilde{Y}_t = \bar{a} - \bar{b}(R_t - \bar{r})$
The monetary policy rule: $R_t^{ff} - \bar{r} = \bar{m}(\pi_t - \bar{\pi})$
The risk premium equation: $R_t = R_t^{ff} + \bar{p}$
The AS curve: $\pi_t = \pi_{t-1} + \bar{v}\tilde{Y}_t + \bar{o}$

a. Assume that the economy began with a zero GDP gap and with inflation at its target level, derive the short-run solution for this economy and show it on an AS/AD diagram.
b. Demonstrate algebraically the long-run effects of such an occurrence.
c. Under what conditions would a risk premium such as $\bar{b}$ lead to the possibility of deflation?

3. Suppose that independent of interest rate movements, economic conditions develop that cause consumers and firms to hold off on further consumer durable and investment expenditures for the indefinite future. How does the presence of a risk premium in the AS/AD model alter the response of the economy to such developments?

CHAPTER 14 SOLUTIONS

True/False Questions

1. False. Investment plunged due at least in part to a huge increase in real interest rates. See Section 14.1.

2. True. The spread between corporate bonds and U.S. Treasury securities reached more than 6 percent by the end of 2008 from less than 2 percent a decade earlier. See Figure 14.1.

3. False. Our experience during the Great Recession underscores the point that the Fed cannot just determine what it would like interest rates to be. See Section 14.2.

4. False. It enters the model the same way as an aggregate demand disturbance. See Section 14.2, The Risk Premium is the AS/AD Framework.

5. False. Just the opposite, it is rising real interest rates. See Section 14.3, The Dangers of Deflation.

6. True. In addition to accounting for a response to inflation issues the Taylor rule also accounts for production/employment issues. See Section 14.3.

7. False. It is the present value of the stocks' future earnings. See the case study "Should Monetary Policy Respond to Asset Prices?"

8. True. An examination of the Fed's assets and liabilities can tell us a lot. See Section 14.3, The Fed's Balance Sheet.

9. False. That funding was part of the fiscal stimulus. See Section 14.3, Fiscal Stimulus.

10. True. Financial institutions insured by the FDIC have less incentive to safeguard their depositors' assets since the government/taxpayers will pick up the tab if they fail. See Section 14.3, Financial Reform.

11. True, in the past. New computing capabilities are allowing current macroeconomists to better account for such economic realities and improve their forecasting abilities. See the case study "Macroeconomic Research after the Financial Crisis."

Multiple-Choice Questions

1. e, each of these was done. See Section 14.1.

2. d, default risk on the part of borrowers. See Section 14.2.

3. e, the difference between R and $R^{ff}(R - R^{ff})$ is $\bar{p}$. See Section 14.2.

4. b, the risk premium equation is combined with the monetary policy rule after which the monetary policy rule accounts for the difference between real interest rates and the rental rate of return on capital when inflation is on target. See case study "Deriving the AD Curve."

5. c, a shift of the AD curve since that is where the risk premium enters the AS/AD model.

6. d, negative inflation rates mean that prices are falling and constitute deflation. See Section 14.2, The Dangers of Inflation.

7. b, with deflation money becomes worth more. See Section 14.2, The Dangers of Deflation.

8. d, borrowers are unwilling to commit to a loan because real interest rates are too high. See Section 14.2, The Dangers of Deflation.

9. c, the Fed was unable to get real interest rates to fall that far. See Section 14.3.

10. b, the 1920s, just before the stock market crash. See Figure 14.6.

11. d, U.S. Treasury securities. See Section 14.3, The Fed's Balance Sheet, and Figure 14.8.

12. b, American Recovery and Reinvestment Act. See Section 14.3, Fiscal Stimulus.

13. d, moral hazard, the incentive to take greater risks in the future. See Section 14.3, Financial Reform.

14. e, Increasing deposit insurance would contribute to the moral hazard problem. See Section 14.3, Financial Reform.

15. a, the limits of technology. See the case study "Macroeconomic Research after the Financial Crisis."

Exercises

1. a. Substitute the risk premium equation into the monetary policy rule by solving it for R_t^{ff} and then solve for $R_t - \bar{r}$ as shown:

$$R_t - \bar{p} - \bar{r} = \bar{m}(\pi_t - \bar{\pi})$$
$$R_t - \bar{r} = \bar{p} + \bar{m}(\pi_t - \bar{\pi})$$

   b. Substitute the monetary policy curve into the IS curve:

$$\tilde{Y}_t = \bar{a} - \bar{b}(\bar{p} + \bar{m}(\pi_t - \bar{\pi}))$$
$$\tilde{Y}_t = \bar{a} - \bar{b}\bar{p} - \bar{b}\bar{m}(\pi_t - \bar{\pi})$$

   Note that at this point we can tell that a positive risk premium will have a negative impact on GDP gaps. Intuitively we know this to be the case since risk premiums cause interest rates to rise.

2. The presence of a risk premium causes interest rates to rise and a reduction in interest-sensitive spending. The AD curve will shift to the left as shown in Figure 1 by AD_2 and generate a negative GDP gap, $\tilde{Y}'$, which leads to downward pressure on inflation. If the previous level of inflation, π_1, was low enough and the downward pressure on inflation is great enough, then those conditions can combine to generate a fall in the price level resulting in deflation as shown by $\pi_2 < 0$ in Figure 1 as a result of the shift of AS_2 along AD_2.

Problems

1. Worked Problem. The problem is worked in the text.

2. a. The derivation for aggregate demand is performed by substituting the risk premium equation into the monetary policy rule and the monetary policy rule into the IS curve as follows:

$$R_t^{ff} = R_t - \bar{p}$$
$$R_t - \bar{p} - \bar{r} = \bar{m}(\pi_t - \bar{\pi})$$
$$R_t - \bar{r} = \bar{p} + \bar{m}(\pi_t - \bar{\pi})$$
$$\tilde{Y}_t = \bar{a} - \bar{b}(\bar{p} + \bar{m}(\pi_t - \bar{\pi}))$$
$$\tilde{Y}_t = \bar{a} - \bar{b}\bar{p} - \bar{b}\bar{m}(\pi_t - \bar{\pi})$$

   Now substitute the AS curve into the AD curve and solve for $\tilde{Y}_t (\tilde{Y}_t'$ in Figure 2) and assume that there are no inflation shocks, i.e., that $\bar{o} = 0$.

$$\tilde{Y}_t = \bar{a} - \bar{b}\bar{p} - \bar{b}\bar{m}(\pi_{t-1} + \bar{v}\tilde{Y}_t + \bar{o} - \bar{\pi})$$
$$\tilde{Y}_t + \bar{b}\bar{m}\bar{v}\tilde{Y} = \bar{a} - \bar{b}\bar{p} - \bar{b}\bar{m}(\pi_{t-1} + \bar{o} - \bar{\pi})$$
$$\tilde{Y}_t(1 + \bar{b}\bar{m}\bar{v}) = \bar{a} - \bar{b}\bar{p} - \bar{b}\bar{m}(\pi_{t-1} - \bar{\pi})$$
$$\tilde{Y}_t = \frac{\bar{a} - \bar{b}\bar{p}}{1 + \bar{b}\bar{m}\bar{v}} - \frac{\bar{b}\bar{m}}{1 + \bar{b}\bar{m}\bar{v}}(\pi_{t-1} - \bar{\pi})$$

   This solution for $\tilde{Y}_t$ allows us to see the impact of a risk premium on the GDP gap absent any changes in inflation since $\pi_{t-1} = \bar{\pi}$ and the second term on the right-hand side becomes zero given our starting conditions so that:

$$\tilde{Y}_t' = \frac{\bar{a} - \bar{b}\bar{p}}{1 + \bar{b}\bar{m}\bar{v}}$$

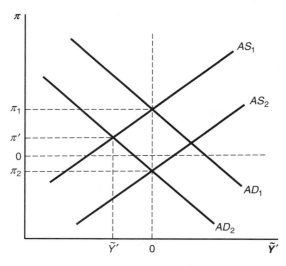

Figure 1

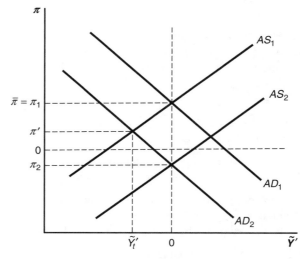

Figure 2

To see the impact of the increased risk premium on inflation, we substitute this value for $\tilde{Y}_t$ back into the AS curve while remembering that both $\bar{a}$ and $\bar{o} = 0$ in this example.

$$\pi_t = \bar{\pi} + \bar{v}\left(\frac{\bar{a} - \bar{b}\bar{p}}{1 + \bar{b}\bar{m}\bar{v}}\right) + \bar{o}$$

$$\pi_t = \bar{\pi} - \frac{\bar{v}\bar{b}\bar{p}}{1 + \bar{b}\bar{m}\bar{v}}$$

Note that in the absence of a risk premium, $\bar{p} = 0$, no shift of the AD curve would occur and the inflation would still equal its target level.

b. To see the long-run effects of a risk premium in financial markets, let the AS curve complete the adjustment process as detailed in Chapter 13 so that it returns the economy of a GDP gap of zero with the risk premium and AD_2 still in place. The effect on inflation is now the effect of interest since we know what the GDP gap will be. We show impact on inflation by solving the AD curve for inflation as follows:

$$\tilde{Y}_t = \frac{\bar{a} - \bar{b}\bar{p}}{1 + \bar{b}\bar{m}\bar{v}} - \frac{\bar{b}\bar{m}}{1 + \bar{b}\bar{m}\bar{v}}(\pi_{t-1} - \bar{\pi})$$

$$\frac{\bar{b}\bar{m}}{1 + \bar{b}\bar{m}\bar{v}}(\pi_{t-1} - \bar{\pi}) = \frac{\bar{a} - \bar{b}\bar{p}}{1 + \bar{b}\bar{m}\bar{v}} - \tilde{Y}_t$$

$$\pi_{t-1} - \bar{\pi} = \left(\frac{1 + \bar{b}\bar{m}\bar{v}}{\bar{b}\bar{m}}\right)\frac{\bar{a} - \bar{b}\bar{p}}{1 + \bar{b}\bar{m}\bar{v}} - \left(\frac{1 + \bar{b}\bar{m}\bar{v}}{\bar{b}\bar{m}}\right)\tilde{Y}_t$$

$$\pi_{t-1} = \bar{\pi} + \frac{\bar{a} - \bar{b}\bar{p}}{\bar{b}\bar{m}} - \left(\frac{1 + \bar{b}\bar{m}\bar{v}}{\bar{b}\bar{m}}\right)\tilde{Y}_t$$

Remember that $\bar{a}$ still equals zero, as does the GDP gap, so that the AD curve provides a solution for inflation that relates the amount of deflation to the strength of monetary policy response to the inflation gap.

$$\pi_{t-1} = \bar{\pi} - \frac{\bar{p}}{\bar{m}}$$

c. Under what conditions would a risk premium such as $\bar{b}$ lead to the possibility of deflation?

The relationship derived in part b above tells us that for deflation to occur, for π_{t-1} to be negative, the risk premium must exceed the target level of inflation by an amount determined by the strength of monetary policy efforts to control inflation. For example, if $\bar{m} = 0.5$, then to cause deflation the risk premium must be more than half the targeted level of inflation.

3. The response to the economy does not change. The AD curve for an economy with a risk premium is $\tilde{Y}_t = \bar{a} - \bar{b}\bar{p} - \bar{b}\bar{m}(\pi_t - \bar{\pi})$ and contains no terms that interact with the elements of $\bar{a}$. The consumers and firms represented in $\bar{a}$ are changing their behavior for some reason other than a risk premium or an interest rate–related development. Thus the impact on aggregate demand surfaces entirely in non-interest-sensitive elements of the economy that existed in the model prior to the inclusion of a risk premium and is shown as a shift of the aggregate demand curve.

CHAPTER 15 | Consumption

OVERVIEW

We now explore in greater detail the behavior of consumers in the largest sector of the economy. Upon finishing this chapter you should be able to explain how the neoclassical consumption model uses the behavior of rational individuals who maximize a lifetime utility function subject to an intertemporal budget constraint to allocate their lifetime wealth over both the current and future periods in their lives. You should also be able to show how this behavior is compatible with the permanent income hypothesis and what implications it has for the size of peoples' marginal propensities to consume when they experience a change in income. Not only should you be able to show how this leads to consumption smoothing, but you should also be able to discuss circumstances where exceptions to this behavior occur. Finally you should have some understanding regarding behavioral economics and its relationship to the neoclassical consumption model and know about the behavior of consumer borrowing and debt during the past few decades leading up to the financial turmoil at the end of the first decade of 2000.

KEY CONCEPTS

The *neoclassical consumption model* is one of the basic building blocks of modern macroeconomic modeling. The micro foundations of this model rely on the assumption that actors are rational and that they maximize lifetime utility subject to a lifetime wealth constraint. In this chapter the model consists of a current and a future period and income that can be earned in both periods.

The neoclassical consumption model allows for *financial wealth* in the form of savings accounts, stock and bonds, and other financial assets.

An *intertemporal budget constraint* requires that the present value of both current and future consumption be equal to the sum of any financial wealth and *human wealth*, defined as the present value of any current and future earnings.

Economists use a *utility function* to represent the satisfaction or benefit that an individual receives from participating in a given activity. In this chapter, that activity is consumption. We assume that more utility, or well-being, is gained from greater consumption, but that utility functions exhibit a characteristic economists' call *diminishing marginal utility*; that is, successive increments of consumption each yield smaller and smaller increases in utility.

The *Euler equation* for consumption is generated in the process of maximizing utility when faced with a wealth, or intertemporal budget constraint, as described above. Euler equations are useful because they allow identification of a state where the consumer is indifferent between another unit of current consumption or another unit of future consumption. In other words, the *marginal utility consumption* today just equals the marginal utility of consumption in the future.

The *permanent-income hypothesis* posits a consumption behavior that depends on an average value of income over an individual's lifetime rather than on the value of that individual's current income in any given time period. The expectation of an average income value does not require, but also does not preclude, a present value calculation as found in the calculation of lifetime wealth in an intertemporal budget constraint.

The *marginal propensity to consume* is the change in consumption that results from a change in disposable income, usually written as a ratio or as a percentage, and can be either short term resulting from a change in current period income or long term resulting from a change in expected average lifetime income.

The principle of *Ricardian equivalence* tells us that the present value of taxation's effect on consumption is invariant to the timing of that taxation. Effectively, it means that a change in taxation at any point in the future will have the same effect on current consumption as an equivalent present value change in taxation would have in the current period.

In some, or even many, cases when individuals are unable to obtain financing at a bank or other lending institution they face what economists call a *borrowing constraint* meaning that they are only able to consume out of current income rather than out of their lifetime earnings. A borrowing constraint will have the effect of increasing the size of an individual's marginal propensity to consume.

Another complicating factor that can influence the size of an individual's marginal propensity to consume has become known as the *random walk view of consumption* and involves the presence of uncertainty about one's lifetime earnings. When anticipated, a change in lifetime earnings should have very little effect on consumption since the change was foreseen and should have been factored into any present value considerations. However, an unanticipated change in lifetime earnings should have a much larger impact since there would have been no way for the individual to have factored that event into her planning horizon.

Income uncertainty also affects the marginal propensity to consume in another way as well. In order to prepare against a sudden drop in one's income, people are likely to set aside part of their income as what is known as *precautionary saving*. This behavior can be seen even when they might be expected to be borrowing because they are in a phase of their life when income is low and they expect to earn more later on. If the risk is great enough that they might lose their income, they may insure against that risk by saving even more while they still have an income.

A recent development in economics is the field of *behavioral economics*. It integrates economic theory and analysis with research findings in the fields of neuroscience and psychology in an effort to better understand how and why individuals make the decisions that they do in the way that they do.

The *personal saving rate* is the percentage of disposable (after tax) income that people save rather than consume.

TRUE/FALSE QUESTIONS

1. Once thought to be outdated, the neoclassical consumption model has seen a recent resurgence in the study of consumer behavior.

2. Financial wealth consists only of stocks and bonds.

3. The intertemporal budget constraint equates the present discounted value of consumption and total wealth, including all financial assets.

4. The principle of diminishing marginal utility applies only to goods and services that can be purchased in large enough quantities that utility can actually diminish.

5. The Euler equation tells us that as interest rates increase, current consumption becomes more expensive.

6. The log utility function is particularly useful because it makes the substitution and income effects easy to identify.

7. Ricardian equivalence means that a change in the timing of taxes does not affect the allocation of consumption across time as long as taxes are only levied on real income.

8. According to the permanent-income hypothesis, consumption will only change when there is an actual change in permanent income.

9. Precautionary saving occurs when individuals set aside part of their income for the occurrence of an unforeseen event, such as an automobile accident or a severe illness.

10. Behavioral economists have seen rich success at validating the neoclassical consumption model through utilizing the laboratory environment similarly to psychologists.

11. In response to the Great Recession, the personal saving rate is now higher than at any point since the oil crisis in the early 1970s.

12. As a consequence of the Great Recession, household wealth has fallen to its lowest level since World War II.

MULTIPLE-CHOICE QUESTIONS

1. Which of the following is not a specific part of the intertemporal budget constraint?
   a. current consumption
   b. future consumption
   c. current financial wealth
   d. future financial wealth
   e. total wealth

2. Which is the correct interpretation of the intertemporal budget constraint?
   a. It is the amount of money available to spend on consumption.
   b. The present value of lifetime consumption is at least equal to the present value of lifetime wealth.
   c. The present value of consumption equals total lifetime wealth.
   d. The value of consumption equals the value of wealth.
   e. Total wealth minus savings equals consumption.

3. Which of the following is the correct form of the Euler equation?
   a. $u'(c_{today}) = \beta(1 - R)u'(c_{future})$

   b. $u'(c_{today}) = \dfrac{1}{\beta}(1 + R)u'(c_{future})$

   c. $(1 + R)u'(c_{today}) = \beta u'(c_{future})$

   d. $u'(c_{today}) = \beta(1 + R)u'(c_{future})$

   e. $u'(c_{future}) = \beta(1 + R)u'(c_{today})$

4. Holding β constant, an increase in the real interest rate causes which of the following to occur?
   a. current consumption to increase
   b. future consumption to increase
   c. current consumption to decrease
   d. both current and future consumption to decrease
   e. both current and future consumption to increase

5. Holding β constant, an increase in the real interest rate causes which of the following to occur?
   a. the marginal utility of current consumption to remain unchanged
   b. the marginal utility of current consumption to increase and of future consumption to decrease
   c. the marginal utility of current consumption to decrease
   d. the marginal utility of future consumption to decrease
   e. the marginal utility of current consumption to increase.

6. Milton Friedman's permanent-income hypothesis depends on all of the following except
   a. the average value of income.
   b. current income.
   c. the present discounted value of income.
   d. the expected value of lifetime income.
   e. none of the above

7. Each of the following helps provide intuition toward understanding the permanent-income hypothesis except
   a. the practice of consumption smoothing.
   b. utility maximization.
   c. diminishing marginal utility.
   d. the Euler equation.
   e. none of the above

8. Ricardian equivalence means that consumption
   a. is subject to a lifetime wealth constraint.
   b. depends on the present discounted value of taxes.
   c. depends on disposable income.
   d. is invariant to the timing of taxes.
   e. Both b and d apply.

9. When an individual faces a borrowing constraint, it means that
   a. the individual is consuming less than this his income.
   b. the intertemporal budget constraint is no longer the correct constraint.
   c. financial conditions may be bad for the entire economy.
   d. the individual's credit history may not be good.
   e. all of the above

10. The random walk view of consumption predicts which of the following?
    a. large changes in consumption for no reason
    b. small changes in consumption for no reason
    c. large changes in consumption independent of the Euler equation
    d. a large change in consumption following an anticipated promotion
    e. small changes in consumption following an anticipated promotion

11. Which of the following explains why the marginal propensity to consume may be larger than the permanent-income hypothesis would predict?
    a. fear of job loss
    b. borrowing constraints
    c. poor credit history
    d. all of the above
    e. none of the above

12. When considering households of above-average wealth, the Euler equation and the permanent-income hypothesis provide which conclusion?
    a. Their consumption response to a temporary income shock is large.
    b. They tend to smooth consumption over time.
    c. They still behave as if they faced a borrowing constraint.
    d. They experience large changes in consumption on a regular basis.
    e. Their consumption behavior is unpredictable.

13. When considering households of above-average wealth, the Euler equation and the permanent-income hypothesis provide which conclusion?
    a. Their consumption response to a temporary income shock is small.
    b. They behave as if they faced no borrowing constraint.
    c. They experience small changes in consumption over time.
    d. Their consumption behavior is very predictable.
    e. Their consumption tends to vary more over time than higher-wealth households.

14. Behavioral economics draws heavily on research and insights from each of the following disciplines except
    a. psychology.
    b. sociology.
    c. neuroscience.
    d. economics.
    e. none of the above

15. Significant changes in household behavior regarding debt and personal saving rates occurred in
    a. 1975.
    b. 1985.
    c. 1995.
    d. 2005.
    e. 2010

EXERCISES

1. Show and explain how the neoclassical consumption model is consistent with Milton Friedman's permanent-income hypothesis.

2. Discuss the tax rebate implications for a stimulus package given the type of behavior modeled by the permanent-income hypothesis.

PROBLEMS

Worked Problem

1. Use the following log utility model and lifetime wealth constraint to complete this problem.

$$\max_{c_{today},\, c_{future}} U = u(c_{today}) + \beta u(c_{future})$$

$$c_{today} + \frac{c_{future}}{1+R} = \bar{W}, \text{ where } \bar{W} = f_{today} + y_{today} + \frac{y_{future}}{1+R}$$

a. Derive the Euler equation for consumption. Begin by solving the budget constraint for c_{future}

$$c_{today} + \frac{c_{future}}{1+R} = \bar{W}$$

$$\frac{c_{future}}{1+R} = \bar{W} - c_{today}$$

$$c_{future} = (1+R)(\bar{W} - c_{today})$$

and substituting it into the utility function such that

$$U = u(c_{today}) + \beta u[(1+R)(\bar{W} - c_{today})].$$

Take the derivative of U with respect to c_{today}, set it equal to zero, and solve for the marginal utility of consumption today to derive the Euler equation.

$$\frac{\partial u}{\partial c_{today}} = u'(c_t) + \beta u'(c_f)(1+R)(-1) = 0$$

$$u'(c_t) = \beta(1+R)u'(c_f)$$

b. Use the Euler equation you derive to explain how consumption is allocated between the present and the future.

   The Euler equation, $u'(c_t) = \beta(1+R)u'(c_f)$, says that consumption will be chosen so that the marginal utility of consumption today is just equal to the discounted value of the marginal utility of future consumption. Note from the budget constraint that future consumption is $1+R$ units greater than deferred current consumption.

2. Use the consumer's budget constraint and the Euler equation you derived in Problem 1 to complete this problem.
   a. Assume that $\beta = 1$ and solve for the level of consumption both today and in the future.
   b. Suppose that an individual discounts future consumption by 10 percent so that $\beta = 0.9$. Show how this will affect both current and future consumption.

3. Suppose that a worker does not discount future consumption and that $\beta = 1$, that utility takes the log form, and that the real interest rate is currently 3 percent. Assume that this worker has financial assets worth $20,000, labor income in the current period of $30,000, and in the future of $60,000.
   a. Using the intertemporal budget constraint determine how much human wealth this person possess.
   b. Now determine the value of this person's total wealth.
   c. What portion of this person's total wealth will be consumed in each period and what is that dollar amount?
   d. If this individual receives an increase salary in the current period of $15,000, how much will consumption in each period be increased?
   e. Suppose instead that this individual knows that the increase in salary will come in the future, what difference would it make for consumption in each period?
   f. Explain why your answers in parts d and e differ.
   g. Refer back to part b and determine what impact a doubling of interest rates would have for this individual on both consumption and wealth?
   h. Suppose that an encounter with identity theft constrains this person from being able to borrow during the current period, how would that experience change this person's consumption stream?

CHAPTER 15 SOLUTIONS

True/False Questions

1. False. The neoclassical consumption model has long been a mainstay in macroeconomic modeling. See Section 15.1.

2. False. It also includes assets such as savings accounts. See Section 15.2.

3. True. Total wealth includes both financial and human wealth. See Section 15.2.

4. False. This principle applies to all types of goods and services regardless of their divisibility. See Utility, Section 15.2.

5. True. This explanation consists of two parts. First, when interest rates increase, the Euler equation requires $u'(c_t)$ to increase, which in turn requires consumption to fall. Current consumption becomes more expensive because any saved consumption now earns a greater return. See Choosing Consumption to Maximize Utility and The Effect of a Rise in R on Consumption, Section 15.2.

6. False. it cannot address substitution and income effects because they cancel each other out. See Section 15.2, The Effect of a Rise in R on Consumption.

7. False. Taxes are levied on nominal income but the statement is otherwise true. See Ricardian Equivalence, Section 15.3.

8. False. Consumption will change even when there is an anticipation of increase in income as long as the individual's perception of a higher average income increases. See Consumption as a Random Walk, Section 15.3.

9. False. It occurs when there is a potential loss of income in the foreseeable future. See Section 15.3, Precautionary Saving.

10. False. These studies have explicitly tested the use of assumptions considered to be more realistic. See the case study "Behavioral Economics and Consumption," Section 15.4.

11. False. It has risen since the Great Recession began, but not to its level during the 1970s. See Figure 15.4 and Section 15.4.

12. False. It is very low, but it was lower in the mid-1970s. See Figure 15.5.

Multiple-Choice Questions

1. d, although future financial wealth is there implicitly as unspent current financial wealth, it is not formally part of the constraint. See Section 15.2.

2. c, lifetime wealth includes today's financial wealth and income plus any future income. See Section 15.2.

3. d, see Section 15.2, equation 15.6.

4. c, a higher interest rate is felt through its presence in lifetime wealth in the present discounted value of labor income. See Choosing Consumption to Maximize Utility and The Effect of a Rise in R on Consumption, Section 15.2.

5. e, see the explanation to multiple-choice queston 4 and combine it with the principle of diminishing marginal utility. In order for $u'(c_{today})$ to increase, less must be consumed.

6. b, each of the other answers approximates the concept of lifetime income used by Friedman's hypothesis. See Section 15.3.

7. e, each of the answers provides insight. See Permanent-Income Hypothesis, Section 15.3.

8. e, Ricardian equivalence assumes the ability to assess lifetime income and make consumption decisions accordingly.

9. b, while one or more of parts a, c, and d may be true, they need not all be true but part b will always apply. See Borrowing Constraints, Section 15.3.

10. e, the random walk still implies consumption smoothing and incorporates large anticipated events. See Consumption as a Random Walk, Section 15.3.

11. d, each of these choices leads to purposefully spending less or an inability to borrow as might otherwise be desired. See Borrowing Constraints and Precautionary Saving, Section 15.3.

12. b, this is the group of households that behaves according to the predictions of the permanent-income hypothesis.

13. e, the permanent-income hypothesis does predict this group of households' behavior very well.

14. b, each of the other disciplines is named in the text. See Evidence from Individual Households, Section 15.3.

15. b, this observation is discussed Aggregate Evidence, Section 15.4 and can be seen in Figures 15.3 and 15.4.

Exercises

1. When making consumption decisions for today, the permanent-income hypothesis relies on the assumption of an average value of income over one's remaining lifetime, rather than just current period income. This can be seen in the solutions for consumption both in the current and in the future time periods where $c_{today} = \frac{1}{2}\bar{W}$, and $c_{future} = \frac{1}{2}(1 + R)\bar{W}$. Note that in both time periods, consumption is proportional to the individual's lifetime wealth constraint, $\bar{W}$, where

   $$\bar{W} = f_{today} + y_{today} + \frac{y_{future}}{1 + R}.$$ Note that in the absence of bequests this model requires that total wealth also be consumed between the two time periods.

2. Since the legislative process makes the occurrence and timing of tax rebates public knowledge for quite some time prior to their implementation, their effect on consumption should be relatively small. The public will have had significant time to adjust its value for expected lifetime income and to choose the corresponding level of consumption. Tax rebates are also seen as temporary, which does not work to change lifetime income and therefore leaves consumption relatively unchanged and the effect of the tax rebate small for a second reason.

Problems

1. Worked Problem. The problem is worked in the text.

2. a. Begin with the Euler equation and budget constraint,

   $$u'(c_{today}) = \beta(1 + R)u'(c_{future}).$$

   $$c_{today} + \frac{c_{future}}{1 + R} = \bar{W}$$

   then use the fact that the derivative of $u'(c) = 1/c$ and make the substitutions into the Euler equation

   $$\frac{1}{c_{today}} = \beta(1 + R)\frac{1}{c_{future}}$$

   which can be arranged as

   $$\frac{c_{future}}{c_{today}} = \beta(1 + R)$$

   and again as

   $$c_{today} = \frac{c_{future}}{\beta(1 + R)}$$

   and if $\beta \neq 1$ can be substituted into the budget constraint

   $$c_{today} + \frac{c_{future}}{(1 + R)} = \bar{W}$$

   as

   $$c_{today} + c_{today} = \bar{W}$$
   $$2c_{today} = \bar{W}$$

   and consumption today becomes

   $$c_{today} = \frac{1}{2}\bar{W}.$$

   Similarly, with using $\beta = 1$ the Euler equation also yields the solution for consumption in the future

   $$c_{future} = (1 + R)c_{today} \text{ or}$$
   $$c_{future} = \frac{1}{2}(1 + R)\bar{W}$$

   b. If $\beta = 1$, then we repeat the steps as follows except that we substitute

   $$\beta c_{today} = \frac{c_{future}}{1 + R}$$

   into the budget constraint as

   $$c_{today} + \beta c_{today} = \bar{W}$$
   $$(1 + \beta)c_{today} = \bar{W}$$

and consumption today becomes

$$c_{today} + \frac{1}{1+\beta} = \bar{W}.$$

Thus if $\beta < 1$, the consumption today will be more than one-half of $\bar{W}$. Similarly, consumption in the future becomes

$$\frac{c_{future}}{c_{today}} = \beta(1+R)$$

$$c_{future} = \beta(1+R)c_{today}$$

$$c_{future} = \beta(1+R)\frac{1}{1+\beta}\bar{W}$$

$$c_{future} = \frac{\beta}{1+\beta}(1+R)\bar{W}.$$

Note that if $\beta < 1$, that $\frac{\beta}{1+\beta}$ will be less than one-half, meaning that $\beta < 1$ and future consumption discounted, consumption will be shifted from the future to the present. Note that $\frac{1}{1+\beta} + \frac{\beta}{1+\beta} = 1$ so that total wealth will still be consumed between the two periods.

3. a. The human wealth portion of the wealth constraint is

$$\text{human wealth} = y_{today} + \frac{y_{future}}{1+R}$$

$$= \$30,000 + \frac{\$60,000}{1+0.03}$$

$$= \$30,000 + \$58,252.43$$

$$= \$88,252.43$$

b. Substituting the appropriate values into the equation for total wealth yields

$$\bar{W} = f_{today} + y_{today} + \frac{y_{future}}{1+R}$$

$$\bar{W} = \$20,000 + \text{human wealth}$$

$$\bar{W} = \$20,000 + \$30,000 + \frac{\$60,000}{1+0.03}$$

$$= \$20,000 + \$88,252.43$$

$$= \$108,252.43$$

c. One-half, $54,126.22, will be consumed in the first period (see the derivation for $c_{today} = \frac{1}{2}\bar{W}$ in part 2a above) and $54,126.22 plus the interest earnings of $1,623.79 for a total of $55,750.01 in the second period (see the derivation for $c_{future} = \frac{1}{2}(1+R)\bar{W}$ in part 2a above).

d. Since $\bar{W}$ increases by $15,000 to $123,126.22 consumption in the first period will be increased by $7,500 to $61,626.22 and in the second period by $7,725 ($7,500 plus 3 percent of $7,500) bringing total future consumption to $63,475.01.

e. If the $15,000 came in the future, lifetime wealth would become

$$\bar{W} = f_{today} + y_{today} + \frac{y_{future}}{1+R}$$

$$\bar{W} = \$20,000 + \$30,000 + \frac{\$75,000}{1+0.03}$$

$$= \$50,000 + \$72,815.53$$

$$= \$122,815.53$$

and current consumption would be $61,407.77, and future consumption would be $63,250.00.

f. The difference between parts d and e is attributable to the interest earnings on the deferred consumption when the $15,000 is received in the first period.

g. An interest rate of 6 percent would make lifetime wealth become

$$\bar{W} = f_{today} + y_{today} + \frac{y_{future}}{1+R}$$

$$\bar{W} = \$20,000 + \$30,000 + \frac{\$60,000}{1+0.06}$$

$$= \$50,000 + \$56,603.77$$

$$= \$106,603.77$$

Since lifetime wealth has fallen by $1,648.66, consumption in the current period will decrease to $53,301.89 × 1.06 - $56,500 for an increase of $56,500 – $55,750.01 or $749.99.

h. When faced with a borrowing constraint, this individual would be constrained to consume only that which is available in the current period, or financial wealth and current human capital, for a total of $50,000.

CHAPTER 16 | Investment

After studying this chapter you should be able to describe several different types of investment that all work to transform current resources into future resources. You should be able to explain how this works for both physical and human capital and for new ideas. You should also be able to explain the distinction between investment in capital stock and in financial assets. Following this chapter you should have a solid understanding of the principle of arbitrage and how it works, including physical, financial, and residential investment. You should also be fluent with the way economists calculate the user cost of capital and how the elements of depreciation, capital gains, and taxation affect that user cost. Finally you should be able to explain how inventory investment behaves relative to the business cycle and provide a couple of potential explanations for that behavior.

KEY CONCEPTS

An *arbitrage equation* allows for the comparison of two different investment alternatives and shows that under profit-maximizing conditions a person would allocate funding between the two options until the returns on each option were identical, that is, until each side of the equation was equal to the other.

A *capital gain* occurs when the price of an asset increases over time. Should the price of that asset decrease over time instead, then its owner would experience a *capital loss*.

The total cost to a firm of employing one more unit of capital is called the *user cost of capital* and includes the interest expense along with any depreciation and capital gains or losses.

When a firm that has issued stocks makes a profit, it generally makes a payment in the form of a *dividend* to its stockholders in order to distribute that profit.

The *price-earnings ratio* is the price of a company's share of stock divided by the earnings it paid on that share.

In a financial market *informational efficiency* exists if the prices in that market fully and correctly reflect all of the available information.

Stock prices follow what economists call a *random walk* when they are just as likely to show gains as declines and when the only thing that causes them to change is unanticipated news.

To avoid the risk involved with owning a single stock, or only a few stocks, people can buy shares in *mutual funds* that pool together the savings of many individuals. These savings are then used to purchase large volumes of stocks and bonds and build a portfolio that most participants in the fund could not acquire on their own.

One way of measuring a firm's value during periods of expansion when adjustment costs to the size of its capital stock are present is to construct a measure known as *Tobin's q*, the ratio of the firm's stock market value to the value of its capital stock. When this ratio exceeds 1, it signals to the firm that it should invest in additional capital, and vice versa when it's less than 1.

The investment component of national income accounting consists of three major categories: *nonresidential fixed investment*, equipment structures purchased by business; *residential fixed investment*, new housing purchased by households; and *inventory investment*, all of the goods produced but not sold during a calendar year.

Production smoothing occurs when firms build up inventories during contractions and draw them down during expansions in order to avoid the costs of increasing and decreasing manufacturing levels during those phases of the business cycle.

Firms will hold some level of raw materials and intermediate goods in inventory in order to carry out their own production activities. Many point to this *pipeline theory* of inventory holdings as a good way to explain the procyclical behavior between GDP and inventories.

The fear of actually running out of goods and customers standing in line leads firms to undertake something called *stockout avoidance* and build up their inventories as a precaution against such an event.

TRUE/FALSE QUESTIONS

1. Investment fluctuates much less than consumption except during expansions, when it rises disproportionately.

2. One important reason to study investment is that it links the present to the future.

3. Firms should invest in capital until the value of its output falls to the value of its user cost.

4. Since corporate stocks are a financial investment and cannot be used to produce new goods and services, the arbitrage equation cannot be applied.

5. The price-earnings ratio is relatively stable as predicted by the arbitrage model.

6. A financial market is said to be informationally efficient if its prices fully reflect all information about that financial market.

7. When stock prices follow a random walk, the only thing that will cause them to change is news that people do not expect.

8. When qualified professionals actively manage mutual funds, they almost always have a higher return than a passively managed fund.

9. The observation of a value for Tobin's q that is less than 1 means that the stock of that firm is undervalued and should be purchased.

10. Since no production occurs when buying an existing home, the arbitrage equation cannot be applied to housing prices.

MULTIPLE-CHOICE QUESTIONS

1. Which form of investment is relevant for economists' work on national income accounting?
   a. the development of new patents and copyrights
   b. the investment in a college education
   c. the acquisition of stocks and bonds
   d. the accumulation of roads, houses, computers, and machine tools
   e. the securitization of mortgages in order to facilitate increased residential housing

2. Which of the following is not a form of capital stock for macroeconomists?
   a. roads
   b. houses
   c. computers
   d. stocks
   e. machine tools

3. An arbitrage equation can be used to address investment questions in
   a. human capital.
   b. new ideas.
   c. financial assets.
   d. all of the above.
   e. only a and b.

4. Firms should continue to put additional capital stock in place as long as
   a. $MPK = R$.
   b. $MPK > R$.
   c. $MPK < R$.
   d. $MPK \geq R$.
   e. $MPK \leq R$.

5. In a profit-maximizing situation investors should choose investment opportunities so that
   a. they are ordered by increasing rates of return.
   b. they are ordered by decreasing rates of return.
   c. rates of return are equal.
   d. only the best returns are chosen.
   e. rates of return increase over time.

6. Which of the following is not a part of the user cost of capital?
   a. capital gains
   b. depreciation
   c. tax rates
   d. dividend payments
   e. interest rates

7. Which is the correct form of the user cost of capital?

   a. $\dfrac{R-\bar{d}+\dfrac{\Delta p_k}{p_k}}{1-\tau}$

   b. $\dfrac{R+\bar{d}-\dfrac{p_k}{\Delta p_k}}{1+\tau}$

   c. $\dfrac{R-\bar{d}-\dfrac{p_k}{\Delta p_k}}{1-\tau}$

   d. $\dfrac{R+\bar{d}-\dfrac{p_k}{\Delta p_k}}{1-\tau}$

   e. $\dfrac{R-\bar{d}+\dfrac{p_k}{\Delta p_k}}{1-\tau}$

8. Suppose that the real interest rate is 3 percent, depreciation is 7 percent, capital gains have been just 2 percent, and the corporate tax rate is 35 percent. What is the user cost of capital?
   a. 18.5 percent
   b. 15.4 percent
   c. 12.3 percent
   d. 4.6 percent
   e. 3.1 percent

9. When applying the arbitrage equation to stocks, a form of financial investment, we solve for the
   a. amount of stock to hold.
   b. optimal dividend payment.
   c. stock's price.
   d. rate of return.
   e. length of time to hold the stock.

10. Which of the following is the correct form of the price-earnings ratio?

   a. $\dfrac{p_s}{earnings} = \dfrac{dividend/earnings}{R+g}$

   b. $\dfrac{p_s}{earnings} = \dfrac{dividend}{R-g/earnings}$

   c. $\dfrac{p_s}{earnings} = \dfrac{earnings/dividend}{R-g}$

   d. $\dfrac{p_s}{earnings} = \dfrac{earnings/dividend}{R+g}$

   e. $\dfrac{p_s}{earnings} = \dfrac{dividend/earnings}{R-g}$

11. Suppose Google will announce its annual profits next week and that they are expected to be extremely low. If markets are informationally efficient and the news is actually worse than expected, then Google share prices will _____ as a result of the announcement.
   a. rise
   b. fall
   c. remain unchanged
   d. fall and then rise again
   e. remain unchanged for a couple of days while the markets examine Google's report and then fall

12. When efficient market principles are applied to the mutual funds market, we find
   a. actively managed funds outperform the index funds.
   b. no differences between actively managed and index funds.
   c. "active index" funds have higher returns than "actively managed" funds.
   d. "passive index" funds have higher returns than "passively managed" funds.
   e. "passive index" funds have higher returns than "actively managed" funds.

13. Evidence finds that each of the following affect the value of Tobin's q except
   a. exogenous changes in tax policy.
   b. the firm's cash flow.
   c. budget deficits.
   d. access to financial markets.
   e. availability of bank loans.

14. Which of the following is not a component of the physical investment measured in the national income accounts?
   a. new housing purchased by individuals
   b. new equipment purchased by firms
   c. a new shopping mall
   d. the acquisition of 100 shares of stock from our brother-in-law
   e. unsold inventory at the end of the year

15. Suppose you put $25,000 as a down payment on a house that costs $125,000. At that point in time, your leverage would be
   a. 20 percent.
   b. five.
   c. $125,000.
   d. $25,000.
   e. one hundred.

16. Suppose that the down payment you are required to make on your new home suddenly decreases from 20 percent to 5 percent, what just happened to the amount of leverage you would be carrying if you made only the minimum down payment?
    a. It would also fall from 20 to 5.
    b. It would rise from 80 to 95.
    c. It would rise from 500 to 2,000.
    d. It would fall from 120 to 105.
    e. none of the above

17. What effect should we see if inventories behaved according to production smoothing?
    a. Inventories decrease as economic growth slows.
    b. Inventories remain relatively constant.
    c. Inventories fluctuate significantly, but inversely, with changes in demand.
    d. Inventories should track the growth of the economy.
    e. Inventories build up as economic growth increases.

18. Which of the following is not an explanation for the procyclical nature of product inventory?
    a. stockout avoidance
    b. pipeline theory
    c. production smoothing
    d. neither a nor b
    e. none of the above

EXERCISES

Worked Exercise

1. Use R for the interest rate on savings, p_k for the price of capital, MPK for the marginal product of capital, Δp_k for any capital gains or losses, and $\bar{d}$ for capital stock depreciation to complete this exercise.
    a. Show how a tax on corporate earnings affects the user cost of capital and thus the required return on capital.

    The solution to this problem requires carefully walking through the complete derivation of the user cost of capital. Begin with the profit-maximizing conditions of the firm, that the marginal product of capital be equal to the interest rate.

    $$MPK = R$$

    Next examine the opportunity cost of just earning interest in a bank versus the rate of return on capital. Note, however, that the rate of return on capital must be adjusted for any change in the value of the capital itself, that is, any capital gains or losses.

    $$MPK + \Delta p_k = R \bullet p_k$$

In order to put both sides of the equation in percentage terms, divide both sides by p_k and normalize setting $p_k = 1$ (but leaving it present in the capital gains term to reinforce that it's in percentage terms). Then move the capital gains term to the right-hand side.

$$\frac{MPK}{p_k} + \frac{\Delta p_k}{p_k} = \frac{R \bullet p_k}{p_k}$$

$$MPK = R - \frac{\Delta p_k}{p_k}$$

Note that the left-hand side now measures the marginal benefit of an additional unit of capital and the right hand-side measures the marginal cost. Note, too, that the type of costs can now be seen more clearly. Since depreciation is one of the reasons that capital stock loses value we can separate it out from the capital gains term as follows by denoting it as $\bar{d}$:

$$MPK = R + \bar{d} - \frac{\Delta p_k}{p_k}.$$

We also need to acknowledge that MPK does not accurately reflect the firm's benefits since it is required to pay income taxes on its earnings. To adjust for this we can multiply MPK by $(1 - \tau)$ and then isolate MPK again:

$$(1 - \tau)MPK = R + \bar{d} - \frac{\Delta p_k}{p_k}$$

$$MPK = \frac{R + \bar{d} - \frac{\Delta p_k}{p_k}}{(1 - \tau)}.$$

Now we can see that as corporate tax rates increase so does the user cost of capital. It also means that the required return on capital increases in order for a firm to undertake an activity.

    b. What impact do capital gains have on the user cost of, and required return on, capital? Explain

    Similarly, from the final equation in part a, we can see that because capital stock depreciates in value over time that both the user cost and the required return on capital increase as a result.

2. Use the data in the accompanying table to complete this exercise.
    a. Calculate Tobin's q for each of the firm's following levels of capital stock:

Units of Capital	Stock Market Value ($ per unit)	Value of Capital ($)	Tobin's q
100	3.50	675	
200	3.75	1,050	
300	4.00	1,385	
400	4.25	1,695	
500	4.50	1,775	

b. If this firm currently holds 250 units of capital, should people buy its stock? Explain.

c. How many units of capital will this firm hold in the long run? Explain.

3. Draw a loanable funds diagram and explain how financial and physical investment or financial and physical capital each impact a different side of this model.

PROBLEMS

1. Suppose that an economy has achieved a steady state but remains concerned that its current level of capital stock is too low for the economy to achieve its desired level of GDP per capita. Discuss any fiscal policy options that the government has at its disposal to address this concern (There are at least two.)

Use the $MPK = \dfrac{R + \bar{d} - \dfrac{\Delta p_k}{p_k}}{1 - \tau}$ equation, the user cost

of capital, to work this problem. Recall that R is the interest rate on savings, p_k is the price of capital, MPK is the marginal product of capital, Δp_k captures any capital gains or losses, and $\bar{d}$ represents capital stock depreciation.

2. Continue on with the economic state of affairs facing the nation described in Problem 1. This time, however, consider the role of monetary policy. What options do monetary authorities have when it comes to trying to the raise the steady-state level or capital stock, thereby increasing per capita GDP? Explain the role that fiscal policy has in determining the effectiveness of monetary policy.

3. Suppose that fiscal and monetary authorities have done all that they can in Problems 1 and 2 to stimulate investment spending given the nature of the model describing the user cost of capital but that the economy remains mired in low-level capital growth and insufficient infrastructure to meet the nation's goals. At this point a young economist suggests the

implementation of an investment tax credit that would let firms write off a portion of the cost of the new capital, rather than depreciate it over several years. This investment tax credit essentially reduces the firm's price of additional capital stock.

a. Let the investment tax credit be represented by *ITC* and show how it affects the user cost of capital, *MPK*.

b. Would a fiscal policy of this type augment or impede the effectiveness of monetary policy? Explain.

CHAPTER 16 SOLUTIONS

True/False Questions

1. False. Investment fluctuates more than consumption. See Section 16.1.

2. True. Deferred consumption is saving. Saving and investing today increase future consumption. See Section 16.1.

3. True. This is exactly what profit-maximizing behavior predicts. See Section 16.2.

4. False. The arbitrage equation applies equally well to corporate stocks as to capital stock. See Section 16.3.

5. False. It actually varies dramatically at times. See Figure 16.3 and Section 16.3, P/E ratios and bubbles.

6. False. Add the word "available" to information and it will be a true statement. See Section 16.3, Efficient Markets.

7. True. The key assumption to this behavior is that markets are "informationally efficient." See Section 16.3, Efficient Markets.

8. False. Just the opposite is true, passively managed funds usually do better. See Section 16.3, Efficient Markets.

9. True. A Tobin's q that is less than one means that the company's market value is less than the replacement value of its capital stock, so buy. See case study "Tobin's q, Physical Capital, and the Stock Market."

10. False. Just the opposite in fact. the arbitrage equation can be applied; the role of production doesn't matter. See Section 16.4, Residential Investment.

Multiple-Choice Questions

1. d, national income accounting counts as investment only those physical things that add to the nation's ability to produce goods and services. See Section 16.1.

2. d, capital stock is used to produce other goods. Stocks represent ownership; they don't produce new goods. See Section 16.1.

3. d, arbitrage analysis applies to each of these. See Section 16.1.

4. b, once $MPK = R$, the firm should stop putting additional capital into place. See Section 16.2.

5. c, the arbitrage equation shows how rates of return equalize over time. See Section 16.2.

6. d, dividend payments are calculated and paid after the cost of capital has been accounted for. See Section 16.2.

7. b, see equation 16.6 in Section 16.2.

8. c,

$$MPK = \frac{R + \bar{d} - \frac{\Delta p_k}{p_k}}{1 - \tau} = \frac{0.03 + 0.07 - 0.02}{1 - 0.35} = 0.1231.$$

See Section 16.2, Example of Investment and the Corporate Income Tax.

9. c, with capital stock the price is already known and quantity to use in the production process is the issue. With financial stock that quantity question has already been solved and the issue is how capital stock's resale price is determined.

10. e, see Section 16.3, P/E ratios and bubbles.

11. b, stock prices will fall as a result of worse information than was already factored into them. See Section 16.3, Efficient Markets.

12. e, actively managed funds generally have lower returns than passively managed funds. See Section 16.3, Efficient Markets.

13. c, each of these is discussed in the text as having an influence on q except for budget deficits. See the case study "Tobin's q, Physical Capital, and the Stock Market."

14. d, the acquisition of the stock is just a transfer of ownership from your brother-in-law to you. See Section 16.4.

15. b, leverage is the value of the asset relative to one's own contribution. See Section 16.4, Residential Investment.

16. c, your leverage would increase from 5 to 20 times the amount of equity you would have in the home.

17. c, in order to avoid the costs of fluctuating production levels, firms would keep production constant as long as they expected growth to resume in the near future and any surge in demand to be only temporary. See Section 16.4, Inventory Investment.

18. c, production smoothing predicts a countercyclical inventory behavior. See Section 16.4, Inventory Investment.

Exericses

1. Worked exercise. This exercise is worked in the text.

2. a. See table below:

Units of Capital	Stock Market Value ($ per unit)	Value of Capital ($)	Tobin's q
100	3.50	675	0.5185
200	3.75	1,050	0.7143
300	4.00	1,385	0.8664
400	4.25	1,695	1.0029
500	4.50	1,775	1.2676

The calculation of the last value for Tobin's q in the table is performed as follows:

$$\frac{500 \times 4.50}{1,775} = \frac{2,250}{1,775} = 1.2726.$$

b. Yes, since Tobin's q is less than one it indicates that the company's market value is less than the value of its capital stock, that it should not acquire additional capital stock at this time, and that its stock value should appreciate, *ceteris paribus*.

c. This company's market value will equal the value of its capital stock when it has acquired approximately 400 units of capital, at which point its holdings of capital stock should stabilize.

3. The S_{LF} consists of savings (forgone consumption) that individuals deposit with financial intermediaries that are able to channel it to borrowers who generate the D_{LF} in order to put large amounts of capital stock in place for productive purposes.

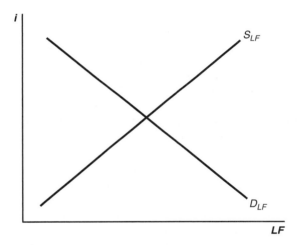

Problems

1. The government could lower the corporate tax rate or allow firms to depreciate their assets at a higher rate on their tax returns. A lower corporate tax rate means that *MPK* can fall, which encourages the use of more capital stock. Allowing a higher depreciation rate lowers the user costs of capital, making it more affordable to put additional capital stock in place.

2. Monetary authorities can influence the expansion of capital stock levels by lowering interest rates, thus making the acquisition and finance of additional capital stock less costly. The influence of fiscal policy will be felt through the level of corporate taxation as discussed in the answer to Problem 1, that is, a lower corporate tax rate means that *MPK* can fall, which encourages the use of more capital stock. The role of allowable depreciation does not interact directly with interest rates and so does not have an immediate influence on the effectiveness of monetary policy.

3. a. An investment tax credit (*ITC*) that reduces the cost of acquiring additional capital stock essentially reduces p_k, thus making the effective cost of capital to the firm $(1 - ITC)p_k$ and the user cost of capital becomes

$$MPK = \frac{R + \bar{d} - \dfrac{\Delta p_k}{(1 - ITC)p_k}}{1 - \tau}$$

Since the firm is now subsidized it will not bear the full cost of its capital acquisition and the necessary return on capital (*MPK*) can be lower.

b. An investment tax credit would augment an expansionary monetary policy since the subsidization and lower interest rates would work together. It would, however, impede a contraction monetary policy since they would be working in opposite directions with the tax credit encouraging investment and monetary policy discouraging it through higher interest rates.

CHAPTER 17 | The Government and the Macroeconomy

OVERVIEW

Government spending determines one-third of the U.S. gross domestic product. In many other countries, the percentage is even greater. For this reason, the importance of this chapter cannot be overstated. It provides a general understanding of government spending and taxation, including the important role of budget deficits and government debt. This chapter's major tool is the debt-GDP ratio, which, along with other important considerations, allows analysis of a country's debt status relative to other countries and its own past experience. A second major focus of this chapter involves understanding the nature of a country's intertemporal budget constraint, that at some point budget deficits require budget surpluses to make payments on the national debt. The economic consequences of the nation's budget deficits and ensuing debt load include their impact on economic growth, inflation (or default), intergenerational equity, and the crowding out of investment spending. Together, all these consequences influence the standard of living experienced by a nation's citizens. Finally, this chapter addresses the major fiscal problem of the current century: the unsustainability of current U.S. policies in the long run. Specifically, the problem centers around financing health care expenditures and understanding why the law of diminishing returns makes their growth unlike that of any other consumption good or service in the economy.

KEY CONCEPTS

The *budget balance* is the difference between government spending and government revenues. When spending exceeds revenues, we have a *budget deficit;* and when revenues exceed spending, we have a *budget surplus.*

When government spending just equals government revenues, we have a *balanced budget.*

Government debt consists of the outstanding stock of government-issued Treasury bonds. Economists distinguish between total amount of the debt ($13.56 trillion at the end of fiscal year 2010) and the publicly held portion of the debt ($9.02 trillion). The difference between the two consists primarily of intragovernment trust funds, which hold a special type of nonmarketable government security issued by the government to itself. The largest of these funds is the Social Security trust fund ($2.4 trillion), almost four times as large as the next closest category. For further reading on this distinction, a Congressional Budget Office document discusses "The Impact of Trust Fund Programs on Federal Budget Surpluses and Deficits" at www.cbo.gov/showdoc.cfm?index=3974&sequence=0. A somewhat critical view citing Office of Management and Budget documents "How Federal Trust Funds Really Work" resides at www.grove.ufl.edu/~leo /fed_trust_funds.html. Current values can be found at www.treasurydirect.gov/NP/BPDLogin?application=np and other trust fund categories identified in the Monthly Treasury Statement, www.fms.treas.gov/mts/index .html.

The *debt-GDP ratio* provides a measure of the size of the government debt relative to the country's GDP. If this ratio becomes too large, the country is seen as an unsafe credit risk. The amount of debt a country can carry safely, however, depends on more than just this ratio. Among other things, a country's past experience with debt, its growth prospects, and the credibility of its government and central bank play crucial roles in determining a country's safe debt-GDP ratio.

The *primary deficit* is the difference between government expenditures and tax revenues, excluding interest payments on the national debt.

The *total deficit* is the total difference between government expenditures and tax revenues, including interest payments on the national debt.

The *flow version of the government budget constraint* consists of an accounting identity with the uses of government funds (purchases of goods and services, transfer payments, and interest payments on the national debt) on one side of the equation and the sources of government funding (tax revenue, borrowings or new debt, and printing money) on the other side.

The government's *intertemporal budget constraint* equates the present value of current and future spending along with any accrued debt and interest payments on it to the present value of current and future consumption.

A government *defaults* on its debt if it announces that it can no longer repay it or that it will only repay it at some percentage of its face value.

Generational accounting recognizes that the people benefiting from government activities today may not be the same ones required to pay for them when the tax bill comes due tomorrow. It provides an approach to fiscal accountability that determines the extent to which future generations will bear the burden for today's current practices and policies on the part of government.

A person's income net of taxes is called *disposable income.*

Crowding out occurs when private savings are diverted away from new investment spending to finance government budget deficits. At issue is the future growth and improvement to a country's standard of living that new investment spending provides. The problem of crowding out is mitigated to the extent that people behave according to Ricardian equivalence.

Current benefits to Social Security recipients are paid by today's workers out of current payroll taxes through a system known as *pay-as-you-go.*

Health spending constitutes the fastest growing segment of the U.S. economy and represents perhaps the most important fiscal issue with which the country has to deal. Its behavior differs from that of most other expenditures. Since another month of life becomes increasingly valuable as one ages and acquires more wealth, health spending fails to experience diminishing returns in consumption like those found with other goods and services.

TRUE/FALSE QUESTIONS

1. Unlike individuals or corporations, the government's budget need not be balanced.

2. The U.S. government spends less money than many other industrialized nations.

3. The intertemporal budget constraint says that the present discounted value of government spending on goods and services must equal the present discounted value of tax revenues.

4. Other things equal, an economy growing more rapidly than its debt load will be deemed a better credit risk.

5. As with the consumption of most consumer goods and services, the consumption of health care is also subject to the law of diminishing returns.

MULTIPLE-CHOICE QUESTIONS

1. During 2007, according to the data presented in the text, government spending as a percentage of GDP was approximately
   a. one-tenth.
   b. one-fifth.
   c. one-fourth.
   d. one-third.
   e. one-half.

2. Which of the following government spending categories receives the highest portion of GDP expenditures?
   a. net interest payments on the national debt
   b. national defense
   c. health care
   d. Social Security
   e. other

3. The federal government receives the largest portion of its revenue from
   a. sales taxes.
   b. payroll (Social Security) taxes.
   c. income taxes.
   d. corporate income taxes.
   e. excise taxes.

4. The largest budget imbalance in U.S. spending in the twentieth century occurred because of
   a. World War I.
   b. World War II.
   c. the Vietnam War.
   d. the Korean War.
   e. the Iraq War.

5. Aside from the World War II period, the highest debt-GDP ratios in the United States were experienced in the
   a. 1950s.
   b. 1960s.
   c. 1970s.
   d. 1980s.
   e. 1990s.

6. Most economists rely on _____ when conducting macroeconomic analyses regarding the consequences of government debt.
   a. total debt
   b. interest-free debt
   c. net debt
   d. foreign-held debt
   e. federal debt

7. Which of the following is not a use of government funds?
   a. purchases of goods and services
   b. Social Security payments
   c. issuing Treasury bonds
   d. interest payments on the national debt
   e. Medicaid payments

8. The stock of a nation's debt in any given year includes
   a. last year's stock of debt plus interest payments on that debt.
   b. last year's stock of debt plus the current year's primary budget deficit.
   c. last year's stock of debt plus the current year's total budget deficit.
   d. last year's stock of debt plus interest payments on that debt plus the total budget deficit.
   e. both c and d.

9. Which of the following issues is not relevant to the determination of how much government debt a country can sustain?
   a. the level of economic growth
   b. the likelihood of high inflation
   c. the crowding out of investment activity
   d. intragovernment debt holdings
   e. intergenerational equity

10. Countries with a high and growing debt-GDP ratio present concerns regarding each of the following except
    a. the possibility of deflation.
    b. the possibility of default.
    c. higher interest rates.
    d. central bank credibility.
    e. devaluation of existing debt.

11. The primary concern of economists pursuing the field of generational accounting is that
    a. people are unaware of the intergenerational equity issues surrounding government debt.
    b. government debt could crowd out future investment spending.
    c. future generations will be unwilling to repay the government debt they inherit.
    d. high and rising debt-GDP ratios imply higher tax rates on future generations.
    e. future growth rates will be too low to accommodate current and projected debt growth.

12. Investment in an economy cannot be financed through
    a. government savings.
    b. foreign savings.
    c. private savings.
    d. trade deficits.
    e. none of the above.

13. Crowding out of investment occurs as a result of each of the following except
    a. budget deficits soaking up funds otherwise available for investment.
    b. people failing to take account of Ricardian equivalence.
    c. higher interest rates brought on by budget deficits and higher government debt.
    d. negative government savings.
    e. none of these; economists have been unable to provide any empirical evidence of its existence.

14. The best description of the fiscal problem of the twenty-first century described in the text is that
    a. government spending is too high.
    b. tax receipts are too low.
    c. current fiscal policies are unsustainable.
    d. health care spending is growing too rapidly.
    e. Medicaid and Medicare spending are grossly underfunded.

15. Which of the following is of least concern when it comes to issues contributing to the unsustainability of current fiscal policies?
    a. Social Security benefits
    b. Medicare spending
    c. Medicaid spending
    d. defense spending
    e. the law of diminishing returns

16. The main culprit behind the fiscal problem of the twenty-first century is
    a. the national debt.
    b. a growing debt-GDP ratio.
    c. Social Security obligations.
    d. spending on health care.
    e. spending on terrorism and national defense.

17. As prices for health care rise, consumers continue to demand more and more health care. This situation is
    a. an example of a violation of the law of demand.
    b. an example of irrational consumers.
    c. primarily a result of the moral hazard involved with a third-party payment system.
    d. a reflection of more income and consumer preferences.
    e. an example of waste and in part fraud by the medical profession.

EXERCISES

1. The government finances its debt primarily through the sale of three different types of Treasury securities to the public: bills, notes, and bonds. It also issues bonds that are held in intragovernment trust funds. Go to www.treasurydirect.gov/tdhome.htm and click on the following links: "Individuals" and then "Treasury Securities & Programs."
   a. Look up the difference between bills, notes, and bonds and explain how they are distinguished from each other.
   b. Look up intragovernmental holdings and report how they are defined (under "Home," "Government," "Resources," "FAQs," "Public Debt," and "Ownership of the Debt"). Then, using the "Monthly Statement of the Public Debt" ("Home," "Government," "Reports," "Public Debt Reports"), report the biggest category of such holdings.
   c. Use the Monthly Statement of the Public Debt to determine how the debt in each of these four categories has grown during the past 20 years. To do so, use data from the fiscal year just ended (the September report) and from the fiscal years ending 10 and 20 years ago. Create a table showing how these categories have changed, and report them both in levels and as percentages of the sum of these four categories during the corresponding years.
   d. What trends do you observe?

2. Return to the TreasuryDirect web site.
   a. Under the government section, go to the Reports section and click on "Public Debt Reports: Debt to the Penny." Report the Debt Held by the Public, the Intragovernmental Holdings, and the Total Public Debt Outstanding for the end of the last fiscal year.
   b. Look at the average interest rate graph under "Charts and Analysis" in the Government section and report the approximate average interest rate for the end of the last fiscal year.
   c. Under the Government section, go to the Interest Reports section and look up "Interest Expense on the Debt Outstanding" and report the amount of interest expense for the last fiscal year.
   d. Using the data collected in this process, determine whether the interest expense reported by the Treasury is for Debt Held by the Public or for the Total Public Debt.

3. For this exercise, go to the Economic Report of the President (www.gpoaccess.gov/eop/index.html), click on the "List of Statistical Tables" and find the table for Federal Receipts and Outlays by major category in the Government Finance section (in 2010, it was Table 80). Click on the link and download the spreadsheet version of this table. Income security programs include unemployment compensation, retirement and disability programs, and benefits such as food stamps and housing subsidies. Health care includes assistance for the poor through Medicaid, health care training, and medical research activities.
   a. Calculate and report in a table the percentage of the federal budget spent on Health, Medicare, Income Security, Social Security, Net Interest and these five categories together, for the most recent fiscal year and for 1970, 1980, 1990, 2000, and 2010.
   b. What implications do these trends have for the issues surrounding the nation's intertemporal budget constraint?

PROBLEMS

Worked Problem

1. Suppose a government began the year with a debt load of $500, an interest rate of 5 percent, and ran a deficit of $50.
   a. At the end of its second year, to maintain the same debt load of $500 with which it began, what would its fiscal policy regarding its budget balance have to be during this government's second year? Using equations (17.3) and (17.4) from the text, to maintain the same level of debt its problem would begin with

$$B_2 = (1+i)B_1 + G_1 - T_1 \quad \text{and} \quad B_3 = (1+i)B_2 + G_2 - T_2$$

Since $B_3 = B_1$, to maintain the same debt load, these equations become

$$B_2 = (1+i)B_1 + G_1 - T_1 \text{ and } B_1 = (1+i)B_2 + G_2 - T_2$$

Solve the second one for B_2 and set it equal to the equation on the left:

$$(1+i)B_2 = B_1 + T_2 - G_2$$

$$B_2 = \frac{B_1}{1+i} + \frac{T_2 - G_2}{1+i}$$

$$\frac{B_1}{1+i} + \frac{T_2 - G_2}{1+i} = (1+i)B_1 + G_1 - T_1$$

$$\left(\frac{B_1}{1+i}\right) + (T_1 - G_1) + \left(\frac{T_2 - G_2}{1+i}\right) = (1+i)B_1$$

Note that, with the exception of the debt term on the left-hand side of the equation, it is exactly the same as equation (17.6) in the text. Remember that, in this problem, we set B_3 equal to B_1 rather than zero. Were B_1 equal to zero, the preceding equation would be exactly the same as equation (17.6). Now solve for $T_2 - G_2$:

$$\left(\frac{B_1}{1+i}\right) + (T_1 - G_1) + \left(\frac{T_2 - G_2}{1+i}\right) = (1+i)B_1$$

$$\frac{T_2 - G_2}{1+i} = (1+i)B_1 - (T_1 - G_1) - \frac{B_1}{1+i}$$

$$T_2 - G_2 = (1+i)^2 B_1 - (T_1 - G_1)(1+i) - B_1$$

To make this clearer, we do the last three lines over, using numbers:

$$\frac{500}{1.05} - 50 + \frac{T_2 - G_2}{1.05} = (1.05)500$$

$$\frac{T_2 - G_2}{1.05} = (1.05)500 + 50 - \frac{500}{1.05}$$

$$T_2 - G_2 = (1.05)^2 500 + 50(1.05) - 500$$

$$T_2 - G_2 = 551.25 + 52.50 - 500$$

$$T_2 - G_2 = 103.75$$

In other words, to maintain the same debt level, the country must run a surplus during the second period large enough to pay interest on the initial debt for two years and repay the first year's deficit along with its interest.

b. To reduce the debt load by 10 percent, what will the government's policy have to be? Here, we have essentially the same problem, except that we need to be left with a debt of 450 instead of 500:

$$\frac{450}{1.05} - 50 + \frac{T_2 - G_2}{1.05} = (1.05)500$$

$$\frac{T_2 - G_2}{1.05} = (1.05)500 + 50 - \frac{450}{1.05}$$

$$T_2 - G_2 = (1.05)^2 500 + 50(1.05) - 450$$

$$T_2 - G_2 = 551.25 + 52.50 - 450$$

$$T_2 - G_2 = 153.75$$

2. Suppose the government begins with a balanced primary budget that grows at the same 3 percent rate as GDP and the interest rate on the national debt is 4 percent. Note, you may find it more efficient to complete this problem on a spreadsheet.
   a. Complete the following table describing the behavior of this country given the assumptions just listed.
   b. What happens to the debt-GDP ratio during this decade?

	Debt-GDP$_t$ %	GDP$_t$ ($)	B_{t+1} ($)	Interest ($)	B_t ($)	G_t ($)	T_t ($)
2020		4,000.00			1,000.00	100.00	100.00
2021							
2022							
2023							
2024							
2025							
2026							
2027							
2028							
2029							

c. Now assume that GDP growth increases to 5 percent and complete the following table again:

	Debt-GDP$_t$ %	GDP$_t$ ($)	B$_{t+1}$ ($)	Interest ($)	B$_t$ ($)	G$_t$ ($)	T$_t$ ($)
2020		4,000.00			1,000.00	100.00	100.00
2021							
2022							
2023							
2024							
2025							
2026							
2027							
2028							
2029							

d. What happens to the debt-GDP ratio during this decade?

e. Under what conditions would the debt-GDP ratio remain constant?

CHAPTER 17 SOLUTIONS

True/False Questions

1. False. The government's budget must be balanced at least over time in present discounted value. See Section 17.1.

2. False. It does spend less than many countries as a percentage of GDP, but its GDP is many times that of most industrialized nations: three times greater than Japan for example, six times greater than the United Kingdom, and over 40 times greater than Sweden. See Section 17.3, Figure 17.3, and the CIA World Factbook online at www.cia.gov/cia/publications/factbook/index.html.

3. False. The statement is almost true. The present discounted value of government spending on goods and services *plus* the national debt does equal the present discounted value of tax revenues. See Section 17.4.

4. True. Without other problems, a country growing faster than its debt load will be a more acceptable credit risk to potential lenders. See Section 17.5.

5. False. While this may be true for health care consumed in a specific time period, the text points out that it is not true for the return to adding months of life and, in that sense, the answer to this question is false. See Section 17.6.

Multiple-Choice Questions

1. d, one-third. See Section 17.1.

2. c, health care. See Table 17.1 and Section 17.2.

3. c, income taxes. See Table 17.1 and Section 17.2.

4. b, World War II. See Section 17.2 and Figure 17.1.

5. a, 1950s. Note that this answer is just barely correct. The 2010s are expected to eclipse the 1950s. See Section 17.2 and Figure 17.2.

6. c, net debt. See Section 17.1.

7. c, issuing Treasury bonds. See Section 17.4.

8. c, last year's stock of debt plus the current year's total budget deficit (since it includes interest payments on the national debt). See Section 17.4.

9. d, intragovernment debt holdings. See Section 17.5.

10. a, the possibility of deflation. See Section 17.5.

11. d, the higher tax rate implied by high and growing debt-GDP ratios. See Section 17.5.

12. e, none of the above. Trade deficits are a tempting answer, but since they are the excess of imports (income to foreign countries) over exports (foreign country expenditures) they essentially amount to foreign savings. See Section 17.5.

13. b, people failing to take account of Ricardian equivalence. If they did take account of this, additional savings would occur and investment spending can remain unchanged. See Section 17.5 and equation 17.7.

14. c, current fiscal policies are unsustainable. See Section 17.6.

15. d, defense spending. See Section 17.6.

16. d, spending on health care. See Section 17.6.

17. d, a reflection of more income and consumer preferences. Rather than a violation of the law of demand, this reflects an increase in the demand for health care services. See Section 17.6.

Exercises

1. a. Bills have a maturity of less than one year. Notes have a maturity between one and 10 years. Bonds have a maturity of greater than 10 years; currently (2010), new issues have 30-year maturities. Notes and bond both pay interest every six months.

    b. Intragovernmental holdings are government account series securities held by government trust funds along with a small amount of marketable securities. Government account series are by far the largest category in the monthly statement's itemization.

    c. Levels:

	Bills ($)	Notes ($)	Bonds ($)	Intragovernmental Holdings (Govt. Agency Accounts) ($)
1990	482,454	1,218,081	377,224	779,412
2000	616,174	1,611,326	635,263	2,242,900
2010	1,783,675	5,252,585	846,054	4,515,925

Percentages:

	Bills (%)	Notes (%)	Bonds (%)	Intragovernmental Holdings (Govt. Agency Accounts) (%)
1990	16.89	42.63	13.20	27.28
2000	12.07	31.56	12.44	43.93
2010	14.39	42.37	6.82	36.42

d. Intragovernmental holdings have grown significantly, while bills and notes have remained relatively constant. Bonds, however, have become a smaller portion of the national debt.

2. a. Your answers will differ from these, but compare them to those from the end of the 2010 fiscal year that were

   Debt Held by the Public:
   $9,022,808,423,453.08
   Intragovernmental Holdings:
   $4,538,814,607,438.71
   Total Public Debt Outstanding:
   $13,561,623,030,891.79

   b. At the end of the 2010 fiscal year, the average interest rate was approximately 3 percent.

   c. Interest expense for the 2010 fiscal year was $413,954,825,362.17.

   d. The interest expense for the fiscal year 2010 was 4.59 percent of the debt held by the public and 3.05 percent of the total debt outstanding. The Treasury most likely is reporting for the Total Public Debt.

3. a. The table for part a is as follows:

Note the consistent growth of Health and Medicare as a portion of the budget. Also noteworthy is the growth rate of total government spending. The 2000–06 period of time experienced an increase of over 60 percent in the average growth rate of total government spending compared to the 1990–99 period of time. This difference helps explain some of the later Income and Social Security and Net Interest behavior.

   b. A larger and larger portion of the federal budget is no longer discretionary. For the most part, these expenditures are not negotiable.

Year	Health (%)	Medicare (%)	Income Security (%)	Social Security (%)	Net Interest (%)	Sum of All Five Categories (%)
1970	3.02	3.17	8.03	15.49	7.36	37.07
1980	3.93	5.43	14.66	20.05	8.88	52.95
1990	4.60	7.83	11.87	19.84	14.71	58.85
2000	8.64	11.02	14.18	22.88	12.46	69.18
2010	10.01	12.29	18.43	19.39	5.05	65.17

Problems

1. Worked Problem. This problem is in the text.

2. a and b. With a growth rate of 3 percent and an interest rate of 4 percent, the debt-GDP ratio grows during this decade:

	Debt-GDP$_t$ (%)	GDP$_t$ (%)	B$_{t+1}$ (%)	Interest (%)	B$_t$ (%)	G$_t$ (%)	T$_t$ (%)
2020	25.0	4,000.00	1,040.00	40.00	1,000.00	100.00	100.00
2021	25.2	4,120.00	1,081.60	41.60	1,040.00	103.00	103.00
2022	25.5	4,243.60	1,124.86	43.26	1,081.60	106.09	106.09
2023	25.7	4,370.91	1,169.86	44.99	1,124.86	109.27	109.27
2024	26.0	4,502.04	1,216.65	46.79	1,169.86	112.55	112.55
2025	26.2	4,637.10	1,265.32	48.67	1,216.65	115.93	115.93
2026	26.5	4,776.21	1,315.93	50.61	1,265.32	119.41	119.41
2027	26.7	4,919.50	1,368.57	52.64	1,315.93	122.99	122.99
2028	27.0	5,067.08	1,423.31	54.74	1,368.57	126.68	126.68
2029	27.3	5,219.09	1,480.24	56.93	1,423.31	130.48	130.48

c and d. With a growth rate of 5 percent and an interest rate of 4 percent, the debt-GDP ratio declines during this decade:

	Debt-GDP$_t$ (%)	GDP$_t$ (%)	B$_{t+1}$ (%)	Interest (%)	B$_t$ (%)	G$_t$ (%)	T$_t$ (%)
2020	25.0	4,000.00	1,040.00	40.00	1,000.00	100.00	100.00
2021	24.8	4,200.00	1,081.60	41.60	1,040.00	105.00	105.00
2022	24.5	4,410.00	1,124.86	43.26	1,081.60	110.25	110.25
2023	24.3	4,630.50	1,169.86	44.99	1,124.86	115.76	115.76
2024	24.1	4,862.03	1,216.65	46.79	1,169.86	121.55	121.55
2025	23.8	5,105.13	1,265.32	48.67	1,216.65	127.63	127.63
2026	23.6	5,360.38	1,315.93	50.61	1,265.32	134.01	134.01
2027	23.4	5,628.40	1,368.57	52.64	1,315.93	140.71	140.71
2028	23.2	5,909.82	1,423.31	54.74	1,368.57	147.75	147.75
2029	22.9	6,205.31	1,480.24	56.93	1,423.31	155.13	155.13

e. When the growth rate of GDP equals the interest rate, the debt-GDP ratio remains constant. To see this, remember that the growth rate of the debt is the interest rate; then think about the debt-GDP ratio itself, and apply the growth rate rules from Chapter 3:

$$g_{\left(\frac{debt}{GDP}\right)} = g_{debt} - g_{GDP} = 0 \quad \Rightarrow \quad g_{debt} = g_{GDP}$$

CHAPTER 18 | International Trade

OVERVIEW

Countries trade goods and services for the same reason individuals do: overall they are better off, or wealthier, as a result. When a country imports more than it exports, as is the case currently with the United States, it must borrow money from other countries to finance the shortfall. At some point in the future, creditors will demand repayment, at which time the debtor nation must produce more than it consumes and run a trade surplus. Comparative advantage drives individuals to improve their living standards by trading with others, because they are relatively more efficient at their specialty than those with whom they trade. Countries do the same as they specialize in the production of the goods and services with the lowest opportunity cost and benefit from the resulting price differences. They do not need to have an absolute advantage or be the lowest-cost producer of a product, they need only to have a comparative advantage or to produce that product by giving up less of some other good to produce their specialty. Absolute advantage, on the other hand, drives workers to migrate to locations with greater productivity in order to improve their standard of living. Trade also benefits a country when it can offset the risk of natural business cycle fluctuations with its trading partners.

KEY CONCEPTS

The *trade balance* is the difference between exports and imports. When imports exceed exports, we have a *trade deficit;* and when exports exceed imports, we have a *trade surplus*. A trade imbalance implies the presence of international borrowing or lending and the eventual necessity of repayment, or a long-run balance of trade.

Risk-sharing occurs in international trade to the extent that trading partners offset each other's business cycle fluctuations that result from natural occurrences or disasters.

Autarky describes the state of a self-sufficient country that conducts no foreign trade with other countries.

Arbitrage describes the process of buying low in one location, or period of time, and selling high in another. This process facilitates gains from trade and helps explain the principle of comparative advantage between individuals as well as regions and countries.

An *absolute advantage* exists when an individual or country is the lowest-cost producer of a good or service when compared to other individuals or countries.

A *comparative advantage* exists when an individual or country has a lower opportunity cost for producing a good or service compared to others, even when that individual or country is not the lowest-cost producer in absolute terms.

Outsourcing refers to the use of resources outside of the firm to complete the production process. In an international trade context, it means the use of resources (typically labor) outside the country to complete the production process.

The *twin deficits* (the budget and trade deficits) are so named because of their relationship with each other. Large U.S. budget deficits use up private savings and crowd out domestic investment spending unless another source of loanable funds exists. U.S. trade deficits provide foreign countries with additional income and thus savings that generate potential loanable funds for offsetting the budget deficits.

Net foreign assets are the difference between U.S. ownership of foreign assets and foreign ownership of U.S. assets. Until 1986, U.S. net foreign assets were positive and the United States was a net creditor to the rest of the world. Since then, net foreign assets have been negative and the United States has held a net debtor position with respect to the rest of the world.

TRUE/FALSE QUESTIONS

1. On any given day, someone else produces virtually every good you consume.

2. International trade mitigates business cycle effects.

3. International borrowing indicates that a country has a trade deficit.

4. Foreign savings in a country are positively correlated to that country's trade deficit.

5. Absolute advantage determines a nation's ability to profit from international trade.

6. Outsourcing violates the principle of comparative advantage.

7. Empirical evidence supports the permanent-income hypothesis implications of international trade theory, that countries run trade deficits to smooth their consumption paths.

8. At some point, the trade deficits of today must be offset by trade surpluses in the future.

9. Economists generally express significant concern about the United States' foreign debt obligations and its ability to keep on borrowing so heavily from the rest of the world.

MULTIPLE-CHOICE QUESTIONS

1. Which of the following decreases did not contribute to the near tripling of foreign trade between the United States and its trading partners in the past 60 years or so?
   a. ocean freight costs
   b. overseas telephone costs
   c. airline revenue per passenger mile
   d. average worldwide tariffs on manufactured goods
   e. None of the above; they all contributed.

2. Foreign trade exceeds 20 percent of their GDP in each of the following countries except
   a. Canada.
   b. France.
   c. Germany.
   d. the United Kingdom.
   e. the United States.

3. Of the following U.S. trading partners—Canada, China, France, Germany, Japan, and the United Kingdom—which share the U.S. distinction of running a trade deficit?
   a. all of them
   b. all of the European nations
   c. only Japan
   d. France and the United Kingdom
   e. Canada and Japan

4. Individuals, as well as countries, engage in trade for several reasons. Which of the following is not one of them?
   a. consuming more than they can produce on their own
   b. increasing the welfare of other producers
   c. placing greater value on what other people produce
   d. increasing their own personal wealth
   e. avoiding certain activities

5. When a country runs a trade deficit, at least one of the following conditions must be met. Which one is not a possibility?
   a. The country expects greater growth in the future.
   b. Its exports exceed its imports.
   c. It has productive investments to make.
   d. The foreign debt it accrues eventually must be repaid.
   e. It is consuming more than it produces.

6. A country has a comparative advantage relative to another country in good X when
   a. it can produce more of good X than the other country.
   b. it can produce enough of good X so it has no need to import it from another country.
   c. its opportunity cost of producing good X is less than the other country's.
   d. its shipping costs are less than those in the other country.
   e. the other country has an absolute advantage producing good X.

7. In the apple and computer example in the text, a worker in the North could produce either 160 apples or 16 computers. What is the lowest price for which the North would sell a computer to the South?
   a. 6 apples
   b. 8 apples
   c. 10 apples
   d. 12 apples
   e. 14 apples

8. Economists generally extol the virtues of free trade for each of the following reasons except that it
   a. makes only one party better off.
   b. improves efficiency.
   c. increases wealth.
   d. exploits comparative advantage.
   e. accomplishes both b and c.

9. The practice of free migration of labor
   a. relies on comparative advantage.
   b. relies on absolute advantage.
   c. improves productivity in the country workers leave.
   d. improves the welfare of all workers.
   e. both b and d

10. The primary reason people in poor countries are poor is because
    a. the capital stock in those countries is too low.
    b. those countries have too many people.
    c. productivity in those countries is very low.
    d. of too little foreign aid.
    e. both a and b.

11. Countries engaging in foreign trade generally experience
    a. job creation.
    b. welfare losses in both countries.
    c. job destruction.
    d. all of the above.
    e. only a and c.

12. The use of outsourcing by domestic firms
    a. increases their production efficiency.
    b. creates more jobs than it destroys.
    c. generates costs to the economy.
    d. all of the above
    e. none of the above

13. Which of the following equations accurately describes domestic saving?
    a. $Y - T - C$
    b. $IM - EX + I$

    c. $IM - EX - I$
    d. $Y - C - G$
    e. $Y - C - G - I$

14. When a country runs a trade deficit, that country can expect to
    a. eventually return more goods than it currently is acquiring.
    b. experience increased holdings of financial assets.
    c. have a large budget deficit.
    d. pay higher interest rates.
    e. become a credit risk if trade deficits become too large.

15. The United States has been a net debtor to the rest of the world since approximately
    a. 1975.
    b. 1985.
    c. 1995.
    d. 2005.
    e. Never. The United States is a net creditor to the rest of the world.

EXERCISES

1. Show that a country's foreign savings are the negative of that country's trade deficit.

2. Without looking back in the text, use the national income accounting identity to show that a nation's level of investment is the sum of its public, private, and foreign savings.

3. Write a response discussing both positive and negative aspects of the question: Are trade deficits good or bad?

PROBLEMS

Worked Problem

1. Using Tables 18.2, 18.3, and 18.4 along with the assumptions from the text of identical workers and equal spending on both goods within each country, create diagrams as instructed in parts a–c.
   a. Draw production possibility frontiers for the representative workers from each country on a single diagram and label the autarky solutions as well as the endpoints and the PPF slopes. Use apples on the horizontal axis. This is shown in Figure 1.

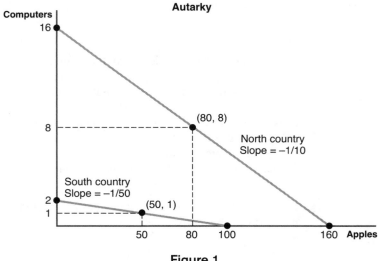

Figure 1

b. Draw production possibility frontiers for each country on a single diagram and label the autarky solutions as well as the endpoints and the slopes for both PPFs. This is shown in Figure 2.

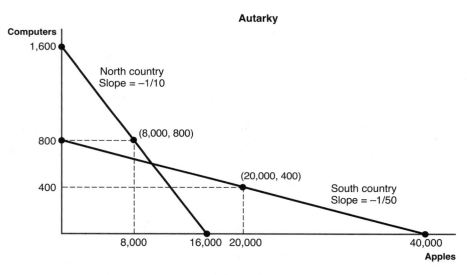

Figure 2

c. Show the free trade solutions on both the individual's and country's diagrams. Figure 3 shows the results for individuals and Figure 4 shows the results for countries.

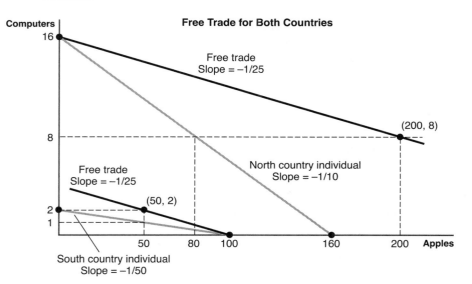

Figure 3

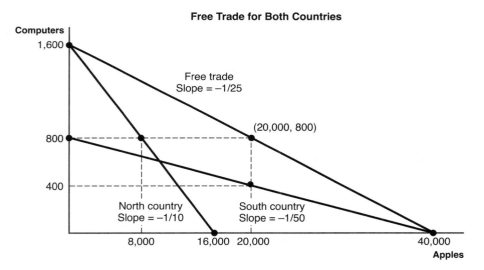

Figure 4

2. Repeat the process found in Problem 1 using the information found in the following table:

	North Country	South Country
Labor force	200	100
Number of pens one worker can produce	180	200
Number of MP3 players one worker can produce	18	50

    a. Create a table equivalent to Table 18.3.
    b. Draw production possibility frontiers for the representative workers from each country on a single diagram and label the autarky solutions as well as the end points and the PPF slopes. Use pens on the horizontal axis.
    c. Draw production possibility frontiers for each country on a single diagram and label the autarky solutions as well as the endpoints and the slopes for both PPFs.
    d. Create a table equivalent to Table 18.4.
    e. Show the free trade solutions on both the individual's and country's diagrams.

3. Use the information from the following table to complete parts a through c in this problem.

	Student A	Student B
Number of pizzas this student can produce	8	10
Number of papers this student can write	2	5

    a. Draw the production possibility frontiers for each student on a single diagram.
    b. Which student has the absolute advantage in pizza production? Paper writing?
    c. Identify each student's comparative advantage both numerically and graphically.
    d. Ignoring the ethical problems of complete specialization in a classroom environment, use the diagram to show how these two students can maximize both pizza and paper production.
    e. What is the range of possibilities for the terms of trade slope? Explain why it exists.

CHAPTER 18 SOLUTIONS

True/False Questions

1. True. The meals you eat might come close to negating the statement if you prepare them yourself, but then who produced the components of your meal? See Section 18.3.

2. True. During a recession, exports can offset at least some of the drag an economy might experience otherwise. See Section 18.4.

3. False. Trade could be balanced at the same time the country has a budget deficit by using international borrowing to finance the budget deficit. See Section 18.4.

4. True. To finance a trade deficit a country must borrow from abroad. Those borrowings become foreign savings in the country with the trade deficit. See Section 18.4.

5. False. The ability to profit from trade derives from production efficiencies by being able to offer goods for sale at a lower price (comparative advantage), not just the ability to offer a lot, or more, of them (absolute advantage). See Section 18.5.

6. False. In fact, it operates along the same lines, just on inputs rather than output. See the case study "Outsourcing: Separating the Fiction and Fact."

7. False. If this were true, the fastest growing countries would be running trade deficits and borrowing against their future income. See Section 18.8.

8. True. At some point foreigners will require payment rather than promises of payment, and this statement will be true. See Section 18.8.

9. False. Only a minority of economists expresses such concerns at the current time. See Section 14.8.

Multiple-Choice Questions

1. e, lower trade barriers, transportation, and communication costs all led to increased foreign trade for the United States. See Section 18.2.

2. e, the United States. See Section 18.2.

3. d, only the United Kingdom. All of the others do not. See Section 18.2 and Figure 18.3. (Our other North American trading partner, Mexico, ran a $400 million trade deficit in 2006.)

4. b, increasing the welfare of other producers. See Section 18.3.

5. b, a trade deficit is when imports exceed exports. See Section 18.4.

6. c, its opportunity cost of producing good X is less. In other words, it is more efficient at producing good X even if it cannot produce as much. See Section 18.5.

7. d, 12 apples. The answers 6, 8, and 10 are prices for which it could produce and trade domestically. It would gain from trade only by selling at a price greater than 10. See Section 18.5.

8. a, that it makes only one party better off. To the contrary, it makes both parties better off. See Section 18.5.

9. b, relies on absolute advantage, but improves the welfare of only the migrating workers. See Section 18.6.

10. c, because productivity in those countries is very low. Some of the other reasons may contribute, but the question asks about the primary reason. See Section 18.6.

11. d, all of the above. See Section 18.7.

12. d, all of the above. See Section 18.7.

13. d, $Y - C - G$. Note that $(Y - T - C) + (T - G) = Y - C - G$. See Section 14.8.

14. a, return more goods than it currently is acquiring. See Section 18.8.

15. b, 1985. Technically it has been so since 1986. See Section 18.8 and Figure 18.6.

Exercises

1. The trade deficit equals $EX - IM$. Foreign savings equal $IM - EX$. Note that the negative of the trade deficit, $-(EX - IM)$, becomes $-EX + IM$ which equals $IM - EX$, or foreign savings.

2. Begin with the national income accounting identity:

$$Y \equiv C + I + G + EX - IM$$

Then, subtract taxes (T) from both sides of the identity:

$$Y - T \equiv C + I - T + G + EX - IM$$

Note the intentional placement of taxes on the right-hand side of the identity. Next, systematically move everything except investment to the left-hand side of the equation:

$$Y - T - C + T - G + IM - EX \equiv I$$

Now, note the natural groupings of private, public, and foreign savings, all providing funding for investment. Note, too, that, if public savings is negative (thus reducing investment), a trade deficit, or positive foreign savings, can increase investment thus offsetting the crowding out of a budget deficit:

$$(Y - T - C) + (T - G) + (IM - EX) \equiv I$$

3. A number of responses are possible to this question. The positive aspects of a trade deficit should include lower prices, better quality, and greater selection of goods and services (basically aspects that benefit the consumer). Also included might be the foreign savings aspects of trade deficits that allow for increased investment. The negative aspects of a trade deficit should include the uneven bearing of costs that come from lower employment in the import-competing industries, costs of retraining workers, and reductions in self-sufficiency (essentially aspects that harm workers). Also included might be the dependence on foreign savings and the payment of interest earning abroad.

Problems

1. Worked Problem. The problem is worked in the text.

2. a. The table equivalent to the autarky position in Table 18.3 in the text looks like this:

	North Country	South Country
Wage, w	180 pens	200 pens
Price of an MP3 player, p	180/18 = 10 pens	200/50 = 4 pens
Consumption of pens (per person)	180 × 1/2 = 90	200 × 1/2 = 100
Consumption of MP3 players (per person)	18 × 1/2 = 9	50 × 1/2 = 25
Fraction of labor working to produce pens	50%	50%
Fraction of labor working to produce MP3 players	50%	50%
Total production in the pen sector	100 × 180 = 18,000	50 × 200 = 10,000
Total production in the MP3 sector	100 × 18 = 1,800	50 × 50 = 2,500

b. For individual workers, the production possibility curves are shown in Figure 5.

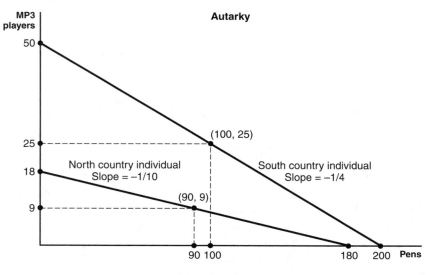

Figure 5

c. For each country, the production possibility curves are shown in Figure 6.

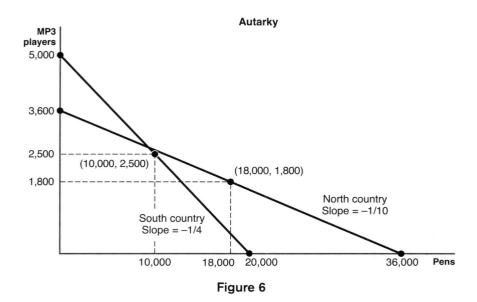

Figure 6

d. The table equivalent to the free trade position in Table 18.4 in the text looks like this:

	North Country	South Country
Fraction of labor working to produce pens	100%	0%
Fraction of labor working to produce MP3 players	0%	100%
Total production in the pen sector	200 × 180 = 36,000	0
Total production in the MP3 sector	0	100 × 50 = 5,000
Wage, w	180 pens	50 × 7.2 = 360 pens
Price of an MP3 player, p	36,000/5,000 = 7.2 pens per MP3 player	
Consumption of pens (per person)	180/2 = 90	360/2 = 180
Consumption of MP3 players (per person)	90/7.2 = 12.5	180/7.2 = 25

e. The free trade solutions for both individual workers (Figure 7) and countries (Figure 8) are shown in those figures.

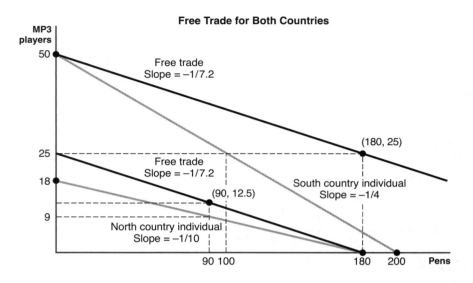

Figure 7

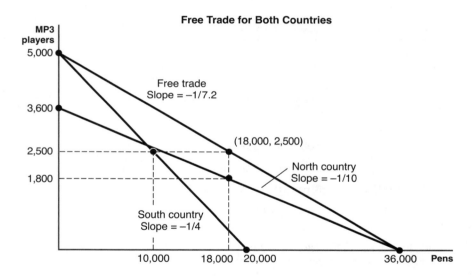

Figure 8

3. a. The production possibility frontiers are shown in Figure 9.

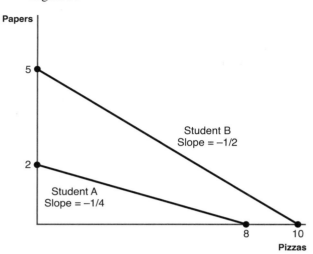

Figure 9

b. Student B has the absolute advantage in the production of both goods as seen by the positioning of that PPF farther away from the origin at both end points.

c. Student A has the comparative advantage in producing pizza with an opportunity cost of one-quarter of a paper (rather than one-half). Student B has the comparative advantage in paper writing with an opportunity cost of only two pizzas (rather than four). Note that these advantages are embodied in the slopes of the individual PPFs. Note, too, that Student B is two and a half times as productive as Student A in paper writing, but only 25 percent more productive in producing pens.

d. Student A will specialize in making pizza and Student B will write papers. They also need to find common terms of trade, then both will be able to consume outside their original PPFs, as shown in

Figure 10, on the solid lines with the same terms of trade for both students.

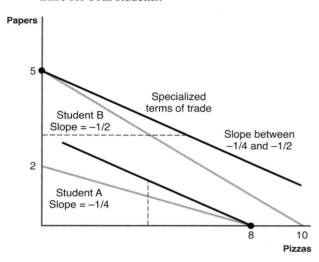

Figure 10

e. As shown in Figure 10, the range of possibilities for the terms-of-trade slope is between $1/4$ and $1/2$, or one paper for a price somewhere between two and four pizzas. Student A gladly would trade four pizzas for anything over one paper since he would then be able to consume more than he could produce all alone. Anything less than one paper per four pizzas (or a cost of more than four pizzas per paper) he could produce without trade. Since Student B can produce a paper for two pizzas without trade he would be willing to trade a paper for anything more than two pizzas. Trade therefore is bounded by a price between two and four pizzas, or a terms-of-trade slope of between $1/4$ and $1/2$. Actual terms of trade would depend on preferences and negotiating power.

CHAPTER 19 | Exchange Rates and International Finance

OVERVIEW

Exchange rates play an important role in determining the level of activity in both the markets for imports and exports and the financial sector. Long-run exchange rates derive largely from the law of one price, whereas short-run exchange rate fluctuations result primarily from financial market activity. Incorporating foreign interest rates into the short-run model developed earlier in Chapters 9–14 produces a richer framework (although of similar appearance) with a more fully developed model of the foreign sector. The new model describes the impact of monetary policy in an increasingly open economy and allows for the consideration of the effect of other countries' monetary policies on our own domestic economy. This chapter also explores the United States' experience with the fixed exchange rate nature of the gold standard, the Bretton Woods system, and its current situation of floating exchange rates. Finally, it explores the lessons learned from other countries' experiences in achieving and maintaining stable currencies in world foreign exchange markets.

KEY CONCEPTS

A *nominal exchange rate* is a financial market price. It is the rate at which one currency exchanges for another or the price of one currency in terms of another.

The *real exchange rate*, by contrast, is the rate, or price, at which real goods and services exchange for one another. Equivalently, it also is the nominal exchange rate adjusted for price level differences between the two countries under consideration.

Depreciation of a currency occurs when it becomes less valuable to other countries, that is, when its price in terms of other currencies decreases.

Appreciation of a currency occurs when it becomes more valuable to other countries, that is, when its price in terms of other currencies increases.

The *law of one price* states that, in the long run, after accounting for differences in taxes, tariffs, and transportation costs, the same goods must sell for the same price in all countries. It includes the expectation that short-run arbitrage (buying low in one place and undercutting a higher price somewhere else) will erode price differences beyond those just enumerated. In the long run, however, when the law of one price does hold, real exchange rates should be equal to 1.

The *international transmission of monetary policy* occurs when interest rate changes in one region of the world cause macroeconomic effects in another part of the world. These impacts are transmitted primarily through their effects on nominal exchange rates and, because of sticky inflation, on real exchange rates as well. The real exchange rate movements directly affect a country's net exports and, consequently, its aggregate demand.

Fixed exchange rates result when a country pegs, or fixes, the price of its currency to the currency of another country.

Floating exchange rates occur when the interaction of supply and demand in foreign exchange markets establishes the value, or price, of a country's currency.

The *policy trilemma* refers to the way monetary authorities are forced to choose among three mutually inconsistent goals in an international monetary system: stable exchange rates, free financial flows, and monetary policy autonomy. All three are desirable, but only two can be accomplished at any given point in time and at the expense of the third.

Foreign exchange reserves become necessary when a fixed exchange rate regime is in place and pegs its own domestic currency to another country's currency. In such cases, foreign exchange reserves constitute the domestic country's holdings of the foreign country's currency to which it has pegged its own currency's value. The domestic country then uses its foreign exchange reserves to intervene in foreign exchange markets and keep its exchange rate constant at its pegged value.

A country that sets a fixed price for its currency, usually artificially low, and then supplies only the quantity that it wishes is operating with a *capital control*.

TRUE/FALSE QUESTIONS

1. The introduction of exchange rates into the short-run model alters that model by significantly changing the relationship of the IS curve.

2. A currency appreciation in the long run means that domestic monetary policy has been more restrictive (tighter) than the monetary policy of its foreign trading partner.

3. Sticky inflation causes anticipated nominal exchange rate movements to cause real exchange rate movements in the short run.

4. The central bank of a country seeking to maintain a fixed exchange rate must adopt the monetary policy of the country to which it is fixing its currency value.

5. A change in the real interest rate in the rest of the world ($\bar{R}^w$) causes the domestic aggregate demand curve to shift to the right or to the left.

6. Net exports that respond to changes in the real interest rate make the IS curve flatter.

7. Restrictive monetary policy abroad (higher foreign interest rates) is harmful to a country's domestic economy.

8. U.S. experience with fixed exchange rates is limited to the brief period of the Bretton Woods agreement.

9. When faced with the international finance policy trilemma described in the text, it is generally best to choose floating exchange rates and allow free financial flows while at the same time maintaining monetary policy autonomy.

10. The United States' movement from trade deficits to trade surpluses would cause an economic expansion in its domestic economy.

MULTIPLE-CHOICE QUESTIONS

1. Which of the following countries does not have its own currency?
   a. Japan
   b. United Kingdom
   c. Germany
   d. China
   e. Canada

2. Which of the following events would cause the nominal exchange rate for the U.S. dollar to appreciate?
   a. increased acceptance of the euro as payment for crude oil
   b. increased imports by the United States
   c. increased exports by the United States
   d. increased interest rates in the European Union
   e. none of the above

3. Which of the following will not keep the law of one price from holding exactly?
   a. taxes
   b. tariffs
   c. transportation costs
   d. quality differences
   e. exchange rates

4. The law of one price is accurately portrayed by which of the following equations, where E is the nominal exchange rate, P is the domestic price level, and P^w is the price level in the rest of the world?
   a. $P/E = P^w$
   b. $P = EP^w$
   c. $PP^w = E$
   d. $P^w = EP$
   e. $P^w = E/P$

5. The problem with the Big Mac index failing to demonstrate the law of one price is
   a. the law of one price is just a theoretical construct.
   b. it does not account for the price of locally produced ingredients.
   c. it does not account for real estate and labor prices.
   d. all of the above.
   e. only b and c.

6. The real exchange rate is
   a. equal to 1 in the long run.
   b. a ratio of foreign to domestic goods.
   c. driven by the law of one price.
   d. all of the above.
   e. only a and c.

7. The primary determinant of nominal exchange rate movement is
   a. international trade.
   b. foreign travel.
   c. fluctuation in world oil prices.
   d. international financial market activity.
   e. unable to tell

8. The main source of hyperinflation is
   a. fiscal policy.
   b. monetary policy.
   c. consumption spending.
   d. excessive export demand.
   e. excessive price increases.

9. Statements 1–5 that follow represent the steps in the process through which monetary authorities can affect the foreign sector. What is the correct order of these steps?

   (1) Higher real interest rates attract financial flows into the country.
   (2) Domestic goods become relatively more expensive, reducing net exports.
   (3) Demand for the domestic currency increases, causing it to appreciate.
   (4) Because of sticky inflation, real exchange rates increase.
   (5) The central bank raises nominal interest rates, and because of sticky inflation, real interest rates increase.

   a. 1, 4, 3, 5, 2
   b. 2, 5, 4, 3, 1
   c. 4, 3, 1, 2, 5
   d. 5, 1, 3, 4, 2
   e. 3, 5, 2, 4, 1

10. Which of the following equations is the new net export function once foreign and domestic interest rates and the marginal product of capital are accounted for?
    a. $NX_t/\bar{Y}_t = \bar{a}_{nx} - \bar{b}_{nx}(\bar{R}_t^w - \bar{r})$
    b. $NX_t/\bar{Y}_t = \bar{a}_{nx} - \bar{b}_{nx}(R_t - \bar{r}) + \bar{b}_{nx}(\bar{R}^w - \bar{r})$
    c. $NX_t/\bar{Y}_t = \bar{a}_{nx} - \bar{b}_{nx}(R_t - \bar{R}^w) + \bar{b}_{nx}(\bar{r} - \bar{r})$
    d. $NX_t/\bar{Y}_t = \bar{a}_{nx} + \bar{b}_{nx}(\bar{R}^w - \bar{r})$
    e. $NX_t/\bar{Y}_t = \bar{a}_{nx} - \bar{b}_{nx}^2(R_t - \bar{r})(\bar{R}^w - \bar{r})$

11. Given the new formulation of net exports, which of the following identifies the elements that now must cause the IS curve to shift?
    a. $\bar{a}_{nx}$
    b. $-\bar{b}_{nx}(R_t - \bar{r})$
    c. $+\bar{b}_{nx}(\bar{R}^w - \bar{r})$

    d. a and b
    e. a and c

12. According to the text, the best (most probable) explanation for the positive correlation between exchange rates and economic performance is that
    a. good economic performance causes low inflation.
    b. low inflation causes good economic performance.
    c. low inflation causes exchange rates to appreciate.
    d. good economic performance causes currency appreciation.
    e. currency appreciation causes good economic performance.

13. The policy trilemma discussed in the text encompasses three mutually unachievable goals. Which of the following is not one of those three goals?
    a. monetary policy autonomy
    b. low and stable inflation
    c. a stable exchange rate
    d. free financial flows
    e. none of the above

14. Which of the following statements does not help explain why a country can achieve only any two of the three open economy goals for international finance?
    a. Defending a fixed exchange rate leads to foreign exchange depletion.
    b. Flexible exchange rates are influenced by both foreign and domestic monetary policies.
    c. Autonomous monetary policy and stable exchange rates require tight control over international financial flows.
    d. Pegging a country's currency to the currency of an economic power, such as the United States, forces adoption of that economic power's monetary policy.
    e. None of the above; they all do.

15. Developing countries have a particularly difficult time maintaining free financial flows and stable exchange rates if
    a. government officials are corrupt.
    b. government budget constraints are out of control.
    c. foreign aid is unreliable.
    d. they have an extremely small number of major trading partners.
    e. both a and c occur in combination.

16. Which of the following is not one of the benefits of a single currency for a large geographical area such as the European Union or the United States?
    a. the elimination of exchange rate risk
    b. the reduction of regional stimulus ability
    c. the reduction of transaction costs
    d. the reduction in the number of central banks pursuing independent monetary policies
    e. increased consistency regarding inflationary expectations

17. The three financial crises presented in the text had several characteristics in common with the current situation in the United States. Which of the following is not one of them?
    a. relatively open capital markets
    b. trade deficits
    c. budget deficits
    d. structural problems in the financial sector
    e. strong economies prior to the crisis

EXERCISES

1. Show that the exchange rate is a ratio of world prices ($\bar{P}^w$) to domestic prices ($\bar{P}$) and that, in the long run, exchange rate growth derives from the growth rates of the foreign and domestic money supplies.

2. Provide an intuitive explanation for whether the IS curve is steeper or flatter with the inclusion of a foreign sector that responds to exchange rates.

3. Use your answer from Exercise 2 and an IS-MP diagram to show whether the impact of a change in interest rates has a stronger or weaker impact on the economy.

PROBLEMS

Worked Problem

1. Begin with the national income identity, $Y_t \equiv C_t + I_t + G_t + EX_t - IM_t$ and the equations for each of the three unchanged sectors: $C_t = \bar{a}_c \bar{Y}_t$, $G_t = \bar{a}_g \bar{Y}_t$, and $I_t/\bar{Y}_t = \bar{a}_i - \bar{b}_i(\bar{R}_t - \bar{r})$. Add to them the new enriched net exports equation $NX_t/\bar{Y}_t = \bar{a}_{nx} - \bar{b}_{nx}(R_t - \bar{R}^w)$ where $\bar{R}^w$ is the world interest rate.
   a. Using the net export equation given in this problem, show how to derive equation (19.7) from the text, repeated here for convenience: $NX_t/\bar{Y}_t = \bar{a}_{nx} - \bar{b}_{nx}(R_t - \bar{r}) + \bar{b}_{nx}(\bar{R}^w - \bar{r})$. Begin with the enriched net export function then add a special form of zero to it as shown in the following (note that the world marginal product of capital, $\bar{r}$ is the same in all countries):

$$\frac{NX_t}{\bar{Y}_t} = \bar{a}_{nx} - \bar{b}_{nx}\left(R_t - \bar{R}^w\right)$$

$$\frac{NX_t}{\bar{Y}_t} = \bar{a}_{nx} - \bar{b}_{nx}\left(R_t - \bar{R}^w\right) + \bar{b}_{nx}\left(\bar{r} - \bar{r}\right)$$

Now rearrange the equation so that both the foreign and domestic real interest rate terms are matched with a marginal product of capital term:

$$\frac{NX_t}{\bar{Y}_t} = \bar{a}_{nx} - \bar{b}_{nx}R_t + \bar{b}_{nx}\bar{R}^w + \bar{b}_{nx}\bar{r} - \bar{b}_{nx}\bar{r}$$

$$\frac{NX_t}{\bar{Y}_t} = \bar{a}_{nx} - \bar{b}_{nx}R_t + \bar{b}_{nx}\bar{r} + \bar{b}_{nx}\bar{R}^w - \bar{b}_{nx}\bar{r}$$

$$\frac{NX_t}{\bar{Y}_t} = \bar{a}_{nx} - \bar{b}_{nx}\left(R_t - \bar{r}\right) + \bar{b}_{nx}\left(\bar{R}^w - \bar{r}\right)$$

   b. Derive an IS curve for the economy described here. As in Chapter 10, begin this process by substituting the equations for each of the sectors except investment and net exports into the national income identity as follows:

$$Y_t = C_t + I_t + G_t + NX_t$$
$$Y_t = \bar{a}_c\bar{Y}_t + I_t + \bar{a}_g\bar{Y}_t + NX_t$$

Divide both sides by $\bar{Y}_t$:

$$\frac{Y_t}{\bar{Y}_t} = \bar{a}_c + \frac{I_t}{\bar{Y}_t} + \bar{a}_g + \frac{NX_t}{\bar{Y}_t}$$

Substitute for $I_t/\bar{Y}_t$ and $NX_t/\bar{Y}_t$:

$$\frac{Y_t}{\bar{Y}_t} = \bar{a}_c + \bar{a}_i - \bar{b}_i\left(R_t - \bar{r}\right) + \bar{a}_g + \bar{a}_{nx} - \bar{b}_{nx}\left(R_t - \bar{r}\right) +$$
$$\bar{b}_{nx}\left(\bar{R}^w - \bar{r}\right)$$

Gather the $\bar{a}$ terms and $\bar{b}_{nx}(\bar{R}^w - \bar{r})$ and subtract 1 from both sides:

$$\frac{Y_t}{\bar{Y}_t} - 1 = \bar{a}_c + \bar{a}_i + \bar{a}_g + \bar{a}_{nx} - 1 + \bar{b}_{nx}\left(\bar{R}^w - \bar{r}\right) -$$
$$\left(\bar{b}_i + \bar{b}_{nx}\right)\left(R_t - \bar{r}\right)$$

Recall that $\dfrac{Y_t}{\bar{Y}_t} - 1 = \dfrac{Y_t - \bar{Y}_t}{\bar{Y}_t} = \tilde{Y}$ and note $\bar{a} = \bar{a}_c +$

$\bar{a}_i + \bar{a}_g + \bar{a}_{nx} - 1 + \bar{b}_{nx}(\bar{R}^w - \bar{r})$ when $\bar{R}^w - \bar{r}$ is the difference between the world interest rate and the domestic rate of return on capital. Therefore, we can simplify, and as in Chapter 10, we still get the same general form of

$$\tilde{Y}_t = \bar{a} - \bar{b}\left(R_t - \bar{r}\right)$$

except that $\bar{b} = (\bar{b}_i + \bar{b}_{nx})$ and $\bar{a}$ now contains the addition intercept term of $\bar{b}_{nx}(\bar{R}^w - \bar{r})$. To graph this new IS curve, we still need to solve for R_t:

$$\tilde{Y}_t = \bar{a} - \bar{b}\left(R_t - \bar{r}\right)$$
$$\bar{b}\left(R_t - \bar{r}\right) = \bar{a} - \tilde{Y}_t$$
$$\left(R_t - \bar{r}\right) = \frac{\bar{a}}{\bar{b}} - \frac{1}{\bar{b}}\tilde{Y}_t$$
$$R_t = \bar{r} + \frac{\bar{a}}{\bar{b}} - \frac{1}{\bar{b}}\tilde{Y}_t$$

Note that, when the economy is fully employed, $\bar{a} = 0$, $\tilde{Y}_t = 0$, and $R_t = \bar{r}$. Note, too, that the slope of the IS curve now is $-\dfrac{1}{\bar{b}_i + \bar{b}_{nx}}$, or smaller than with just $\bar{b}_i$ in the denominator.

c. Draw a graph showing how the IS curve in this problem differs from the standard IS curve developed in Chapters 9–12 when net exports were modeled simply as $EX_t = \bar{a}_{ex}\tilde{Y}_t$ and $IM_t = \bar{a}_{im}\tilde{Y}_t$. Note that the IS curve modeled in this problem (Figure 1) has a flatter slope than the earlier one from Chapter 10.

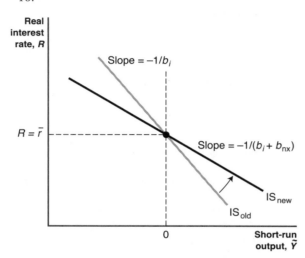

Figure 1

2. Use the standard monetary policy rule [$R_t - \bar{r} = \bar{m}(\pi_t - \pi)$] and the aggregate supply curve ($\pi_t = \pi_{t-1} + \bar{v}\tilde{Y}_t + \bar{o}$) from Chapter 13 and the IS curve derived in Problem 1 to work this problem.
   a. Derive an aggregate demand curve, invert it by solving for inflation, and show it on an AS/AD diagram.
   b. Using the slope of the AD curve from part a, show whether this AD curve is steeper or flatter than the one from Chapter 13.
   c. How would an inflation shock in an open economy like this one differ in its effects from an inflation shock in an economy like the one modeled in Chapter 13? (For simplicity, assume that the inflation shock originates within the country itself.)
   d. Will the central bank in this economy need to pursue a policy as aggressive as the one it would need to pursue in the Chapter 13 economy to restore short-run output to its full employment level?

3. When including the influence of exchange rates on net exports, the text indicates that the IS curve retains its basic shape. In fact, it states that "what has changed, however, is that we have an additional mechanism at work in the economy that causes short-run output to decline by even more for a given change in the interest rate." Use the solution for output derived in part b of Problem 1 to show that this statement is correct and explain the economic intuition behind this result.

4. Use the AD curve derived in Problem 2 to answer this problem. Assume for the purposes of this problem that real interest rates in the rest of the world have increased relative to those at home.
   a. Show the impact of this occurrence on an AS/AD diagram.
   b. Show what happens in the long run if world interest rates remain at their new level.

CHAPTER 19 SOLUTIONS

True/False Questions

1. False. The model does not change significantly. The IS curve becomes flatter, but its downward-sloping relationship between real interest rates and short-run output remains unchanged. See Section 19.1.

2. True. A more restrictive monetary policy at home means that the domestic money supply has grown more slowly than in the other country, hence less inflation and a lower price level, ceteris paribus. See Section 19.2.

3. False. This statement would be true if the nominal exchange rate movements were unanticipated, but as is, people take into account the exchange rate movements they anticipate. See Section 19.3.

4. True. This is a key feature of fixing exchange rates. See Section 19.4.

5. True. The parameter $\bar{a}$ now contains an additional term, $+\bar{b}_{nx}(\bar{R}^w - \bar{r})$. Recall that, whenever $\bar{a}$ changes, the AD curve shifts. See Section 19.5.

6. True. Both investment and net exports now provide channels for interest rate movement to affect economic activity. See Section 19.5.

7. False. Higher interest rates abroad lead to lower exchange rates, which stimulate domestic exports and reduce imports, thus stimulating the economy. See Section 19.5.

8. False. The United States spent 100 years on the gold standard, which effectively fixed exchange rates between any other countries also on the gold standard. See Section 19.6.

9. False. There are costs and benefits to each goal, and deciding which two to pursue must remain an individual choice for each country. See Section 19.7.

10. False. It could cause an expansion, but it depends on how the change from trade deficits to trade surpluses takes place. If it involves higher interest rates, the reduced interest-sensitive spending could well offset the increased demand for exports or the decreased demand for imports. See Section 19.8.

Multiple-Choice Questions

1. c, Germany. As part of the European Union, Germany uses the common currency of the euro. See Section 19.2.

2. c, increased U.S. exports. This would cause demand for the dollar to increase in foreign exchange markets. See Section 19.2.

3. d, quality differences. Quality differences mean we no longer are talking about the same goods in both countries. See Section 19.2.

4. d, $P^w = EP$, or $EP = P^w$. Prices in foreign countries should equal prices in domestic countries adjusted by the exchange rate.

5. c, the cost of real estate and labor. Both are nontradable goods, where arbitrage is not possible. See the case study "The Big Mac Index."

6. d, all of the above. See Section 19.2.

7. d, international financial market activity. See Section 19.3.

8. a, fiscal policy. See Section 19.4 and Section 8.5.

9. d, 5, 1, 3, 4, 2. See Section 19.5.

10. b, $\dfrac{NX_t}{\bar{Y}_t} = \bar{a}_{nx} - \bar{b}_{nx}\left(R_t - \bar{r}\right) + \bar{b}_{nx}\left(\bar{R}^w - \bar{r}\right)$. See Section 19.5. See also the worked problem (Problem 1) to see how part c actually is used in the derivation of part b.

11. e, answers a and c. Answer b is not correct because a change in R_t causes only a movement along the IS curve. See Sections 19.5.

12. d, good economic performance causes currency appreciation. See Section 19.5.

13. b, low and stable inflation. This is a general, domestic, monetary policy goal and would exist even in a closed economy. See Section 19.7.

14. e, none of the above. Each statement corresponds to why one of the goals cannot be achieved. Both parts a and d refer to the loss of monetary policy autonomy when pursuing stable exchange rates and allowing free financial flows. See Section 19.7.

15. b, government budget constraints are out of control. Absent tax increases, large budget deficits require either more financial inflow or increases in the money supply. More financial inflow causes currency appreciation. Increased money supply leads to inflation, financial outflow, and currency depreciation. Default on government debt may be another concern contributing to financial outflows. See Section 19.7.

16. b, the reduction of regional stimulus favoritism. The Fed, for example, cannot use monetary policy to stimulate economic activity only in the Midwest. See the case study "The Euro."

17. d, structural problems in the financial sector. The text puts these in the category of other problems, dissimilar to those of the United States. The United States has had problems, but they were individual and not structural. See Section 19.8.

Exercises

1. Start with equation (19.1) ($EP = P^w$) and rewrite it, imposing long-run values as shown in equation (19.3), ($\bar{E} = \bar{P}^w/\bar{P}$). Recall from Section 8.2 that, in the long run, velocity is constant and output is predetermined. Use the quantity theory of money ($M\bar{V} = P\bar{Y}_t$) to establish that the growth rate of money equals inflation as shown here:

$$g_m + g_v = g_p + g_y$$
$$g_m + 0 = g_p + 0$$
$$g_m = \pi$$

Finally, return to equation (19.3) and show that exchange rate growth depends on money supply growth in both countries:

$$\bar{E} = \frac{\bar{P}^w}{\bar{P}}$$
$$g_E = g_{\bar{P}^w} - g_{\bar{P}}$$
$$g_E = \pi^w - \pi$$
$$g_E = g_m^w - g_m$$

2. Answers here will vary somewhat but should include references to the original IS curve developed in Chapters 9–14, where net exports were simply a function of domestic income. In that model, the slope of the IS curve was determined by the response of investment to changes in the real interest rate. Recall that the only component of GDP modeled in Chapter 14 as a function of real interest rates was investment $[I_t/\bar{Y}_t = \bar{a}_i - \bar{b}_i(R_t - \bar{r})]$. Setting up this discussion also requires that the positive relationship between

exchange rates and interest rates be made a bridge to the new specification of net exports [$NX_t/\bar{Y}_t = \bar{a}_{nx} - \bar{b}_{nx}(R_t - \bar{R}^w)$]. Now we see that two responses to changes in real interest rates occur: the previous response from investment ($\bar{b}_i$) and the additional response from net exports ($\bar{b}_{nx}$). Since both components of aggregate demand respond negatively to real interest rate changes, short-run output responses to the same change in interest rates will be stronger. From a mathematical perspective, as will be shown in Problem 1, the slope of the IS curve now becomes $-1/(\bar{b}_i + \bar{b}_{nx})$ and the addition of $\bar{b}_{nx}$ to $\bar{b}_i$ makes the IS curve flatter.

3. Figure 2 shows that the short-run output response on the new IS curve (modeled with net exports responding to real interest rates) is greater than its response in the original model represented by the old IS curve.

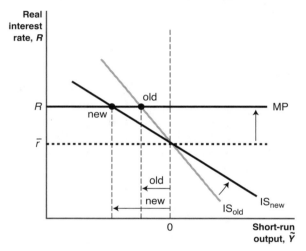

Figure 2

Problems

1. Worked Problem. The problem is worked in the text.

2. a. Substitute the MP curve $R_t - \bar{r} = \bar{m}(\pi_t - \bar{\pi})$ into the IS curve $\tilde{Y}_t = \bar{a} - (\bar{b}_i + \bar{b}_{nx})(R_t - \bar{r})$:

$$\tilde{Y}_t = \bar{a} - (\bar{b}_i + \bar{b}_{nx})(R_t - \bar{r})$$
$$\tilde{Y}_t = \bar{a} - (\bar{b}_i + \bar{b}_{nx})[\bar{m}(\pi_t - \bar{\pi})]$$
$$\tilde{Y}_t = \bar{a} - \bar{m}(\bar{b}_i + \bar{b}_{nx})(\pi_t - \bar{\pi})$$

Now solve for inflation:

$$\tilde{Y}_t = \bar{a} - \bar{m}(\bar{b}_i + \bar{b}_{nx})(\pi_t - \bar{\pi})$$
$$\bar{m}(\bar{b}_i + \bar{b}_{nx})(\pi_t - \bar{\pi}) = \bar{a} - \tilde{Y}_t$$

Divide both sides by $\bar{m}(\bar{b}_i + \bar{b}_{nx})$ and move $\bar{\pi}$ to the right-hand side of the equation to generate the graphing form of the AD curve:

$$\pi_t - \bar{\pi} = \frac{\bar{a}}{\bar{m}(\bar{b}_i + \bar{b}_{nx})} - \frac{1}{\bar{m}(\bar{b}_i + \bar{b}_{nx})}\tilde{Y}_t$$
$$\pi_t = \bar{\pi} + \frac{\bar{a}}{\bar{m}(\bar{b}_i + \bar{b}_{nx})} - \frac{1}{\bar{m}(\bar{b}_i + \bar{b}_{nx})}\tilde{Y}_t$$

b. The slope is now flatter due to the $\bar{b}_{nx}$ term in the denominator of the coefficient on $\tilde{Y}_t$. That is, $1/\bar{m}(\bar{b}_i + \bar{b}_{nx}) < 1/\bar{m}\bar{b}_i$, where $1/\bar{m}\bar{b}_i = 1/\bar{m}\bar{b}$ from the AD curve in Chapter 14.

c. With a flatter AD curve, inflation would rise by less and short-run output initially would fall by a greater amount, as shown below in Figure 3. Note that the arrows refer to the situation involving only the AD curve developed in this problem.

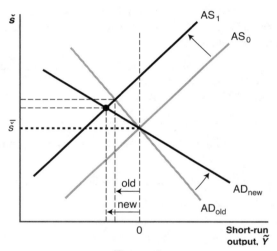

Figure 3

d. The central bank will need to pursue a less aggressive policy, now that the foreign sector also responds to interest rate movements. As the central bank lowers interest rates to stimulate the economy, greater investment spending will occur as before. However, spending on domestic production now will be augmented by additional foreign spending, as exchange rates fall in response to lower interest rates and imports decrease in response to the same currency depreciation.

3. The solution for output from part b is: $\tilde{Y}_t = \bar{a} - (\bar{b}_i + \bar{b}_{nx})(R_t - \bar{r})$. In the earlier model, this solution was $\tilde{Y}_t = \bar{a} - \bar{b}_i(R_t - \bar{r})$. To show the validity of the statement in question, we must show that, for all positive values,

$\bar{b}_i + \bar{b}_{nx}$ is greater than $\bar{b}_i$: $\bar{b}_i + \bar{b}_{nx} > \bar{b}_i$. The intuition is the same as in Problem 2, part b: For any given change in real interest rates, additional foreign spending occurs and augments the original investment spending.

4. The AD curve derived in Problem 2 is $\pi_t = \bar{\pi} + \dfrac{\bar{a}}{\bar{m}\left(\bar{b}_i + \bar{b}_{nx}\right)} - \dfrac{1}{\bar{m}\left(\bar{b}_i + \bar{b}_{nx}\right)}\tilde{Y}_t$, where the parameter $\bar{a} = \bar{a}_c + \bar{a}_i + \bar{a}_g + \bar{a}_{nx} - 1 + \bar{b}_{nx}\left(\bar{R}^w - \bar{r}\right) = 0$ at full employment.

a. An increase in $\bar{R}^w$ causes foreign currencies to appreciate relative to the domestic currency, making domestic goods relatively less expensive. This causes an export boom and, at the same time, makes foreign goods relatively more expensive, causing a decreased demand for imports. This increase in net exports causes $\bar{a}$ to become positive, the AD curve to shift out to the right, and inflation to increase, as shown in Figure 4.

b. If the world interest rate differential remains at its new level in the long run, short-run output will return to full employment but with a new and higher level of inflation, as firms and individuals adjust their expectations regarding the location of the AD curve. At this point, this country's central bank either must accept a new and higher target-level inflation, as shown in Figure 5, or raise interest rates and cause a recession to get inflation to return to its original level.

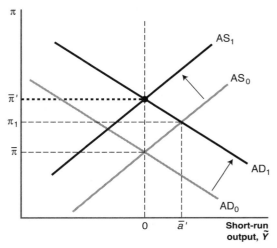

Figure 5

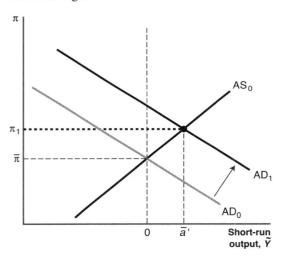

Figure 4